Framing the Rhetoric of a Leader

Also by Marta Degani

HE HIRINGA, HE PŪMANAWA: Studies on the Māori Language (with Alexander Onysko and Jeanette King)

INTRODUCTION TO COGNITIVE SEMANTICS

LANGUAGES AND CULTURES IN CONTACT: Maoridom in the Short Fiction of Witi Ihimaera and Patricia Grace

Framing the Rhetoric of a Leader

An Analysis of Obama's Election Campaign Speeches

Marta Degani
University of Verona, Italy

First published 2015 by
PALGRAVE MACMILLAN

Palgrave Macmillan in the UK is an imprint of Macmillan Publishers Limited, registered in England, company number 785998, of Houndmills, Basingstoke, Hampshire RG21 6XS.

Palgrave Macmillan in the US is a division of St Martin's Press LLC, 175 Fifth Avenue, New York, NY 10010.

Palgrave Macmillan is the global academic imprint of the above companies and has companies and representatives throughout the world.

Palgrave® and Macmillan® are registered trademarks in the United States, the United Kingdom, Europe and other countries.

ISBN 978–1–137–47158–1

This book is printed on paper suitable for recycling and made from fully managed and sustained forest sources. Logging, pulping and manufacturing processes are expected to conform to the environmental regulations of the country of origin.

A catalogue record for this book is available from the British Library.

A catalog record for this book is available from the Library of Congress.

Typeset by MPS Limited, Chennai, India.

Contents

List of Figures and Tables

Figures

Tables

Acknowledgments

This book grew out of an interest in American political discourse that has become stronger after Barack Obama turned into an acclaimed public figure and his rhetoric started being praised by many commentators. Since then, insightful readings have enlarged my horizons, stimulated my ideas and given me the opportunity to create my own path. I am, therefore, first of all grateful to all the scholars and writers who have contributed to my own development through their inspirational work.

Many people, indeed, have accompanied the different phases of this very long journey. I would like to thank my colleagues and friends at the Department of Foreign Languages and Literatures at the University of Verona and, in particular, Roberta, Cesare, Roberto, Paola and Anna for their support and encouragement during the making of this book. I am also grateful to Paolo and Maria Ivana for jointly organizing a conference in which I could present parts of the project discussed in this book.

I feel indebted to the two anonymous reviewers for their gracious and generous comments on the first version of the manuscript.

I would also like to thank the staff at Palgrave Macmillan for accepting my work for publication and managing its production so efficiently and professionally. Many thanks to Rebecca Brennan, Libby Forrest, K. Nithya and Ian Kingston, who, each in their own role, have made it all possible.

My special and deeply felt thanks go to Alexander for his unrestrained devotion to the 'cause' of this book. I am profoundly grateful for the time we spent discussing linguistic and political ideas, comparing opinions and growing together. As a concluding note, I would like to thank Maurizio, my dad, and Chiara, my sister, for their constant love.

1
Introduction

American presidents represent the kind of public figures who cannot escape the headlines. They fatally attract the media, generate rumors and make the entire world talk about them. Their public image is constructed piece by piece in the different phases that mark their ascendancy to the presidency, from the early stage of the pre-primary election up to the general election. This means that by the time the competition is reduced to a direct confrontation between a Democratic and a Republican frontrunner, people already know a lot about both candidates. In this last and heated phase of political contest, the words of the candidates on how they would lead the country have been repeated often enough to have found their way into people's minds and hearts. Thus, the stage is prepared for the *grand finale* when the president elect is acclaimed with standing ovations.

What happened to America on 4 November 2008 was more than the election of the 44th President. The ascendancy to the American presidency of Barack Hussein Obama was taken as a sign that the time of change had finally come to America and to the world. Obama was the first African-American President and his victory was taken to mark the beginning of a new chapter in the history of America. The front pages of newspapers and magazines all over the world celebrated this historic event. The outburst of enthusiasm could not be silenced and Obama was soon made into a world celebrity.

Obama no doubt happened to be the right person at the right time. After two terms of Republican administration, the country was ready and eager to be led by a President who promised renewal. Significantly enough, Obama's election campaign focused on change and hope. These very concepts responded to the needs and wishes of the American people, and they could be truthfully supported by Obama himself. In other words, change and hope represented what the American electorate was looking for and they depicted the Democratic candidate Obama as the right option for the ballot.

Obama was young and non-white, and he represented a powerful embodiment of the American Dream. His own personal story could tell Americans that everyone can make it, notwithstanding all odds. He was also the man of the new global era. As proved by his successful communication through new media technology, Obama was able to engage young voters and obtain their support (see McKinney and Banwart 2011). His genealogy and upbringing also gave him a very special status. Being the son of a white mother and an African father, he could be seen as reconciling the deep racial divide between Whites and Blacks in the US. At the same time, the presence of an Indonesian stepfather and the experiences he could collect from three different continents (Asia, Africa, America) facilitated drawing an image of him as the cosmopolitan citizen or, to put it differently, the universalist who cannot deny particularity. In this way, he could attract the sympathies and embrace the aspirations of many different people: ethnic groups, immigrant communities, white liberals and even radicals. In addition to this, the fact that he was raised by a single parent, his mother, and received caring affection by other female figures in his extended family, was probably appreciated by many 'untraditional' American families.

Besides embodying and communicating so many positive messages, Obama has been credited with very skillful use of linguistic devices throughout the 2008 election campaign. For instance, Alim and Smitherman (2012) have recently emphasized Obama's flexibility in language usage as one typical feature of his rhetorical style during his first run for the presidency. In particular, they refer to Obama's unusual capacity to aptly switch his mode of expression from Standard American English to African American Vernacular English, depending on the context and on the receivers of his varied oral deliveries.

Language was central to Obama's victory. His electoral speeches, which constitute the long-lasting core of his hard-fought campaign, proved his rhetorical ability. Here, Obama's words seemed to prove an innate disposition for crafting messages that can speak to and inspire many different Americans. Obama's speeches also seemed to demonstrate his sensitivity for recognizing the real problems affecting people. Furthermore, they showed his pragmatic approach in making reasonable proposals to face problems effectively.

Obama's mastery in leading discussions and mediating perspectives is a facet of his personality and subjectivity that his biographers like to emphasize. So, for instance, when discussing Obama's experiences at Harvard Law School, Remnick (2010: 189) observes how 'Obama attracted attention at Harvard for the confidence of his bearing and his way of absorbing and synthesizing the arguments of others in a way that made even the most strident opponent feel understood'. An additional proof of Obama's talent for successful communication is given by his admission to the group of excellent students who were selected out of hundreds for contributing to the *Harvard Law Review*.

In his manifest inclination for talking publicly, Obama excels previous presidents by standing out as a virtuoso of rhetoric. This personal gift emphasizes the centrality of speechmaking for modern American presidents. Speechmaking, indeed, represents a key component of modern presidential campaigns. The art and craft of speechmaking has been an essential quality for any American politician running the presidential race from the twentieth century onwards. In a way, one could say that the modern American president has turned into a loquacious public figure by necessity (see Tulis 1987, Kernell 1993, Perloff 1998, Metcalf 2004). Irrespective of their talents, modern American presidents feel the urge to address their audience publicly and enchant them with moving and well-designed political messages. For this reason, the preparation of an electoral campaign involves the hard work of collaborators who work in teams to facilitate the job of the would-be president. They are the so-called speechwriters. Candidates establish a special relationship with their speechwriters, since the end product of the speechwriters' work, the electoral speech, needs to echo the voice of the candidate. This is a crucial point of the whole process.

As a specific textual type, electoral speeches respond to certain needs (see Trent and Friedenberg 2000). They typically contain information on the candidate, the election campaign, political opponents, failures of past policies, proposals for improvements and so on. Furthermore, they can be characterized by a focus on, for example, foreign or domestic affairs, depending on what is perceived as the 'real' political issue at that particular moment. Speeches also need to follow a general structure of presentation that prescribes, among other things, the inclusion of speech modules: sections of variable length that appear again and again during a campaign.

Given a basic textual grid to which speeches tend to conform, the interest of researchers in political communication obviously resides in the recognition of a politician's distinctiveness. Politicians are remembered for the traits that make their rhetoric different from (or similar to) that of previous political leaders. There is indeed a tradition of rhetorical studies investigating presidential language, and this tradition is quintessentially American. A large number of scholars working in this framework have explored different facets of American presidential language. Some of these scholars were concerned with emphasizing the role of history in political speeches and the related idea of communicating continuity within change (see, for example, Smith and Smith 1994, Campbell and Jamieson 1995, Perloff 1998). Others considered aspects of meaning creation in their semantic content analyses and focused on the effects of lexical usage (see, for example, Hart 1984, 2000, Lim 2002). Still others were interested in exploring the communicative relationship between speaker and listener to account for the impact and hence effectiveness of political speeches (see, for example, Wilson 1990, Dayan and Katz 1992, Kernell 1993, Teten 2003).

Even though rhetorical studies occupy a very large portion of American scholarly interest, there are also works that look at political discourse from a different perspective. In particular, provocative suggestions on how to interpret ideological oppositions in the domain of politics were put forward by Hunter (1991). The sociologist proposed a theory about opposing views in American culture for which he coined the expression 'culture war'. In brief, the theory refers to a values divide in US culture and explains cultural oppositions in American society in terms of people's moral assessments of reality. Since people's belief systems are expected to have important repercussions on their political behavior, the theory has been used primarily to study disagreements over public policy and political candidates. Influential as Hunter's idea of a culture war in American society has been, ever since its publication in the 1990s, it has caused heated discussions among political scientists. It was received by some with skepticism and by others with enthusiasm. Notwithstanding reactions, it is a truism that Hunter's theory has strongly influenced the understanding of American politics. This is a fact that should be kept in mind for appreciating the cultural relevance of the linguistic analyses presented in this book.

Very significantly, Hunter's (1991) ideas about American culture and politics seem to reverberate in Lakoff's (1996) view of American politics. With all the necessary adaptations and a good range of expansions, Lakoff appears to interpret and translate an influential socio-cultural theory into a promising linguistic framework.

In Lakoff's view, what makes conservatives different from progressives is a distinctive way of thinking about politics that is based on two specific family-based moral systems. Reasoning from a cognitive linguistic perspective, Lakoff assumes that the people's choice to side with either Republicans or Democrats is based on the existence of two different idealized cognitive models: the Strict Father (SF) and the Nurturant Parent (NP). While the SF model is in line with Republican ideology, the NP one is coherent with a Democratic understanding of reality. Each of the two models explains a specific worldview where certain moral values have priority over others. Thus, for instance, authority plays a key role in the SF morality model, whereas nurturance is central to NP morality.

In various publications, Lakoff (1996, 2004, 2006, 2008) also claimed that the models underlie American right-wing versus left-wing political rhetoric. In other words, the models provide the grounding for how politicians discuss matters or, to put it more technically, for how politicians frame political issues. Thus, Republican political leaders are expected to talk in line with SF morality, whereas Democratic politicians are envisaged to express their ideas according to a NP worldview.

Having said this, doubts still remain on the actual applicability of Lakoff's suggestions. His hypotheses are very stimulating and they have potential to shed light on politicians' use of language as well as on the effects of their words on prospective supporters. However, Lakoff did not couple his hypotheses with any empirical data. Furthermore, the very small amount of research that tried to apply the SF and NP models to the analysis of American political language (Cienki 2004, 2005a, 2005b, Ahrens 2006, 2011, Ahrens and Yat Mei Lee 2009) could not provide any clear support for their validity. This paucity of results calls for further investigations.

The challenge of putting Lakoff's hypotheses further to the test is taken up in this book. In light of Obama's great success during the 2008 election campaign, the question arises of whether he conformed to Lakoff's prediction about Democratic politicians and their supposed NP framing of issues. To explore this question, Obama's electoral speeches are taken as the testing ground for empirically proving, or disproving, the validity of Lakoff's models.

Given the importance of working with a coherent and representative pool of data, a corpus was created that gathers speeches during the whole period of Obama's first election campaign for the American presidency. The corpus brings together Obama's much acclaimed primary night speeches as well as a good range of other speeches in which he tackles issues that have relevance for his political message to the American electorate.

Testing Lakoff's models is not an easy task. The complexity of the models invites a book-length investigation that can test their validity from different angles. The study presented in this book intends to propose a new way of applying the models that is based on different levels of linguistic analysis. In this sense, the book is also aimed at shedding new light on the potential usefulness of Lakoff's models for understanding American political discourse. Indeed, a thorough analysis of Obama's speeches in terms of Lakoff's models demands a combined quantitative and qualitative approach, which is based on close reading and contextual analysis.

When applying Lakoff's models, it is first of all important to stress that moral values are at the core of the models. Thus, moral values are the starting point of the analysis presented in this book. Since it is values which define the opposing SF and NP morality models, they need to be searched for in a corpus of political language. Values motivate not just the selection of issues to be discussed during an election campaign, but, most importantly, determine how a politician frames his or her discourse. Accordingly, the first step in the linguistic analysis that is shown here consists in the identification and classification of individual values addressed by Obama in his electoral speeches.

Clearly enough, values do not exist in a vacuum. On the contrary, during an election campaign, values can be woven into the fabric of an elaborate narrative. Obama's electoral narrative is at the same time personal, social and historical. In his speeches, he talks about himself and his family, he refers to the American people and he celebrates America as a great nation and a beacon of light for all of humanity. The political values addressed by

Obama need to be understood against this general background. They occupy a specific role and a defined textual space within the larger whole of his political and moral message to the American electorate.

His values also take part in the architecture of a discourse that is finely assembled for the purpose of reaching and conquering a large audience. For this reason, the analysis is not limited to identifying and classifying the values expressed in his speeches. In addition to that, it also considers the range of rhetorical strategies on which Obama relied for a successful communication of values. The book provides details on the amplitude of values that Obama expressed in his electoral speeches and on the strategies that he employed to give voice to the values in the context of his electoral narrative.

One of the central questions of how Obama uses language to frame his values is whether he relies on metaphors to reach that aim. The use of metaphors in political discourse has a long tradition in research, particularly from the perspective of cognitive linguistics (see Chilton 1996, Musolff 2000a, 2000b, 2003, 2004, Beer and De Landtsheer 2004, Charteris-Black 2004, 2005, 2006, 2013, Carver and Pikalo 2008). Metaphors are also central to Lakoff's family-based models, and this has actually led to interpretations that put the underlying values as second to metaphors. It is thus a further aim of the book to focus on the actual role of metaphorical expressions and their relation to values in Obama's speeches. This empirical quest for metaphors sheds new light on a previously assumed direct relation between metaphors and Lakoff's models.

Closely related to a contextual analysis of values and metaphors is an investigation of lexical choices. Thus, the book also deals with highly frequent words in Obama's speeches. In detail, looking at the usage of the most prominent words in context serves as an additional test for checking Obama's framing of issues. The lexical analysis is prompted by two major objectives. On the one hand, it is important to find out which lexical items are the most signifying 'carriers' of Obama's electoral message. On the other hand, it is crucial to check whether or not links can be established between the expression of a moral worldview and the use of specific lexical items that can, in principle, be associated to Lakoff's models. The results of this exploration highlight that Obama's lexical preferences can be seen as indicative of the (moral) reality he constructs in his speeches.

Overall, this book illuminates the role of Lakoff's SF and NP models for understanding and analyzing political language. Moreover, the particular application of Lakoff's models presented in this work offers a novel way of approaching the complex relation between political language and cognition.

2
Political Discourse in the US

> All life therefore comes back to the question of our speech, the medium through which we communicate with each other; for all life comes back to the question of our relations with one another. These relations [...] are verily constituted, by our speech. [...] The more it suggests and expresses the more we live by it [...]. (Henry James, The Question of Our Speech, 1998: 44)

While the primary objective of this book remains the presentation of a new way for testing the applicability of Lakoff's models to the analysis of Obama's election campaign speeches, it is important, first of all, to explore the larger context of previous research on American political discourse. Accordingly, this chapter offers a comprehensive overview of the major concerns and areas of research that have attracted American scholars with an interest in political discourse. In particular, the chapter highlights the significance of speech-making, drawing on major approaches in the field of rhetoric, the role of speechwriters and the function of speeches as a form of communication that is characteristic of election campaigns.

Throughout the discussion, these issues are illustrated with examples from Obama's 2008 election campaign speeches, alluding to the fact that an analysis that is in line with the American tradition of rhetorical studies can yield further interesting insights. In addition, the chapter introduces Hunter's notion of a cultural divide between orthodox and progressive people in the US and suggests a striking similarity to how Lakoff constructs his models of political morality. This aspect is of great importance for the book since it grounds the linguistic investigation in a broader cultural dimension.

2.1 Political discourse and rhetoric: from classical oratory to contemporary speech-making

Political discourse is such a vast area of enquiry that any attempt at exhaustively describing its multiple components and making them fit into a coherent whole is very likely to undermine even the stamina of the most zealous scholar. Driven by a wide range of different and diverging reasons, political philosophers, political and social scientists, discourse analysts, experts in communication and linguists of various beliefs have made the relation between language and politics the subject matter of their investigations. As a result, an immense number of books and articles dealing with political language, discourse and communication (the terms are often used interchangeably) have been published and are currently available to the avid reader.

In line with the field of rhetoric, which goes back to the time of the Sophists and Aristotle, political discourse has often been studied in terms of political oratory. There is indeed a very tight connection between politics and rhetoric. As pointed out by Gill and Whedbee (1997: 157), 'the essential activities of rhetoric are located on a political stage. For example, all the major writers on rhetoric from antiquity – Isocrates, Plato, Aristotle, Cicero, Quintilian – believed that politics was the principal locus of rhetoric, and, therefore, they designed their theories of rhetoric for use by political agents'. The influence of classical rhetoric, and of Aristotle's work in particular, on modern studies of political communication cannot be overemphasized (see Corcoran 1979: 35–51). While the Sophists and Plato suggested an interpretation of rhetoric as the art of persuasion based on emotional appeal, Aristotle can be regarded as the first philosopher who was able to raise the status of rhetoric from subjective art to objective science. This was accomplished with great mastery by turning rhetoric into a systematic method that incorporated logic. In other words, Aristotle enlarged what up to his time had been the traditional domain of rhetoric so as to embrace logic, the science of knowledge. The result was the creation of a method for public communication that combined the rapturous character of artful eloquence with the organizational and demonstrative requirements of logical reasoning.[1]

In Aristotle's accounts (*Rhetorica*, ch. 3, Book I, see Ross 1924: 1358^{b}– 1359^{a}), political oratory stands for one component of a tripartite division of rhetoric, the other components being forensic (legal) and epideictic (ceremonial) oratory. What makes the political rhetorician distinct from the forensic or ceremonial orator is that kind of knowledge that allows him to act for the common good of the whole community. In a society where the knowledge of things coincided with the knowledge of their purposes, the political rhetorician as a man of outstanding education and exquisite understanding was expected to act for the benefit of the polis. Therefore, the spiritual and ethical well-being of his citizens were the raison d'être of the political orator when speaking in public. As convincingly expressed by Corcoran in his description of classical rhetoric (1979: 43) 'political rhetoric was conceived as a method of special competence in arranging, testing and refining broad areas of information, all with a view to articulating this information as an argument on behalf of policies and actions contributing to the public good'.

Describing classical political rhetoric as public 'performance' is an apt way to underline yet another feature of political communication. Performativity is part and parcel of delivering a political speech, and it is precisely this aspect of political communication that gives the audience the decisive role of a judge (*Rhetorica*, Book I, see Ross 1924: 1354ª–1377ª). If words are uttered so as to provoke certain kinds of reactions in the listeners, the power of the orator essentially depends on his capacity to use language convincingly. The political rhetorician may well be considered a man of special skills, but his authority is not unquestioned and the truthfulness of his words is not a given. This is why it is important for the political orator to know his audience and to understand their needs. Thoughts need to be expressed in a logical manner, which means that the political speech has to be structured according to specific rules that determine how to present ideas. This makes the speech into a piece of rational argumentation based on the presentation of premises, facts and probabilities. However, already Aristotle stressed the fact that rational argumentation alone is not enough for securing the support of an audience. The political orator also needs to have an affective and charismatic power over his listeners (*Rhetorica*, Book II, III, see Ross 1924: 1377ᵇ–1419 ᵇ). It is only when the audience is rationally convinced by logical expression and emotionally stirred by the lyrical quality of speech that the political orator is very likely to gain credit and appreciation. Indeed, emotions are a central concern in Aristotle's accounts of rhetorical ability. In his view, the good orator is the one who knows the nature of his listeners' feelings and can use emotions strategically to instill new ideas in the audience.

If we now move from the ancient time of classical political rhetoric to current political discourse in the US, it is worth noticing how 'ancient' considerations are still valid in the modern context. In particular, the importance of emotional involvement for successful communication in general is an aspect that is strongly emphasized by modern cognitive linguistics (see Johnson 1990, 2007, Lakoff and Johnson 1999). New discoveries in the cognitive sciences have demonstrated that people do not just base their judgments on facts (see Damasio 2000). They rather reason using the logic of frames, metaphors and narratives, and they make decisions relying on emotion. Cognitive scientists and neuroscientists have strongly criticized the long-held practice of viewing reason and emotion in dualistic opposition by demonstrating that emotional experience precedes cognitive processes and how this makes rational thinking possible (for an application to politics see Marcus 2002). According to this view, which is embraced in this book and presented in the following chapters, the type of Cartesian rationality that supports the body/mind dichotomy should be abandoned in favor of a new interpretation of reason as embodied.

The ability of the rhetorician to use language skillfully and to move people's emotions would, however, be of little advantage in the absence of other kinds of knowledge. Indeed, the political orator is required to have a profound knowledge of his people, their needs, their values and their expectations so as to be able to successfully connect to the public. In other words, the orator has to connect successfully to the collective mindset of his people in order to obtain their favor. Once again, this is a point that lies at the core of cognitive linguistic explanations of political discourse (see Lakoff 1996). In the political domain, being able to gain people's support essentially means understanding their moral framing and addressing their values. But more on this aspect will be described in the following chapters.

In the context of American political discourse, the tradition of rhetorical studies still plays a key role in the 'field' and in the 'laboratory'. On the one hand, politicians and their spin doctors seem to be well aware of the importance of employing the art and science of rhetoric for communication in the public domain, especially at crucial times such as during election campaigns (see, for example, Trent and Friedenberg 2000, Friedenberg 2002, Stockwell 2005). On the other hand, rhetoric continues to be used as a method and a theoretical framework for the study of political discourse (see, for example, Windt and Ingold 1987, Jamieson 1988, Stuckey 1990, Kelley 2001, Browne 2003, Metcalf 2004, Wood 2007).

In America, scholarship that intersects rhetoric and politics has typically been concerned with either the study of electoral politics as represented in the speeches of presidential candidates or with the speeches of presidents in office. These studies can be observed to center on three broad areas of examination: the role of history, the creation of meaning and the impact of the political message.

First of all, studies highlighting the role of history in presidential discourse have often taken into consideration the temporal and spatial situatedness of political speeches. This contextual information is seen as decisive for the creation of historical narratives that underline continuity within change. This point is stressed by, among others, Smith and Smith (1994: 126) when they write that 'policies are grounded in historical narratives' and observe that presidents need to establish an essential grounding of their policies in shared American values and national myths. More precisely, American political narratives can be said to be historical in that they construct a sense of community and shared national identity by linking current events to a long temporal chain of events. As Shenhav (2009: 201) acutely points out:

> Political narratives' capability of embedding current events in a chain of experiences is a major way in which they can construct a sense of continuity. The use of narratives in the political domain situates contemporary occurrences in a broad temporal context of collective experiences and bestows upon the individual a story of collective agency, as in "the Nation" or "our State". Thus narratives enfold present political events in a time frame which can exceed the current event, giving their audience a sense of familiarity with events that they personally could have never

experienced. Situating contemporary occurrences within an ongoing course of events offers political leadership an opportunity to shift a single event into a larger chain of national events. Consequently current political affairs can be interpreted, conceived and explained as part and parcel of "our" mutual story.

As the producers of political narratives, politicians exploit temporal fluidity to give 'substance' to what appears as ephemeral. By connecting the fleeting present to a stable chain of past events, political candidates can locate individual American stories in the larger frame of American national history. By doing so, they can also make every citizen feel that they are part of a communal fate. Quite significantly, presidents are often defined as storytellers who recall the past to describe the present. This binding relation to the past often emerges in the use of linguistic patterns that evoke former presidents and public figures to establish identification with their purposes and to use their authority for interpreting current situations (see Fields 1996 for an account of presidential eloquence that illustrates both constancy and change across the same type of speeches by different presidents). In his study of Obama's proverbial language, Mieder (2009) observes how Obama uses certain clichés and fixed phrases that were previously heralded by presidents of the caliber of Lincoln, Douglass and King. As he points out,

> [...] Obama shares a certain predilection to proverbial language with Lincoln, Douglass and King. He certainly read them, and he must have been impressed and at times moved by some of their deeply felt statements that were quite often couched in proverbial language. Abraham Lincoln's use of the biblical proverb "A house divided against itself cannot stand" (Mark 3, 25), Frederick Douglass's use of Jefferson's declaration turned proverb "All men are created equal", and Dr. Martin Luther King's insistence on the golden rule "Do onto others as you would have them do unto you" (also used by Lincoln and Douglass) readily come to mind. There is doubtlessly some direct or indirect rhetorical influence here [...]. (Mieder 2009: 2)

Besides these, Mieder also refers to the influence that other presidents seem to have had on Obama's shaping of his public rhetoric. In particular, he mentions Obama's frequent quoting of Franklin D. Roosevelt and John F. Kennedy (2009: 68–71). Far from rejecting his debt to a long history of American political oratory, Obama appears very proud to add his own voice to the chorus that throughout centuries has incessantly celebrated the American spirit and mission. Besides shaping his campaign speeches in ways that are reminiscent of previous presidential rhetoric, Obama also admires the achievements of former presidents. This happens, for instance, when he refers to Jefferson and Franklin's active contribution to the improvement of public infrastructure.[2]

(1) Now is not the time for small plans. Now is the time for bold action to rebuild and renew America. We've done this before. Two hundred years ago, in 1808, Thomas Jefferson oversaw an infrastructure plan that envisioned the Homestead Act, the transcontinental railroads, and the Erie Canal. One hundred years later, in 1908, Teddy Roosevelt called together leaders from business and government to develop a plan for a 20th century infrastructure. Today, in 2008, it falls on us to take up this call again – to re-imagine America's landscape and remake America's future. That is the cause of this campaign, and that will be the cause of my presidency. (21 June 2008)[3]

Obama takes the American presidents Jefferson and Roosevelt as the models who can inspire a nation to take action and change the course of events. In Obama's words, the American people have already proven their capacity for 'bold action' and they have the moral fiber to do it again.

Another common practice is that of recalling the nation's founding fathers and the great accomplishments of previous American presidents. A case in point can be found in one of Obama's election campaign speeches when he recalls the 'moral mission' of presidents Roosevelt, Truman and Kennedy by stating the following:

(2) Change is facing the threats of the twenty-first century not with bluster, or fear-mongering, or tough talk, but with tough diplomacy, and strong alliances, and confidence in the ideals that have made this nation the last, best hope of Earth. That is *the legacy of Roosevelt, and Truman, and Kennedy.* (20 May 2008, my emphasis)

American presidents Roosevelt, Truman and Kennedy are taken by Obama as exemplary models for the kind of moral values and ideals they strongly sustained while in office. After all, the need to rely on shared American values when crafting one's public image is made explicit in Obama's personal and political manifesto, *The Audacity of Hope* (2006), when he writes that

[...] shared values – the standards and principles that the majority of Americans deem important in their lives, and in the life of the country – should be the heart of our politics, the cornerstone of any meaningful debate about budgets and projects, regulations and policies [...] We hang on to our values, even if they seem at times tarnished and worn; even if, as a nation and in our own lives, we have betrayed them more often than we care to remember. What else is there to guide us? Those values are our inheritance, what makes us who we are as people. (Obama 2006: 64, 83)

In this passage, shared American values appear as the enduring foundation of the strong national edifice.

From a linguistic point of view, continuity within change can be observed on the levels of both content and form. As for content, emphasizing moral values, virtue and the need to follow the Constitution and God has been common practice since Washington's presidency (Perloff 1998: 102). In the words of the highly respected Alexander Hamilton, one of the founders of the Constitution: 'if it were to be asked, what is the most sacred duty and the greatest source of security in a republic? The answer would be, an inviolable respect for the Constitutions and Laws – the first growing out of the last …' (quoted in Morgan 2001: 96). The inalienable truths expressed in the Constitution typically inform the public oratory of American political leaders. By inciting a feeling of communal and historically rooted American identity, references to the Constitution can successfully cling to the hearts of the electorate. In his famous and often quoted speech, 'A More Perfect Union', Obama celebrates foundational moments in American history by recalling the signing of the Declaration of Independence in 1787, the industrious work of the founders and the all-encompassing significance of the Constitution, with its emphasis on the basic human values of equality, liberty and justice.

(3) Two hundred and twenty one years ago, in a hall that still stands across the street, a group of men gathered and, with these simple words, launched America's improbable experiment in democracy. Farmers and scholars; statesmen and patriots who had traveled across an ocean to escape tyranny and persecution finally made real their declaration of independence at a Philadelphia convention that lasted through the spring of 1787.

The document they produced was eventually signed but ultimately unfinished. It was stained by this nation's original sin of slavery, a question that divided the colonies and brought the convention to a stalemate until the founders chose to allow the slave trade to continue for at least twenty more years, and to leave any final resolution to future generations.

Of course, the answer to the slavery question was already embedded within our Constitution – a Constitution that had at is very core the ideal of equal citizenship under the law; a Constitution that promised its people liberty, and justice, and a union that could be and should be perfected over time. (18 March 2008)

If the Constitution, as such, is relied upon by both Democrats and Republicans in their speeches, divisions emerge once it is used to justify political action and policies. As a matter of fact, the interpretation of the Constitution has divided historians and legal theorists for a very long time. Should people endow the Constitution with a transfixed character or should they rather emphasize its potential for flexibility? This question is by far too complex to give it adequate treatment here. However, I would like to simply hint at this issue by offering an anecdote that succinctly illustrates Obama's own view of the American Constitution and his interpretation of it.

What the framework of our Constitution can do is organize the way by which we argue about our future. All of its elaborate machinery – its separation of powers and checks and balances and federalist principles and Bill of Rights – are designed to force us into a *conversation*, a "deliberative democracy" in which all citizens are required to engage in a process of testing their ideas against an external reality, persuading others of their point of view, and building shifting alliances of consent. [...] In sum, the Constitution envisions a road map by which we marry passion to reason, the ideal of individual freedom to the demands of community. (Obama 2006: 110, 111, 113, my emphasis)

Obama's emphasis on the dialogic nature of the Constitution ('a conversation') and the need to see it in relation to new people and new situations is in line with one of the major aims expressed throughout the whole 2008 campaign: the necessity to bring change to America. Furthermore, since change implies motion, Obama's second metaphor – the one about a journey that is expressed by the phrase 'road map' – fits in coherently. While the metaphor of the Constitution as a conversation is apt in endowing that concept with an idealistic, humanitarian touch ('politics is for and about the people'), the image of the map adds a more practical and down to earth note to it. This can be seen as Obama's personal way of combining immanence with transience and emotiveness with rationality.

During Obama's 2008 election campaign, the emphasis on following and being inspired by the Constitution is paired with the expression of religious belief. Obama communicates to his electorate how religion could give him the drive to face the most difficult situations when he says: 'I'm a person of deep faith, and my religion has sustained me through a lot in my life. I even gave a speech on faith before I ever started running for President where I said that Democrats, "make a mistake when we fail to acknowledge the power of faith in people's lives"' (14 April 2008). Later in the campaign, he locates faith and values at the core of his ethical project to renew the country.

(4) We know that faith and values can be a source of strength in our own lives. That's what it's been to me. And that's what it is to so many Americans. But it can also be something more. It can be the foundation of a new project of American renewal. And that's the kind of effort I intend to lead as President of the United States. (1 July 2008)

In this project, supporting faith and values means making the American people stronger and more capable of coping with everyday problems. Obama's emphasis on the role of faith in American private and public life leads to an appreciation of religion not just as an individual moral force but as a real civic force. In this way, Obama's project appears as an attempt to reconcile religion and liberal democracy and transcend the distrust that each of them has towards the other. After eight years of Republican dominance among religious voters, Obama offers the American people the possibility to forge a new relationship between religion and politics (see Copeland 2009).[4]

Moving on with our discussion, we now consider how the notions of continuity and change also affect the linguistic form of political oratory. Even though there is a lot of controversy about how to define political genres, political speeches are generally categorized according to their specific situation, their purpose and the type of audience: for example, inaugural addresses, state of the union addresses,[5] announcement speeches, acceptance addresses, veto messages, farewell addresses, hortatory or moralistic addresses, pardoning rhetoric and so on (see Simons and Aghazarian 1986, Kiewe 1994, Campbell and Jamieson 1995, Perloff 1998, ch. 7). 'Rhetorical situation' is another general expression used to describe how the creation of political messages is influenced by different factors. As Bitzer (1968) explains, the rhetorical situation is defined first of all by the reasons that urge a politician to communicate, secondly by the public that will receive the message and thirdly by more general constraints and influences. Rhetoric at crisis times, or crisis rhetoric, continues to be a popular research subject among political scientists worldwide. Early studies like that of Lasswell (1949) demonstrated how rhetoric at crisis times is characterized by an emotive, ornamental and repetitive style. Also De Sola Pool (1956) emphasized how crisis rhetoric is far less varied and more simplified than rhetoric at times of peace. More recently, De Landtsheer (1994) has observed how rhetoric during periods of economic crisis tends to be more metaphorical and persuasive; the same is true when military missions fail and politicians use emotive and impressive language to keep the level of anxiety in society under control (De Landtsheer and De Vrij 2004).

Returning to the American context and its specificities, Campbell and Jamieson (1990: 2) note how 'the impact of earlier rhetoric on the discourse of subsequent presidents is illustrated by presidential war rhetoric, in which the lines of argument available and the timing of its appearance, although not its essential form, have been strongly influenced by precedents'. Presidential political speeches contain the traces of a long rhetorical tradition while being shaped by the particular presidency and system to which they belong. Whenever a political leader talks in public, there are expectations that go with his/her speech. The audience is more or less consciously aware of the historical events to which the contents of the oral text refer and/ or respond to. At the same time, the audience evaluates political speeches to varying degrees in light of certain parameters that define a political text and its corollary of typical lexical choices, syntactical structures, argumentative moves and narrative appeals. Thus, while categorizing political speeches

according to genres may be captious even for expert analysts, everyone listening to politicians' talk has intuitive expectations on discourse structure
in relation to genre. This point is lucidly explained by Bakhtin:

> Speech genres organize our speech in almost the same way as grammati-
> cal (syntactical) forms do. We learn to cast our speech in generic forms
> and, when hearing others' speech, we guess its genre from the very first
> words; we predict a certain length (that is, the approximate length of the
> speech whole) and a certain compositional structure; we foresee the end;
> that is, from the very beginning we have a sense of the speech whole,
> which is only later differentiated during the speech process. (1990: 956)

This generic expectation of genre can help the analyst to understand reactions and responses from an audience. So, if one takes the example of election
campaign speeches, there are generic expectations for this type of discourse.
The candidate running for president is expected to talk about current issues
and to present solutions to problems that afflict the country. He/she is also
expected to provide persuasive argumentation and sound explanations. In
the end, the aim of political campaigning is that of obtaining people's support in order to be selected as the candidate for the presidency. To put it
simply, winning the presidential race means convincing the electorate that
one will be able to lead the country better than any other competitor.

As far as studies on meaning creation in political discourse are concerned,
scholars have adopted the critical lens of rhetoric for interrogating the
nuances of meanings and thus bringing to the fore questions of ideology
and power. Hart (1984), for instance, created a computer program, called
DICTION, that allows to make assessments of people's speech by grouping
their words according to a set of attitudinal categories, Activity, Optimism,
Certainty, Realism, Embellishment, Self-Reference, Variety, Familiarity,
Human Interest, Complexity and Symbolism. In his computerized content
analysis of political discourse, Hart (1984) compared presidential words and
phrases from Harry Truman to Ronald Reagan with those of other leaders
such as chief executives, social activists, religious prelates and political candidates to find out which features characterize presidential language. What
he could observe was that presidents use more optimistic language, more
realism, and less complexity. Presidents also show a tendency to refer to
themselves more frequently. Hart also adduces reasons for these presidential
linguistic traits. Presidents use optimistic language to uplift the nation, they
avoid complexity so as to be understood by everyone and they personalize
their discourse to sound more convincing. Apart from these generalizable
commonalities, presidential speeches also exhibit more idiosyncratic traits,
especially in so far as they reflect the personalities of different political
leaders. Thus, the rhetorical style of presidents is marked by individual
differences as well. For instance, Truman's style was simple and certain,

Carter's was complex and equivocal. Self-reference was common practice for Nixon and Ford but it rarely marked the rhetoric of other presidents such as Truman, Eisenhower and Kennedy. In a later work on the 1996 presidential election campaign, Hart (2000) explains Bill Clinton's success over Bob Dole by referring to the different ways the two candidates used language. 'Dole was conspicuously more ambivalent, more likely to talk about bureaucratic procedures and personalities than about concrete realities, more self-absorbed' (Hart 2000: 4), whereas Clinton used more human-interest language (*you, us, people, family*). 'Clinton stressed the common ties among the American people' (2000: 4). In this respect, certain similarities can be glimpsed from Clinton's use of language and Obama's lexical choices during the 2008 election campaign, especially in so far as Obama's use of family-based terminology is concerned. This aspect will be dealt with in more detail in Chapter 7.

Lim's study (2002) also considers facets of meaning creation in presidential rhetoric. Similarly to Hart, Lim conducts computer assisted content analysis but with the different aim of detecting changes in American presidential speeches from the nineteenth to the twentieth century. More precisely, Lim analyses presidential inaugural addresses and state of the union addresses from 1789 up until 2000. The major finding of his diachronic study concerns the identification of a distinct rhetorical trend marking the speeches of twentieth century presidents. Compared to nineteenth century presidential rhetoric, the rhetorical style of twentieth century presidents appears as marked by five distinctive traits. It is more anti-intellectual, more abstract, more assertive, more democratic and more conversational.

Presidential rhetoric sounds more anti-intellectual as a result of a language where reference to cognitive processes and states (for example, *know*) is little, as well as causal inferences and legal/judicial terms.[6] While anti-intellectualism makes presidential rhetoric sound like the rhetoric of the common man, a sense of linguistic abstraction is more likely to be associated with poetic language. In fact, abstraction comes out from the reiterated use of other distinctive linguistic elements. Lim observes that the number of references to expansive rhetorical categories like time, space, nature and its processes has progressively increased. The use of idealistic terms and lofty concepts (for example, *ideal, dream*) has also become more frequent and the same has occurred with religious words and invocations of God. As Lim observes, anti-intellectualism and abstraction are categories that normally do not match since abstract reference normally requires some theorizing. One of the possible effects of this combination is 'pontification without explanation', an expression referring to the fact that abstract rhetoric is 'seldom a prelude to a substantial argument' (Lim 2002: 334).

Besides becoming more anti-intellectual and more abstract, presidential speeches also communicate a sense of increased assertiveness. Lim notes that words implying an active orientation tend to be used more. Also references to strength, power and influence are more recurrent. In short, presidential rhetoric appears as more and more pervaded by an air of can-doism with positive projections into the future. This is linguistically expressed by frequent references to the concepts of commencement, renewal and hope and a parallel disappearance of terms such as fate and providence. Significantly enough, these observations about the development of a presidential rhetoric that is more activist, more realist and more confident seem also confirmed by president Obama's use of language. Suffice it to consider his catch phrase during the 2008 election campaign: 'Yes, we can'.

Another general rhetorical shift that Lim deduces from his analysis is that towards democratization. Lim observes that 'modern presidents have rhetorically represented themselves increasingly as protectors and defenders of the people', while becoming 'less verbally concerned with the other branches of government' (2002: 339). This is linguistically expressed in many ways. The use of words denoting kinship, and especially the term *children*, has increased a lot, whereas references to the legislature, the Senate, the House of Representatives and the Supreme Court have drastically diminished. References to the reified authority of the Constitution have also declined, while the figure of the president has acquired more centrality, as shown by the frequent use of inclusive and exclusive self-reference (for example, the personal pronouns *we* and *I*). This has contributed to the rise of a rhetoric that is more people-oriented. The sense of inclusiveness is communicated not just through the use of personal pronouns but also by the use of the term *America*, which modern presidents seem to prefer over *United States*. The word *America* alludes to a type of unity among people that is more humanly connoted than the one evoked by the term *United States*. While the expression *United States* implies a union among bounded territories, the term *America* is more suggestive of a union among other kinds of pluralities: races, communities and individuals. Lim also notes that certain traditionally Republican terms, such as *republic, citizen, character, duty* and *virtuous*, have become uncommon. 'In contrast, references to leader, people, democracy have increased dramatically over time' (2002: 340). As part of this process of democratization, language has also become more compassionate and emotive, as suggested by the frequent employment of terms indicating supportiveness, affiliation, affect and concern for the well-being of people. In addition to this, political language is now more egalitarian than in the past, as proved by the increased use of the words *poverty* and *help*. The analysis presented in Chapters 5, 6 and 7 will show in which ways Obama's rhetoric is in line with this general democratic orientation.

Lastly, Lim observes that the rhetorical style of modern presidents has become more conversational. Presidents' tendencies to be anecdotal and their use of a more intimate language signal this trend. It has become common practice among modern politicians to refer to other political figures and to the stories of American citizens as a form of paying reverence to the wisdom of American people. This habit also features in Obama's 2008 election campaign speeches and will be discussed in Chapter 5. Furthermore, Lim notes that alongside an increase in self-referentiality there has been a concomitant increase in the use of singular pronouns directed to the other, which he interprets as a sign of affiliation rather than distance. As the following discussion describes, the use of personal pronouns as a rhetorical strategy is a feature of presidential language that has been analyzed in a number of studies.

The rhetorical works considered so far have basically emphasized two aspects of presidential speeches: the tight relation between tradition and innovation, and the skillful use of words and phrases that help define the president as an individual and in his relation to the public. This last facet of presidential rhetoric has also been observed with a more specific focus on the effects that presidential language can produce on people. Thus, there are studies that, following on from Aristotle's concerns, explore the communicative relationship between speaker and listener to account for the impact or effect of a political speech. In these accounts, the success or persuasiveness of a communicative act is dependent on the skillful use of rhetorical strategies that reduce the distance between speaker and listener and eventually suggest their identification with each other. This aspect is described, for example, in Tannen (2007, ch. 6), who mentions repetition in the form of both parallel structures and recursive formulas, dialogue, and the use of various images and figures of speech as techniques used by politicians in their speeches to create a sense of involvement. Another much quoted technique is the use of personal pronouns to suggest a symbolic identification between the president and the nation (see, for example, Schlesinger 1959, Dayan and Katz 1992, Ryfe 1999, Teten 2003). The personal pronoun *we*, in particular, is used to create a sense of communal sharing and indicate that the president is in touch with the whole country. The strategic use of personal pronouns enables politicians to construct and change their identities and roles as political actors (see Wilson 1990). Thus, political leaders can strategically decide to use the pronouns *we*, *us* and *our* to communicate their supposed will to act as spokesmen for ordinary people. This is accomplished thanks to the opacity of the actual referents. When American candidates for the presidency employ the pronoun *we* in their public speeches they actually rely on a certain degree of semantic ambiguity of this term since the personal pronoun could refer to the American people at large, to one of the two major parties, to both parties, to the presidential candidate and the electorate and so on. On the whole, the use of these so-called inclusive pronouns helps politicians legitimize their opinions by seeming to anticipate people's needs and wishes (see Chilton 1987, 1990). The corpus of election campaign speeches analyzed in this book shows Obama's preference for inclusive over exclusive pronouns.[7]

A political leader's capacity to convince the public and elites to support them is actually the essence of the contemporary approach to presidential rhetoric as expressed by the two concepts of 'rhetorical presidency' and 'going public'. The rhetorical presidency is a theoretical construct according to which:

- Presidents' addresses can be as important as their policies;
- Presidents' words are deeds, since they bring the force and majesty of the office with them;
- Even presidential directives will not achieve their goals if presidents cannot persuade the public and the press to support their aims;
- Presidents have a variety of ways to influence opinions, including speeches, press conferences and the news;
- Presidential messages are the outgrowth of modern marketing techniques.

(Perloff 1998: 105)

In Tulis's view (1987), 'rhetorical presidency' is based on the popular appeal of the president and is characterized by its heavy reliance on speech-making and the coincidence of speech with action. According to the critic, reliance on speech-making is so strong that 'presidential speeches themselves have become the issues and events of modern politics rather than the medium through which issues and events are discussed and assessed' (179).[9]

'Going public', on the other hand, is a 'strategy whereby a president promotes himself and his policies in Washington by appealing to the American public for support' (Kernell 1993: 2). The major difference between the two notions lies in the fact that 'going public' is more closely connected to institutional factors. It more specifically refers to the strategy employed by American presidents to make direct appeals to voters and in so doing put pressure on the Congress to pass legislation that the president stands for. In a nutshell, 'going public' is a strategy of leadership that looks for the immediate support of voters to avoid negotiation with a divided Government.

2.2   Speech-making as a form of political campaign communication

The term *political discourse* has no doubt vast applicability. Since the political arena is made up of many different participants – political institutions, politicians, citizens, voters, protesters, dissidents, grassroots organizations, pressure and issue groups and so on – the concept of political discourse can appear as rather elusive (see Van Dijk 1997). In principle, it can refer to any of the multiple expressions of 'political text and talk' (see Chilton and Schäffner 2002) that are produced in a political dimension. Furthermore, in line with suggestions from critical discourse analysis, any instance of discourse can be politically connoted in so far as it promotes forms of power, dominance, control, ideology and discrimination (see Fairclough 1989, 1995, Wodak 1989, Kress and Hodge 1993, Fairclough and Wodak 1997; for an examination of political (in the broad sense) ideologies through the descriptive tools of cognitive linguistics see Dirven et al. 2001). It is therefore important to make it clear that the concept of political discourse is used in this book, unless differently specified, with reference to political leaders' 'talk' as exemplified by president Obama's speeches during the 2008 election campaign.

Having specified how the notion of political discourse is interpreted here, it is now necessary to spend a few words on how politicians speak in public. This is one of the most fundamental communicative practices during any political campaign and certainly a crucial practice during presidential election campaigns. As pointed out by Gelderman, 'a president who wishes to lead a nation rather than only the executive branch must be a *loquacious president* [...] *Speeches are the core of the modern presidency*' (1997: 8–9, my emphasis). Today, speeches occupy such a central space in the realm of political communication that one needs to be reminded that this used not to be the case at the beginning and in the early phase of American presidential history (Perloff 1998, ch. 6). Indeed, during the eighteenth and nineteenth centuries the role of presidential oratory was minimal. The Founding Fathers avoided speaking in public as much as possible. Fearing that their words could stir unpredictable and uncontrollable mass reactions, they devised a political system that gave power to the institutions of government (states, Congress, presidency). Democracy was far less participatory back then, and the president's power was expected to derive directly from the Constitution. For this reasons, presidents used to limit their public speaking to ceremonial occasions and to craft their speeches around general topics. Abraham Lincoln, taking the oath of office in 1861, is admittedly one of America's greatest orators and one who could elevate the country with his inspirational messages. Among others, his Gettysburg Address has been acclaimed as a monumental instance of presidential rhetoric. However, while recognizing the importance of public opinion, Lincoln did not regularly speak in public (Tulis 1987: 79–83). During his presidential years, he made no more than a hundred speeches and many of them were very short (Metcalf 2004: 235). President Woodrow Wilson was probably the first to fully recognize that his power would crucially depend on his ability to influence and lead mass opinion. While he was in office, between 1913 and 1921, he relied extensively on his public speaking (Kernell 1993: 19). Since then, presidents have been more and more concerned about communication with their audiences, to the point that the expressions 'going public' and 'rhetorical presidency' have been coined. As Hart (1984: 2) remarks, in 1976 Gerald Ford gave seven times more speeches than Dwight Eisenhower twenty years earlier; more recently, 'it has become possible to conceive of a corrupt president or an inept or a truculent president, but it is not now possible to imagine a quiet president' (Hart 1984: 4).

Over the last decades, verbal communication has become a major part of the presidency as well as an essential component of presidential election campaigns. In their need to speak to the public, presidential candidates are faced with two basic tasks. First they need to decide who are the people they intend to address, and consequently they have to devise an appropriate message to be communicated (see Trent and Friedenberg 2000). In order to analyze audiences, political campaigns have increasingly employed two tools: the study of past voter statistics and the public opinion poll. Both tools have flourished in recent years due to developments in computer technology. Knowing voters' preferences and inclinations can help presidential candidates to choose which states should be targeted more specifically. However, the use of polling and of issue polls in particular has not always been seen favorably. Issue polls are intended to scrutinize the electorate to find out which topics and issues are of utmost concern and what the opinions and beliefs of voters are. In this way, issue polls provide candidates with a list of themes that can be addressed during the campaign. Furthermore, issue polls can affect the development of politicians' positions on certain issues. Absolute reliance on polls, at the expense of elaborating one's own program and taking a personal approach to issues, is a practice that was first strongly criticized by president Harry Truman. In 1954, at a time when polling had just started to develop as a tool of campaigning, Truman wrote: 'It isn't polls or public opinion of the moment that count. It is right and wrong leadership – men with fortitude, honesty, and a belief in the right – that makes epochs in the history of the world' (quoted in Trent and Friedenberg 2000: 180).

Today, many politicians probably agree with the implications of Truman's message that polls can help understand the electorate better, but they cannot and should not determine the course of a campaign. This position is also taken and promoted by the cognitive linguist George Lakoff. In *Thinking Points* (2006), a handbook for the grassroots progressive community, Lakoff mentions 12 traps that progressives should avoid if they intend to win elections. The second of these is the 'poll trap', where the label refers to the erroneous habit of slavishly following polls to find out which position to take, instead of leading people to new positions. The relevance of these comments will become clearer in the following chapters.

If we now zoom in on the message of the election campaign, a few more details can be added. Election campaign speeches are expected to provide information about the candidate him/herself, the election as a whole, the particular policies that will be supported if the candidate is elected, political opponents and enemies, and the bad politics of the past to which alternatives are proposed. As the analysis in the following chapters will show, in the 2008 election campaign, Obama appeared as the embodiment of the contemporary American success story – a man with an extraordinary life and a great personality. This probably reinforced, on a general level, his message of unity and change. Obama could also rely on a general dissatisfaction with Republican governance and particularly with a loss of public confidence in Republican foreign and domestic policy. The war in Iraq, the mismanagement of Hurricane Katrina and congressional corruption feature as frequent targets of Obama's criticism, especially in the initial phase of the race.

Political campaigns can also be distinguished by their focus on either foreign or domestic affairs. For instance, after 9/11, American politicians running for the presidency in 2004 could not avoid discussing foreign policy and national security – a dimension of 'talk' that overall benefited the Republicans as the self-proclaimed better defenders of the nation from foreign attacks. The following election in 2008 was only initially concerned with foreign affairs and the war in Iraq. In particular, the main subject of Obama's agenda was domestic affairs, including education, health care, (un) employment, taxes and, above all, the economy. The emphasis on the economy was evident in his campaign speeches starting from August 2008 and reaching its climax by mid-September due to a severe crisis in some of the nation's financial institutions. These observations are supported by statistical analyses which demonstrate a gradual shift in the frequency of Obama's lexical choices during 2008 (Savoy 2010). In particular, the term *Iraq* undergoes a very sharp decline, starting from April 2008, and it nearly disappears from the speeches Obama delivered in September and October. Conversely, in these two months a significant increase in the use of the word *jobs* is recorded. Furthermore, Obama's general orientation toward domestic policy and his focus on American citizens is indicated by his marked preference for terms such as *labor, worker, manufacturing, women, school, insurance* and *crisis* throughout the whole election campaign.

Apart from the content as such, the success of political campaign speeches is also dependent on the overall structure and sequence of presentation. In this respect, a remarkable feature of political speeches is the presence of 'modules': sections of variable length that reappear with slight variation during the campaign. As the demand for public speaking has increased, politicians are faced with the need to address different audiences on a wide range of topics. Under these circumstances, resorting to the use of 'speech modules' appears as a necessary move. This strategy was noted and commented upon during the 1980 primaries, when the *New York Times* reported that the presidential candidates of the two major parties

> make hundreds of speeches in their campaigns, speeches that vary in content depending on where they were given and the audience addressed. But every candidate has a body of material, usually presented in every speech that varies little from audience to audience. This material represents the heart of his message to the voters as he moves around the country. (quoted in Trent and Friedenberg 2000: 181)

Trent and Friedenberg (2000: 182–5) describe the 'speech module' as an independent unit of a speech that can be delivered in a time span varying from two up to seven minutes. The length of the module essentially depends on the presence or absence of examples, statistics, illustrations or other support materials. Candidates normally have a speech module for each of the major topics under discussion (health, environment, unemployment, education, taxes and so on). Typically, speech modules share a common structure. They open with some attention-gaining device and then move to describe a problem and present a solution. Sometimes the solution can be visualized in more detail, as when, for example, the candidate describes what would happen if he/she were elected. Key modules are generally devised at the beginning of the campaign, but new modules can emerge throughout, as certain political issues may become more relevant due to unforeseen circumstances. For example, this might have played a role in Obama's focus on the economy in his campaign speeches at the time when the economic crisis was at its worst (in late summer 2008). Via partial reiteration, speech modules have the pragmatic function of reinforcing a candidate's position on the major issues. Furthermore, being tailored to specific audiences and occasions, speech modules have the potential to convince different components of the electorate that certain policies are valid.

The analysis of Obama's 2008 election campaign rhetoric brings forth some interesting examples of speech modules. In particular, if one considers the last couple of months before the final election, speech modules can be identified that elaborate on the global financial crisis and the American (Obama's) strategy of intervention. The module reported below has been observed to reoccur without modification in three distinct speeches that Obama held in September. This example also shows how long such stretches of unaltered speech can be.

(5) We meet here at a time of great uncertainty for America. The era of greed and irresponsibility on Wall Street and in Washington has led us to a financial crisis as serious as any we have faced since the Great Depression. They said they wanted to let the market run free but they let it run wild, and in doing so, they trampled our core values of fairness, balance, and responsibility to one another.

Everywhere you look, the economic news is troubling. But for so many Americans, it isn't really news at all.

600,000 workers have lost their jobs since January. Home values are falling. Your paycheck doesn't go as far as it used to. It's never been harder to save or retire; to buy gas or groceries; and if you put it on a credit card, they've probably raised your rates. In so many cities and towns across America, it feels as if the dream that so many generations have fought for is slowly slipping away.

I know these are difficult days. But here's what I also know. I know we can steer ourselves out of this crisis. Because that's who we are. Because that's what we've always done as Americans. Our nation has faced difficult times before. And at each of those moments, we've risen to meet the challenge because we've never forgotten that fundamental truth – that here in America, our destiny is not written for us, but by us.

There are many to blame for causing the crisis we are in, and that starts with the speculators on Wall Street who gamed the system and the regulators in Washington who looked the other way.

This Administration started off by asking for a blank check to solve this problem. I said absolutely not. I said it was unacceptable to expect the American people to hand this Administration or any Administration a $700 billion check with no conditions and no oversight when a lack of oversight in Washington and on Wall Street is exactly what got us into this mess. If the American people are being asked to help solve this crisis, then you have a right to make sure that your tax dollars are protected. That's why I laid out a few a conditions for Washington.

First, I said we needed an independent board to provide oversight and accountability for how and where this money is spent at every step of the way.

Second, if American taxpayers are financing this solution, I said that you should be treated like investors. That means that Wall Street and Washington should give you every penny of your money back once this economy recovers.

Third, I said that we cannot and will not simply bailout Wall Street without helping the millions of innocent homeowners who are struggling to stay in their homes. They deserve a plan too.

Finally – and this one is important – I said that I would not allow this plan to become a welfare program for the Wall Street executives whose greed and irresponsibility got us into this mess.

Now, my opponent, John McCain, talks about getting tough on Wall Street now, but he's been against the common-sense rules and regulations that could've stopped this mess for decades. He says he'll take on the corporate lobbyists, but he put seven of the biggest lobbyists in Washington in charge of his campaign. And if you think those lobbyists are working day and night to elect my opponent just to put themselves out of business, well I've got a bridge to sell you up in Alaska.

The truth is, when my opponent first reacted to this crisis by saying that the fundamentals of our economy are strong, he didn't just make a mistake. He revealed an out-of-touch philosophy he's followed for decades in Washington – the idea that if we give more and more to those with the most, prosperity will trickle down to everyone else; the idea that no harm will be done if we let lobbyists shred consumer protections and fight against every regulation as unwise or unnecessary.

Well what we have seen over the last few weeks is nothing less than the final verdict on this failed philosophy. And I am running for President of the United States because the dreams of the American people cannot be endangered anymore.

We have a different way of measuring the fundamentals of our economy. We know that the fundamentals that we use to measure economic strength are whether we are living up to that fundamental promise that has made this country great – that America is a place where you can make it if you try; that everyone should have the chance to live their dreams.

I know I wouldn't be standing here today without that promise. And I know that's the promise we must keep once more.

When I talk to those young veterans who come back from Iraq and Afghanistan, I see my grandfather, who signed up after Pearl Harbor, marched in Patton's Army, and was rewarded by a grateful nation with the chance to go to college on the GI Bill.

In the face of that young student who sleeps just three hours before working the night shift, I think about my mom, who raised my sister and me on her own while she worked and earned her degree; who once turned to food stamps but was still able to send us to the best schools in the country.

And when I listen to another worker tell me that his factory has shut down, I remember all those men and women on the South Side of Chicago who I stood by and fought for two decades ago after the local steel plant closed. These are my heroes. Theirs are the stories that shaped me. And it is on their behalf that I intend to win this election and keep the promise of America alive as President of the United States. (24, 27, 28 September 2008)

This speech module follows a clear structure. The opening paragraph sets the ground for the main issue to be discussed – the financial crisis – and also provides a motivation for that (the greed and irresponsibility of people working in Wall Street and in Washington) and a moral evaluation (these people have trampled on American fundamental values). After this brief and condensed introduction, Obama employs three paragraphs to describe the major effects of the economic crisis on the lives of the American people (increasing unemployment and reduced purchasing power) and to combine this message with an optimistic note. In fact, in the last of this group of paragraphs he empowers Americans with a patently patriotic statement. Since Americans have already proved their capacity to cope with the most difficult situations, they won't be defeated this time. They can decide their destiny and hence turn the crisis into another American victory against adverse conditions. Then, in the following six paragraphs, Obama elaborates a bit more on the actual causes of the crisis and offers his own solution to that. While many people can be 'blamed for causing the crisis', Obama is very straightforward in directing his accusations against Wall Street speculators, Washington legislators and the current Republican Administration. These groups of people are held responsible for the crisis. To contrast the tragic consequences of their misbehavior, Obama proposes a political action plan. His plan to restore economic stability is articulated in four points that revolve around some basic Democratic values: responsibility (an independent board should check how money is spent), fairness in economic dealings (American taxpayers should be treated like investors) and care for the people who really need help (innocent homeowners instead of guilty Wall Street executives). This coherent articulation gives the impression of a thoroughly planned political design that responds to the need for logos in political rhetoric. Furthermore, Obama is able to accommodate political ethos and pathos by relying on people's emotional reaction to convey basic moral values. The speech module continues with two paragraphs where the target of Obama's blame becomes more specific. John McCain, his Republican opponent, is accused of incoherent and contradictory political behavior because of his apparent criticism of Wall Street and corporate lobbyists and his concomitant enduring support of their special interests. McCain is depicted as the prototypical Republican candidate who believes in unregulated free markets and the moral right of rich people to get more because they are the ones who can make the country prosper. In what follows, Obama presents the rationale for his participation in the presidential race and explicitly refers to the people who would benefit from his leadership. In order to sound more convincing and be emotionally more involving, he draws some parallels between his personal story and the stories of ordinary American people. To the Republican failed philosophy that only makes rich people richer, he opposes a vision of America as the land of opportunity where everyone is given an equal chance to succeed. The credibility of this message is immediately manifest. Notwithstanding all odds, Obama could make it. He openly embodies the very logic he puts forth and the ideals he sustains. Obama's closeness to the American people and his trust in their capacity to face the crisis is expressed via references to his own life and that of his family. Young American veterans coming back from Iraq and Afghanistan are compared to Obama's grandfather, who fought in the war and was rewarded with a chance to go to college on his return. Students who work hard to pay for their education remind Obama of his mother and the struggles she went through to get a university degree and sustain a family. Finally, the situation of workers who have recently lost their jobs allows for even more personal reminiscences. Obama evokes his own past experience as a community organizer on the South Side of Chicago when he helped people go on with their lives after the local steel plant had closed and people lost their jobs. Obama concludes his speech module with a promise to the

American people, the promise to give each and every American the possibility to realize their dreams.

Another element of political strategic planning is the crafting of a short statement that can epitomize the candidates' message throughout the campaign, the so-called 'why I am running' statement. Faucheux, a political analyst and public affairs strategist, suggests that candidates should develop 'a sentence or short paragraph that summarizes the reason why the voters should elect you, keeping in mind your strengths, the opposition's weaknesses, and your points of inoculation' (1994: 49). In 2008 Obama repeatedly spelled out the reasons that made him run the presidential race. The explicit and direct phrasing 'that's why I'm running for President (of the United States)' alternates with expressions like 'I'm running (for President of the United States) because', 'the reason I'm running for President is' and 'it is why I'm running for President'. The same ideas are sometimes channeled by replacing the typical causal clause with a temporal or a hypothetical subordinate ('when I am President, I will' and 'If I'm President, I will'), or a simple declarative ('I will be the President who'). Almost every speech of Obama's 2008 campaign contains at least one of these statements, where the Senator makes his electoral promises and in so doing tries to gain the voters' support. This means that each of the issues variously addressed during the long campaign is also framed in this standardized format. As a way of exemplification, part of a speech containing five such statements is reported below:

(6) The woman I met in Indiana who just lost her job, and her pension, and her insurance when the plant where she worked at her entire life closed down – she can't afford four more years of tax breaks for corporations like the one that shipped her job overseas. She needs us to give tax breaks to companies that create good jobs here in America. She can't afford four more years of tax breaks for CEOs like the one who walked away from her company with a multi-million dollar bonus. She needs middle-class tax relief that will help her pay the skyrocketing price of groceries, and gas, and college tuition. *That's why I'm running for President.*

The college student I met in Iowa who works the night shift after a full day of class and still can't pay the medical bills for a sister who's ill – she can't afford four more years of a health care plan that only takes care of the healthy and the wealthy; that allows insurance companies to discriminate and deny coverage to those Americans who need it most. She needs us to stand up to those insurance companies and pass a plan that lowers every family's premiums and gives every uninsured American the same kind of coverage that Members of Congress give themselves. *That's why I'm running for President.*

The mother in Wisconsin who gave me a bracelet inscribed with the name of the son she lost in Iraq; the families who pray for their loved ones to come home; the heroes on their third and fourth and fifth tour of duty – they can't afford four more years of a war that should've never been authorized and never been waged. They can't afford four more years of our veterans returning to broken-down barracks and substandard care. They need us to end a war that isn't making us safer. They need us to treat them with the care and respect they deserve. *That's why I'm running for President.*

The man I met in Pennsylvania who lost his job but can't even afford the gas to drive around and look for a new one – he can't afford four more years of an energy policy written by the oil companies and for the oil companies; a policy that's not only keeping gas at record prices, but funding both sides of the war on terror and destroying our planet in the process. He doesn't need four more years of Washington policies that sound good, but don't solve the problem. He needs us to take a permanent holiday from our oil addiction by making the automakers raise their fuel standards, corporations pay for their pollution, and oil companies invest their record profits in a clean energy future. That's the change we need. And *that's why I'm running for President.* (6 May 2008, my emphasis)

As this passage shows, Obama presents his own solutions for different problems affecting American people. In detail, he suggests the following: (a) introducing a new system of taxation that is less oppressive on the middle class, (b) reforming healthcare so that not only rich people are insured, (c) showing more empathy for veterans and their families and (d) investing in clean energy for a safer environment. From a textual point of view, each of the four paragraphs containing the statement 'that's why I'm running for President' is structured in a similar way. First, Obama refers to ordinary American citizens and the problems they face in their daily lives. Then, he calls for immediate action to cope with these problems. At the end of each textual unit, the solution to all of this finally comes: it is Obama himself epitomized in the statement of 'that's why I'm running for President'. Obama also skillfully combines a clear line of reasoning with a captivating emotional appeal, which proves his rhetorical ability.

Sometimes presidents are charged with accusations regarding the authorship of their public speeches. It is a fact that American presidents have made recourse to speechwriters since the foundation of the nation (Trent and Friedenberg 2000: 189–96). George Washington had four different speechwriters. Abraham Lincoln often received advice from his secretary of state, William Seward. Andrew Johnson could rely on the refined knowledge of the historian George Bancroft. Calvin Coolidge and Herbert Hoover called upon the same speechwriter. Franklin D. Roosevelt committed himself to the expertise of different people for preparing his speeches. With the remarkable exception of Dwight Eisenhower, all presidents can be said to have received help and advice in preparing their speeches. The masses, however, only started to become aware of this practice after Roosevelt's time in office. People have realized that the demands on public figures are simply too big to be all faced individually. This realization has smoothed down criticism and helped people cast a milder judgment on the use of speechwriters. After all, the person voicing a speech remains its author and the one who can be either blamed or praised for its contents. For this reason, one is inclined to agree with a speechwriter who once noted:

> I don't think it occurs to the general public that a speech is ghostwritten. Even if someone in the audience has read somewhere that Congressman X has a ghostwriter and he knows it as the man speaks, he forgets it. He's listening to the man, and he's holding him responsible, and he's responding to him for everything that is said. (quoted in Trent and Friedenberg 2000: 197)

The individual contribution of political leaders to 'their' public speeches is also hinted at in Charteris-Black (2005). In his outline of the 'art of speech making', Charteris-Black deals with the question of authorship of and personal responsibility for political speeches by writing that

> The political speaker is more than a mere mouthpiece [...] because ultimately he or she has the opportunity to edit the content of the speech and to improvise in its style of delivery. Though the words he or she utters may originate in the minds of invisible others, the politician is ultimately accountable for them. What is said is recorded in official sources (e.g. *Hansard*) and may subsequently be quoted back to the source who cannot deny or disown it. The role of speechwriters is, then, to support the marketing of a 'brand' that is created by the individual politician and therefore it is the politician who must be considered as the author of his or her speeches. (2005: 8)

As these words suggest, political leaders can adjust their rhetoric as they deliver their speeches. More importantly, though, this quote illustrates that in official contexts where speech is recorded, it is always the person having delivered a speech who is held accountable as the author of the speech.

Acting behind the scene, ghostwriters are often perceived as occupying a marginal space on the political stage. They are not the protagonists in the play of politics, but their job is nonetheless commendable considering how much it contributes to the final result (see Lehrman 2010 for an instructional and well-documented resource on speechwriting).

After all, speechwriters are expected to act as a kind of presidential alter ego (see Schlesinger 2008 for a lively and entertaining narration of the unique relationships between US presidents and their speechwriters/advisors from the 1930s until the Bush 2001 administration). Since they need to portray a faithful image of the candidate, it is necessary for them to establish a close relation with him. This will allow them to grasp the true nature of the candidate's life philosophy, to unveil his personal value system, to comprehend his position on the major issues, to understand his decision process and to capture the typical traits and vagaries of his language and behavior. After having absorbed this bulky amount of diverse information, speechwriters are expected to act as ventriloquists who give voice to someone else's mind. The end product should sound like an echo of the candidate's own ways of using language and it should appear as an accurate reflection of his whole person. In addition to knowing the candidate, speechwriters also need to know how to gather information about different topics of political interest and about audiences and occasions of speech delivery. Due to the diversified expertise that is needed, speechwriters are often organized in teams typically made up of three groups: the researchers, the stylists and the media or public relation advisors. The first group basically conducts background research. The second group composes the speeches taking heed of how the candidate in his personal style recounts stories, tells jokes, expresses indignation and uses a particular jargon or a set of metaphors. The third group concentrates on identifying good strategies to please the audience. What should be stressed at this point is that throughout the entire creative process the candidate remains the major editor, writer and creator. The speechwriting team usually meets with the candidate and minutely writes down and records his words on the different issues. Many drafts of the speeches would then be sketched until the final version is approved by the candidate, who can see himself reflected in the pages.

For president Obama, one of the chief interlocutors during his 2008 election campaign was the 'wunderkind' Jon Favreau, a then 27-year-old speechwriter (see Philp 2009, Pilkington 2009). The two men first met in 2004 and since then Favreau has been studying with almost obsessive accuracy Obama's speech patterns and cadences. He learnt by heart the much acclaimed speech that Obama gave at the Democratic National Convention in 2004, and he is said to carry a copy of Obama's autobiography *Dreams from my Father* wherever he goes. Favreau is one of the few people who had the opportunity to get so close to the president as to 'absorb his ideas and language' and obtain his trust in representing them. Throughout the campaign he worked in close connection with the president. In the words of the journalist Ashley Parker (20 January 2008), 'Mr Favreau used time to master Mr Obama's voice. He took down almost everything the senator said and absorbed it. Now, he said, when he sits down to write, he just channels Mr Obama – his ideas, his sentences, his phrases'. Since Obama is not only an enchanting orator but also a very well-versed writer, the work with his 'mind reader' has always been extremely collaborative, with drafts of the speeches being sent back and forth between the two of them. In addition to this, Favreau could rely on a team of advisers who supplied him with essential information about crucial times in American history and remarkable speeches by former presidents. In particular, Favreau could benefit from the assistance by Adam Frankel and Ben Rhodes, two highly valued consultants in the presidential rhetorical team. Notwithstanding these joint efforts, Obama alone should be taken as the true author of his speeches, the unmistakable voice who finds expression in remarkable pieces of political eloquence. Controversial as it may be, this is the opinion that Newton-Small (28 August 2008) shares with his readers in explaining how Obama writes his speeches:

> Obama takes an unusually hands-on approach to his speech-writing, more so than most politicians. His best writing time comes late at night when he is all alone scribbling on yellow legal pads. He then logs these thoughts into his laptop, editing as he goes along. This is how he wrote both of his best-selling books – *Dreams from my Father* and *The Audacity of Hope* – staying up after Michelle and his two young daughters had long gone to bed, raveling in the late night quiet. For this speech [28 August 2008] Obama removed himself from the distractions at home and spent many nights in a room in a Park Hyatt Hotel in Chicago. These late-night sessions produced long, meandering texts that were then circulated to a close group of advisers, including David Axelrod and Obama's speech-writer Jon Favreau [...]. 'When you work with senator Obama the main player on a speech is senator Obama', Axelrod said. 'He is the best speech-writer in the group and he knows what he wants to say and he generally says it better than anyone else would'.

While we may disagree with the enthusiastically supportive tone of these words, it is by now common knowledge among scholars of political rhetoric that 'at the presidential level, there is simply no truth to the charge that words are being put into the president's mouth' (Ritter and Medhurst 2003: 9). So, the master and chief wordsmith of Obama's speeches cannot be anyone but Obama himself.

Another practice that is fairly common during election campaigns is the selection of so-called 'surrogate speakers' who can speak on behalf of the candidate when time constraints do not allow him to be on duty (see Trent and Friedenberg 2000: 198–201). Since surrogate speakers should have a clearly identifiable connection to the candidate, they are normally appointed from among family members, cabinet members and legislative allies. Sometimes, surrogates can replace the candidate very successfully, such as when they are capable of relating to a particular audience in a very convincing manner. So, for example, on 24 September 2008, while Obama was talking in Dunedin (Florida), his wife Michelle presided a roundtable discussion with Pennsylvania military spouses. That was not the first time that Michelle addressed this type of audience. Indeed, throughout the whole election campaign she put a lot of effort into creating an image of herself and her husband as a couple who are particularly sensitive to the needs of military families. In August 2008, for instance, at a roundtable with military spouses in Vancouver, she emphasized the kindred spirit of her husband by saying: 'The commander in chief doesn't just need to know how to lead the military, he needs to understand what war does to military families'. Talking to military spouses on several occasions gave Michelle the unique opportunity to reinforce her somewhat doubted patriotic feelings.[8] Furthermore, it protected Barack Obama from stepping onto unstable ground. After all, a direct comparison between a man with no military service and an ex-Navy pilot and war hero was more likely to favor the second (the role of presidential spouses as a surrogate is described in Benoit, Blaney and Pier 1998, ch. 9).

So far, the discussion has alluded to the fact that every speech responds to specific needs. American political speeches, however, can also be grouped according to common purposes that reflect the different phases in the confrontation between candidates. Basically, every election campaign passes through four relatively discrete stages that can be categorized as preprimary, primary, convention and general election (see Trent and Friedenberg 2000, ch. 2). Here, the discussion is restricted to the primary and general election stages due to their absolute significance and their relevance with respect to the speeches analyzed in this study. Primaries have been described as 'America's most original contribution to the art of democracy' (Keech and Matthews 1976: 91). Primary elections serve the purpose of selecting one candidate for each of the two major parties to run in the general election. In other words, through primaries voters determine the front-runners for the nomination. Primaries are important occasions for voters to see candidates in action and to get first-hand impressions of how they behave both verbally and non-verbally. In addition, they provide candidates with some general feedback from voters, which can determine a repositioning in terms of stands on issues, images and overall campaign strategies. The increase in the number of primaries in the last few decades has enlarged citizens' involvement in the democratic process for a number of reasons. Primary campaigning is a phase in which candidates crisscross states and cities and can even meet individual voters. It is a stage in the campaign when large sums of money are spent in the primary states and there is a lot of media coverage. Finally, and most importantly, it is during this time that candidates make promises about what they will do if elected, and this generally has a strong impact on voters (for an insightful discussion on the nature and quality of communication during presidential primaries over a period of 80 years, starting from 1912, see Kendall 2000).

Once the leading contenders for the nomination have been determined through primary elections and legitimized via national conventions, the final stage of the election starts, that of the general election campaign. This last phase is of utmost importance since it represents the climax of the election campaign. This is the period when communication becomes more intense and direct.

In the case of Obama's 2008 election campaign, 5 February, also known as Super Tuesday, was the day when the largest number of primaries were held. On that day Obama won 13 contests while Hillary Clinton came first in only ten of them. Between 5 February and 10 June more primaries were held in different states, which confirmed Obama as the Democratic candidate for the presidential election. After it was clear that Obama was the candidate of choice for the Democrats, the general election campaign continued throughout summer up until November with intense speech-making. From then on until election day, Obama's speeches were aimed at obtaining the support of the larger electorate, not just Democrats, but particularly swing voters and Independents.

2.3   Political discourse as a battleground for competing worldviews

In the last two decades, the general debate on American politics and ideology has been informed and enriched by the insights of a well-known sociologist from the University of Virginia, James Davison Hunter. In 1991, Hunter proposed a theory about opposing views in American culture that goes by the name of 'culture war' and, in a nutshell, concerns a 'values divide' in US culture. The theory was primarily intended to describe cultural oppositions in American society and to account for them in terms of people's moral assessments of reality. The theory has been primarily used for studying disagreements over public policy and political candidates. This means that the 'cultural divide' has been taken as a template to analyze how views on the whole range of political issues are shaped and how political behavior is affected by that.

Besides having become extremely influential in the US, Hunter's theory has also caused heated discussions, especially among circles of academic sociologists and political scientists. In fact, since the publication of Hunter's work, scholars and professionals of various creeds have evaluated his theory in relation to their own scientific paradigms and have come up with often contradictory results. Reviewing data from the General Social Survey and the National Election Study from the early 1970s to the mid-90s, DiMaggio and colleagues (1996) rejected the idea of a cultural divide by claiming that, with the sole exception of abortion, there was 'no support for the proposition that the United States has experienced dramatic polarization in public opinion on social issues' (738). In their view, Americans, if anything, were becoming more and more similar. Shortly after, this opinion was reinforced by results from a qualitative study conducted by Wolfe (1998). This showed that middle-class Americans did not occupy two 'hostile camps' (321). More recently, Fiorina and co-authors (2005) have tried to remove any doubts about the existence of polarization in American politics by claiming that polarization is no more than a myth. Conversely, on the other side of the intellectual debate, many books have been published over the last few years which have gathered new evidence to prove that America is, indeed, split by cultural and political polarization (see Bowman 2010 for an overview of some of these studies). Thus, skepticism has alternated with amicable response and unfavorable criticism with praise. In this vortex of competing opinions, no voice may sound sufficiently loud and no reasoning may appear convincing enough to be taken as definitive. One fact, though, remains: Hunter's theory, be it embraced or refuted, has strongly contributed to shaping the understanding of American politics. Furthermore, Hunter's ideas about American culture (and politics as a reflection of it) tie in with Lakoff's view of American politics (1996). While the sociologist has identified deep connections between morality and cultural (by derivation also political) divisions, the linguist has provided a framework that illuminates the kind of links existing between morality, parenting style and political affiliation. More about Lakoff's linguistic model and its applicability to the analysis of political discourse will be said in the following chapters. For the moment, in view of its historical and cultural significance, this section is intended to introduce the reader to Hunter's theory.

In 1991, Hunter coined the expression 'culture wars' to describe the 'values divide' between 'red' (Republican) and 'blue' (Democratic) Americans. Since then, the concept has entered the language of political debate, making its first public appearance in 1992 when presidential candidate Pat Buchanan declared at his speech at the Republican National Convention that 'there is a religious war going on in our country for the soul of America. It is a cultural war, as critical to the kind of nation we will one day be as the Cold War itself'. On that particular occasion, the use of a martial metaphor to define American religious and cultural disputes was not received very favorably, since both progressives and many conservatives were expecting a more appealing message (Hunter and Wolfe 2006: 1). However, the concept of a 'culture war' as such was destined to influence the debate on cultural politics for years to come. But what is actually meant by 'culture war' and how far can we talk of a 'cultural conflict' within America? Hunter (1991) provides a clear answer to this question.

To start with, the sociologist very neatly explains that for him 'cultural conflict' is 'political and social hostility rooted in different systems of *moral understanding*' (1991: 42, my emphasis). In other words, differing worldviews rather than theological or ecclesiastical divisions can be held responsible for social and political opposition among Americans. Ultimately, social divisions that are politically consequential can be traced back to the matter of moral authority. According to Hunter, the way in which moral authority is envisioned has an effect on how political issues are debated as diverse as abortion, childcare, funding for the arts, affirmative action and quotas, gay rights and so on. What is meant by moral authority is 'the basis by which people determine whether something is good or bad, right or wrong, acceptable or unacceptable' (*ibid.*).

People make their moral judgments according to their own view of morality and this inevitably affects human relations in so far as affinities and dissimilarities are perceived. People sharing similar moral views tend to stick together and define themselves in contrast to those whose moral views are different. In Hunter's words 'it is the commitment to different and opposing bases of moral authority and the world views that derive from them that creates the deep cleavages between antagonists in the contemporary culture war' (43). Thus, competing moral visions are at the base of today's cultural war.

This, however, doesn't mean that opposing moral visions surface in clearly defined, fully articulated and unambiguously differentiated world views. 'These moral visions take expression as *polarizing impulses* or *tendencies* in American culture' (43, emphasis in the original). In line with their understanding of moral authority and consequential approach to reality, Americans can be split into two major groups: orthodox and progressive. Many Americans, however, are found to occupy a middle space in between the two large groupings. These are people who lean towards one side or other, but who cannot fully identify themselves with either of the two poles. For this reason, when Hunter describes the deep cleavage in the American culture war he refers to 'the impulse toward orthodoxy' and 'the impulse toward progressivism'. Somewhat apologetically, Hunter admits that 'the terms are imperfect, but each aspires to describe in shorthand a particular locus and source of moral truth, the fundamental (though perhaps subconscious) moral allegiances of the actors involved in the culture war as well as their cultural and political dispositions' (43). Adding to this, one may also feel inclined to praise Hunter's labeling, since the two expressions adequately capture the complexity implicit in any act of categorization, even more so when dealing with people.

Another aspect that needs to be elaborated in more detail is Hunter's interpretation of the terms 'orthodox' and 'progressive'. These words are taken by the sociologist to indicate 'formal properties of a belief system or world view'. What defines orthodoxy is 'the commitment on the part of adherents to an external, definable and transcendent authority' (43). This authority, which lies outside and beyond individuals – in God, the Scriptures and the holy texts – defines boundaries between good and bad, right and wrong, acceptable and unacceptable. Besides providing a consistent measure of value and dictating lines of conduct, this transcendent authority gives meaning to people's existence and purpose in life, at both a personal and a collective level. By contrast, 'within cultural progressivism, moral authority tends to be defined by the spirit of the modern age, a spirit of rationalism and subjectivism' (44). In this view, moral authority as the source of truth is perceived as transient rather than transcendent. Truth is nothing fixed or predetermined. On the contrary, it is subject to the unfolding flux of history and the indeterminacy of multiple subjectivities. Moral authority resides in personal experience and rationality as they interact with the contingency of particular cultural or religious traditions. Even though there may be distinctions among people sharing this vision, 'what all progressivist world views share in common is the tendency to resymbolize historic faiths according to the prevailing assumptions of contemporary life' (44–5). Furthermore, since what divides the orthodox from progressives is a contrasting view of morality and not religiosity, the cultural cleavage Hunter describes cuts across older lines of conflict among Protestants, Catholics and Jews to create new alliances. Due to their common views, interests and concerns, orthodox wings of Protestantism, Catholicism and Judaism establish solidarity among each other and build strong connections. The same is true of progressive sectors within different faith communities.

Not surprisingly, once applied to the context of American politics, these moral orientations fit two divergent political inclinations. Moral orthodoxy resonates in conservative thinking, whereas progressivist morality finds expression in a liberal political agenda. If we then consider that orthodoxy and progressivism are best interpreted as tendencies, we also understand why people can take a conservative position on certain issues and a liberal one on others. Hence, the antagonists in the culture war are cultural conservatives or traditionalists on the one side and cultural progressives or liberals on the other. While indulging in these classifications, Hunter also puts forward a cautionary note by claiming that 'the danger of using these "political" labels, however, is that one can easily forget that they trace back to prior *moral commitments* and more basic *moral visions*' (46, my emphasis). Immediately after that he adds, 'we subtly slip into thinking of the controversies debated as political rather than *cultural* in nature' (46, my emphasis). What these words emphasize is that political controversy is no more than a reflection of a larger and more complex cultural cleavage whose roots are moral in nature. Summing up his perspective Hunter writes the following:

> The culture war emerges over fundamentally different conceptions of moral authority, over different ideas and beliefs about truth, the good, obligation to one another, the nature of community, and so on. It is, therefore, cultural conflict at its deepest level. [...] a struggle over national identity – *over the meaning of America.*(1991: 49–50, emphasis in the original)

This is an important aspect to mention because it can help prevent reductionist approaches to Hunter's work. The author first and foremost describes a cultural conflict that divides Americans into two opposing fronts. He then takes American politics as an exemplary battleground where these two cultural factions compete against each other. This means that specific issues dividing Republicans from Democrats in the domain of American politics cannot be taken as the proper indicators to measure the validity of Hunter's culture war theory. Since the culture war entails much more than the sum of social issues that are customarily debated in the political arena, it is both misguided and misleading to test Hunter's theory on the basis of citizens' political identification and opinion on matters of political debate. Indeed, this is the approach that was taken in the vast majority of empirical studies aimed at testing the theory. Based on either public opinion surveys or face-to-face interviews, these studies unanimously rejected the argument of division among Americans (see, for example, Davis and Robinson 1996, DiMaggio et al. 1996, Wolfe 1998, Baker 2005).

Reasoning along similar lines, the opposition between cultural conservatives and cultural progressives should not be conflated with a conflict between religious conservatives and religious progressives. Just as politics, religion is also considered as an expression of culture. Religion, though, is given a privileged status within the theory. Adherence to a particular system of belief, be it traditionalist faith or secular creed, explains the type of link that can be established between private and public culture. 'Systems of faith or belief [...] locate the individual and community in the larger social order, offering not only moral explanations of where they fit and why but of where they should fit in as well' (58). Systems of beliefs provide explanations for all the sorts of issues people confront themselves with on an everyday basis. They give reasons for the existence of poverty, richness, success, failure, sufferance, appreciation, dislike and so on. At the same time, these belief systems are normative in that they prescribe what kind of action should be taken and which principles should be followed.

This emphasis on systems of belief to account for American cultural conflict is grounded in history. As Hunter suggests (61–3), America has constructed its national identity very differently from Europe. Lacking millennia of tradition, America has devised great myths about its origin and its calling in the future. In the eyes of Puritan settlers America appeared as a 'new Jerusalem' and its citizens as 'people set apart for a special purpose'. Later on in the nineteenth century, Protestants believed that America would be the nation for Christ's kingdom to flourish, and Catholics and Jews saw America as the land of spiritual promise. American history has always been depicted in moralistic terms, even in secular discourse. Every single war has been framed as a necessary crusade for maintaining spiritual well-being. Still today, public debate is not just about competing interests, but is rather 'a struggle between good and evil'. Furthermore, America keeps on offering itself as 'model of democracy and freedom to the nations of the world'.

After having shed some light on the crucial nexuses in Hunter's theory, we may now better appreciate his description of the cultural war that divides American public opinion and debate:

The central dynamic of the cultural realignment is not merely that different public philosophies create diverse public opinions. These alliances, rather, reflect the *institutionalization and politicization of two fundamentally different cultural systems*. Each side operates from within its own constellation of values, interests and assumptions. At the centre of each are two distinct conceptions of moral authority – two different ways of apprehending reality, of ordering experience, of making moral judgments. Each side of the cultural divide, then, speaks with a different moral vocabulary. Each side operates out of a different mode of debate and persuasion. Each side represents the tendencies of a separate and competing moral galaxy. They are, indeed, "worlds apart". (1991: 128, emphasis in the original)

This excerpt provides a concise account of the factors which, according to Hunter, determine divergent approaches to politics in the US. As his words suggest, people's understanding of morality has repercussions on the way they perceive reality and make sense of it. The quote also indicates that moral values have an impact on the verbal expression of thoughts and on the use of certain rhetorical strategies.

As mentioned at the beginning of this section, Hunter's ideas have been extremely influential among US academics and beyond. Possible reverberations of his theory in the wide-ranging domain of the social sciences and humanities may therefore be expected. Indeed, in his writings on politics and morality, the cognitive linguist Lakoff describes a framework for understanding politics that can be connected to Hunter's theory. Thus, even though Hunter's name is not mentioned in any of Lakoff's publications dealing with political discourse, it remains quite striking how much the ideas proposed by the two scholars appear to complement each other. Lakoff's approach seems to reflect Hunter's notion of a culture war, with the difference that Lakoff builds a fully-fledged cognitive model that accounts for the conceptual differences between conservatives and liberals in the contemporary American political landscape. Notwithstanding similarities, the proposals put forward by the two scholars are of a different nature. On the one hand, Hunter looks at the cleavage between red and blue Americans as essentially a cultural and social phenomenon motivated by a different understanding of morality and moral authority. Lakoff, on the other hand, scrutinizes this phenomenon from the vantage point of cognitive linguistics. His focus is on lexical choices, rhetorical habits and ways of framing issues, and his analytical tools provide explanations in terms of divergent conceptualizations and opposing metaphorical systems. Language, the starting point of Lakoff's analysis, is not taken as a neutral system of communication. The major assumption is that language reflects specific frames, conceptual metaphors, narratives and emotions that are grounded in our conceptual system. This will be discussed in more detail in the next chapter.

3
Cognition and Politics

The reason why man is a being meant for a political association ... is evident. Nature, according to our theory, makes nothing in vain; man alone of the animals is furnished with the faculty of language ... [this faculty] serves to declare what is advantageous and what is the reverse, and it therefore serves to declare what is just and what is unjust. It is the peculiarity of *man*, ... that he *alone possesses a perception of good and evil, of the just and the unjust ... and it is association in these things which makes a family and a polis.*

(Aristotle, *Politics*, quoted in Zashin 1974: 290, my emphasis)

While the previous chapter focused on some important aspects of scholarly research on American political discourse that are relevant for the type of linguistic investigation carried out in the book, this chapter concentrates on the relation between political language and cognition, and provides the theoretical foundation for the analysis presented in the following chapters.

The discussion sets out to introduce Lakoff's cognitive linguistic approach to the study of political language. This functions as a general background for the detailed description and critical evaluation of Lakoff's Strict Father and Nurturant Parent models of political morality. As a sideline, the chapter also provides a succinct review of research on conceptual metaphor in politics, which has been the most widely explored area in cognitive linguistic analyses of political language so far. As mentioned in the introduction, testing Lakoff's models represents the major aim of this book. For this reason, it is vital to examine the few studies that have already implemented elements of Lakoff's models. A close look at these publications is crucial not only to ground the current investigation in previous work, but also to show how the present study moves beyond former approaches.

3.1 Exploring the cognitive links between metaphor, morality and politics

In 1980, the publication of *Metaphors We Live by* (Lakoff and Johnson) – a seminal book on conceptual metaphors – cleared the way for the development of a new field of linguistic enquiry: conceptual metaphor theory (CMT). Since then, CMT has been extremely prolific and its ideas have been applied to the study of a wide range of domains, including economics, corporate communication, science, visual art, literature, education and politics (for an overview on the application of conceptual metaphor theory to different discourse domains, see Semino 2008).

In a nutshell, CMT is based on the assumption that metaphor is fundamentally a cognitive phenomenon and not merely a linguistic one. Metaphorical expressions that populate our everyday language are seen as the reflection of deep-seated ways of conceptualizing certain notions. These notions typically represent quite abstract domains, which, in the process of metaphorizing, become frequently connected with our physical and embodied experience. We can consider just one among the many examples given in Lakoff and Johnson (1980), that about the metaphorical understanding of the notion of theory. Lakoff and Johnson take a few conventionalized English expressions involving the notion of theory to postulate that this notion is metaphorically understood in terms of the notion of building. The linguistic expressions which they provide are the following:

The theory needs more *support*. Here are some more facts to *shore up* the theory. We need to *buttress* the theory with *solid* arguments. The theory will *stand* or *fall*. They *exploded* his latest theory. We will show that theory to be without *foundation*. So far we have put together only the *framework* of that theory. (Lakoff and Johnson 1980: 46, emphasis in the original)

Relying on these and similar phrases, Lakoff and Jonhson claim that our understanding of the abstract domain THEORY (called the Target domain) is partly understood in terms of a more concrete domain, that of a BUILDING (the Source domain). The relation between the two domains is expressed by the conceptual metaphor THEORIES ARE BUILDINGS.

Lakoff and Johnson shared with other cognitive linguists a general dissatisfaction with formalist analyses of language, and, like others, they were stimulated by discoveries in the cognitive sciences (for example, experiments on human categorization with findings relating to prototype structure and basic level categories; see Rosch 1975, 1977, 1978, Rosch and Mervis 1975). Among cognitive linguists, however, they were the first to place metaphor at the core of cognition. Their provocative ideas about the largely metaphorical, unconscious and embodied nature of human thought (for a detailed and more recent account of these aspects of cognition see Lakoff and Johnson 1999) had an international resonance and boosted a lot of scholarly interest and reactions.

After providing an explication for the metaphorical and cognitive basis of most of our everyday language, Lakoff decided to apply conceptual metaphor to the analysis of political thought. Thanks to his expertise as a linguist and as a cognitive scientist, Lakoff (1996) devised a widely influential metaphorical framework for understanding American politics. In fact, from the mid-1990s onwards, he has embarked on an intellectual crusade to serve the Democratic cause in the US (Lakoff 2004).

In Lakoff's view (1996, 2004), what divides conservatives from progressives, or Republicans from Democrats as one may prefer to call them, is a distinctive way of thinking and talking about politics that is based on two specific family-based moral systems. Lakoff emphasizes the role of morality in steering people's minds when dealing with politics. His understanding of morality is informed by discoveries in the cognitive sciences, which can explain how morality works in people's lives and what exactly connects morality to politics.

According to Lakoff, the notion of morality, one among other 'contested concepts' (a concept that would have radically different meanings for different Americans)[1] is understood to a large part metaphorically: it is conceptualized according to a system of roughly two dozen metaphors. These metaphors highlight various facets of morality, and they can help us understand why people support certain policies while opposing others. For instance, they can help us understand why conservatives are against abortion but in favor of the death penalty, or why they see a need for budget cuts but do not object to spending more and more public money for building new prisons. According to Lakoff, this can all be explained in terms of adherence to a particular worldview that is intrinsically metaphorical.[2]

In order to appreciate the explanatory value of individual metaphors that define contrasting moral worldviews, it is necessary to start considering how our notion of morality emerges and is molded by the way we as physical beings interact with the world. In other words, preliminary thoughts on metaphorical morality should not overshadow the embodied nature of morality and its experiential grounding in our everyday experiences. As Lakoff points out (1996, part II), the very notion of morality is founded on experiential human well-being. Modern Western morality essentially concerns promoting experiential well-being in others. By contrast, causing experiential harm to others is immoral. Lakoff also provides a partial definition of well-being by saying that:

> [...] other things being equal, you are better off if you are *healthy* rather than sick, *rich* rather than poor, *strong* rather than weak, *free* rather than imprisoned, *cared for* rather than uncared for, *happy* rather than sad,

whole rather than lacking, *clean* rather than filthy, *beautiful* rather than ugly, if you are functioning *in the light* rather than the dark, if you can *stand upright* so that you don't fall down, and if you live in a community with *close social ties* rather than in a hostile or isolated one. (1996: 41–2)

These conditions form the grounding for our system of moral metaphors. In other words, metaphors for morality are based on non-metaphorical experiential morality, that is on forms of well-being, and, as a result, the whole metaphorical system that accounts for morality is far from arbitrary. As Lakoff explains, these metaphors establish correlations between the domain of morality and a range of non-moral domains, including health, wealth, strength, boundedness, empathy, nurturance, happiness, wholeness, purity, light and verticality. Since it is better to be rich than to be poor, morality is conceptualized in terms of wealth. As people function better in the world if they are strong rather than weak, we expect morality to be conceptualized in terms of strength. Because it is better to be cared for than uncared for, it seems very natural that morality is conceptualized as nurturance. Since it is better to be healthy than sick, it is not surprising that morality is defined in terms of health and can be interpreted through the notions of cleanliness and purity. One could continue this list of consequential reasoning. The key question to answer, however, is how the correlations between morality and the individual concepts of wealth, strength, nurturance, health and so on are understood by different people or, in other words, how different people frame these notions according to their particular moral worldview.

If metaphor can explain the nature of morality, framing links metaphorical morality to the real world. In Lakoff's view, people sharing a particular (metaphorical) moral view will frame issues by relying on the same kind of logic. Since they embrace a distinctive kind of morality, Democrats and Republicans frame reality differently. Understanding this difference in framing crucially means understanding why liberals and conservatives think, talk and act the way they do.

At this point, it is important to clarify the notion of frame. On a par with conceptual metaphor, the term *frame* relates to another foundational theory in cognitive linguistics. Apart from linguistics, the concept of frame has found applications in many other fields, such as psychology, anthropology, sociology, philosophy, social science and artificial intelligence (see Cienki 2008 for an overview).

To put it simply, a frame is a knowledge structure that unites and organizes all the information we have about a concept. To take a simple linguistic example, if we consider the concept 'house', our understanding of this notion is dependent on the types of semantic associations we can establish when thinking about it. We all know that a house is made up of distinct structural parts: a roof, walls, windows, floors, rooms and so on. We also know that a house is a dwelling for people, but may host animals as well.

Furthermore, a house can be seen as a material good that is subject to commercial transactions, or it can be endowed with affective meaning as a private place belonging to a family. All these and many other semantic components can get activated in our minds when we think about the concept 'house' (Givón 2005: 70). This activation will depend on the relative salience that a particular component has for us and this, in turn, depends on various contextual and cultural factors. Like *house*, all words are understood relative to a frame.

If we now place the linguistic treatment of frame in a historical perspective, Fillmore requires special mention as the 'founding father of frame theory'. In a number of publications, Fillmore (1961, 1968, 1971, 1975, 1977, 1982, 1985, 1986, 1987) developed and progressively expanded the notion of frame. From initial experiments on the distributional properties of individual verbs (1961), Fillmore moved to the identification of specific semantic roles that could explain the structures associated to those verbs (1968), and subsequently saw those structures in terms of larger cognitive domains (1971). The development of Fillmore's notion of frame also bears the traces of concomitant research on prototypes. As Fillmore states, 'I use the term *frame* for any system of linguistic choices – the easiest cases being collections of words, but also including choices of grammatical rules or linguistic categories – that can get associated with prototypical instances of scenes' (1975: 124, emphasis in the original). The term *scene*, which Fillmore would later admit using as a synonym of frame, schema, domain and script (1986), is elaborated further in his analysis of the 'commercial event' scene (1977), where he shows how the verbs *sell*, *buy*, *spend* and *cost* are all related by way of evoking different aspects of the same scene. In later publications (1982, 1985, 1987), Fillmore's understanding of frame within cognitive linguistics becomes more evident, since there the notion is explained as a kind of semantic (in the broad sense) structure that is consonant with an encyclopedic view of meaning. As knowledge structures, frames are the lenses through which people make sense of reality. As we know, the same issue may be subject to different interpretations, each of them depending on the particular frame that has been applied for understanding that issue. In Fillmore's words, 'from a frame semantics point of view, it is frequently possible to show that the same "facts" can be presented within different framings, framings which make them out as different "facts"'(1982: 125). It is in this latter sense that the notion of framing is employed in this study, following Lakoff (1996, 2004, 2006, 2008), to indicate the way political leaders present 'facts' to their electorate. In the political arena framing is crucial since different framing results in apparently different 'facts' and this, clearly, has an impact on people's reactions and judgments. In Lakoff's words,

> frames are mental structures that shape the way we see the world. As a result, they shape the goals we seek, the plans we make, the way we act,

and what counts as a good or bad outcome of our actions. In politics our frames shape our social policies and the institutions we form to carry out policies. To change our frames is to change all of this. Reframing *is* social change. (2004: xv)

What Lakoff seems to introduce as a new element in his theory is the idea of reframing. This is described as an essential strategy that politicians (read Democratic politicians) should adopt to regain ideas that have been appropriated by someone else's (read Republican) powerful framing. As Lakoff comments (2006: 12), 'in politics, whoever frames the debate tends to win the debate. Over the past thirty-five years, conservatives have framed most of the issues in American political discourse'. Put straightforwardly, if Democrats want to win they need to do a lot of reframing. Thus, for example, Lakoff suggests Democrats should do away with the phrase *tax relief* which constructs an image of taxes as an affliction (2004: 4–5). The phrase was first introduced by George W. Bush and due to its reiterated use came to occupy a privileged space in political speeches, replacing the expression *tax cut*. The fact that the term *tax relief* was used so frequently made the particular frame it evokes (taxation as an affliction) accepted as common sense. To put it in more linguistic terms, the repetition of the term *tax relief* made the corresponding frame entrenched in people's minds. To contrast this powerful framing, Democrats need to elaborate and propose a reframing of it. In Lakoff's view, Democrats should avoid talking of a *tax relief* and start finding the proper way to reframe the notion of taxation in positive terms. As the discussion will show in Chapters 5 and 6, Obama skillfully reframes *tax relief*.

To return to the exploration of morality, we can now say that Lakoff frames morality as tightly connected to experiential well-being, and, in so doing, he turns a complex notion that is historically, culturally and socially connoted into an easily graspable concept. However, he offers a definition of well-being that resembles a patchwork of different concepts whose individual contribution to our understanding of morality is not spelled out.[3] This is a point that will become clearer below when Lakoff's two family-based moral systems of American politics are described. Another point to consider is that the types of source domains for morality that Lakoff provides are not all equally susceptible to moral framing. Hence concepts such as strength, authority, boundaries, self-interest, nurturance, happiness and self-development are subject to different interpretations according to different models of moral framing. Conversely, when morality is understood in terms of concepts such as essence, wholeness and purity, these notions do not leave much space for accommodation in terms of a particular moral view. In a way, these concepts prescribe a certain interpretation of reality. Thus, we can think of strength as related to the enforcement of rules or, alternatively, we can consider strength as the support we give to others. These are two distinct ways of interpreting the concept of moral strength. By contrast, if we think of a notion like essence, we can either make it part of our belief system or decide not to do so.

There is yet another metaphorical understanding of morality that is given prominence in the system. The ubiquitous conception of well-being as wealth reveals the fundamental economic metaphor for morality. According to Lakoff, we all conceptualize an increase in well-being as a gain and a decrease in well-being as a loss or a cost. This results in two possible uses of the general metaphor MORALITY IS WEALTH, namely MORALITY IS ACCOUNTING and MORALITY IS FAIR DISTRIBUTION. Morality is conceptualized in terms of accounting (MORALITY IS ACCOUNTING)[4] when the aspect of morality that is highlighted is human interaction and its results. When two people interact with each other they are thought of as being involved in a transaction where each of the two parts transfers an effect to the other. If the effect helps, it is conceptualized as a gain; if it harms, it is seen as a loss. In the same way as it is important to maintain a balance between debit and credit in financial transactions, it is vital to keep a balance between social gain and loss in moral action. Similarly, the imperative to pay one's financial debts translates into an obligation to pay one's moral debts. These are the basics for understanding why moral action is a form of financial transaction. The moral accounting metaphor is then realized in a small number of moral schemes, the most central being those of reciprocation, retribution, restitution and altruism. Each of them is defined by using the metaphor of moral accounting, but they differ in how they make use of it. Furthermore, the schemes are governed by two general principles. According to the first principle, it is moral to give something of positive value and immoral to give something of negative value. In line with the second principle, there is a moral imperative to pay one's moral debts and the failure to do so results in immoral action. Lakoff (1996: 46–50) describes these moral schemes as summarized below:

- **Reciprocation**: if you do something good to me, I 'owe' you something equally good. If I give this positive value back to you, I 'repay' my debit and we are even. The financial and moral books are balanced.
- **Retribution**: if I do something to harm you, I give you something of negative value or, in terms or moral arithmetic, I've taken from you something of positive value. This places you in a moral dilemma. You are now in a condition to 'owe' me something of equally negative value, and you can decide either to pay me back or not to do so. If you pay me back with equal negative value you act according to the second moral principle while violating the first. Conversely, if you decide not to repay me with negative value you follow the first moral principle while violating the second. People who decide to equally 'harm' the ones by whom they have been 'harmed' adopt a morality of retribution. On the other hand, those who decide not to respond to the harm received by inflicting

the same amount of harm on others embrace a morality of absolute goodness. This distinction in moral framing can help us understand why death penalty is moral for conservatives (who share a morality of retribution/punishment) and immoral for liberals (who support a morality of absolute goodness).

- **Restitution**: if I give you something of negative value and thus deprive you of some positive value, I can decide to balance the moral transaction by giving you back something of equally good value.
- **Altruism**: if I give you something of positive value by doing something good for you, then you are in my 'debt'. I can decide to cancel this debt and reject anything in return. By doing so I nonetheless augment my moral 'credit'.

As these moral schemes illustrate, thinking of morality in terms of accounting means focusing our attention on people as moral agents and their social interactions. There is yet another way of conceptualizing morality in economic terms. If we look at morality in terms of wealth and the related concept of distribution, another metaphor emerges: MORALITY IS FAIR DISTRIBUTION. Once again, there are many versions of what is to count as fair distribution, each of them depending on the kind of moral priorities people have. This point will be clarified below when presenting Lakoff's family-based moral models.

3.1.1   Lakoff's family-based models of political morality

As expounded in the previous chapter, Hunter (1991) interprets conservative and progressive thinking as a reflection of a particular kind of moral belief. Lakoff (1996) makes the connection between politics and morality even stronger by demystifying the role of the family. By locating the family at the core of his moral models, Lakoff is able to offer a comprehensive explanation that sounds naturally convincing. The family is the first social space where our basic moral values form via interaction among its members. This kind of moral education, which we are exposed to from an early age, substantially informs the development of our worldviews. For Lakoff, our upbringing markedly affects the formation of moral values, according to which we will relate to politics later in life. What motivates this link between family-based morality and politics is a very common metaphorical way of conceptualizing a nation as a family, with the government as a parent and the citizens as the children. The nation-as-family metaphor turns family-based morality into political morality, providing the essential links between conservative/progressive family values and conservative/progressive political policies.

What makes the conservative worldview and the constellation of conservative political positions distinct from their progressive counterparts is reliance on a different family model. Lakoff (1996) distinguishes two basic family models: the Strict Father (SF) model, characterizing conservative morality, and the Nurturant Parent (NP) model, which is typical of progressive morality. Each model of the family induces a set of moral priorities which play a significant role in the political agenda. Both models are idealized or, to use Lakoff's terminology (1987: ch. 4), they are Idealized Cognitive Models (ICMs). Similar to frames, ICMs are structures that enable the organization of knowledge. They function according to certain cognitive structuring principles (for example, prototype, metaphor, metonymy, image schema) and they are idealized in the sense that they represent abstractions from the complexities of the physical world. This means that in reality there are more than just two forms of family-and-political morality, since each of the two models is subject to variation. Furthermore, many people 'live by' some version of each of the two models, which explains why they apply different models to different life situations and political issues. Lakoff also acknowledges the complexity of political ideologies by admitting that his models do not account for everything in politics, since other factors that are not included in his analysis can influence political positions. Indeed, political candidates can also be supported for a number of other reasons. For example, they can have a convincing rhetorical style, they can appear as people to be trusted, their personality can exert some form of fascination on voters or they can just represent an alternative to someone else who is disliked.

Taking a closer look at the two models, we will start the discussion with an overview of each of them by synthesizing Lakoff's description. The SF model revolves around the notion of discipline. The major assumptions underlying the model are that 'people are inherently bad, life is difficult, and the world is fundamentally dangerous' (Lakoff 1996: 65). Children are born bad because they instinctively want to do what they like rather than what is right. For this reason, they need to be made good by a strong and strict father. The notions of right and wrong represent two absolute categories. Life is difficult because only the strongest are expected to succeed and prosper. People are therefore classified as either winners or losers. The world is a dangerous place and one needs to be ready to face threats at all times. This leads to the third binary opposition, that between good and evil. Evil itself is either external (enemies, temptations) or internal (uncontrolled desires).

The SF model is based on a traditional (patriarchal) view of the nuclear family where the father has primary responsibilities for supporting and protecting the family and overall control of the household. The mother, instead, is expected to support her husband and to take care of minor day-to-day responsibilities and the details of child raising. The father is the center of authority in the family, and he has the role to prepare his children for a tough, competitive and hierarchical world. To do this, he sets strict rules and exerts punishment for their violation. This helps children develop discipline, which is at the base of moral strength. It is only through 'tough love' (strictness) that children can develop self-control and self-denial, which are necessary to build moral character and moral strength. By respecting and obeying their parents, children build character, self-discipline and self-reliance, which are essential qualities for succeeding in life. Self-discipline is necessary for developing an unwavering foundation of character and integrity that helps survival in our difficult and competitive world. Self-reliance gives children authority over their own destinies and prevents parents from meddling in their lives once they are adults. Competition is also encouraged as a means to promote hard work, to advance personal responsibility and to reinforce the natural order. According to the model, people who fail to demonstrate moral strength are a threat to an orderly society, since they blur the lines between morality and immorality.

As mentioned before, a number of metaphors define morality in people's conceptual system. Some of them have priority in the SF model and Lakoff presents them as summarized below (1996: ch. 5):[5]

- MORAL STRENGTH: this has the highest priority in the model and explains the crucial notion of self-discipline. Having self-discipline means being strong and therefore capable of opposing internal and external evils. It also means being fit to compete in the world and likely to be successful. Moral strength to defeat external evils (hardships of different sorts) takes the form of courage, whereas moral strength to fight against internal evils (various passions and desires) is a matter of self-control and self-denial. The opposite of self-control and self-denial – self-indulgence – is seen as a vice in this metaphor. Thus, the moral strength metaphor imposes a form of asceticism. In line with the metaphor, moral weakness is the prelude to immoral action, since a person who is morally weak is likely to fall and give in to evil forces. Hence, moral weakness is condemned and punished. Giving moral strength the highest priority in one's morality system means looking at the world as a place of constant war between the forces of good and those of evil which must be fought ruthlessly. Fighting against evil (adversaries) is morally justified and encouraged as a form to uphold moral order. This imposes a strict us/them dichotomy on human relations and categorizes people into groups of good and bad.
- MORAL AUTHORITY: this notion is modeled on the role of parents in the family and on that of the father in particular. Since the father knows what is best for his children, he determines what is good behavior. If the children respect the moral rules of good behavior, they become strong and self-reliant and gain authority over their own lives.
- MORAL ORDER: this notion is rooted in the belief about the existence of a moral hierarchy which places God above man, man above nature, adults above children, Western culture above non-Western culture and America above other nations. Moral order is often extended to other hierarchical power relations, including men above women, whites above non-whites,

Christians above non-Christians and straights above gays. This metaphor legitimizes the authority of some individuals or groups of people over others.

- MORAL BOUNDARIES: the concept implies a metaphorical interpretation of morality as motion within prescribed boundaries or on a prescribed path. Any transgression of boundaries or deviation from the path equals immoral action and needs to be punished. Transgressors are dangerous for society because, by deviating from accepted standards, they blur the clear-cut distinctions between right and wrong, and they can lead other people astray.
- MORAL ESSENCE: this notion is based on a metaphorical understanding of a person as an object. Being conceptualized as an object, the person is seen as made up of some essential components (virtues and vices), which define his/her character or moral fiber. Essence is determined by past actions and is taken as a reliable indicator of future behavior.
- MORAL WHOLENESS: this concept emphasizes the importance of unity, stability and homogeneity. Wholeness of form is also seen as an essential ally of moral strength.
- MORAL PURITY: the notion of purity implies a metaphorical interpretation of a person as a substance that can be corrupted and thus lose its uniformity. This metaphor is closely related to that of moral wholeness.
- MORAL HEALTH: according to this metaphor, morality is a form of physical well-being that should be preserved. On the contrary, immorality is a contagious disease that should be kept away and under control. Immorality is dangerous because it can spread rapidly and in unpredictable ways.
- MORAL SELF-INTEREST: this metaphor provides the crucial link between self-discipline (which makes one strong) and self-reliance (which is a sign of individual success). The metaphor is based on a folk interpretation of an economic idea. It is a version of Adam Smith's view of capitalism, which holds that, if each person seeks to maximize his own wealth (self-interest in the metaphor), then, by an invisible hand, the wealth (interest) of all will be maximized. From this it follows that pursuing one's own interest is a moral activity because by helping yourself you are helping everyone. The metaphor also implies that prosperity is moral whereas poverty is immoral. Discipline is what makes you moral and allows you to prosper. By this logic, being poor means a lack of discipline to be moral and become rich. For this reason, you deserve to be poor. According to the metaphor, the gap between poor and rich reflects a natural order and is good. In addition, the poor should not be helped since they are regarded as having caused their own troubles. Those who help poor people are believed to change the system by immoral action.
- MORALITY AS NURTURANCE:[6] this metaphor serves the purpose of specifying when helping people is moral. According to SF morality, help should

never interfere with the development of self-discipline and individual responsibility; otherwise, it would blamefully promote moral weakness. Hence, nurturance is conditional: it is given as a reward for moral (disciplined) behavior and it is suppressed as a form of punishment in case of immoral (undisciplined) action. Nurturance must serve the function of discipline, strength and authority.

As these metaphors illustrate, SF morality is defined by a range of different moral values whose order of presentation reflects an actual ranking of importance according to Lakoff. The highest priorities in conservative morality are defined by the so-called 'strength group', which comprises MORAL STRENGTH, MORAL AUTHORITY, MORAL ORDER, MORAL BOUNDARIES, MORAL ESSENCE, MORAL WHOLENESS, MORAL PURITY and MORAL HEALTH. Next to the strength complex is moral self-interest, which functions as the means to achieve self-reliance, a goal of moral strength. Moral nurturance occupies the last position, since it has no more than an ancillary function. Nurturance works in service of the moral strength group and of moral self-interest.

As hinted at above, the metaphors defining SF morality and the conservative worldview surface in Republican rhetoric and policies. Lakoff (1996: 30) provides a list of typical conservative terms and phrases that seem to emerge from the moral metaphors.[7] They include expressions such as: *character, virtue, discipline, tough it out, get tough, strong, self-reliance, individual responsibility, backbone, standards, authority, heritage, competition, earn, hard work, enterprise, property rights, reward, freedom, intrusion, interference, meddling, punishment, human nature, traditional, common sense, dependency, self-indulgent, elite, quotas, breakdown, corrupt, decay, rot, degenerate* and *deviant lifestyle*.

Lakoff also suggests how the different SF moral metaphors find expression in actual conservative policies. In line with moral strength, Republicans abhor any kind of social programs helping poor and weak people. According to the metaphor, it is immoral to give something to those people because they have not earned it and therefore do not deserve it. Giving support to those who are not worthy of it creates immoral forms of dependency by discouraging the development of self-discipline and self-reliance. Punishment, instead, that comes in the form of no help can act as a stimulus to develop moral strength. Thus, Republicans oppose student aid because morally strong students should be self-reliant and able to pay fully for their tuition fees. Following the same logic, prenatal care programs to lower infant mortality are not to be funded because morally strong mothers should be able to provide for their own prenatal care. The same applies to postnatal care, health care for children, and care for the aged and infirm, all of which are seen as matters of purely individual responsibility. Conservative opposition to abortion is also a consequence of SF morality. According to the model, mothers who opt for abortion typically belong to two social groups. They are either unmarried teenage mothers whose undesired pregnancies are seen as the result of unrestrained sexual behavior or they are women who are career oriented and see pregnancy as an obstacle to the achievement of their professional goals. For SF morality, both types of mothers should be punished by making them keep their unwanted babies. The fact that anti-abortionist positions are better understood as a form of punishment rather than as an expression of respect for life under any circumstances becomes evident once considered on a par with death penalty support. Following the retribution moral scheme, people who caused death must pay with their own life for that. As these examples show, social forces and social class are not even considered for explaining certain conditions. The only explanations that are admitted are those in terms of immoral behavior that needs to be punished. On the contrary, morally strong people whose discipline is reflected in their prosperity should be rewarded with a reduction in taxes. Elaborating more on this metaphor, since in SF morality protection translates into strength, it is deemed very sensitive not to limit the possession of guns that help fathers protect their families against offenders and aggressors. The country itself should have a strong judicial system for punishing criminals and a strong military force for fighting fiercely against any enemies who could menace the social order. The fight against enemies (internal and external) also involves a battle against progressive ideas and programs that are considered as a form of threat.

According to the metaphor of moral authority, the federal government as the father figure should not meddle in people's lives. The no-meddling condition, which is typical of conservative thought and of American culture, is visible in Republican antipathy towards forms of government intervention. For many conservative Americans federal authority should either be transferred to local governments or be eliminated altogether. Government regulation is also seen as standing in the way of free enterprise and therefore conservatives believe it should be minimized. Beyond this distinctive way of looking at and judging government's actions, the metaphor of moral authority also explains why any deviant behavior is understood as disobedience to authority and hence deserves punishment.

The moral order metaphor justifies exploitation of the environment on the assumption that God has given men dominion over nature. Nature is conceptualized as a resource for human prosperity and profit and not as a treasure that should be cared for and respected. Once applied to foreign policy, the metaphor of moral order places America on top of all other nations as the world's moral authority and the leader to be followed and admired. Moral order also imposes strict roles within the family and results in a no same-sex marriage policy, since homosexual marriages do not fit the traditional view of the family.

Consonant with the metaphors of moral boundaries and with that of moral wholeness, multiculturalism should be avoided as much as possible. Different cultures in the US should not preserve their distinctive traits, but rather be assimilated into mainstream American culture, since they would otherwise count as a threat to the established order of values. Indeed, multiculturalism is considered the evil of all evils, because it allows for a multiplicity of alternative views on what is moral, thus acting against moral wholeness, moral boundaries, moral authority and moral strength in so far as it blurs the good vs. evil distinction. The metaphor of moral wholeness also makes Republicans very critical of sexually explicit art, which is conceived of as a dangerous attack on the solid edifice of traditional sexual values.

To finish the description of how SF moral views, in Lakoff's opinion (1996), affect Republican reasoning about political issues, moral self-interest and moral nurturance need to be addressed. According to the metaphor of moral self-interest, conservatives strongly support corporations that seek to maximize their profit, since they essentially exist to maximize investors' profits, besides providing goods and services. Individuals should be free to pursue their own interests because this is seen as the only condition that allows people to succeed in life. For this reason, government regulations need to be kept to a minimum. As for moral nurturance, this applies with restrictions. For instance, irresponsible and undisciplined people should not be helped because they are seen as the cause of their misfortune. Obligation to help people is felt exclusively when someone is affected by external disasters, such as floods, earthquakes or explosions.

Lakoff (1996) claims that in opposition to SF morality, the NP family model gives priority to nurturance over discipline. The general assumption of NP morality is that children are born good and can be made better. This can be accomplished when parents take great care in nurturing their children and in teaching them how to become nurturers of others. In this way, not only can children become better people, but the world at large can be made a better place. As a moral notion, nurturance basically means empathy and responsibility towards other people. The microcosm of the family represents the most basic form of community. Here, children learn the essential values of love, nurturance, support, protection and responsibility toward others. In this social space, children learn that they have commitments growing out of empathy for others.

According to the NP model, a family is made up of either two parents or just one. When there are two parents neither of them has moral authority over the other. Close bonds between parents and their children derive from the kind of empathic and loving relations parents have to their children. These also help children form secure attachments that will play an important role in their life, especially in their capacity to affirm themselves and establish positive interpersonal relations. Good communication is regarded as an essential component of growth. Thus, parents feel a need to explain their decisions, and they are open to questions coming from their children. Protection against external dangers also plays a significant part in nurturant child-raising, since it is a very basic form of caring. Besides the most obvious evils, such as drugs and crime, other dangers against which parents should protect their children include, for example, pesticides in food, diseases, pollution and so on. Parents feel a moral responsibility to protect their children from all of these. In contrast to the SF family model, obedience does not result from fear of punishment in the NP family. Children obey their parents because they love and desire to please them. Still differently from SF morality, when children do something wrong in a NP family, parents generally prefer to adopt a moral scheme of restitution rather than retribution, and do not physically harm their children. As an additional contradiction of the SF model, in a NP family it is not through sufferance, deprivation and castigation that children become responsible, self-disciplined and self-reliant, but rather through being cared for and being respected, as well as by caring for others. Children are also taught self-nurturance, since in order to become good nurturers they first of all need to take care of themselves. Indeed, the major goal of nurturance is for children to be happy and fulfilled in their lives. Here, fulfillment stands for a nurturant life, that is a life committed to responsibilities within the family and the community. In this process, parents help children develop their potential for achievement and enjoyment. According to NP logic, self-realization means having positive relations to others, contributing to one's community, developing one's own potential and finding joy in life. Work is the means to achieve all of these goals, and strength and self-discipline are required to obtain that. Once again, in contrast to SF morality, strength and self-discipline are not narrowly bound to individual efforts, but rather they are realized thanks to the constant support and attachment of the people who love and care about you. Since NP morality does not assume that humans are depraved, children are essentially taught to empathize with others and develop social responsibility. As a result, cooperation and compassion are preferred over Darwinian competition. Accordingly, immorality is not defined as lack of discipline, but as lack of compassion, empathy and nurturance.

Compared to the SF model, a NP family induces a different set of moral priorities that are encapsulated in a set of metaphors. Lakoff's (1996, ch. 6) list of basic NP metaphors for morality is summarized below:

- MORALITY AS NURTURANCE: this is the most direct expression of the nurturance ethic. From this it follows that helping people in need is a moral responsibility, whereas to avoid doing so is immoral. Nurturance essentially requires empathy, and it involves sacrifices for the good of others.
- MORALITY AS EMPATHY: empathy is a necessary precondition for nurturance and hence of the highest importance in the model. Empathy is not simply the capacity to relate to and project oneself onto others. Empathy means being able to understand others and connect to them according to their value system. Being capable of doing that is a moral activity and it should guide a person to become nurturant.

- MORAL SELF-NURTURANCE: this metaphor emphasizes the moral obligation that everyone has for taking care of themselves in order to be able to take care of others. This means, among other things, to secure a living and to maintain one's health.
- MORALITY AS SOCIAL NURTURANCE: this is necessary for nurturance within a wider community. In order to empathize with one another and help one another, people living in a community must attend to the cultivation of social ties. They have a moral responsibility to do so. Community-building, service to the community and cooperation are all moral values.
- MORALITY AS HAPPINESS: this metaphor is based on the assumption that people who are happy can be better nurturers because unhappy people are less likely to be empathetic. Cultivating one's own happiness goes hand in hand with developing an empathetic approach to others. Thus, morality does not coincide with ascetic behavior. It is not immoral to enjoy and find pleasure, provided that it doesn't hurt others. Communion with the natural world is also considered as an aesthetic experience which makes nurturance toward nature a form of morality.
- MORALITY AS SELF-DEVELOPMENT: this makes the development of human potential, in oneself and others, into a moral calling.
- MORALITY AS FAIR DISTRIBUTION: according to this metaphor morality is understood in terms of fairness, and fairness in turn is conceptualized as the even distribution of material objects. In the liberal worldview fair distribution follows three basic models: equal distribution, impartial rule-based distribution and rights-based distribution. This metaphor brings issues of equality and equitability into the moral system.
- MORAL GROWTH: this is promoted through nurturance and can continue throughout one's lifetime, since there is no fixed end to moral development and personal improvement.
- MORAL SELF-INTEREST: this has a subservient role within the system. It basically operates to promote other moral values, such as self-nurturance, self-development and happiness. On a general level, the violation of nurturant ethics is not considered in anyone's self-interest in this system.
- MORAL STRENGTH: strength is crucial to nurturance and works at its service. Hence, it translates into strength to be nurturers and care for others. This subservient role of moral strength in the system vastly affects its meaning. The metaphor stresses the central position of protection in NP morality and defines a number of moral virtues and failings. Moral failings include lack of social responsibility, selfishness, self-righteousness, narrow-mindedness, inability to experience pleasure, aesthetic insensitivity, lack of curiosity, uncommunicativeness, dishonesty, insensitivity to feelings, inconsiderateness, uncooperativeness, meanness, self-centeredness and lack of self-respect. Conversely, moral virtues are just their opposites and identify with social responsibility, generosity, respect for the values of others, open-mindedness, a capacity for pleasure, aesthetic sensitivity,

inquisitiveness, ability to communicate, honesty, sensitivity to feelings, considerateness, cooperativeness, kindness, community-mindedness and self-respect. A person of good character is a person who has these virtues.
*   MORAL BOUNDARIES: these are defined by actions that produce non-nurturant effects.
*   MORAL AUTHORITY: this is not the ability to set and enforce rules. Moral authority is earned trust deriving from successful nurturance and a sense of responsibility in doing that. Good nurturers simply establish their authority through what they do for others.

As previously observed for SF metaphors, also NP metaphors are ranked within the model. As the name of the cognitive model suggests, metaphors that are given the highest priority in liberal thought are those concerning nurturance (MORALITY AS EMPATHY, MORALITY AS NURTURANCE, MORALITY AS SELF-NURTURANCE, MORALITY AS SOCIAL NURTURANCE, MORALITY AS SELF-DEVELOPMENT, MORALITY AS HAPPINESS, MORALITY AS FAIR DISTRIBUTION, MORAL GROWTH). Self-interest is interpreted differently in each of the models according to their foundational values. In the case of SF morality, self-interest operates to promote strength, while in NP morality it works at the service of nurturance. In contrast to the SF model, nurturing morality places strength metaphors (MORAL STRENGTH, MORAL AUTHORITY, MORAL BOUNDARIES) at the lowest end of the hierarchy.

As there are words and phrases which, according to Lakoff (1996: 30–1), characterize conservative discourse, so there are expressions that are indicative of progressive talk. They include the following: *social forces, social responsibility, free expression, human rights, equal rights, concern, care, help, health, safety, nutrition, basic human dignity, oppression, diversity, deprivation, alienation, big corporations, corporate welfare, ecology, ecosystem, biodiversity* and *pollution.*

If we now apply NP moral metaphors to politics, we get an explanation of the liberal political worldview and of progressive policies. Nurturance can be seen to motivate the largest part of liberal views on a wide range of topics. As a nurturing parent, the government is expected to provide every citizen with their basic needs, including food, shelter, education and healthcare. Thus, liberals are in favor of social programs and welfare. They support well-funded and expanding public education systems and believe that every American should have access to an affordable healthcare system. Providing safe and affordable abortion is seen as an additional form of nurturance. The government is also expected to act openly by telling the truth to citizens and in so doing earning the trust of Americans. The government has social responsibilities toward people. Its fundamental job is to provide sufficient protection for everyone, broader prosperity, better health, more freedom, greater democracy and opportunities for all Americans by guaranteeing equal rights for everyone. Liberals support feminism and gay rights because nurturant parents want their children to fulfill their potential. Since differences are celebrated rather than looked upon with suspicion, multiculturalism is encouraged. The government should also build and maintain public infrastructure and work to reduce violence and diminish exploitation of the environment. Indeed, the government should strive to make the environment safe, clean and healthy. To achieve this aim, major investments should be made in renewable energy. Regulation is deemed necessary to keep control of various threats, such as pollution, nuclear waste, unsafe products and workplace hazards. In fact, the economy should function for the benefit of the people and be centered on innovation to create millions of well-paying jobs in order to provide every American with a fair opportunity to prosper. Reasoning in terms of the strength metaphor, America should protect its people from external threats by building and maintaining strong diplomatic alliances and pursuing wise foreign and domestic policy. One of the ideas underlying liberal foreign policy is that America's leading role in the world will be strengthened by helping people around the world to have a better life. Strength to be nurturers is another fundamental nurturant value which motivates policies on taxation. In a nurturant family, older and stronger children have a moral obligation to help out those who are younger and weaker. In the same way, the wealthier citizens of the nation have a moral duty to help those who are less prosperous.

3.1.2 A critical look at Lakoff's models

What have been described so far are two Idealized Cognitive Models (ICMs) as Lakoff conceived them. This means that both the SF and the NP models, as they have been introduced here, represent instances of prototypical conservative and liberal morality. In reality, though, each of the two models is subject to variation, which is reflected in the range of conservative and liberal approaches to political issues. This is an important point to mention, since it accounts for flexibility internal to the models and, as a consequence, for fluctuation between proto-typical conservative and liberal positions. Furthermore, this way of devising the models connects to Hunter's definition of orthodox and progressive as two polarizing tendencies in American culture. Both writers reject static and monolithic interpretations of political siding by preferring explanations that fit reality more accurately.

To take the discussion a bit further ahead in the intellectual debate, we can say that while the term *idealized* in the phrase Idealized Cognitive Model appears as felicitous, an unhappy fate befell the word *cognitive*. Following Lakoff's first detailed explanation of ICMs (1987), scholars, notably Quinn and Holland (1987), complained about the lack of an explicit cultural core in this theorization. Others, like Shore (1996), postulated the existence of cognitive models and cultural models as distinct types, the former being mental models proper and the latter kinds of constructions which are dependent on institutions and social practices. This opposition between cognitive and cultural models is indeed a reflection of a long-held assumption about the incompatibility of cognition and culture.[8] Thus, even though each of the two terms does not necessarily exclude the other, there is a strong tendency not to use the expressions 'cognitive model' and 'cultural model' as synonyms (see Gibbs 1999). In light of these critiques, Lakoff's work (1996) might have benefited from having some space devoted to explaining the reasons for describing the family-based models as ICMs. After all, the description of SF and NP morality is grounded, as Lakoff himself mentions, in American culture.

To return to Lakoff's discussion of the two morality models in relation to people's moral/political thought and behavior, another observation can be made. Lakoff takes great pains to explain that some people have both a conservative and a liberal moral system at their disposal and can apply them to different issues. Lakoff describes the American electorate as being made up of roughly three groups of people: 40 per cent are conservative, 40 per cent are liberals and the remaining 20 per cent are 'multidimensional', meaning that they are neither pure conservatives nor pure liberals. 'Multidimensional' people can in turn be subdivided into 'biconceptuals' and 'pragmatists'. The former are people who dispose of both models and may use either model in framing political issues. The latter are either conservatives or progressives who are more willing to compromise for practical reasons than, let's say, ideological conservatives and progressives.

If these words shed light on the usefulness of applying the two metaphorical models for analyzing and understanding American political discourse, Lakoff's methodology for arriving at these models may be subject to some criticism. Indeed, Lakoff's claims about the existence of the SF and NP family models are based on the observation of a limited set of 'surface' phenomena. To support his distinction, Lakoff merely provides an impressionistic list of well-known American expressions such as *founding fathers, fatherland, sons of this country* and *Uncle Sam* (1996: 153–4). This is not surprising, since early studies in cognitive semantics were characterized by a general lack of considering usage-based data, whereas more recent research advocates the need for rigorous empirical methodologies and corpus-based analyses (see, for example, Charteris-Black 2004, Deignan 2005, Stefanowitsch and Gries 2006, Cameron and Maslen 2010, Glynn and Fisher 2010). This is why testing Lakoff's models on corpora of political language, as carried out in the present study, can prove particularly insightful (see also Cienki 2004, 2005a, 2005b; Ahrens and Yat Mei Lee 2009, Ahrens 2011; cf. section 3.3).

Another aspect of the morality models which should be pointed out is their internal structure. If we compare SF to NP basic metaphors some interesting observations can be made. If we focus on SF and NP metaphorical source domains, we realize that certain moral notions are included in both models, and they are simply given a distinctive framing and a different priority. The source domains which characterize SF as well as NP morality are the following: STRENGTH, AUTHORITY, BOUNDARIES, SELF-INTEREST and NURTURANCE. With the exception of nurturance, the rest of these moral notions appear to have a larger 'share' in SF than in NP morality. They actually define SF morality more accurately than NP morality. If we then consider the kind of moral notions that uniquely define each of the two models other forms of unbalance arise. SF source domains that are absent in NP metaphors include: ORDER, ESSENCE, WHOLENESS, PURITY and HEALTH. These are moral notions that uniquely describe and define SF morality and which cannot find any equivalent in the NP moral view. Conversely, NP source domains that do not feature in SF metaphors comprise EMPATHY, SELF-NURTURANCE, SOCIAL NURTURANCE, HAPPINESS, SELF-DEVELOPMENT, FAIR DISTRIBUTION and GROWTH. These typically NP notions outnumber the set of uniquely SF source domains; however, their contribution to moral framing is of a different kind. The notions of self-nurturance and social nurturance are no more than elaborations on the general concept of nurturance, which is contained in both models. The concepts of self-development and growth are problematic in two respects. On the one hand, they overlap quite substantially. On the other hand, one cannot exclude a possible SF framing of them. Indeed, in a SF worldview the idea of self-development/growth is closely connected to that of strength. A similar observation can be made for the concepts of happiness and fair distribution, which can also be seen to play a role in SF morality. The SF model describes how one can achieve self-fulfillment (and be happy) by becoming self-reliant and successful in life. It also alludes to what is considered fair distribution in so far as it creates an opposition between people who deserve a lot and people who don't deserve anything. For all these reasons one can say that, judging by the internal structure of the two models, the SF model comes out as the most elaborately devised. This may actually be a consequence of American social and political reality. As Lakoff himself observes, Republicans are aware of the importance of communicating clear moral values and have worked for a long time on the framing of these values, both intellectually and practically. This situation places Republicans in a position of 'moral' advantage over Democrats. This can also be a reason that explains the imbalance between the two models in terms of their internal design.

To conclude with a note on Lakoff's presentation of the two models, it is necessary to say that his fully fledged explanation of conservative and progressive worldviews is not as detached as one may imagine. Indeed, his description is value laden and Lakoff does not abstain from taking side with the liberals. Close to the end of the book, he fully abandons his scientific neutrality and turns into a strong advocate of liberal morality by defining the NP conceptual model as the better one.

Lakoff praises conservatives for their ability to see the links between politics, family and morality. Compared to liberals, conservatives have a better understanding of how politics works and they have a long track record of funding think tanks for the cultivation and spread of conservative ideas.

In this sense, conservatives appear as more mindful of the underpinnings of their political worldview than liberals. Over the past decades, they have defined their ideas and carefully devised their own language to express them in public. Lakoff, however, is not neutral when detailing SF morality, and his explanations often demonize conservatives as violent and irrational pursuers of individualistic goals. In other words, Lakoff's descriptions of the two models make one instinctively feel closer to liberal thought. NP morality generates positive, almost rosy, feelings, whereas the impressions coming from SF morality are rather negative and unequivocally gloomy. Conservative morality appears as unhealthy for society, since it fosters a culture of exclusion and blame. Lakoff is very apt in provoking emotional responses to the models while providing scientific evidence to disprove the validity of conservative understanding of human nature and behavior. As he points out, over the past century, cognitive psychology and neuroscience have demonstrated that children are not born bad, discipline does not breed self-discipline, obedience in childhood does not lead to self-reliance in adulthood, people do not always act in their own interest and a folk behaviorist belief in stimulus-response is wrong (see Lakoff 2006: 434–47).

Lakoff's sympathy for the liberals and his involvement in the political arena becomes evident once we consider his active role in a number of political initiatives. First of all, he contributed to the foundation of the Rockridge Institute in 1997.[9] This progressive think tank was aimed at making people aware of the importance of framing and of its manipulative use by the Republicans. The institute was set up to support progressives by encouraging the expression of their values and ideas in public discourse and, equally, by showing how conservatives' success was largely dependent on their use of a language that could capture their value system. Lakoff also acted as a consultant of progressive groups and participated in Democratic gatherings where his expertise as a linguist was called upon to disclose the essential links between language, cognitive science and politics. One of the results of his work and research with political leaders was the dissemination of his credo in a few publications essentially addressed to American progressives. They include *Don't Think of an Elephant* (2004), *Thinking Points* (2006), *Whose Freedom* (2006) and *The Political Mind* (2008). Rather than writing as a linguist, Lakoff follows an explicit political agenda in these books. The rediscovery and celebration of traditional American values that Lakoff sees as closely connected to the progressive vision lie at the core of his political message. He tries to incite liberals to take action and move from a defensive towards an offensive stance in the battlefield of politics. Due to his assertive prose style, Lakoff resembles a semi-belligerent activist who thrusts the sword of framing (and reframing) as an effective tool for gaining political power. Progressives are hence instructed on how to fight back by countering conservative arguments, but countering doesn't simply mean attacking one's opponents. Instead, liberals are taught to herald their own values and present a clear moral vision to the nation. After all, as Lakoff argues, people vote for their values and identities, even if these can conflict with their interests. In particular, progressives are invited to use simple and compact expressions that are an immediate reflection of a NP moral view and can effectively activate this frame in voters. Furthermore, Lakoff calls for an elaboration of certain values, such as protection, and a re-appropriation of contested concepts, like freedom, that are subject to political manipulation.

Even though Lakoff's aim in writing these books is primarily political, he still relies on linguistic examples, which sound convincing and provocatively intriguing as they are grounded in the practice of everyday political communication. An example is the reiterated use of the expression *tax relief* that marked George W. Bush's 2004 campaign. As Lakoff explains, this wording is based on the metaphor TAXATION IS AN AFFLICTION, and as such depicts taxes as an oppressive burden and the person who takes them away as a kind of hero. Once Bush is seen as a hero, the fact that a reduction in taxes is proposed for the wealthiest remains hidden, as well as the idea that fair taxation can help every citizen.

Lakoff's argumentation becomes more scientific in *The Political Mind* where he recalls the role of cognitive science in understanding how the human brain works, and provides a biological explanation to account for moral and political thought processes. In this work, reason is described not just as unconscious, metaphorical and embodied, but (and most significantly) as tied to empathy, an emotion that is intimately connected to the activities of our mirror neuron circuitry. In Lakoff's words, 'our mirror neuron circuitry and associated pathways connect us both physically and emotionally with others, allowing us to feel what others feel. In other words, they provide the biological basis of empathy, cooperation and community. We are born to empathize and cooperate' (2008: 118–19). This quote shows Lakoff's efforts to find support in natural science in order to make his claims even stronger. Since empathy is defined as a foundational disposition, embracing a NP philosophy results as the most natural way of understanding reality. Lakoff goes even beyond that and places the concept of empathy at the base of evolutionary theories by suggesting a non-conformist interpretation of the Darwinian struggle for survival.[10] Lakoff employs the following excerpt from Darwin's *The Origin of Species* (1859) to tie the notion of empathy in with evolutionary theory:

> I use this term [struggle for existence] in a large and metaphorical sense including dependence of one being upon another, and including (which is more important) not only the life of the individual, but success in leaving progeny. Two canine animals, in times of dearth, may be truly said to struggle with each other, which shall get food and live. *But a plant on the edge of the desert is said to struggle for life against the drought, though more properly it should be said to be dependent on the moisture.* (Darwin in Lakoff, 2008: 201, my emphasis)

Lakoff comments on Darwin's words by saying that the scientist himself considered the notion of 'struggle' as a misleading metaphor. In his opinion, Darwin's use of the term 'struggle' was embedded in nineteenth-century culture. That word was in common use in that particular historical period and its circulation was, on the one hand, the outcome of dominant economic ideas about competitiveness and, on the other hand, the result of a Christian emphasis on a SF view of God as a Strict Father. As a consequence, the word 'struggle' was also employed to refer to those concepts that would nowadays rather be called 'symbiosis', 'structural independence' and 'mutuality' (Lakoff 2008: 202), or, in other words, empathy. To further support his theory, Lakoff mentions recent research by H. Kern Reeve and Bert Hoelldobler according to which 'evolution [...] selects groups on the basis of in-group cooperation, not competition – whether ants, biological films, or human beings' (Lakoff 2008: 205). Here, Lakoff's apotheosis of NP morality reaches its climax. The linguist justifies the absolute priority of empathy within our moral system by endowing this concept with quintessential relevance for the theory of evolution.

As described, in *Political Mind* (2008) Lakoff suggests an interpretation of the Darwinian struggle for survival that fits a NP worldview. Curiously enough, in his critique of the SF and NP models, Goatly (2007) complains about Lakoff's silence on the ideological implications of certain economic metaphors. Goatly connects Lakoff's ideas about morality and politics to his own work on metaphors and sees SF and NP moralities as in line with a '(neo)Darwinian emphasis on competition versus the more modern Gaian[11] emphasis on interdependence and symbiosis' (2007: 385). Goatly's criticism is primarily targeted at the fallacies he detects in SF morality. In his view, conservative attitudes, which according to Lakoff are grounded in a SF morality, are actually based on an 'ideological competitive struggle for power or wealth or privilege' (2007: 383). The right wing is intimately driven by a capitalist ideology that informs many of the SF metaphors. Thus, even Lakoff's basic metaphor for morality, WELL-BEING IS WEALTH, is, according to Goatly, the mere result of capitalist ideology. As Goatly writes, 'instead of rejecting this metaphor, as a right wing capitalist one, he [Lakoff] distinguishes a right wing and a left wing interpretation of it' (2007: 384). In fact, Lakoff's reliance on the metaphorical capitalist core of morality could be the reason why the SF model is more elaborately described than the NP one; after all, to rephrase Goatly's words, capitalism fits better to right wing ideology. As a solution to this impasse, Goatly suggests taking a broader perspective on metaphors used particularly by seventeenth-century economic philosophers to understand today's (moral) politics. Starting from the general assumption that metaphors, besides being experientially grounded, are also historical and cultural constructs (see Quinn 1991, Geeraerts and Grondelaers 2003, Kövecses 2005, Musolff 2010, Musolff *et al* 2012), Goatly calls for a more accurate analysis of metaphorical politics. As he points out, since politics is fundamentally metaphorical in nature, one should not underestimate the fact that

> [...] many of the most significant metaphor themes have been created by, nurtured by, or used to express and reinforce a philosophical tradition which can be traced back at least as far as the first part of the capitalist era, the dawn of the Scientific and Industrial Revolutions in 17th century Britain. Beginning with Thomas Hobbes this tradition can be followed, with variations, through Hume, Adam Smith, Thomas Malthus, who, in turn, had considerable influence on Darwin, and represents ideologies which have begun to acquire a new ascendancy since the last quarter of the 20th century. (Goatly 2007: 335)

If all these philosophers can be said to have contributed to the definition of a wide range of general economic and political metaphors (for example, POWER/ACHIEVEMENT/SUCCESS IS GOOD, QUALITY IS WEALTH, ACTIVITY IS FIGHTING, FREEDOM IS SPACE TO MOVE, RELATIONSHIP IS PROXIMITY/COHESION), it was Hume ([1940] 1969) who more specifically theorized on morality. As Goatly observes, the significance of Hume's metaphorical understanding of morality as pleasure and sympathy should be accounted for in any theory of morality (2007: 388). Not by accident, one could argue, Hume's MORALITY IS PLEASURE metaphor, which sees selfish pleasure (read advantage) as the basis of morality, ties in with Lakoff's interpretation of morality as self-interest. Conversely, the counterbalancing metaphor of MORALITY IS SYMPATHY appears as closely connected to Lakoff's view of morality as empathy. In general, this discussion shows that Goatly's critique is very helpful for expanding the understanding of the cultural implications in (moral) politics.

Besides playing a key role in Lakoff's SF and NP models, conceptual metaphors have also been used outside of these models to analyze political discourse. Thus, in order to provide a more comprehensive picture of cognitive linguistic analyses of political discourse, the following section explores this issue in more detail, discussing major works on conceptual metaphors in political discourse.

3.2   Conceptual metaphors in political discourse: an overview

It is a truism that metaphor inhabits discourse, and it is also a fact that people are often unaware of the metaphorical nature of the language they use. To take just an example, the phrase *election campaign* is one of those common expressions whose reference to the military can easily go unnoticed. As the *OED* reminds us, the term *campaign* comes from military vocabulary and indicates 'the continuance and operations of an army "in the field" for a season or other definite portion of time, or while engaged in one continuous series of military operations constituting the whole, or a distinct part, of a war'. Once the term *campaign* is employed in combination with election in the (battle)field of politics, the result is the identification of candidates in the political campaign as military opponents fighting against each other. Election campaigns turn into competitions over ideas or over different interpretations of the same ideas; they become battles to define public problems and to find solutions to them. In line with the military metaphor, winning an election is like winning a war: it requires strategy and planning.

As in many other types of discourse, that of politics blooms with metaphors. Miller (1979: 157) provides a useful list of general sources that inform our common metaphorical understanding of politics. The list, though by no means exhaustive, gives an idea of the wide range of concepts that contribute to shaping the general domain of politics. It includes the following source domains:

- *Human relationships of everyday life*, such as those in the family (father to children, husband to wife, master to slave, brotherhood), those in the sphere of exchanges, contracts and promises, and those in sporting activities and games or in warfare and military life;
- *Making and doing things through the arts*, such as medicine, gymnastics, generalship, horsemanship, tending sheep, piloting, building, tailoring, painting, acting, flute-playing, and engineering on a large scale;
- *The characteristics of artifacts*, such as a building and its foundation, a pyramid, a wheel, a pair of scales, a web or cloth woven from thread, clocks, machines, pumps, engines, computers and communication networks;
- *Capacities of human beings*, such as references that treat a community or institution as a person that plans or exercises foresight and experiences such human emotions as love, hatred, pride, sympathy and magnanimity;
- *Activities or processes in nature*, such as animal behavior [...], organic processes common to human and nonhuman beings (conception, birth, maturation, health and disease, death), and the natural properties or motions of bodies (revolution, attraction, repulsion, the exertion of force);
- *Mathematical relations* and proportions of various kinds. (Miller 1979: 157)

As this list illustrates, the domain of politics is understood by and large via metaphorical associations to a wide range of concepts.

The relevance of certain metaphorical sources for political targets like democracy, war and peace, and globalization is an issue addressed in Beer and De Landtsheer (2004). The two political scientists draw upon linguistics, and cognitive linguistics in particular, to propose the arguments for the study of metaphor in world politics. They place the human body at the core of a metaphorical constellation of source domains as the notion that underlies a lot of contemporary political discourse and that is historically rooted in political theory.[12] As they remind us

Traditional political philosophy relied heavily on the implied metaphor of the "body politic", giving a corporeal form to an abstract, intangible entity, the state. Plato's ideal state, the Republic, was modeled on the ideal citizen. The frontispiece of Hobbes's *Leviathan* was a picture of a giant man, within whom were multitudes of smaller men. *The Federalist Papers* moved in the direction of a more mechanical metaphor, but again the political machine was composed of human beings. (2004: 16)

According to Beer and De Landtsheer, this embodied interpretation of the state (and of politics) is responsible for the development of additional political metaphors that are related to the human body in its physiological, interactive and socio-cultural dimensions. In detail, sports appear as a frequent source domain in the speeches of Western political leaders. For instance, US former president Lyndon Johnson 'used the "starting line" metaphor to describe the need to establish equal competitive conditions. Reagan emphasized the "runners" idea in stressing that competitors need to rely on athletic character' (2004: 17). Furthermore, it is commonplace to talk of political election campaigns in terms of races. The family and different family types (as explained by Lakoff's SF and NP models) is another source of political metaphors. Not surprisingly, a father role has been attributed more than once to American national leaders.

The metaphorical 'father' was applied to the first four presidents and to the Civil War president. Washington was the 'father of this country'. John Adams was 'the father of American independence'. Jefferson was 'the father of the Declaration of Independence'. Madison was 'the father of the Constitution'. Lincoln was 'Father Abraham'. (2004: 23)

For describing crisis situations or extremist ideologies, disease and insidious or repellent living organisms (microbes, rats) are very popular as metaphorical sources. References to landscape and technology also function as rich resources for interpreting political reality. Nature and everyday life metaphors tend to have a reassuring effect on the audience and they are typically used by Democratic politicians to communicate a sense of prosperity. Metaphorical political life is seen very frequently via associations to various kinds of machines. Thus, the checks and balances of the American Constitution were inspired by Newton's laws of celestial mechanics, the smelting furnaces of the Industrial Revolution prompted the melting pot metaphor and the modern network metaphor originates in cybernetics. Political metaphors can also be used to suggest escape from reality; this occurs when the metaphorical sources are games or forms of spectacle.

The incorporation of scientific metaphors into politics is the major concern of a few contributors to Carver and Pikalo's volume (2008). Among them, Akrivoulis (2008) considers the impact of metaphorical explanations characterizing Newtonian physics on two distinct phases of American politics: its founding era and the early Cold War years. The use of Newtonian metaphoricity in the founding act of American society, it is argued, had a tremendous effect on how America started conceiving of itself and its relation to other states. 'In the Newtonian imaginary, with everything reflecting harmony and order, and also being sanctioned by it, whatever existed in society and politics was considered legitimate, as long as it could correspond to the mechanized, harmonious and balanced view of political reality' (2008: 20). Moving forward in time, political conceptualizations that reflect Newtonian balance became prominent in the Cold War period when 'state-policies are fixed like planetary movements and regulated by measurable state-interests, as if they followed calculable orbits in a *cosmos* (international system) that itself provides these legitimate and infallible patterns of behavior' (2008: 21). Akrivoulis then demonstrates how this ideological schematization has a bearing on three levels of US foreign policy: project of action, level of motivation and power to act.

Pikalo (2008) explores the rise and fall of metaphors from the natural sciences that have been used throughout history to conceptualize political realities (for example, body, machine, network, flow). According to Pikalo, metaphors based on imageries of nature tend to be time-specific and to evolve on a par with the developments of theories of nature. Classical Newtonian mechanistic imagery, however, seems to defy the 'laws of nature' being still very influential in politics and political theory. As he claims:

> Although the natural sciences have seen the introduction of self-reflexive theories, especially in the form of quantum physics and the theory of relativity, and the social sciences have introduced various post-positivist and post-empiricist methodologies, 'the political' is predominantly still thought and imagined in relation to this tradition of mechanical metaphor [Newtonian physics]. (2008: 52)

This metaphorical 'naturalization' of politics provides a schematic and simplified template for understanding political realities. Following the rules of Newtonian physics, politics is interpreted as a complex of physical objects governed by the laws of nature. This interpretation, however, blatantly obscures the unpredictability of human and social factors that escape the determinism of a cause–effect logic.

The discussion so far has illustrated how political metaphors can serve the general purpose of making abstract, complex and inaccessible concepts more graspable and thus simpler. Furthermore, it has alluded to the fact that political metaphors can be employed in a manipulative manner. As an instance of planned discourse, political 'text and talk', to use Chilton and Schäffner's terminology (2002), makes an ideological use of metaphor. Figurative devices are often used by politicians for rhetorical and persuasive purposes. In a way, they are the food of political thought.

The function of metaphor as an essential ingredient for achieving political persuasiveness is emphasized, among others, by Charteris-Black (2005). In his book, which focuses on the analysis of the strategic use of metaphor by successful twenty-first-century political leaders in Britain and the US, he claims that

> Metaphor is an important characteristic of persuasive discourse because it mediates [...] – between cognition and emotion – to *create a moral perspective on life* (*or ethos*). It is therefore a central strategy for legitimization in political speeches. Metaphor influences our beliefs, attitudes and values because it uses language to activate unconscious emotional associations and it influences the values that we place on ideas and beliefs on a scale of goodness and badness. It does this by transferring positive or negative associations of various source words to a metaphor target. (2005: 13, my emphasis)

As Charteris-Black's words indicate, the power of metaphor resides in its capacity to shape reality. Here lies its essential ethical dimension. By providing a particular interpretation of the world around us, metaphor confronts us with a set of propositions and assumptions about the world itself and the way we behave in it. These sets of underlying messages conveyed by metaphorical language use are the salt and pepper that activate our emotional reactions. One can say that the success of a certain metaphor depends on the types of associations it is based upon. To take an example, a metaphorical source domain like WARFARE used to define foreign policy can trigger different reactions in types of audience who do not share a common value system. Recalling Lakoff's two political and cognitive models, Republicans can be thought of as supporters of a lexicon of conflict that is in line with their moral values. Conversely, Democrats are more likely to favor a lexicon of cooperation. As Charteris-Black argues, politicians deliberately select metaphors that can better serve their ultimate goals since 'metaphor is both pervasive and persuasive when employed discursively in the rhetorical and argumentative language of political speeches' (2005: 28). But metaphor alone is not enough for granting political success. To revert back to Charteris-Black: 'political leaders become persuasive when their metaphors interact with other linguistic features to legitimize policies' (2005: 17), and also 'it is the combined effect of various strategies that is most effective in political speeches. The overlapping of diverse rhetorical strategies creates a powerful interplay that ensures persuasive political communication' (2005: 5).

A wide range of rhetorical figures of speech typical of political communication is summarized in Tuman (2008: 69–73) and portrayed below:

- *Accumulation*: two or more clauses are used in succession within a speech, saying essentially the same thing. This is often done for emphasis and/ or clarity.

- *Anaphora*: repetition of a word or phrase at the beginning of successive phrases, clauses or lines. Like accumulation, this is done for emphasis or clarity.
- *Antithesis*: clauses in a speech set in opposition to one another, usually to distinguish between choices, concepts and ideas.
- *Catalogue*: a speaker offers a list of things, ideas or arguments. Often this is done in conjunction with a logos appeal to suggest evidence or support for a claim the speaker is making. Beyond making the message appear logical, the effect of this figure may also be to strengthen a speaker's ethos as an expert and trustworthy source by making it appear as if he has considered all the possibilities.
- *Definition*: involves a statement of the precise characteristic of a concept, a thing, or even an individual. This is often used to bring clarity to a point and to create a common reference for the audience.
- *Example:* a citation of a specific instance of something from the past. This may be necessary to help the audience follow a political speaker's otherwise vague point.
- *Exemplum*: involves the use of a direct quotation from another individual in the speech. Political leaders often employ this because they desire to have the audience make an association between themselves and the individual they quote.
- *Hyperbole*: probably the most common of all figures used in political rhetoric. It refers to an intentional exaggeration of the truth.
- *Personification*: the assignment of human characteristics to impersonal, nonhuman things. This is often used to create a positive or negative association with something, by imbuing it with characteristics the audience may more easily understand.
- *Praeteritio*: this can be found in any situation where a speaker refers to something or someone by clearly suggesting (and thus pretending) they are going to do so. Here, the candidate pretends he will not address his opponent's shortcomings, but by listing what he will not talk about, he still manages to sneak them into his speech and raises the audience's awareness of them.
- *Prolepsis*: this refers to anticipatory refutation. In this situation the speaker anticipates a criticism or counterargument to the one being presented, and actually voices the response to it before it can be made.

Other general rhetorical strategies that characterize the oral delivery of political leaders are mentioned in Atkinson (1984), Beard (2000) and Charteris-Black (2005). They include:

- *Sound bites* (also called parallelisms): short and memorable phrases that encapsulate an argument. They are easily quotable and typically consist of pairs of clauses.

- *Contrastive pairs*: they contain two parts which are in some ways in opposition, but in other ways use repetition to make the overall effect.
- *Three-part lists*: they provide a sense of unity and completeness by having information organized in three parts, which seem to mimic the sequence of initiation, response and required third part as in spoken interaction.

After this brief excursion into common rhetorical strategies in political discourse which can closely interact with conceptual metaphors, some major book-length studies focusing on conceptual metaphors in the political arena have to be discussed. On returning to Charteris-Black (2005), his empirical study on both memorable and representative speeches of six well-known political leaders (Winston Churchill, Martin Luther King, Margaret Thatcher, Bill Clinton, Tony Blair and George W. Bush) highlights a few important points. One of the major findings concerns the effectiveness of metaphor, especially when used in combination with other rhetorical strategies. Recourse to antithesis, in particular, seems rather appealing for the audience, since it triggers basic cause–effect reasoning. Margaret Thatcher's talk is presented as a clear example of successful rhetoric that mingles metaphor with antithesis by proposing sets of common oppositions such as us vs. them, good vs. bad, moral vs. immoral and healthy vs. ill, all with the aim of communicating an image of political reality that is based on conflict. In addition to the interplay of different rhetorical devices, metaphors are also significantly persuasive when they occur in combination in what Charteris-Black defines as 'nested metaphors', 'a term used to describe the rhetorical practice of placing a metaphor from one source domain within a metaphor from another source domain' (2005: 53). This occurs, for instance, in Winston Churchill's wartime speeches, when light and fire metaphors are inscribed in a more general and overarching journey metaphor. Charteris-Black also demonstrates how metaphors are skillfully used by politicians for the creation of specific myths that fit their personality as well as the historical time and the aims they intend to achieve. This explains why different political leaders can show a preference for diverse metaphors. Thus, for example, George Bush Sr. and Jr. appear as the only politicians among the ones analyzed that show a liking for crime and punishment metaphors (as one would actually expect relying on Lakoff's SF morality model) and for finance metaphors (still in line with Lakoff's description of the moral accounting metaphor). Indeed, it is often the case that the same metaphor is used by politicians who exploit the power and richness of metaphor for their own purposes. The journey metaphor is such a case. As pervasive as it is, this metaphor inhabits the dialectical space of all political speeches, but the trajectories it describes are of a distinct nature. Thus, Martin Luther King describes the civil rights movement in terms of a spiritual journey of salvation, whereas Bill Clinton's use of journey metaphors either creates nostalgic links to some sort of idealized American history or represents projections into the future of the nation. Besides journey metaphors, personifications are also very recurrent in political talk. The metaphorical identification of the nation as a person is resonant in Churchill's wartime oratory, in which the marked contrast between England as a hero and Germany as a villain is a distinctive trait. According to Charteris-Black, personification is even more frequent in American than in British political discourse. The NATION IS A PERSON metaphor is employed by the Bush administrations to suggest a positive evaluation of the US and an opposing negative evaluation of terrorists as sub-human.

While Charteris-Black focuses on the strategic use metaphor, Chilton (1996) devotes his attention to the metaphorical processes intrinsic to the formation and use of political concepts. His study revolves around the concept of security,[13] one among many so-called contested concepts. In the book, Chilton considers how this notion, far from conceptually isolated, is indeed embedded in a nexus of other political concepts. Security, state and sovereignty are part of the same metaphorical conceptual system and therefore closely interconnected. These notions are grounded in four basic experiential gestalts, the CONTAINER, PATH, FORCE and LINK image schemas and the related UP–DOWN and CENTRE–PERIPHERY schemas. According to Chilton, it is necessary to understand how these image schemas and their connected metaphors have structured much thinking about states and the relations between them in order to make sense of the institutionalized discourse of international relations and that of the policy-making community (1996, chs 2 and 3). In other words, understanding politics means bringing to the fore what political theorists have long assigned to a place of oblivion: the role and relevance of metaphor. As Chilton points out, political scientists and international relations theorists have both tacitly and sometimes admittedly supported the marginalization of metaphor in political language, following a tradition that goes back to Thomas Hobbes's claims about language in *Leviathan* ([1651] 1988). In Chilton's view, Hobbes looks at metaphor as simply senseless and thinks that language should be used according to the principles of 'disembodied', 'objective' reason and science. The influence of these ideas on subsequent epistemology, philosophy of language and politics is enormous and can be retraced 'in the realist and neorealist mentality which dominated Western theory of international relations in the Cold War period' (Chilton 1996: 18–19). Up until the cognitive linguistics turn of the 1970s, there was in fact a strong tendency to interpret political concepts along the lines of formal semantic theories that were unwilling, or perhaps just incapable, of explaining metaphor. Furthermore, until that time, political theory considered the presence of metaphor in theoretical discourse as suspect and studies of political behavior did not pay much attention to the way policymakers used metaphors. The rhetorical approach to politics is probably the only remarkable exception. Its view of metaphor as an effective means of political persuasion, however, is by no means reductive when compared to that of cognitive semantics. What Chilton suggests for the study of political language is a framework that brings together insights from cognitive linguistics and (critical) discourse analysis and interprets metaphor both as 'a cognitive process which enters substantially into the formation of mental models' (1996: 73) and as a constitutive component of text, language and discourse.

> One of the main ways in which texts are coherent wholes, and also cohere with the surrounding context (both the immediate political situation and a historical tradition), is the use of metaphor. This means that the analysis of metaphor must be a key component in understanding not merely the minds of political actors but also the political culture that supports them. (1996: 29)

Politics, like any type of discourse in natural language, inevitably uses metaphor, and the metaphors it selects to describe political reality do actually create that reality. As Chilton explains, the metaphors of container, balance and pressure have 'become natural to narrate Cold War history and military doctrines' (1996: 245) and were introduced after the Second World War by realist theorists and policymakers who rejected metaphor in favor of an 'objective' description of reality.

The need for an integrated approach to the study of metaphor in political discourse also emerges in Musolff (2004), who combines insights from cognitive semantics with suggestions from the fields of pragmatics and discourse analysis to scrutinize public discourse about European integration in Great Britain and Germany. In detail, Musolff explores metaphorical scenarios underlying politically mediated discourse in Great Britain and Germany to shed some light on the different attitudes to European integration in the two countries and to test the commonly held assumption about a mere opposition between British Euro-skepticism and German Euro-enthusiasm. The study covers a time span of approximately a decade, from 1989 to 2001, which represents a period of great changes as determined by the collapse of communism, the unification of Germany, the rise of sovereign nation states in Eastern Europe, the birth of the European Union and the subsequent Treaties of Maastricht and Amsterdam.

For his analysis Musolff works with texts from British and German newspapers and magazines, using two bilingual English–German corpora, EUROMETA I and II. In addition, empirical findings from initial work with these bilingual corpora are validated though an extension of the data pool so as to include large and comparable portions of two bigger corpora, the British COBUILT and the German COSMAS. This means that in a first phase political metaphors for 'attitudes towards Europe' were identified in the smaller bilingual corpora and later the same metaphors were searched for in a much larger collection of data.

Musolff's own contribution to the study of metaphor does not simply consist of an extensive and thorough analysis of a wide range of metaphorical scenarios. Rather, he suggests enriching the cognitive semantic study of political metaphors with both argumentative and historical dimensions. On the one hand, he claims that it is important to see how different discourse communities exploit the argumentative potential of metaphorical scenarios beyond predictable prototypicality effects. On the other hand, he stresses that it is also necessary to consider the evolution of metaphorical scenarios and the creation of new conceptual mappings over the years. This enlarged approach proves particularly helpful for investigating attitudes towards political issues, since they necessarily involve emotional and evaluative components and are subject to variation over time. Thus, when exploring political attitudes to European integration through an analysis of the path–movement–journey metaphorical domain, it is essential to consider the specific scenarios of modes of transport (train, ship, airplane and so on) and related notions of punctuality, efficiency, speed, delay, obstacles and so on. Other observations concern the life–body–health domain and its instantiations. As Musolff points out, the conceptualizations of economy as health and of nations as people motivate the metaphorical depiction of European countries as either healthy or sick persons depending on the state of their economies. However, these conceptualizations cannot be used to explain different attitudes, since other factors come into play. As Musolff explains, the expression 'sick man of Europe' was first used in the German press to refer to the poor British economy in the early 1970s. Later on, the same expression was utilized in the British press to revert the stigma label onto Germany and criticize German involvement in EU integration. This, clearly, cannot count as a proof of British Euro-skepticism and should rather be seen as a reaction to stigmatization.

Musolff's integrated approach to political metaphor also allows for his personal re-reading of Hobbes's *Leviathan*. In Hobbes's work Musolff spots a discussion of analogical reasoning according to which the relationship between a source and a target domain not only involves a transfer of semantic structure, but opens up to emotive and evaluative aspects as well. These very aspects are indeed responsible for apparently self-evident conclusions. In Musolff's words 'Hobbes consistently advocates a critical attitude towards seemingly unproblematic analogies that lead to dangerous conclusions. This disqualification of *metaphor* is not to be equated with the (vacuous) recommendation to speak or think only in literal terms' (2004: 171, emphasis in the original).

Another valuable contribution to research on metaphor in political discourse is that of Ahrens (2009). Her volume brings together a number of articles that explore the relation between gender and metaphor in political language from a range of theoretical and methodological standpoints which include cognitive linguistics, semantics, rhetoric, sociolinguistics, applied linguistics and political science. As Ahrens reports, sociolinguistic studies have already proved that men and women use language differently in the workplace (see Tannen 1994, Holmes and Stubbe 2003), and findings in critical discourse analysis have demonstrated how the language of business is characterized by masculine metaphors (see Koller 2004). Politics, however, still remains a vast area to be investigated for the potential presence of gendered metaphors. Thus, Ahrens's (2009) aim in editing this volume is to shed light on the type of metaphors that female and male politicians use, and to observe whether they differ. Ahrens's volume is subdivided into three parts. Studies in part I consider conceptual metaphors that female and male politicians of different nationalities (German, Italian, American and Irish) used in speeches and interviews. Part II focuses on the metaphorical language employed by politicians of different gender and nationalities (British, German and American) engaging in face-to-face interactions. Unlike parts I and II, part III deals with mediated discourse and examines how women are constructed by advertisements in Singapore, pundits in the US and policy statements in the Netherlands and Spain. The majority of studies in parts I and II demonstrate that in the political domain there are no striking differences between the metaphors used by men and women.[14] When differences emerge, factors other than gender appear to motivate them. These include political orientation, type of audience addressed and specific goals to be attained.

Apart from these monographs and edited volumes, there is a bulk of literature that mainly appeared in the form of journal articles concerned with different facets of political discourse in relation to conceptual metaphor. The following recent, and fairly recent, publications may give an idea of the range of topics discussed. Presidential talk is the issue under scrutiny in a number of studies. Among others, Semino and Masci (1996) analyze football metaphors in the discourse of Silvio Berlusconi; Hodgkinson and Leland (1999) compare Clinton's use of construction metaphors to Bob Dole's use of metaphors of tradition through an analysis of their presidential speeches; Bates (2004) explores the types of metaphors pertaining to the CIVILIZATION and SAVAGE clusters that George Bush Sr. employed during the First Gulf War; Ferrari (2007) discusses the role of metaphor and other persuasive strategies in George Bush Jr.'s speeches from 2001 to 2004; Duman and Locher (2008) investigate Hillary Clinton and Barack Obama's uses of the VIDEO EXCHANGE IS CONVERSATION metaphor in their video clips on YouTube; and Lu and Ahrens (2008) provide a detailed analysis of BUILDING metaphors and their ideological implications in Taiwanese presidential speeches.

The ideological and manipulative use of metaphors and other rhetorical devices is at the core of Bhatia's (2008) accurate study of the complex sociopolitical construct of terrorism as it emerges from the Bush Administration's National Strategy for Combating Terrorism devised in 2003. Previous research has also shown how metaphor systems are used discursively by politicians to advocate their own policies and oppose those of 'others', that is to say to legitimize and delegitimize. Lakoff (1991), for example, discusses the kinds of metaphors used to explain international relations and to justify the war in the Gulf. Jansen and Sabo (1994) focus on the use of sport and war metaphors for mobilizing patriarchal values and sustaining masculinity during the Persian Gulf War. Rohrer (1995) illustrates the metaphors used by George Bush Sr. to conceptualize the political situation in the Persian Gulf before the war. Sandikcioglu (2000) explores news coverage of the Persian Gulf War, with a focus on the metaphorical representation of the West as civilized, mature, rational and stable in opposition to the 'other', which is depicted as barbarous, immature, irrational, weak and instable.

Studies of metaphor in political press reports are numerous and they generally emphasize how the use of certain metaphors can influence the reader's interpretation of current political issues. Burnes (2011) deals with newspaper reports of elections, comparing the 2008 parliamentary election in Pakistan to Obama's 2008 election. Flowerdew and Leong (2007) examine the discursive role of metaphor in the construction of patriotism in post-colonial Hong Kong through an analysis of opinion pieces and reports from local newspapers. Zinken (2003) devotes his attention to the functions and effects of intertextual metaphors in ideological discourse through an analysis of Polish newspapers on the occasion of the tenth anniversary of the end of communism. Press reports are also the source of data for Santa Ana (1999), who examines the framing of immigration by analyzing metaphors in hundreds of articles from the *Los Angeles Times*. The role of metaphors in shaping immigration policy is also discussed in Charteris-Black's (2006) study of right-wing strategies in the 2005 British election campaign.

The function of metaphor as an instrument of legitimization is emphasized in McEntee (2011) as well. She analyzes speeches delivered by the Secretary General of the United Nations to explore how metaphor is employed to legitimize an international organization identity and to construct a common image of international diplomacy. The power of metaphor to construct (supra)national identities is an issue addressed in research on political language in the European Union. Chilton and Ilyn (1993) look at political discourse in the EU as a form of 'conversation' among European countries and adopt a translinguistic and transnational perspective to analyze the metaphor of the 'common European house' in Russian, French and German texts. The same metaphor and its ideological implications are also discussed in Schäffner (1996). Along similar lines, Musolff (2000a) concentrates on the metaphorical source domains of HOUSE and CONSTRUCTION and their different realizations in British and German media texts and their respective national debates. In subsequent studies on the reporting of political issues in the British and German press, Musolff (2000b, 2003) considers metaphors from the domains of HEALTH and TRANSPORT and discusses how some of them have changed over time so as to adapt to the specific needs of users and to the specificities of discourse contexts. Straehle *et al* (1999) report on the EU discourse on unemployment and its metaphorical conceptualization as a STRUGGLE by examining two different genres produced by the EU: presidency conclusions and commissioners' speeches.

Language is in a constant flux and metaphors partake in its life cycle. This means that while a few metaphors become old and 'die' a few others are given birth and start circulating. Billig and Macmillan (2005) are interested in metaphors which have attained the status of idioms and focus on the *smoking gun* idiom in particular. Relying on Glucksberg's property attribution model of metaphor, they consider the use of the *smoking gun* idiom in the rhetoric of blame and compare its appearance in the Watergate controversy to that in the dispute about the search for weapons of mass destruction in Iraq. While Billig and Macmillan (2005) focus on a specific type of lexicalized metaphor, Hobbs's study (2008) revolves around new metaphors or new uses of existing metaphors. As she observes, new metaphors are designed to attract attention, but become problematic if rejected, as was the case with Bush's military plan to increase US forces in Iraq.

Vertessen and De Landtsheer (2008) have taken a broader approach to metaphor and applied a theory originally crafted for the study of crisis rhetoric (Crisis Communication Combination theory) to analyze the language used by politicians at election time. They start from the general assumption that politicians make an extra rhetorical effort during election campaigns in order to be persuasive. To achieve this aim, politicians craft messages where the degree of metaphoricity is generally high, conceptual complexity tends to be low and modality is typically of the epistemic type. Their definition of a 'metaphor power index' based on the three variables of metaphor frequency, intensity and content is of particular interest.

Finally, authors like Schäffner (2004) and Sharifian (2007, 2009) have lucidly reasoned on the kinds of problems and challenges one may encounter when trying to successfully translate conceptual figurativity into political language.

While this section has been intended to provide a general overview of the linguistic studies that have looked at the role of conceptual metaphor in political discourse, the following section more specifically describes and comments on the contributions offered by Cienki (2004, 2005a,b), Ahrens and Yat Mei Lee (2009) and Ahrens (2011) to the analysis of political language. Since these studies present applications of Lakoff's family models to the analysis of political speeches, it is important to discuss these works in more detail.

3.3   Linguistic applications of Lakoff's metaphorical morality models

The level of elaboration and detail with which Lakoff engaged to describe the SF and NP models of morality seems to have acted more as a deterrent than as an incentive for linguistic research. So far, linguistic attempts to test the empirical validity of the suggested models have been few and far between.

The earliest linguistic applications of the models are attributable to Cienki (2004, 2005a, 2005b). Combining quantitative and qualitative methods of analysis, Cienki (2004) embarks on an investigation that has the aim of empirically testing Lakoff's models. For this, he assembles a corpus of roughly 41,000 words which consists of three 90 minute transcriptions of televised debates between George W. Bush and Al Gore before the US presidential elections in October 2000. Cienki is very precise in explaining the reasons for the selection of these data. Among the various motivations, particular emphasis is placed on striking a balance between the two candidates in terms of their number of words spoken as well as lexical density and range of topics discussed. In addition, Cienki narrowed his focus to debates taken from a late stage in the campaign, since it could be expected that the positions of the two competitors would be distinctively clear at that time. As a starting point for his analysis, Cienki takes the central metaphors for SF and NP morality that he deduces from chapters 5 and 6 of Lakoff's book (1996). He also provides a summary of these metaphors in two appendices at the end of his article. In other words, he focuses on the actual manifestations of these sets of metaphors in a carefully compiled corpus of political language to measure the validity of Lakoff's models as conceptual structures that can explain American politics.

In detail, Cienki's linguistic analysis (2004) is divided into four parts. First he conducts a search for metaphorical expressions (at or below the sentence level) that can be taken as a direct reflection of central SF and NP metaphors. As a further step, he also looks for metaphorical and non-metaphorical entailments of these metaphors. The analysis is then complemented by frequency counts of key words that reflect source domains of both SF and NP metaphors. Lastly, he provides a comparison of stylistic differences between Bush and Gore in the way they employ SF and NP metaphors. Methodologically, Cienki expresses his general concerns about the reliability of findings and the replicability of studies. In order to avoid these pitfalls he had all his data tested by a second analyst. These methodological concerns are reiterated in later publications (2005a,b) and become even more evident if we consider his involvement in the Pragglejaz Group (2007), who devised an explicit procedure for identifying metaphorically used words in a text. In so doing, Cienki (2004) reflects a new emphasis in cognitive linguistic research for studies that are empirically based and clear in their methodological procedures. This new orientation, which is also embraced in this book, can contribute greatly to an advancement of research in conceptual metaphor theory.

As far as Cienki's (2004) results are concerned, the findings related to the presence of direct linguistic expressions of SF and NP central metaphors in the corpus proved insignificant. While each candidate was observed to have used some direct SF and NP metaphors and each of them used more direct metaphors of the predicted type (that is, Bush used more direct SF metaphors and Gore more direct NP metaphors), the total amount of metaphorical language that directly reflected SF and NP metaphors was very small. On the other hand, the analysis of metaphorical and non-metaphorical logical entailments[15] of SF and NP metaphors revealed that, on the whole, they were used much more often by both candidates. Results also demonstrated that, altogether, Bush produced more entailments than Gore and that his assortment of SF and NP entailments was more balanced, which possibly contributed to his depiction by the media as a 'compassionate' conservative.

The explanation that Cienki (2004) suggests for the fact that SF and NP metaphors do not find much direct metaphorical expression in the data is based on Clausner and Croft's (1997) notions of schematicity and productivity.

> Clausner and Croft (1997) make an important distinction between kinds of metaphors which is relevant here. They note that conceptual metaphors differ according to their degree of (a) schematicity, and (b) productivity. By schematicity, they are referring to the range of source or target domain concepts that are consistent with a given metaphorical mapping. For example, the mapping ARGUMENT IS WAR has a high level of schematicity because the domains involved encompass many possible sub-domains: so the type of 'argument' could be rational or irrational, philosophical or commonplace. Similarly, the source domain encompasses many possible aspects of war, such as strategy, physical interaction, possible outcomes, etc. However, they observe that a metaphor like THE CONVINCINGNESS OF AN ARGUMENT IS THE STRUCTURAL INTEGRITY OF A BUILDING is much less schematic, since the range of concepts which we normally use to characterize either how convincing an argument is or how solid a building is, are much more limited. By productivity, Clausner and Croft mean the number of roughly synonymous expressions by which the metaphorical mapping is manifested. They note that orientational metaphors, such as GOOD IS UP / BAD IS DOWN, are on the high end on the scale of productivity because of the many expressions which appear, in English as well as many other languages, that describe the positive and the negative in terms of opposing ends of the vertical scale. In terms of the present study, we see that the SF and NP metaphors (Appendices 1 and 2) are not productive in the context of these data, and we can surmise that they are probably not productive in Bush's and Gore's language overall. Indeed, they are likely not productive metaphors in American English at all. However, they appear to be schematic metaphors, many of which represent high-level mappings which subsume a number of subcases. (Cienki 2004: 415)

Following Clausner and Croft's (1997) observation, the two notions of schematicity and productivity seem to go hand in hand. The explanation they provide suggests that the more a conceptual metaphor is schematic, the more it is expected to be productive. Thus, a schematic metaphor like ARGUMENT IS WAR finds abundant manifestation in language, whereas a less schematic metaphor, like THE CONVINCINGNESS OF AN ARGUMENT IS THE STRUCTURAL INTEGRITY OF A BUILDING, is less likely to give rise to verbal expressions. This interdependence between schematicity and productivity has been explored by other cognitive linguists, notably Bybee (1985) and Langacker (1987), who first used these terms for describing morphological properties. Among the morphological examples they provide, the -ed morpheme represents a clear case of a schematic structure that finds expression in the paradigm of regular verbs and is hence productive. Clausner and Croft (1997) present their own study as an extension of these morphological theories to the semantic domain of metaphor by claiming: '*We argue that metaphors vary in both their schematicity and productivity, and the Bybee/Langacker cognitive linguistic view of grammatical organization provides a theoretical foundation for describing this variation*' (1997: 248, emphasis in the original). If, as these studies indicate, schematicity can be taken as an indication of productivity, one actually wonders why Cienki decided to rely on these two notions for explaining his findings. Since he states that SF and NP metaphors are not productive in his data (and possibly in American English), one would expect him to claim that these metaphors are non-schematic. However, Cienki describes SF and NP metaphors as schematic. At this point, the correlation between lack of productivity and schematicity appears striking and counterintuitive, and one would expect a detailed account of why that happens to be the case.

Cienki (2004) also observes that a few complexities emerged in the process of coding the data for metaphors and entailments. In particular, there were cases when what on a surface level appeared as a SF or NP expression was actually motivated by the opposite goal. Cienki gives the example of Gore saying 'Well I think we need <u>tough</u> enforcement of the civil rights laws' (2004: 419, emphasis in the original). This example is analyzed by Cienki in the following way: 'tough enforcement of the law follows the SF ideal of setting standards and enforcing them. However, Gore is talking about civil rights laws, and so is supporting the NP ideal of fair distribution and equal opportunity' (*ibid.*). What remains unclear is how Cienki eventually decided to classify such ambiguous cases. Indeed, if seen from a different perspective, this example would rather appear as an uncontroversial instance of the strength to be nurturers ideal that Lakoff describes as part of the NP model. Another aspect for which Cienki's analysis admittedly does not account for is criticism of the opponent's model. Indeed, both candidates are observed to use such criticism (that is, Bush negatively comments on ideas coherent with the NP model and Gore does the same with the SF model), and it would be worthwhile analyzing this type of criticism in more detail.

Another component of Cienki's analysis (2004) is based on the observation that certain words related to both the SF and NP models were used frequently. Following this observation, Cienki conducted frequency counts which showed that 'Gore used more NP buzz words than SF; however, Bush matched Gore's use of NP buzz words and exceeded him in the use of SF language' (2004: 422). An interesting detail regards the term *fight*, which Gore used twice as often as Bush. Since the word *fight* evokes the moral strength metaphor that is at the base of SF morality but also features in the NP worldview, it would be important to consider how it is used. This type of information would help us understand whether the term *fight* is employed to support SF or NP morality.

Furthermore, Cienki's (2004) analysis of the rhetorical strategies typical of the two candidates highlights a marked contrast. Bush's persuasiveness comes out as the result of a communicative style which is characterized by the repetition of small phrases, often including metaphorical SF key words. On the contrary, Gore prefers to use language in a more diversified manner, speaking at length and quite literally.

Still in the same study, Cienki (2004) moved beyond the level of language to consider how gestures could also reflect SF and NP conceptual metaphors. Since gestures are to a certain extent more unconscious than verbal language, the presence of SF or NP metaphorical gestures to accompany SF or NP linguistic expressions can be taken as evidence for the existence of Lakoff's morality models as deep structures located in our brains. In detail, Cienki observed whether there were differences in the kinds of gestures accompanying Bush's and Gore's SF and NP linguistic expressions, and, in the case that there were, whether these gestural differences could be reconciled with central metaphors in the two morality models.

The analysis of gestures was conducted on a smaller set of data. It focused on the video of the second televised debate, since there the hands of the candidates were shown more consistently. This analysis highlighted significant differences between them. Bush's gesturing was observed to be coherent with SF morality: his highly frequent use of two-handed gestures, with both hands tense and communicating solidity and upright nature, is resonant with the source domains of SF metaphors. Furthermore, the analysis pointed out that these SF gestures were also produced when Bush uttered NP phrases. Cienki comments on this finding, saying that 'if his gestures are in fact reflecting how he was thinking while formulating his speech, then it would suggest Bush's conviction in the SF model even when he is using NP language' (2004: 428). This is indeed a finding that makes one wonder about the classification of Bush's NP linguistic expressions. Were they really NP phrases or were they so just on a surface level, while actually being motivated by SF aims? And, if that is the case, wouldn't it make more sense for this type of analysis to classify language according to its 'real' semantic content without making a distinction between what is said and what is meant? Stated differently, wouldn't it be more reasonable to classify as either NP or SF those parts of text that are motivated by the relative logic and then emphasize how both a NP and a SF logic can be manifested manipulatively in language via expressions that appear to contradict that logic?

To continue with Cienki's semiotic analysis, in contrast to Bush, Gore used a larger array of gestures that reflected a plurality of messages and a more complex rhetorical style. Cienki provides an interpretation of these results that emphasizes basic conceptual differences between SF and NP source domains. While source domains of SF metaphors are based on image schemas (objects, forms, positions), many NP source domains appear as culturally dependent. Thus, Cienki states, '(the source domain of) metaphors in the SF model may simply lend themselves better to metaphoric gestural expression than the (source domains of) metaphors in the NP model' (2004: 430).

Cienki (2004) concludes his study claiming that the data do not provide the type of evidence that is typically found in studies of conceptual metaphors. Some evidence of reasoning in terms of the two models is found in entailments of the SF and NP metaphors, but gestures appear as the most promising field for further investigations.

In a companion article (Cienki 2005a), the results of the earlier study are taken as a basis for further methodological and theoretical consideration about metaphors and cognitive models. Thus, in this publication, Cienki (2005a) makes it very clear that the central SF and NP metaphors he has deduced from Lakoff (1996), though structured in a parallel fashion, contain a lot of differences.

> First, consider the target domains other than morality itself. In the SF model, the target domains are more varied, and many of them represent ideas that, I would argue, are talked about more frequently (e.g., being good or bad, rights, persons); whereas in the NP model, they are concepts that are used less frequently in normal discourse, and, indeed, are more specific to the realm of morality itself (e.g., moral agents, moral actions, moral growth). [...] in addition, there are noticeable differences in the source domains. Many of the source domains for SF metaphors represent simple objects (object, paths), orientations (being upright, being low), or abstract nouns captured by single lexemes (wholeness, purity, health). However, a number of source domains that are important in the NP model represent concepts that are themselves more involved, that (revealingly) require multi-word characterizations (fair distribution, children needing nurturance, the nurturance of social ties). (Cienki 2005a: 285)

According to Cienki, if we compare SF and NP central metaphors, their differences cannot go unnoticed, and they can actually motivate the relative paucity of NP expressions in the data. This is, however, an observation that needs further reflection. If we take a look at Lakoff's description of SF and NP morality as rooted in two sets of basic metaphors (see Section 3.1.1), all these metaphors (often presented as metaphorical concepts) have MORALITY as their target domain, and each of them represents a complex metaphorical construct that can best be explained making recourse to other metaphors. Thus, the metaphor of MORAL STRENGTH, which is foundational for SF morality, subsumes other metaphorical notions like BEING GOOD IS BEING UPRIGHT, BEING BAD IS BEING LOW, or DOING EVIL IS FALLING, EVIL IS A FORCE (Lakoff 1996: 72). In fact, these metaphors essentially serve the purpose of explaining why morality is conceptualized in terms of strength. The roughly two dozen metaphors listed in Section 3.1.1 constitute, so to say, the building blocks of the SF and NP models. Each of them describes a particular moral view, a way of looking at (political) reality according to certain values and principles. This is the reason why each of the metaphors has morality as its target domain and takes a general notion as its source (for example, STRENGTH, AUTHORITY, ORDER, ESSENCE, WHOLENESS, EMPATHY, NURTURANCE, SELF-DEVELOPMENT, FAIR DISTRIBUTION and so on). Taking these general notions (the source domains of the basic metaphors) as guidance for identifying the expression of SF or NP moral values in a corpus of political language appears to be a procedure that is more in line with Lakoff's proposal.

In *Moral Politics* and in later publications that elaborate on the same topic (Lakoff 2004, Lakoff and The Rockridge Institute 2006), Lakoff insists on the importance of Democratic politicians framing their discourse according to clear moral values based on NP morality. Lakoff sees values as the core of politics; in his view, values can be expressed explicitly or they can be more indirectly symbolized and evoked by issues and policies. As he points out,

> Politics is about values [...]. Issues are secondary—not irrelevant or unimportant, but secondary. A position on issues should follow from one's values, and the choice of issues and policies should symbolize those values. (Lakoff and The Rockridge Institute 2006: 8)

From this, it follows that, if we intend to measure a politician's degree of adherence to either SF or NP morality, we need to look for the kinds of values they express. Values such as 'opportunity for children' or 'fair working conditions' can be taken as the expression of deep-rooted moral views according to which morality is metaphorically conceived as empathy and nurturance. This is the approach that, differently from Cienki, is pursued in this book.

Implicit in this approach is also the idea that morality as such is what triggers linguistic expressions that are framed according to the general notions describing the source domains of the basic metaphors (for example, STRENGTH, AUTHORITY, ORDER, ESSENCE, WHOLENESS, EMPATHY NURTURANCE, SELF-DEVELOPMENT, FAIR DISTRIBUTION and so on). Once we take the SF and NP models as morality models (and that's what they are!), what we expect from them is to describe morality (a rather vague concept) in terms of other notions that we are more familiar with because of the physical environment where we live (for example, STRENGTH, WHOLENESS, ESSENCE) and the type of social relations we have with other people (for example, EMPATHY, AUTHORITY). In this sense, the models describe our moral view on the world via a set of moral metaphors. The morality part of the metaphors (the Target domains) describes this intellectual and emotional position. Therefore, if one decides to look for manifestations of SF and NP metaphorical morality in a corpus of political language, the morality component of the metaphors should be assigned, so to say, to the beliefs expressed by the politicians. The source domains of the basic metaphors (for example, STRENGTH, AUTHORITY, ORDER, ESSENCE, WHOLENESS, EMPATHY, NURTURANCE, SELF-DEVELOPMENT, FAIR DISTRIBUTION and so on), instead, are expected to be expressed in a politician's speech when they talk about the economy, foreign affairs, education, security and so on. To be more precise, the source domains of the metaphors represent those notions that allow political framing according to specific values (for example, security, freedom, equality, opportunity, protection, community, service and cooperation). In line with these considerations, it is difficult to agree with Cienki (2005a) when he explains the lack of SF and NP metaphorical expressions in his data as possibly dependent on politicians' tendencies not to explicitly mention morality in their speeches.

> One explanation is that rather than talking about morality per se, the candidates were discussing other domains, such as foreign policy, economic issues, etc. Any metaphors they used may have related more to target domains which are different from those proposed in the models, namely domains which are more contextually specific than morality, the moral order, or moral action. (2005a: 288)

To bring the morality models back to their inventor, Lakoff (1996, 2004) suggests that political candidates would frame their discourse according to their moral views. He is not expecting (or predicting) politicians would talk about morality *per se*.

Cienki also proposes alternative ways to test Lakoff's models. Thus, for example, he suggests all kinds of metaphorical expressions should be extracted from the data and some non-experts should classify them in a pile sort task. According to Cienki, this could allow for the emergence of other, not yet considered, metaphorical groupings to complement (or maybe replace) the ones Lakoff presents in *Moral Politics*. This shows that Cienki's dissatisfaction with Lakoff's models centers around the metaphorical level. This is why he also claims 'another possibility could be that the two candidates simply did not use much metaphorical language in the debates, in which case it would be difficult to ascertain whether or not the models are correct' (2005a: 288). This is an observation that can be contradicted. If SF and NP metaphors describe (as they do) our 'moral' relation to the world in terms of basic notions, what is vital for a linguistic analysis is testing up to what extent and how (literally or metaphorically) these basic notions find expression in a corpus of political language.

Significantly enough, when Cienki (2005a) considers the large number of SF and NP entailments (both literal and metaphorical) that he found in his data, he eventually becomes more cautious regarding the use of metaphors and writes the following:

> [...] more striking was the high number of non-metaphorical expressions which were entailed by the two models, totaling 745. This provides rather strong support for the argument that the *SF and NP models as wholes, and not strictly in terms of the metaphorical parts of their structure, played a role* in the logic of the two speakers' arguments. (2005a: 292, my emphasis)

The presence of SF and NP entailments demonstrates that the models find linguistic expression in the data. This is indeed a sign that the models 'as wholes' can be taken as valid instruments for analyzing politics. Furthermore, the abundance of literal entailments indicates that the models are not necessarily expressed through metaphors. Towards the end of his article, Cienki elaborates more on this point and seems to recognize, though a bit tentatively, that the presence of metaphorical language expressing SF and NP morality cannot be taken as the only criterion for establishing the validity of Lakoff's models.

> Cognitive models may motivate reasoning in terms of sets of metaphors, but contrary to expectation, *this reasoning may be manifested much more through non-metaphorical language* than through verbal metaphoric expressions. (2005a: 304, my emphasis)

There is yet another component of Lakoff's models that Cienki probes in more detail. In a subsequent study conducted on the same pool of data, Cienki (2005b) questions the validity of Lakoff's morality models as family-based. The study is set to test two specific hypotheses. According to the first hypothesis 'the ratio of metaphorical expressions to non-metaphorical entailments should be higher for the subset of utterances with "family" words (such as *family, children, parents*) than in the corpus overall' (2005b: 27). The second hypothesis predicts that '"Family" words should be used in (a) metaphorical expressions and/or (b) entailments of the NP and SF models more frequently than other words in the debates that occur with similar frequencies' (*ibid.*). In Cienki's view, if the two hypotheses were proved true, then data would linguistically support Lakoff's belief in family-based morality. In order to test these hypotheses, Cienki looks for the occurrence of the terms *family, parent* and *child/ren* (and its variant *kid/s*) in his corpus.

Contrary to his expectations, Cienki (2005b) finds out that family terms are used more literally than metaphorically. He also provides some qualitative information on the actual use of the family terms in non-meta-phorical entailments. He observes that these words are frequently employed in buzz phrases and mottos, that is, the candidates' slogans. He also makes a few grammatical considerations concerning the use of family terms. He notes that Bush tends to use the word *child/ren* (*kid/s*) in direct object con-structions where the children's role appears as subjugated to their parents' authority, whereas Gore uses the same word more as an indirect object to talk about what society should do for children. While contradicting Cienki's first hypothesis, these findings shed light on the fact that family plays a role in the logic of SF and NP morality. They also indicate how SF and NP models can find expression in non-metaphorical language.

As for the first part of the second hypothesis, Cienki (2005b) notices that family terms are not used in SF/NP metaphorical expressions more than other comparably frequent lexical items (*country, difference, plan, man, doc-tor, government, teacher, woman*).[16] However, family words occur more often in SF/NP entailments than the other frequent terms, which confirms the second part of Cienki's second hypothesis.

Overall, these findings do not seem to disprove the validity of Lakoff's models as family-based. They rather make one wonder about the appropri-ateness of restricting the application of the two models to metaphorical lan-guage. Cienki himself concludes his study with an allusion to the potential usefulness of finding new ways to test the models that do not focus primar-ily on the identification of metaphors.

This two-part study shows that family terms do play an important role in this corpus of political language, often being used in statements which support the logic of the NP or SF models. However, the family words studied do not play as much of a role as one might expect in the direct expression of conceptual metaphors proposed as part of the NP and SF models. [...] We are left with questions about how to test the validity of proposed sets (or models) of metaphors, [...] *perhaps we need some new theorizing and methodology concerning non-metaphorical entailments.* This could make more explicit what entailments, as opposed to metaphori-cal expressions, can and cannot be expected to reveal about conceptual metaphors. (2005b: 36, my emphasis)

While Cienki's study (2005b) focuses on the terms *family, parent* and *child/ren* (and its variant *kid/s*) in a corpus that assembles three fairly recent debates between Gore and Bush, Ahrens (2006) conducts a diachronic study of general terms referring to people in American presidential speeches.

Ahrens compiles a corpus that brings together State of the Union addresses from 1945 to 2006, and she observes how the use of the terms *humankind, mankind, man* (*men*), *woman* (*women*), *mother(s)*, *father(s)* and *parent(s)* has changed over this span of time. The aim of the study is to uncover how

American presidents exercise power through their use of language that refers to people and how, on a related note, this use of language can be seen as a reflection of a particular value system. The study is based on the hypothesis that presidential language has become more inclusive from the middle of the twentieth century to the beginning of the twenty-first century as a result of societal and legislative changes. The passing of the Civil Rights Act in 1964 and the signing of Title IX[17] into law in 1975 are expected to have had an impact on the linguistic habits of American presidents. The specific hypotheses brought to the fore are the following: (a) the use of the term *mankind* to refer to all human beings should decrease, (b) the use of *man* to stand for all people should also diminish, (c) references to *woman* (*women*) should not be restricted to motherhood, and (d) the use of *mother(s)* and *father(s)* should reflect the variety of social and familiar roles that each parent plays. As the linguistic analysis shows, data corroborate these hypotheses only partially. In relation to hypotheses (a) and (b), Ahrens demonstrates that the use of the term *mankind* to refer to all human beings and of *man* to refer to all people has markedly decreased in the last decades, but with significant differences among presidents. Thus, Democratic presidents like Carter and Clinton clearly avoid using these terms. On the contrary, Reagan, Bush Sr. and Bush Jr. (all Republican), often use *mankind* to refer to humankind, and Reagan and Bush Sr. also use *man* to stand for human being. As Ahrens suggests, findings about *mankind* could be taken as a linguistic indication of adherence to SF morality and its view of the world as man-ruled. Moving to hypothesis (c), the data prove that, on the whole, presidents talk far less about women than about men and that women are never taken as an example for emulation but rather as the target of compassion (for instance, their economic and social status need to improve). Ahrens interprets these findings by stating that women still need to battle to have their deeds recognized. While this is undeniably true, one could also consider that this use of language actually reflects a situation where women are still and often in a position of disadvantage. As for the last hypothesis, the data seem to demonstrate that 'fathers are still primarily considered the providers and the mothers are primarily nurturers' (2006: 389). What is more telling is the use of the term *parent*, which has received a general increase since 1980 (a time when the issue of child-rearing gained more importance in domestic policy), but appears to be used differently by presidents. Significantly, the term *parent* shows a marked increase in use from Reagan to Clinton and a drastic drop from Clinton to Bush Jr. This finding is in line with NP morality and the gender neutral attribution of family roles that it predicts for Democratic politicians. While this study alludes to Lakoff's family models, in later publications Ahrens and Yat Mei Lee (2009) and Ahrens (2011) explore the Lakovian models more closely.

Ahrens and Yat Mei Lee (2009) adopt a corpus-based methodology to investigate the use of lexemes associated to the SF and NP models in American senatorial language. The corpora they use assemble US Senate floor speeches by male and female senators, both Republicans and Democrats, delivered between 2000 and 2007. For each of the two morality models, they consider the top source domains: STRENGTH and AUTHORITY for the SF model, NURTURANCE and EMPATHY for the NP model. Then, they employ WordNet 3.0, a large lexical database of English words, to select the appropriate sense for each of the four concepts (STRENGTH, AUTHORITY, NURTURANCE, EMPATHY). This allows them to create a list of SF lexemes (*authority, authorization, control, decision, determine, direct, dominance, force, forcefulness, intensity, order, potency, power, right* and *strength*) and one of NP lexemes (*aid, anguish, attention, care, empathy, feeling, nourishment, nurturance, provide, share, sorrow, sympathy, tend, treatment* and *understand*). The selected SF and NP lexemes consist of concrete nouns and verbs and direct hypernyms for which searches and statistical analyses are run in each of the four corpora (female, male, Democratic, Republican senators). The study is aimed at uncovering whether gender, party affiliation, or a combination of the two influence the conceptual models invoked by senators via their lexical usage. The specific hypotheses on which the investigation is based are the following:

> [...] if ideology is the overriding factor, male and female Republican senators will have comparable levels of usage of both SF lexemes (high) and NP lexemes (low) in their Senate floor speeches, while Democratic male and female senators will have the opposite pattern. This finding would be the strongest support for Lakoff's proposal that Republicans and Democrats have different views of morality as expressed in different conceptual models. However, if gender overrides ideology, than we may find that women senators of both parties have a high usage of NP lexemes, and a low usage of SF lexemes. (2009: 68)

The findings do not confirm these hypotheses and thus appear to contradict Lakoff's predictions about the two models and their use in political language. The analysis reveals that gender does not play a significant role, since senators as a group do not invoke a particular model on the basis of gender. In relation to ideology, the NP model results as the one invoked most often by all senators. However, exceptions to this last general trend occur when the individual data for senators Barack Obama and John McCain are considered. Both Obama (Democratic) and McCain (Republican) use more SF lexemes than NP ones.

How to interpret these findings? Do they really refute Lakoff's predictions? Are there elements in the analysis which could have skewed the results? Ahrens and Yat Mei Lee are rather cautious and allude to potential shortcomings. Thus, for instance, results for NP lexemes can be affected by highly frequent collocational patterns. A case in point is the combination *health care*, which has the highest frequency both among men and women. Health care was an issue that received great attention during senate floor discussions in the time span considered. As a result, the expression *health care* was uttered very frequently by senators. This happened irrespective of the senators' gender and plausibly of any specific NP framing. For this reason, it would be necessary to ascertain how this high-frequency collocational pattern is actually used. Checking details concerning how the notion of health care is framed could reveal a scenario that is different from the one that the study depicts. In this respect, Ahrens and Yat Mei Lee also admit

> Yet, it is also necessary to see how 'health care' is used in context to determine if the speaker is arguing for or against it or has a neutral stance; that is, to determine if the use of 'health care' should be categorized as an NP lexeme. In fact, when the data are examined more closely, it can be difficult to interpret. Almost every senator is for 'health care' as an abstract concept (which would seem to be in line with our coarse-grained method of counting it as an instance of a lexeme being used in the NP model), but the devil is in the details: who deserves it, who pays for it and who administers the health care programme (that is, the government or private insurance companies). Thus, depending on the level of discrimination one would like to see, it may be that the current frequency-based lexical analysis is too coarse-grained to get at the differences between how men and women are using language. (2009: 71)

Another point which needs further consideration is the apparent lack of differentiation between Democrats and Republicans regarding which SF and NP lexemes and collocational patterns they use. In fact, data show that Democrats use *civil rights* and *voting rights* much more frequently than Republicans. In particular, from the examples and explanations Ahrens and Yat Mei Lee provide, it appears that the collocational pattern *voting rights* is used recurrently by Democrats to support the NP values of inclusivity, nurturance and fair distribution. Conversely, this expression is used only five times by Republicans and all of them by the same person. This person, Senator Graham, talks about *voting rights* not with the aim of supporting them but rather to inquire 'about the details of the act itself' (2009: 72). This is an observation that should make us reflect for two reasons. First of all, it shows that a term such as *right*, which is included in the list of lexemes associated with a SF worldview, can be used with a NP meaning. Secondly, it shows how the collocation *voting rights*, for which a qualitative analysis has been given, indicates an ideological fracture between Democrats and Republicans.

Findings related to Obama and McCain hint at the potential danger of considering groups of politicians (male, female, Democratic and Republican senators) rather than individual politicians. Reasoning in terms of groups has the drawback of homogenizing results and leveling differences. This is another shortcoming that Ahrens and Yat Mei Lee recognize in their discussion of results when they claim: 'It seems from the analysis done above and previously (Ahrens forthcoming) that more information can be gained from an analysis of lexical frequency patterns at the individual level, as opposed to looking at a particular cultural group' (2009: 76). These words encourage future research to focus more attentively on the language use of individual politicians.

Ahrens and Yat Mei Lee also mention how genre can have influenced results. In comparison to state of the union addresses and other types of speech, senate floor speeches are more circumscribed in terms of issues discussed and audience addressed. Such a limitation on the level of expression may reduce the chances of showing one's own SF or NP worldview. In this respect, election campaign speeches can be thought as a better suited terrain for testing Lakoff's models.

Towards the end of the article, Ahrens and Yat Mei Lee indicate with humbleness the kinds of challenges they were unable to face by stating that

> First, given the number of examples involved, we were unable to examine if the sense of the word matched the sense that is associated with the particular conceptual model [...] Second, not all lexemes that we looked at were used to the same extent. [...] Third, we were unable to more than cursorily examine how lexemes were used in a particular context. (2009: 76)

The first and third limitations are particularly significant and call for a different kind of linguistic analysis that can harmoniously integrate a quantitative with a qualitative approach. Lexemes associated to the two models can also be used outside of the models. Thus, we cannot expect that politicians exclusively employ these sets of NP and SF lexemes to address the values as explained by the models. When politicians use NP and SF terms to describe the relation between the government and American citizens, we can say that they are framing discourse according to a NP or a SF moral view. However, if these terms are used for other purposes, they cannot count as linguistic manifestations of either NP or SF morality. This is a crucial distinction for the analysis and one that forces linguists to consider how words are used in context before assigning them to a moral view. For these reasons, one cannot but agree when Ahrens and Yat Mei Lee claim

> It is hoped that future research will be able to look more closely at the use in context (in addition to overall frequency and collocational patterns) so that a more accurate and detailed analysis can be obtained. [...] collocational patterns should be investigated, as should (ideally) each example found, in order to ascertain that the keyword has been used in that particular context in a way that agrees with the conceptual model that it is associated with. This latter goal is ambitious (and fraught with difficulties about what it means to 'agree with' a conceptual model). Nonetheless,

it would be beneficial to integrate aspects of corpus-and frequency-based analyses with aspects of textual and discourse analyses in order to have a richer understanding of both language use and meaning. (2009: 77–8)

As the following chapters will show, the present study takes up this challenge by proposing a different application of Lakoff's models to political language.

Interestingly enough, the findings presented in Ahrens and Yat Mei Lee (2009) are contradicted by those in Ahrens (2011). In this later study, Ahrens focuses on data regarding four individual politicians – Reagan, Bush Sr., Clinton and Bush Jr. – and she works on two other political genres, namely State of the Union addresses (SOUAs) and radio addresses (RAs), in a period from 1981 to 2006. As previously, Ahrens identifies sets of lexemes that she attributes to either SF or NP morality. This time, though, the lists of lexemes are a bit smaller and include nine terms for each of the groups (*sympathy, nourishment, sorrow, feeling, care, aid, attend, nurturance* and *nourish* for the NP model, and *dominance, authorization, potency, intensity, force, control, dominate, strengthen* and *authorize* for the SF model).

The study is based on the general hypothesis that 'patterns of lexical usage found in well-defined corpora can reflect underlying cognitive models' (2011: 168). Thus, the significant frequency of occurrence of SF/NP lexemes in a corpus that assembles carefully selected speeches of a politician is taken by Ahrens as an indication that the politician is crafting his/her talk according to a SF/NP cognitive model. A further and more specific hypothesis regards the constraints demanded by a particular audience. As Ahrens states, 'a comparison of the frequency of different sets of keywords in a corpus of speeches will reflect either the different ideological leanings of that speaker or the different audience demands of a particular speech corpus' (2011: 169). Since SOUAs and RAs are targeted at different audiences (general American public for SOUAs and core constituents for RAs), it is also important for Ahrens to test how far the type of audience can affect the use of SF and NP lexemes or, to put it differently, 'to determine whether they [politicians] modulate their lexical usage based on the audiences that they are addressing' (2011: 169).

The findings confirm these hypotheses. Among the four American presidents, Clinton stands out as the prototypical Democrat and Reagan as the prototypical Republican. Clinton uses NP lexemes much more often than the other three Republican presidents and he does so both in his SOUAs and RAs. His Republican counterpart, Reagan, uses many more SF lexemes in all of his speeches. Thus, both Clinton and Reagan follow the conceptual viewpoint prototypically postulated for a Democratic and a Republican president respectively. Differently from Reagan, Bush Jr. appears to modulate his language according to the audience he is talking to. Thus, in his SOUAs, Bush Jr. uses an almost equivalent number of SF and NP lexemes, whereas in his RAs SF lexemes outnumber NP ones. Ahrens remarks that

Bush Jr. is able to modulate his language to appeal to the general American population by using more compassionate terminology (hence, the reason for his title as a "compassionate conservative") in the general SOUAs, while using more authoritative and strength-related lexemes when talking to his base in the RAs. (2011: 174)

Data concerning Bush Sr. are somewhat inconclusive. On the one hand, his use of NP lexemes is very similar to that of Clinton, which contradicts expectations for a Republican president. On the other hand, his use of SF lexemes is higher in his SOUAs than in his RAs, which runs counter to expectations about audience constraints. Ahrens justifies these results by claiming: 'Bush Sr.'s small corpus size, especially with respect to his RAs, leaves open the possibility that the findings presented for his corpus could potentially change if the word count increased' (2011: 177). Corpus size is thus seen as responsible for these findings that do not align with the general trend.

Ahrens also alludes to the usefulness of considering collocational patterns, which are obtained by extending the lexical search to the words that immediately precede or follow the selected SF and NP lexemes. This kind of analysis demonstrates, for example, that Clinton uses the collocations *health care* and *child care* much more extensively than the Republican presidents. It also shows that Clinton's discussion of care includes expressions such as *quality care, preventive care* and *home care*, which support a NP moral view and do not feature in the corpora of the Republican presidents. The analysis of collocational patterns, however, becomes more intricate when the lexeme *force* is the base for the search. Data demonstrate that Clinton is focused on *work force* and *task force*, whereas Republicans also use collocations such as *air/multinational/military force*. If the collocations for the lexeme *force* can indicate an ideological divide between the Democratic president and the Republican, the fact remains that in Ahrens's analysis the lexeme *force* counts as one that is related to the SF worldview. Ahrens herself admits 'if lexical meanings are taken into account, such that the use of *force* in *work force* is not counted as an instance that has to do with STRENGTH, the data presented above would change' (2011: 179, emphasis in the original). This observation highlights a pitfall in methodology. In fact, Ahrens devises her study with great care and she looks with a critical eye at previous attempts to apply Lakoff's family-based morality models to the analysis of political language. At the very beginning of her article, Ahrens openly discards Cienki's method of testing cognitive models by solely searching for cognitive metaphors, and she criticizes the circularity implicit in this procedure by claiming the following:

[...] it is essential to avoid postulating a cognitive model based on conceptual metaphors and then saying that the conceptual metaphors are evidence for that particular cognitive model. This *circulus in probando* can be avoided if it is first shown that a particular cognitive model exists based on evidence other than conceptual metaphors themselves or if, once conceptual metaphors have been postulated, other linguistic evidence is brought to bear on the issue. (2011: 167)

As a way to solve this conundrum, Ahrens proposes to examine lexical frequency patterns in small and narrowly focused corpora of political language. More precisely, she suggests linguists should conduct corpus-based analyses of political speeches searching for lexemes and collocational patterns related to the SF and NP models.

Moving the analysis from the identification of SF and NP metaphors (Cienki's approach) to the investigation of SF and NP lexemes (Ahrens's approach) might appear to be a better way to find linguistic evidence for the actual use of the two metaphorical models by politicians. Ahrens also sounds particularly convincing when she claims that the SF and NP lexemes she used for the analysis actually represent salient keywords of political language.

All presidents use the NP lexemes and the SF lexemes significantly more frequently than is found in the BNC [British National Corpus] (p < .05). The fact that both SF lexemes and NP lexemes occur more frequently in RAs and SOUAs than in the general corpus indicates that these lexemes represent a distinctive part of political language. (2011: 173)

The SF and NP lexemes Ahrens selects are not just words that happen to be used frequently in the SOUAs and RAs she analyzes. They are words that occur more frequently in the specific corpora she considers than in a general and much larger corpus of English like the BNC. This is an interesting observation and one that, though indirectly, supports Lakoff's models. Since the models are based on certain core notions (STRENGTH, AUTHORITY, NURTURANCE and EMPATHY) that can be linguistically expressed through the sets of SF and NP lexemes that Ahrens provides, the fact that these lexemes mark political language can be seen as in line with Lakoff's interpretation of political reality.

Ahrens's method, however, has its own limitations, especially in so far as it restricts the analysis to specific lexical items which are presupposed to stand unambiguously for the models. Words need to be interpreted in their larger context of use; neither lexemes nor collocational patterns can provide enough information about a politician's framing of an issue or a policy. Therefore, the type of approach that is proposed in the present study takes discourse as the initial level of analysis. It considers how meaning is expressed in the text and how specific SF and NP values (not metaphors, not lexemes) find expression in language. Once expressions of SF or NP values have been detected in the text, attention can reasonably be given to the particular lexemes or metaphors that have been used for that purpose. As the discussion in the following section will show, SF and NP values lie at the core of Lakoff's metaphorical models and they can be verbalized in many different ways. In fact, one cannot expect that politicians communicate their moral values exclusively via metaphors. Similarly, even though certain lexemes are connected to SF and NP values, one cannot expect that politicians will use these lexemes solely and unambiguously to refer to SF and NP values and the moral views they stand for.

3.4   A new procedure for applying Lakoff's models to the analysis of American political language

As the discussion in the previous section has shown, a few studies have already addressed the question of how to apply Lakoff's models to the analysis of political language. These studies (Cienki 2004, 2005a,b, Ahrens and Yat Mei Lee 2009, Ahrens 2006, 2011) were the first attempts to put Lakoff's elaborate theory into the 'tough' practice of analyzing and understanding how politicians shape their speeches. Each of them was based on a clearly defined methodology and tested specific hypotheses in scrupulously compiled corpora of political language. However, notwithstanding their meticulous design, they could not avoid certain shortcomings.

This study is intended to overcome the kind of limitations that have just been described by presenting an alternative way of interpreting and applying Lakoff's models. As observed earlier (Sections 3.1, 3.1.1, 3.1.2), Lakoff's SF and NP models represent abstractions and idealizations of Democratic and Republican thought. In Lakoff's view (1996), they are models that Americans grow up knowing implicitly. Living by a SF or a NP cognitive model implies thinking, talking and behaving in a certain manner. Each of the two Idealized Cognitive Models marks a distinctive ideological leaning and is expected to have a bearing on the way politicians talk and on the decisions they take. Stated differently, Lakoff's prediction is that if politicians invoke either a SF or a NP moral view, this will influence their framing of issues and the kinds of policies they propose.

The models are metaphorical for basically two reasons. First of all, they represent a moral standpoint (hence, they are morality models) and morality is such an abstract concept that its understanding cannot but be guided by metaphor. Secondly, the models are based on the assumption that the relation between the government and American citizens can be seen in terms of the types of relations existing between parents and children in a family (hence, they are family-based models). The models are therefore metaphorical constructs that are aimed to shed light on American politics. As such, the SF and NP models are built upon an array of central moral metaphors, which are in turn related to and informed by other metaphors.

Table 3.1   List of SF and NP central metaphors

SF central metaphors	NP central metaphors
MORAL STRENGTH	MORALITY AS NURTURANCE
MORAL AUTHORITY	MORALITY AS EMPATHY
MORAL ORDER	MORAL SELF-NURTURANCE
MORAL BOUNDARIES	MORALITY AS SOCIAL NURTURANCE
MORAL ESSENCE	MORALITY AS HAPPINESS
MORAL WHOLENESS	MORALITY AS SELF-DEVELOPMENT
MORAL PURITY	MORALITY AS FAIR-DISTRIBUTION
MORAL HEALTH	MORAL GROWTH
MORAL SELF-INTEREST	MORAL SELF-INTEREST
MORALITY AS NURTURANCE	MORAL STRENGTH
	MORAL BOUNDARIES
	MORAL AUTHORITY

The central moral metaphors are those that have the highest priority in each of the two models. They were mentioned at the beginning of this chapter and, to facilitate the discussion, are listed schematically in Table 3.1.

Lakoff (1996) defines these metaphors as central for SF and NP morality. These basic SF and NP metaphors represent, so to say, the backbone of his metaphorical models. Each of them helps us understand why Republicans and Democrats look at the world and speak the way they do. Lakoff also provides some indication of the hierarchical structure that each of the two models imposes on their constitutive metaphors. The hierarchies internal to the SF and NP models can be represented as summarized below (1996: 102, 138):

SF Moral priorities:

1. The Strength Group (MORAL STRENGTH, MORAL AUTHORITY, MORAL ORDER, MORAL BOUNDARIES, MORAL ESSENCE, MORAL WHOLENESS, MORAL PURITY, MORAL HEALTH)
2. Moral Self-interest
3. Moral Nurturance

NP Moral priorities:

1. The Nurturance Group (MORALITY AS NURTURANCE, MORALITY AS EMPATHY, MORAL SELF-NURTURANCE, MORALITY AS SOCIAL NURTURANCE, MORALITY AS HAPPINESS, MORALITY AS SELF-DEVELOPMENT, MORALITY AS FAIR-DISTRIBUTION, MORAL GROWTH)
2. Moral Self-interest

3. The Strength Group (MORAL STRENGTH, MORAL BOUNDARIES, MORAL AUTHORITY)

In particular, the notions that have the absolute highest priority in each model (strength and authority in SF morality, nurturance and empathy in NP morality) are expected to play a significant role in the respective framing of political issues.

From Lakoff's lengthy discussion of SF and NP central moral metaphors (1996: chs 5–6), we can also deduce the following: (a) some moral metaphors are particularly complex and informed by a range of other metaphors, (b) less complex moral metaphors are informed by just one or two metaphors and (c) certain moral metaphors are not informed by any other metaphor. SF/NP central metaphors and their sub-metaphors are summarized below, alongside with an indication of their individual ranking in each of the models.

MORAL STRENGTH (highest priority in SF morality, lowest priority and different framing in NP morality):
  − BEING GOOD IS BEING UPRIGHT
  − BEING BAD IS BEING LOW
  − DOING EVIL IS FALLING
  − EVIL IS A FORCE (either internal or external)

MORAL AUTHORITY (highest priority in SF morality, lowest priority and different framing in NP morality):
  − A COMMUNITY IS A FAMILY
  − MORAL AUTHORITY IS PARENTAL AUTHORITY
  − AN AUTHORITY FIGURE IS A PARENT
  − A PERSON SUBJECT TO MORAL AUTHORITY IS A CHILD
  − MORAL BEHAVIOR BY SOMEONE SUBJECT TO AUTHORITY IS OBEDIENCE
  − MORAL BEHAVIOR BY SOMEONE IN AUTHORITY IS SETTING STANDARDS AND ENFORCING THEM

MORAL BOUNDARIES (highest priority in SF morality, lowest priority and different framing in NP morality):
  − LIFE IS A JOURNEY
  − RIGHTS ARE PATHS

SELF-INTEREST (explains the relation between strength and nurturance in both models):
  − WELL-BEING IS WEALTH

MORALITY AS NURTURANCE (highest priority in NP morality, lowest priority and different framing in SF morality):

−THE COMMUNITY IS A FAMILY
−MORAL AGENTS ARE NURTURING PARENTS
−PEOPLE NEEDING HELP ARE CHILDREN NEEDING NURTURANCE
−MORAL ACTION IS NURTURANCE

MORAL ORDER (highest priority in SF morality, absent in NP morality):
−THE MORAL ORDER IS THE NATURAL ORDER

MORAL ESSENCE (highest priority in SF morality, absent in NP morality):
−A PERSON IS AN OBJECT
−HIS ESSENCE IS THE SUBSTANCE THE OBJECT IS MADE OF

MORAL WHOLENESS (highest priority in SF morality, absent in NP morality):
−IMMORALITY IS DEGENERATION

MORAL PURITY (highest priority in SF morality, absent in NP morality):
−IMMORALITY IS IMPURITY

MORAL HEALTH (highest priority in SF morality, absent in NP morality):
−IMMORALITY IS DISEASE

MORALITY AS EMPATHY (highest priority in NP morality, absent in SF morality):
−no sub-metaphor

MORAL SELF-NURTURANCE (highest priority in NP morality, absent in SF morality):
−no sub-metaphor

MORALITY AS SOCIAL NURTURANCE (highest priority in NP morality, absent in SF morality):
−MORAL AGENTS ARE NURTURING PARENTS
−SOCIAL TIES ARE CHILDREN NEEDING CARE
−MORAL ACTION IS THE NURTURANCE OF SOCIAL TIES

MORALITY AS HAPPINESS (highest priority in NP morality, absent in SF morality):
−no sub-metaphor

MORALITY AS SELF-DEVELOPMENT (highest priority in NP morality, absent in SF morality):
−no sub-metaphor

MORALITY AS FAIR-DISTRIBUTION (highest priority in NP morality, absent in SF morality):
−no sub-metaphor

MORAL GROWTH (highest priority in NP morality, absent in SF morality):
—THE DEGREE OF MORALITY IS PHYSICAL HEIGHT
—MORAL GROWTH IS PHYSICAL GROWTH
—MORAL NORMS FOR PEOPLE ARE PHYSICAL HEIGHT NORMS

As the above list clearly shows, some of the sub-metaphors have aspects of morality as their target domain (moral behavior, moral agents and so on). While these specific moral metaphors enrich our understanding of the central SF/NP morality metaphors, the remaining metaphors are not exclusively related to morality and can be seen as more general metaphors which also motivate our understanding of other domains. Thus, the metaphorical up–down orientation (cf. MORAL STRENGTH) is used in language to describe emotions (HAPPY IS UP, SAD IS DOWN), evaluations (GOOD IS UP, BAD IS DOWN) and status (HIGH SOCIAL STATUS IS UP, LOW SOCIAL STATUS IS DOWN), in addition to morality (MORAL IS UP, IMMORAL IS DOWN). Along similar lines, one can say that the source domain of family (cf. MORAL AUTHORITY, MORALITY AS NURTURANCE, MORALITY AS SOCIAL NURTURANCE) can be used in language to metaphorically conceive of various kinds of social groups and the relationships among their members (a class, a team, an organization, a party and so on). Metaphors which reify human beings and suggest to look at them in terms of some intrinsic substance they are essentially made of (cf. MORAL ESSENCE), can also be used outside the realm of morality to refer to a range of personality traits (for example, 'she is a waterfall' to refer to a very talkative person). Finally, the LIFE IS A JOURNEY metaphor (cf. MORAL BOUNDARIES) is possibly one of the most productive conceptual metaphors in English as well as in other languages.

Since Lakoff presents the SF and NP models as metaphorical, their explanation could not but be based on the description of their constitutive metaphors. Hence, when approaching the models we are faced with a relatively large number of metaphors. According to Lakoff, central SF/NP moral metaphors chiefly contribute to our understanding of the models. From his explanation, one can also deduce that additional moral metaphors and other general metaphors simply support the basic moral metaphors. All these metaphors serve basically to explain how the models are structured. In other words, they are structural components and serve the purpose of specifying the internal conceptual design of the models. Given that the models presuppose a metaphorical interpretation of morality and political reality, they can best be described through metaphors that fit this metaphorical view, and that's what SF and NP metaphors actually do. However, what lies at the very core of the SF and NP theoretical models is the idea that a SF or a NP moral worldview is encapsulated in moral values. This is the key for understanding how the level of metaphorical theorization can be linked to that of political language use.

In *Moral Politics* (1996), Lakoff's earliest publication on the relation between politics and moral views, the relevance of moral values is constantly alluded to, though neither openly addressed nor extensively discussed. After all, Lakoff's major concern in writing this book is that of presenting the Idealized Cognitive Models and justifying their existence. The centrality of moral values is given more direct recognition in *Don't Think of an Elephant* (2004), a manual written for Democrats, to make them aware of the importance of framing political discourse according to NP morality. Significantly enough, the full title of this later publication reads like this: *Don't Think of an Elephant. Know Your Values and Frame the Debate.*[18] At the very beginning of this text, Lakoff emphasizes how moral values are fundamental in politics by stating that

> People will make decisions about politics and candidates based on their value system, and the language and frames that invoke those values. Their values – strict authoritarian values in the conservatives' case – are what motivate them to enter the voting booth. (2004: xiii)

Later, when he describes family-based morality and its reverberations in the political sphere, he also provides a list of core NP values:

- *If you want your child to be fulfilled in life, the child has to be free enough to do that. Therefore* **freedom** *is a value.*
- *You do not have very much freedom if there is no opportunity or prosperity. Therefore* **opportunity** *and* **prosperity** *are progressive values.*
- *If you really care about your child, you want your child to be treated fairly by you and by others. Therefore* **fairness** *is a value.*
- *If you are connecting with your child and you empathize with that child, you have to have* **open, two-way communication**. *Honest communication. That becomes a value.*
- *You live in a community, and that community will affect how your child grows up. Therefore* **community-building, service to the community**, *and* **cooperation in a community** *become values.*
- *To have cooperation, you must have* **trust**, *and to have trust you must have* **honesty** *and* **open two-way communication**. *Trust, honesty and open communication are fundamental progressive values – in a community as in a family.*

> These are the nurturant values – and they are the progressive values. [...] Every progressive political program is based on one or more of these values. That is what it means to be a progressive. (2004: 13, emphasis in the original)

As if reciting a mantra throughout the book, Lakoff sticks to his political message by repeating that progressive core values are family values which emerge from a nurturant moral worldview. This leads to a more comprehensive overview of progressive values that can be sketched as follows (2004: 91):

- Caring and responsibility, carried out with strength
- Protection, fulfillment in life, fairness
- Freedom, opportunity, prosperity
- Community, service, cooperation
- Trust, honesty, open communication

The list above can be taken as an indication of the type of moral values that are dear to progressives and that, in Lakoff's view, Democratic leaders should invoke more consistently in their speeches. According to Lakoff, appealing to NP values gives politicians a great chance to win over the minds and hearts of voters who, at least partly, share a NP moral view. To put it briskly, values are what counts, be they expressed directly or alluded to through plans and policies.

Having said all this and having clarified which are the components of Lakoff's models and which are their functions, the question arises of how to make use of these models for investigating political language. How can we possibly test politicians' framing of issues and policies according to a SF or NP morality? What should we look for? Are there any linguistic signs and traces that can be reconciled with either a SF or a NP moral view? Answering these questions is not an easy task, but this study intends to take up the challenge.

What has emerged from the discussion of Lakoff's work (1996, 2004) is that values are at the core of his models, and it is the values that are expressed in political language. Thus, if we intend to analyze political discourse along the lines of Lakoff's models, the values are the elements that need to be at the center of attention. Assuming this perspective, however, leaves a few questions open for discussion. What is the actual cognitive status of moral values? How do they find expression in language? This study suggests to look at moral values in a way that can be visualized as follows.

Figure 3.1 visualizes the centrality of moral values in Lakoff's models. In addition, Figure 3.1 illustrates how the models are rooted in cognition and how they can relate to language. As discussed earlier, Lakoff describes moral values relating to the SF and NP cognitive models through an array of metaphors. Here, they are grouped into moral metaphors, having morality as their target domain, and general conventional metaphors that support our understanding of certain SF/NP moral values. The connection between metaphors and values is represented by a dotted line in the drawing.

As already pointed out by Lakoff, morality is grounded in cognition. Figure 3.1 emphasizes the fact that the two basic components on which morality is grounded in cognition are embodied experience and socio-cultural knowledge. This means that our notion of morality derives basically from our interaction with the physical world and the type of reactions/emotions it provokes. Furthermore, morality is strongly influenced by the culture we share and the social group we live in. Most importantly, embodied

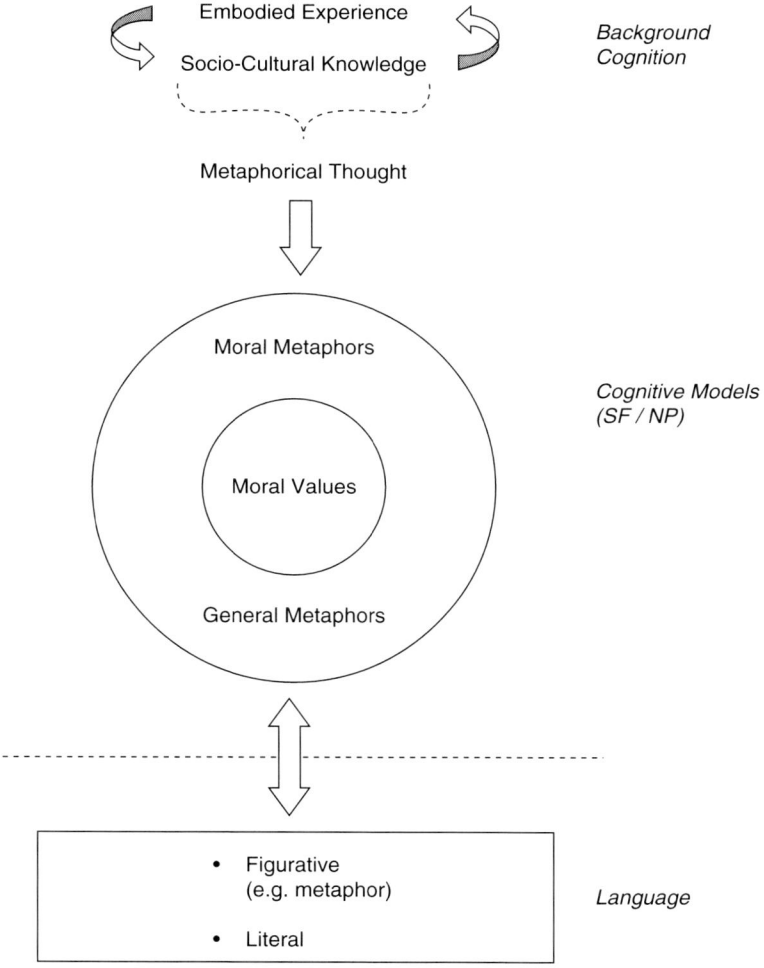

Figure 3.1   Moral values in cognition and language

experience and socio-cultural knowledge do not act as monads but interact with each other. This is graphically represented by the two bent arrows in Figure 3.1. In line with the most recent developments in conceptual metaphor theory (see Steen 2011), the combination of inputs from physical and socio-cultural experience can be seen as responsible for the emergence of metaphorical thought. Cognitive/cultural models (for example, SF and NP) are formed when metaphorical thought is organized in a system that accounts for a particular notion, as for example morality. For this reason, cognition is depicted as being at the basis of SF/NP morality, and the vertical arrow symbolizes the fact that background cognition gives rise to the models.

While moral values can be considered as rooted in metaphorical thought and thus understood via conceptual metaphors, they are not necessarily expressed in language via metaphors. As Figure 3.1 shows, literal language can also play an important role. This aspect, however, has not been sufficiently addressed in research on Lakoff's models so far and even Lakoff himself does not discuss the importance of literality for expressing SF/NP moral values.

The present study intends to address these pitfalls by giving full recognition to both metaphoricity and literality and, more specifically, to the metaphorical and literal manifestations of moral values in political language. The analysis will be conducted on a corpus assembling 30 of Obama's 2008 election campaign speeches. This study takes a holistic approach in that Lakoff's models will be tested by considering both metaphorical and literal language use as well as supportive rhetorical strategies. This is indeed a very succinct description of the aspects that are considered for the linguistic analysis of Obama's speeches. It is the aim of the next chapter to provide a detailed account of all the methodological concerns involved in this investigation.

4
Methodology and Introduction to the Analysis

This chapter prepares the ground for the actual linguistic analysis that will be discussed in Chapters 5, 6 and 7. It combines an explanation of the methodology adopted for the study with an introduction to the analysis. Accordingly, the chapter provides details of a range of methodological concerns that include: (a) the rationale for selecting the corpus, (b) the main features characterizing the corpus, (c) the identification of values in the corpus, (d) the textual units of the analysis and their coding and (e) the procedure for analyzing the data. In addition to this, the chapter also suggests looking at Obama's speeches in terms of a narrative space whose structure and internal organization are dependent on the objectives of the campaign and the strategies adopted.

4.1 Corpus selection and implementation of hypotheses

Lakoff himself admits to a lack of empirical proof for the SF and NP models of political morality that he explains in *Moral Politics* (1996: 158). As he points out when he discusses his theory of SF and NP morality, 'it [the theory] does not have the degree of confirmation that one would expect of more mature theories' (1996: 158). He also remarks that 'survey research has not yet developed an adequate methodology to test for the presence of complex metaphorical cognitive models such as these' (*ibid.*).

In light of these observations, the present study centers on an empirical investigation of Lakoff's SF and NP cognitive models of political morality. The book is aimed at providing a possible method for testing the usefulness of Lakoff's models for understanding American politics and its main actors (that is, political leaders) in particular.

Considering how place, time and target audience affect any linguistic act, this study focuses on American political language as it was used by then Senator Barack Obama at a crucial time of his political career, namely during his first run for the presidency of the US. After eight years of Republican leadership, the 2008 election campaign had the potential to be decisive for a radical change of perspective, and the Democratic party played some of its best cards to allow for that possibility. The election campaign was therefore as heated as ever and the candidates carefully selected (a woman and a young black man). Given this situation, working on Obama's use of language during his first presidential campaign appears promising.

In addition to the specific significance of the 2008 election campaign in terms of the Democratic urge for a new American leadership, election campaigns, in general, represent a prime time for analyzing presidential rhetoric. The 2008 campaign was no exception to that. It was indeed a clear example of successful rhetoric by the main representative of the Democratic party. Obama was almost unanimously commented upon for his skillful rhetorical ability and masterful oral deliveries. This is further indication that the 2008 election campaign provides a solid ground for investigating Obama's use of language. Obviously, an entire election campaign involves a lot of speech making. This has to be considered when deciding to compile a corpus that is at the same time representative of this time span and manageable for close analysis by a researcher.

Therefore, the corpus compiled for the study consists of the transcripts of 30 significant speeches delivered by Barack Obama during the 2008 election campaign and obtained from Barack Obama's website (http://www.barackobama.com/speeches/index.php, last accessed in August 2010 and no longer available). The time span considered for the initial selection ranges from 5 February 2008 (Super Tuesday, the day when Obama was elected as the candidate for the Democrats) to 3 November 2008 (the day before the presidential election). The total number of speeches downloaded from the mentioned website in this period was 119. From these, six were excluded because they were not given by Obama. The excluded speeches were the following:

- 24 October 2008 'Excerpts of Senator Joe Biden's Remarks'
- 24 September 2008 'Remarks of Michelle Obama: Roundtable Discussion with Pennsylvania Military Spouses'
- 18 September 2008 'Remarks of Michelle Obama: North Carolina Economic Roundtable with Working Women'
- 15 September 2008 'Remarks by Senator Joe Biden: the case for Change'
- 25 August 2008 'Remarks of Michelle Obama and Craig Robinson – Democratic National Convention'
- 26 June 2008 'Remarks of Michelle Obama to the Democratic National Committee's Gay and Lesbian Leadership Committee'

Out of the remaining 113 speeches that Obama delivered himself, only 30 were kept for building the corpus. Different criteria were followed for this close selection: (a) the inclusion of all primary speeches, (b) the inclusion of one representative speech for those that were repeated with slight variation throughout the campaign, (c) coverage of speeches in different states, (d) coverage of different topics (for example, economy, education, foreign policy and military) and (e) exclusion of the shortest speeches. The corpus so compiled consists of the speeches listed below in chronological order:

1. 5 February 2008 'Remarks of Senator Barack Obama: Super Tuesday'
2. 12 February 2008 'Remarks of Senator Barack Obama: Potomac Primary Night'
3. 4 March 2008 'Remarks of Senator Barack Obama: March 4th Primary Night'
4. 18 March 2008 'Remarks of Senator Barack Obama: A More Perfect Union'
5. 20 March 2008 'Remarks of Senator Barack Obama: The Cost of War'
6. 14 April 2008 'Remarks of Senator Barack Obama: AP Annual Luncheon'
7. 15 April 2008 'Remarks of Senator Barack Obama: Town Hall Meeting with Veterans and Military Families'
8. 22 April 2008 'Remarks of Senator Barack Obama: Pennsylvania Primary Night'
9. 3 May 2008 'Remarks of Senator Barack Obama: Plan to Fight for Working families and Take on Special Interests in Washington'
10. 6 May 2008 'Remarks of Senator Barack Obama: Primary Night'
11. 20 May 2008 'Remarks of Senator Barack Obama: Forging a New Future for America'
12. 3 June 2008 'Remarks of Senator Barack Obama: Final Primary Night'
13. 21 June 2008 'Remarks of Senator Barack Obama: A Metropolitan Strategy for America's Future'
14. 28 June 2008 'Remarks of Senator Barack Obama: National Association of Latino Elected and Appointed Officials'
15. 30 June 2008 'Remarks of Senator Barack Obama: The America We Love'
16. 1 July 2008 'Remarks of Senator Barack Obama: Council for Faith-Based and Neighborhood Partnerships'
17. 10 July 2008 'Remarks of Senator Barack Obama: Women's Economic Security Town Hall'
18. 13 July 2008 'Remarks of Senator Barack Obama: 80th Convention of the American Federation of Teachers'
19. 16 July 2008 'Remarks of Senator Barack Obama: Summit on Confronting New Threats'
20. 1 August 2008 'Remarks of Senator Barack Obama: Town Hall on the Economy'
21. 5 August 2008 'Remarks of Senator Barack Obama: Energy Town Hall'
22. 23 August 2008 'Remarks of Senator Barack Obama: Vice President Announcement'
23. 9 September 2008 'Remarks of Senator Barack Obama: A 21st Century Education'

24. 12 September 2008 'Remarks of Senator Barack Obama: On taxes'
25. 20 September 2008 'Remarks of Senator Barack Obama (Daytona Beach, FL)'
26. 27 September 2008 'Remarks of Senator Barack Obama (Greensboro, NC)'
27. 10 October 2008 'Remarks of Senator Barack Obama (Chillicothe, OH)'
28. 15 October 2008 'Remarks of Senator Barack Obama (Londonderry, NH)'
29. 20 October 2008 'Remarks of Senator Barack Obama (Tampa Bay, FL)'
30. 27 October 2008 'Senator Barack Obama's Closing argument Speech: One Week'

The speeches were downloaded and saved as Microsoft Word documents. Obama's words in each speech were counted with the word count feature. The heading (that is, 'Remarks of Senator Barack Obama: Super Tuesday') was always omitted. Information about where and when the speech was delivered (that is, Chicago, IL | 5 February 2008) was also omitted from the word count. In short, every effort was made to include all and only the words that Obama used. The average length of each speech is 2,588 words, with the longest speech consisting of 4,916 words (18 March 2008; this is the famous 'Race speech') and the shortest counting 1,083 words (28 June 2008). The corpus consists of 77,641 words in total. Specific information regarding the number of words of each speech is provided in the next chapter (see Table 5.1).

The speeches were delivered in oral form from a prepared text. The analysis is focused on scripted speech rather than spontaneous language use since the former is expected to provide a better ground for detecting political strategies. The version of the speeches that is analyzed here is the one provided for the written, historical records. For this reason, there might be minor differences between the written texts analyzed in this study and the oral texts that Obama produced during his election campaign. While this is a fact that needs to be recognized, the slight difference between the written and the oral texts of Obama's speeches is not expected to affect the analysis in any substantial way. After all, even though in politics the official version of political speeches is usually the spoken one, the written version can be said to reveal the candidate's intent very accurately.

As explained in Chapter 3, previous studies applied Lakoff's theory to the analysis of American political language. In particular, Cienki (2004, 2005a,b) worked on the identification of SF and NP metaphors, while Ahrens (2006, 2011) and Ahrens and Yat Mei Lee (2009) searched for SF and NP lexemes in different corpora. Here, in line with Lakoff's suggestions, the focus of the analysis is on values. As Patent and Lakoff say 'There are always underlying moral reasons for supporting certain policies and opposing others. The first task then becomes *identifying the values* behind any given policy' (2006, from Rockridge archive, my emphasis). The aim of this study is thus to find instantiations of either NP or SF values in Obama's 2008 election campaign speeches. Accordingly, as a preliminary step to the actual analysis, it is important to single out core SF and NP values.

In *Moral Politics*, the book which contains a fully fledged description of the SF and NP models, Lakoff writes about the importance of values, but he does not explicitly list them in the same way as he does for metaphors.[1] As illustrated in Chapter 3, Lakoff (1996) constructs his models by describing what defines each of the two types of family. In a later publication, Lakoff (2004) focuses more directly on values, with the purpose of inciting Democratic politicians to frame their discourse according to their NP values. These include, among others, care and responsibility for others, strength for nurturance, protection, fulfillment in life, fairness, freedom, opportunity, prosperity, community, service, cooperation, trust, honesty and open communication. A general list of core SF and NP values can be deduced from how Lakoff explains the specific character of the SF and NP models and relates these models to a value system. Table 4.1 provides an overview of the type of values that, according to Lakoff's models, fit either a SF or a NP worldview.

Table 4.1 List of core SF and NP values (deduced from Lakoff 1996)

Core SF values	Core NP values
Strength	Care/nurturance
Authority	Cooperation
Order	Equality
Hierarchy	Community/service
Obedience	Fairness
Self-discipline	Opportunity
Self-reliance	Protection
Individual responsibility	Social responsibility
Freedom	Freedom

Following Lakoff's ideas, the general expectation is that Obama, as the main representative of the Democratic party, frames his political speeches according to a NP morality model. Therefore, NP values are expected to abound in his political narrative. This is, however, a hypothesis yet to be tested.

The task of detecting how idealized cognitive models like the SF and NP ones are manifested in a corpus of presidential language cannot be assigned to automated systems. The identification of SF and NP values calls for a different kind of semantic analysis. This activity requires the patient and meticulous scrutiny of an individual who can give meaning to individual words relying on both co-textual and contextual knowledge. These practical reasons make the study of large corpora extremely difficult and motivate the relatively small size of the corpus that is here under investigation. Furthermore, this study picks up Cameron and Deignan's (2003) proposal that one can first test a research question on a small and representative corpus and later expand the search working on a larger amount of data.

For the analysis, the paragraph was considered as the textual unit of semantic investigation. The framing of an issue requires an argumentative space that is larger than a few clauses. This makes the paragraph a better unit of semantic analysis than the sentence or the phrase. The paragraph structure provided in the online version of the speeches was maintained for the analysis since the organization of paragraphs in the written records clearly reflect the topic sequence of the entire texts. One-line paragraphs are quite exceptional in the speeches and were excluded from the analysis since their contribution to the political message was considered irrelevant. On the whole, they chiefly consist of instantiations of Obama's campaign motto ('Yes we can'), rhetorical questions and closing formulae. All together, one-line paragraphs account for 4 per cent of a total of 1,114 paragraphs in the entire corpus.

Since the analysis is aimed at finding out whether or not Obama's speeches contain framings of specific moral views, it is necessary to code each paragraph in relation to whether a NP or SF value is present. Different possibilities exist for the coding. In theory, a paragraph can contain either a NP value or a SF value, no value or both values, or it can even feature a value that is criticized by Obama. This gives the following list of possible codings of the data:

a. Neutral: paragraphs with neither NP nor SF moral values
b. NP: paragraphs with at least one NP value
c. SF: paragraphs with at least one SF value
d. Contra SF: paragraphs with at least one instance of criticism of a SF value
e. Contra NP: paragraphs with at least one instance of criticism of a NP value
f. NP + SF: paragraphs characterized by the combined presence of at least one SF and one NP value
g. Contra NP + SF: paragraphs characterized by the combined presence of at least one SF value and one instance of criticism of a NP value
h. Contra SF+NP: paragraphs characterized by the combined presence of at least one NP value and one instance of criticism of a SF value

Out of this range of possibilities, only the five options reported in Table 4.2 were actually found in the corpus.

Previewing the analysis, it is striking to observe already at this point that only one SF paragraph was found in the whole corpus.

Table 4.2 Types of paragraphs in Obama's speeches

Neutral paragraphs
NP paragraphs
SF paragraphs
Contra SF paragraphs
Contra SF + NP paragraphs

In order to give the reader a first impression of the different types of paragraphs that are analyzed in the next chapter, an example of each of them is provided below:

Neutral paragraph

Well, the polls are just closing in California and the votes are still being counted in cities and towns across the country. But there is one thing on this February night that we do not need the final results to know – our time has come, our movement is real, and change is coming to America. (5 February 2008)

This paragraph has been coded as neutral because it neither evokes nor criticizes any of the core NP and SF values mentioned in Table 4.1. In fact, it is an opening paragraph where Obama prepares the ground with a few introductory lines before moving to the actual political contents of the speech.

NP paragraph

Change is a health care plan that guarantees insurance to every American who wants it; brings down premiums for every family who needs it; that stops insurance companies from discriminating and denying coverage to those who need it most. (20 May 2008)

This paragraph is an instance of a NP paragraph because Obama describes change, one of the key concepts during his 2008 election campaign, in terms of health care. Obama suggests that change consists in taking care of people who do not have any health coverage so that everyone can be granted the right to receive medical assistance when they get sick.

SF paragraph

The people I've met in small towns and big cities across this country understand that government can't solve all our problems – and we don't expect it to. We believe in hard work. We believe in personal responsibility and self-reliance. (6 May 2008)

This is the only example of a SF paragraph identified in the corpus. The paragraph has been classified as SF because Obama explicitly addresses the SF values of individual responsibility and self-reliance by emphasizing the fact the people cannot just rely on government to solve their problems.

Contra SF paragraph

Ronald Reagan called this trickle-down economics. George Bush called it the Ownership Society. But what it really means is that you're on your own. If your premiums or your tuition is rising faster than you can afford, you're on your own. If you're that Maytag worker who just lost his pension, tough luck. If you're a child born into poverty, you'll just have to pull yourself up by your own bootstraps. (14 April 2008)

This has been considered as a contra SF paragraph because it contains a clearly expressed criticism of the so-called Bootstrap logic (the principle according to which 'you are on your own') that many Republicans sustain. Thus, in the paragraph Obama objects to the SF value of self-reliance.

Contra SF + NP paragraph

Change is building an economy that rewards not just wealth, but the work and workers who created it. It's understanding that the struggles facing working families can't be solved by spending billions of dollars on more tax breaks for big corporations and wealthy CEOs, but by giving the middle-class a tax break, and investing in our crumbling infrastructure, and transforming how we use energy, and improving our schools, and renewing our commitment to science and innovation. (3 June 2008)

This is an instance of a mixed paragraph where Obama both criticizes values that are at the base of a SF worldview and supports core NP values. In detail, the target of Obama's criticism is the SF value of moral order according to which the rich deserve more than the poor and should pay fewer taxes. The expressed disapproval of a core SF value is coupled with the celebration of the nurturant values of care and protection. Obama talks about care for people who need a decent job and good education, and he also talks about care for the environment by alluding to investments in alternative energy sources. Furthermore, protection is evoked in the form of safer infrastructures.

As portrayed in the examples above, the codification of paragraphs was done for the entire corpus. However, the act of classifying paragraphs needs to be supported by a set of more specific considerations which are outlined below as research questions.

- What are the functions of neutral paragraphs? How can we explain their presence in the corpus?
- If the paragraph is NP, SF, contra SF or contra SF + NP, which are the specific values addressed and how are they expressed?
- Which values are evoked more frequently? Are values evoked reiterating certain linguistic expressions?
- Are there specific rhetorical strategies that are used to convey certain values?
- Do NP, SF, contra SF or contra SF + NP paragraphs contain metaphorical lexical units?
- Do metaphorical lexical units relate to SF and NP morality models?
- Are there specific SF/NP lexical items? What is the relation between SF/NP words and SF/NP framing of political discourse?

Since the aim of this study is to test Lakoff's models, answers to these questions are part of the book's main objective and will be pursued in the following chapters.

Due to the fact that the identification of specific values plays a crucial role for the analysis, it is important to make clear at this point that within a paragraph a specific value is only counted once, even when it is evoked by more than one linguistic expression. The reiteration is simply considered as an instance of rhetorical accumulation and it does not affect the fact that the value is present.

It is also necessary to spend a few words on the procedure adopted for exploring metaphoricity. While the presence of different metaphors was observed throughout the whole corpus, the metaphorical analysis was limited to value-laden paragraphs (that is, all but neutral paragraphs). The reason for that has to do with the assumptions underlying some of the research questions. Testing Lakoff's models requires searching for instantiations of the values that can fit each of the two models in the corpus. In this approach, metaphoricity only comes into play once the different values (and thus the paragraphs that contain them) have been identified. Accordingly, value-laden paragraphs were searched for metaphorical expressions. For the analysis only metaphorical content units were considered. This means that metaphorical function words were not taken into consideration. Appendix 1 provides an overview of the whole range of metaphorical expressions that were found. In the process of identifying metaphorical expressions in value-laden paragraphs, it was also important to make a distinction between: (a) metaphors that express the values and (b) metaphors unrelated to the value-contents of the paragraph.

Finally, lexemes associated to the SF and NP models were searched across the corpus. This task was accomplished using Wordsmith Tools 4. As a first step, Wordlists were created in order to find out the frequency of specific SF and NP words as established in previous studies (Ahrens 2009, 2011, Ahrens and Yat Mei Lee 2009). Differently from previous research, this analysis also involved the important step of checking the concordances (that is, the contexts) of the selected lexical items. This was crucial in order to assign each of the lexical occurrences to a specific type of paragraph and hence to investigate the relation between supposed SF/NP lexemes and their actual relation to SF/NP framing of political discourse.

4.2   Obama's election campaign as a narrative space

Chapters 5, 6 and 7 will take the reader on a journey through the words, the ideas and the values that inhabit Barack Obama's 2008 campaign speeches. This rhetorical space is so vast to allow for meandering peregrinations. The path we will take has been anticipated in the preceding chapters: we will go through Obama's speeches with the aim of testing Lakoff's models. In order to do so, the analysis will be located on different levels.

The analysis starts by considering the immediate context of Obama's selected speeches: the presidential election campaign as it was run from the beginning of February until the end of October 2008. As a natural unfolding of events, the campaign overarches various phases from Obama's initial antagonism with another Democratic candidate (Hillary Clinton) to his competition with the Republican rival (John McCain), leading to his ultimate victory. This long period is interpreted here as an encompassing narrative space. In other words, the election campaign is taken as the macro-narrative to access the analysis of Obama's speeches. Invoking a narrative structure is very helpful for the analysis of Obama's election campaign speeches since it gives meaning to the composite nature of his political campaign and it also motivates his general framing of discourse.

Every narration, be it frolic or staid, requires certain key components. A story essentially needs a spatial location, a temporal setting, a fact (or some facts) to be told and participants taking part in the action. The spatial and temporal coordinates give the story some concrete grounding by inscribing events in the context of a 'tangible' reality. Facts typically represent the prerequisite for action – they prepare the ground, so to say – and allow listeners/readers to foresee a possible course of events. The number, type and relevance of participants depend on the scope of the narrative and on the actual or intended target audience. The entire narrative is framed by its story-teller, who basically decides on the elements to include in his/her narration and on their internal relation, since every part of the puzzle is expected to fit into a larger (at times visionary) design. In this mapped territory nothing is neutrally conveyed (assuming that something like neutrality may even exist) and language functions like a litmus paper to indicate ideological leanings.

As a narration, Obama's campaign has a precise spatio-temporal situatedness. It runs throughout the year 2008, with following steps marked by the dates when and the locations where the presidential candidate Obama publicly addressed different sections (and factions) of the American electorate. In this narrative, the facts consist in the problematic situations that Obama describes, including (towering) unemployment, (rising) costs of life, (inefficient) public systems, (the prolonged and expensive) war in Iraq, (unfair) taxation, (gender) inequality and so on. Clearly enough, while general issues are talked about by every candidate, what really counts is how each of these issues is framed and presented to the audience (consider the adjectives in brackets). For a political leader, deciding what to discuss is as important as deciding how to discuss it. For the analyst, considering how candidates select and combine their words for the purpose of winning an election is never a futile exercise and may even turn into a revelatory practice. But a presidential candidate does not run alone. The political arena of the election campaign calls for a bustling, at times almost belligerent, competition. After all, there are no silver or bronze medals in this race! On the narrative level, this rivalry determines the emergence of antithetical pairs: hero vs. antihero and allies vs. enemies. In our narration, Obama functions as the chief storyteller and the hero. Notwithstanding the fact that Obama encounters minor antagonists along the way (consider for instance Hillary Clinton), his anti-hero *par excellence* is the Republican candidate John McCain. Thus, the stage is carefully set for the two of them to perform their play, and the intensity of final applause will determine their eventual fate and fame. The hero vs. anti-hero dichotomy is then responsible for the creation of yet another opposing set, that between the supporters of Obama and McCain. Considering our vantage point for the analysis, the former group represents that of the allies whereas the latter characterizes the enemies. Allies include members of Obama's family and supporters of his vision and electoral mission. This is extended to the people Obama meets during his campaign and for whom he promises his help. Conversely, the class of enemies counts advocates of the Republican cause and McCain's supporters. Once these general participant roles have been assigned so as to adjust to the well-known us/them binary that characterizes 'political' (in a broad sense) discourse, the political storyteller is given leeway to emphasize ideological contrasts and manufacture consent, so to say. Accordingly, Obama is very keen on expressing his own solutions to the problems that afflict the nation, and in so doing he marks the ideological distance between himself and McCain.

In addition to the elements described so far, the macro-narrative represented by the election campaign also contains a few narrative substructures that, for ease of description, we will call micro-narratives. In theory, micro-narratives could be seen as standalone narrative threads, but their presence within the larger frame of the macro-narrative is not fortuitous. Similarly to the play within the play theatrical artifact, micro-narratives gain significance once they are considered on the background of the overall macro-narrative for which they serve an ancillary function. In fact, in the context of

Obama's election campaign, micro-narratives reinforce the general electoral message by relying on a strong emotional appeal.

Three distinct types of micro-narratives have been identified in the analysis of Obama's speeches. One of these structures contains Obama's own personal story. Throughout the campaign, Obama frequently mentions his family, including his mother, his grandparents, his father, his wife Michelle and his two daughters, Sasha and Malia. Obama refers to them through affectionate anecdotes and loving words. These people are not just close to him: each of them has played a role in shaping the man who is now addressing the Unites States of America and Obama likes sharing this with the American people. Obama also likes giving details about himself, how he grew up and the type of professions he went through from community organizer to Senator. These personal stories generate Obama's public image and give rise to the creation of a fictional persona: Obama as the incarnation of the American Dream, the living proof that in America if you try hard you can make it, no matter who you are and where you were born. All these personal stories about Obama himself and his family members co-construct one micro-narrative.

A second micro-narrative results from the stories Obama reports about ordinary American citizens. In his speeches, Obama frequently talks about the people he encountered in the different states and cities he visited throughout the campaign. They are men and women, young and old people, each with their own personal, and yet communal, stories to tell. Obama becomes their spokesman by giving voice to their truly American stories. Obama talks about Americans who lost their jobs because a local steel plant closed and jobs were sent overseas to some distant location. He draws the attention of the audience to the situation of people in need of medical assistance who cannot pay for it. He spends words to describe the living conditions of people who cannot afford to pay for their children's basic needs, let alone their tuition fees. These and similar stories depict human scenarios that cry out loud for help. In this context, Obama emerges as the one who can lead Americans who suffer out of the crisis. His plans, the initiatives he proposes and the policies he sustains are presented, in a way, as the panacea that will cure this profound and expanding social sickness.

A third narrative micro-structure embraces the story (or history) of the American people as a nation. This proudly patriotic celebration of the US touches on different facets of national identity. Obama recalls heroic figures of national history, including the American Presidents Abraham Lincoln, Harry Truman, Franklin Roosevelt and John Kennedy. He unsparingly shows his praise for Americans by characterizing them (and thus himself as well) as generous and decent people, folks used to work, ready to suffer for a common purpose, and prone to sacrifice. America itself is depicted as the land of opportunity, the place where ambitious aspirations are justified and constantly encouraged, the sole country where dreams can come true. Obama is also unrestrained in describing American supremacy. Since America, according to Obama, has raised some of the most talented and productive people in the world, America stands out as the world leader in technology and innovation and as the beacon which should guide the entire globe in the twenty-first century. Obama's celebration of American greatness is as passionate as the small but neat portraits he is able to draw when talking of suffering and struggling Americans.

Each of these narrative threads contributes to giving shape and substance to the larger narrative frame of Obama's election campaign. Looking at Obama's speeches in light of this articulate narrative structure is a preliminary step for the actual analysis that is conducted in this book. What is suggested here is to consider each of the analyzed textual units (every speech) on the background of the outlined macro- and micro-narratives to realize how they fit in this heuristic system. This means becoming aware of how every speech functions within the larger narrative frame of the evolving election campaign, with its participants and their action and interaction. At the same time, it also means recognizing how every speech additionally contains a few traces of a story within a story, be it personal (about Obama and his family), social (about ordinary American people) or cultural/historical (about America as a nation). The focus of this analysis, however, is on the story-teller and on the way he frames all of these stories according to his moral worldview.

This study is aimed primarily at testing Lakoff's morality models (see Chapter 3). As already explained, the models predict that Republican leaders conform their speech to a SF worldview and Democratic politicians adhere to a NP moral vision. The general expectation, therefore, is that Obama shapes his discourse so that it reflects NP moral values and thus, more broadly, a NP moral view. Accordingly, the analysis is devised so as to disclose whether or not Obama evokes NP values and, if he does, which particular NP values he relies upon to construct a coherent narrative, and how he linguistically communicates NP values.

In order to explore these aspects of Obama's political moral framing, the analysis has been structured in three parts. The first part (Chapter 5) focuses on the different types of paragraphs identified in the corpus (see Table 4.2) and explains what makes each type distinct from the others in terms of values and functions. The second part of the analysis (Chapter 6) concentrates on value-laden paragraphs and discusses metaphoricity in relation to the expression of moral values. In the third part of the analysis (Chapter 7), findings are presented and discussed that concern the use of specific lexical items in the whole corpus. The lexical items that are investigated include high-frequency content words as well as SF and NP terms as they were identified in previous studies (cf. Ahrens 2006, 2011, Ahrens and Yat Mei Lee 2009).

5
The Expression of Values in Obama's Speeches

This chapter introduces the reader to the semantic analysis of Obama's speeches and focuses on the values with which Obama framed his electoral message during the 2008 campaign. The chapter starts with an overview of the results in the whole corpus of speeches. In particular, information will be provided on the different types of paragraphs that have been coded for their values. This introductory part is followed by the analysis of each of the identified paragraph types, as outlined in the previous chapter. Neutral paragraphs are described primarily in relation to the different functions that they perform. The discussion of NP paragraphs shows the range of NP values expressed in Obama's speeches and it sheds light on the rhetorical strategies employed by Obama to communicate these values to his electorate. Contra SF paragraphs are commented upon for the SF values that Obama criticizes and also for the rhetorical devices that he uses for that aim. Finally, the analysis of contra SF + NP paragraphs provides insights into the ideological contrasts between Republicans and Democrats that are at the core of Obama's speeches.

5.1 General results

As outlined in the methodology chapter, the corpus used for the analysis of Obama's political speeches during the 2008 presidential campaign consists of 77,641 words. The corpus has been compiled by selecting 30 significant speeches in a time span that ranges from the beginning of February 2008 until the end of October of the same year. In addition to primary night speeches, the corpus includes speeches that are relevant either because they contain general issues frequently addressed during the whole campaign or because they deal, more specifically, with a less debated topic. Thus, the rationale for generating this corpus was to provide sufficient thematic coverage to allow for an analysis of the individual values shining through this long electoral 'narrative'.

The textual unit of analysis of this corpus is the paragraph. For this reason, the analysis started with the counting of paragraphs for each of the speeches. The number of paragraphs per speech is a value dependent on the length of the speech. Thus, longer speeches contain more paragraphs than shorter ones. The next step was assigning each of the paragraphs to one of the five categories signaled by the following labels: neutral (N), nurturant parent (NP), strict father (SF), contra SF (CSF) or a mixing of contra SF and NP (CFS + NP). Clearly enough, the task of categorizing each individual paragraph required close reading and consideration of the larger context in which they occurred. As simple as it may appear, this activity was in no way straightforward and, on a few occasions, it benefited from consultations with colleagues in the field.

In Table 5.1 details are provided for every speech concerning their length, their total number of paragraphs and the subdivision of paragraphs into the five aforementioned different types.

Table 5.1 Distribution of paragraphs across speeches

No.	Date	Total no. words	Total no. Para.	N para.	NP para.	SF para.	CSF para.	CSF + NP para.
1	5 February 2008	1682	30	13	12	0	4	0
2	12 February 2008	1861	33	13	11	0	5	3
3	4 March 2008	1832	33	17	12	0	3	1
4	18 March 2008	4916	59	38	19	0	2	0
5	20 March 2008	2223	34	22	10	0	2	0
6	14 April 2008	2161	32	15	7	0	10	0
7	15 April 2008	1424	18	9	9	0	0	0
8	22 April 2008	2003	34	19	8	0	7	0
9	3 May 2008	3190	41	27	12	0	2	0
10	6 May 2008	2324	32	17	11	1	0	3
11	20 May 2008	2182	30	15	12	0	1	2
12	3 June 2008	2451	31	16	7	0	4	4
13	21 June 2008	2978	34	9	18	0	7	0
14	28 June 2008	1083	15	7	7	0	1	0
15	30 June 2008	3410	35	27	8	0	0	0
16	1 July 2008	1415	17	8	9	0	0	0
17	10 July 2008	2007	40	20	19	0	0	1
18	13 July 2008	1624	23	8	14	0	1	0
19	16 July 2008	2183	23	12	11	0	0	0
20	1 August 2008	2194	22	5	15	0	2	0
21	5 August 2008	2229	32	19	12	0	1	0
22	28 August 2008	4694	81	50	27	0	4	0

(continued)

Table 5.1   Continued

No.	Date	Total no. words	Total no. Para.	N para.	NP para.	SF para.	CSF para.	CSF + NP para.
23	9 September 2008	3950	50	26	24	0	0	0
24	12 September 2008	1863	28	8	12	0	5	3
25	20 September 2008	2934	40	18	19	0	3	0
26	27 September 2008	2734	45	20	17	0	7	1
27	10 October 2008	3547	40	13	23	0	2	2
28	15 October 2008	3259	44	17	22	0	1	4
29	20 October 2008	3339	44	19	23	0	0	2
30	27 October 2008	3949	49	24	20	0	5	0
	Total	77,641	1,069	531	430	1	79	26

As Table 5.1 shows, the length of individual speeches is quite variable. While the mean value is 2,588 words per speech, the longest speech (28 August 2008) counts 4,694 words and the shortest one (28 June 2008) consists of only 1,033 words. The length of a speech is directly related to the number of paragraphs per speech. Accordingly, the longest speech has 81 paragraphs, while the shortest consists of just 15 paragraphs. In between these two extremes there is some variability, with a mean value around 35 paragraphs per speech.

Neutral and NP paragraphs are by far the most frequent in the corpus. Contra SF paragraphs account for 7.4 per cent of all paragraphs and CSF + NP paragraphs merely account for 2.4 per cent. The corpus contains only one instance of a SF paragraph.

Neutral paragraphs constitute 49.7 per cent of all the paragraphs, and if we look at their distribution across individual speeches we can observe that their presence is significantly high there as well. In particular, the relative frequency of N paragraphs is higher than 60 per cent in the following speeches: 18 March 2008 (64.4 per cent), 20 March 2008 (64.7 per cent), 3 May 2008 (65.8 per cent), 30 June 2008 (77.1 per cent) and 28 August 2008 (61.7 per cent). The only speeches where their frequency is lower than 30 per cent are the ones made by Obama on 21 June 2008 (26.5 per cent), 1 August 2008 (22.7 per cent) and 12 September 2008 (28.6 per cent).

Next to N paragraphs, NP paragraphs take a large share in the corpus. They represent 40.2 per cent of all paragraphs. While their distribution across speeches is consistent, their frequency is particularly remarkable in the following ones: 21 June 2008 (52.9 per cent), 13 July 2008 (60.9 per cent), 1 August 2008 (68.2 per cent) and 10 October 2008 (57.5 per cent). Only in two speeches is the frequency of NP paragraphs lower than 25 per cent: 14 April 2008 (21.8 per cent) and 22 April 2008 (23.5 per cent). The actual distribution of N and NP paragraphs across the 30 speeches is graphically represented in Figure 5.1.

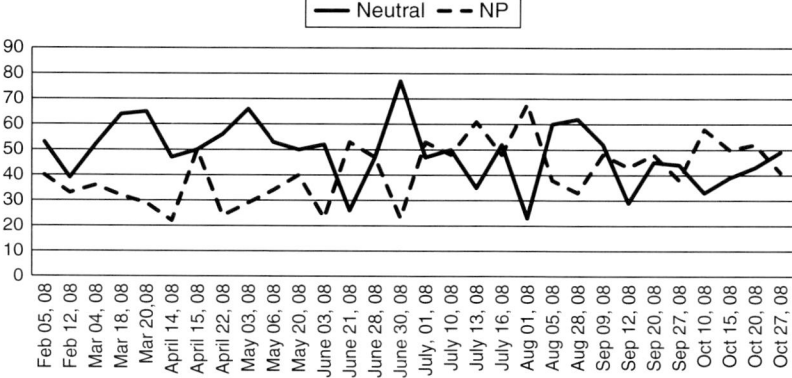

Figure 5.1   Distribution of N and NP paragraphs across speeches

As Figure 5.1 shows, there is some variability with which N and NP paragraphs occur in each of the speeches. While N paragraphs are more frequent than NP paragraphs in most of the speeches, there are a few exceptions where the rate of NP paragraphs exceeds that of neutral ones. In general, the amount of NP paragraphs varies between 21 per cent and almost 70 per cent in the individual speeches. This emphasizes that throughout the election campaign, Obama indeed constantly employed NP values in his speeches.

In the following sections each of the distinct types of paragraph will be described and ample evidence will be given for each of them.

5.2   Neutral paragraphs

Neutral paragraphs are the textual units of analysis where neither NP nor SF values are expressed and/or criticized. Stated differently, they are paragraphs where no value is explicitly evoked that could fit either a NP or a SF worldview. They are neutral because, in contrast to the other types of paragraphs, they cannot be defined as explicitly value-laden.[1]

In relation to the overall number of paragraphs, neutral ones are very frequent: half of all paragraphs (49.7 per cent) are classified as neutral. The reason why neutral paragraphs are so frequent in the corpus has to do with the range of functions they can perform.

5.2.1   Marking a temporal sequence

A general function of neutral paragraphs is that of marking the unfolding of different stages in the election campaign. Many neutral paragraphs locate a speech on a clear spatio-temporal dimension and they often do so by relying on the source–path–goal image schema and the related journey conceptual metaphor.[2] Let us consider a few examples. On Super Tuesday, Obama opens his speech with a general statement that immediately sets the scene and enthusiastically inspires the audience:

(7) Well, the polls are just closing in California and the votes are still being counted in cities and towns across the country. But there is one thing on this February night that we do not need the final results to know – our time has come, our movement is real, and change is coming to America. (5 February 2008)

February 5th is a crucial moment for candidates, since it is the date on which presidential primaries are held in the largest number of states. Due to its significance, this moment of the nomination phase greatly attracts the attention of the media, both national and international.

About one week later, Obama mentions the first achievements and describes the election campaign in terms of the well-known and much exploited journey metaphor (consider the expressions 'we are on our way', 'how much further we have to go' and 'our road').

(8) We won the state of Maryland. We won the Commonwealth of Virginia. And though we won in Washington D.C., this movement won't stop until there's change in Washington. And tonight, we're *on our way*.

But we know how much *farther we have to go*.

[...]

We know *our road* will not be easy. (12 February 2008, my emphasis)

Obama is passionate and cautious at the same time. He knows that the real race has just started and he reminds American people that the way to go is still very long.

After a bit less than a month, Obama strikes a first balance in the competition between himself and his Democratic competitor, Senator Hillary Clinton. This is yet another crucial step in the race for the Democratic nomination, as marked by the following neutral paragraph:

(9) Well, we are in the middle of a very close race right now in Texas, and we may not even know the final results until morning. We do know that Senator Clinton has won Rhode Island, and while there are a lot of votes to be counted in Ohio, it looks like she did well there too, and so we congratulate her on those states. We also know that we have won the state of Vermont. And we know this – no matter what happens tonight, we have nearly the same delegate lead as we did this morning, and we are *on our way* to winning this nomination. (4 March 2008, my emphasis)

Obama is aware that Clinton is a strong opponent and he customarily congratulates her on her victories. He also believes that with the votes of his supporters he can still reach the first target in the long run (winning the

Democratic nomination) and that's why he incites the electorate to sustain his cause. This type of neutral paragraph is recurrent throughout the corpus and it is used skillfully by Obama to invoke the cooperation of the American people by emphasizing how every little step and any sign of advancement in the election journey is the result of communal effort. To this aim, besides relying on the conventional journey metaphor (THE ELECTION CAMPAIGN IS A JOURNEY) to describe the natural sequence of political events, Obama consistently employs the first plural personal pronoun *we* to praise the American people for what is indeed his own success and, implicitly, to call for yet further action. This doesn't mean that other options for addressing his audience are not to be found. When the occasion for the speech is particularly significant, Obama shows a tendency for addressing Americans in a more direct way with the use of the pronoun *you*. This is another skillful strategy that empowers voters by assigning them a decisive role in shaping the electoral process. To illustrate this point we can take two examples. When Obama is elected the Democratic nominee for President of the United States, he makes a speech where he compliments his supporters in the following way:

(10) Tonight, after fifty-four hard-fought contests, our primary season has finally *come to an end.*

Sixteen months have passed since we first stood together on the steps of the Old State Capitol in Springfield, Illinois. Thousands of miles have been travelled. Millions of voices have been heard. And because of what you said – because you decided that change must come to Washington; because you believed that this year must be different than all the rest; because you chose to listen not to your doubts or your fears but to your greatest hopes and highest aspirations, tonight we mark *the end of one historic journey with the beginning of another – a journey* that will bring a new and better day to America. Tonight, I can stand before you and say that I will be the Democratic nominee for President of the United States. (3 June 2008, my emphasis)

Obama is celebratory in addressing the people who cast the ballot for him. The explanation for his first victory over Senator Hillary Clinton is encapsulated in the formula 'because you', that is repeated four times. With their vote, American people determined the end of one journey and the beginning of a second and more important one. Obama claims that the agency of his supporters was essential for arriving at this result. By saying this, he also implies that it can only be 'because of them' that real change is brought to America in the final election. As the election day approaches, Obama is more explicit about that, and he attributes to the American people a decisive role in determining the course of national history. One week before the election he uses the following words:

(11) In one week, at this defining moment in history, you can give this country the change we need.

We *began this journey* in the depths of winter nearly two years ago, on the steps of the Old State Capitol in Springfield, Illinois. Back then, we didn't have much money or many endorsements. We weren't given much of a chance by the polls or the pundits, and we knew how *steep our climb would be*. (27 October 2008, my emphasis)

Since the journey is getting close to its conclusion, Obama recalls the route and describes it as a tough walk uphill. Travelers knew since the very beginning that the climb would not be easy but in the face of all adversities they kept on marching together. That's why now, at this decisive moment, they are asked to take the final step and bring change to America.

5.2.2   Criticizing adversaries

Apart from describing the different phases of the election campaign, neutral paragraphs are often the textual territory where Obama gives voice to his criticism of the Republican adversaries, and of John McCain in particular. Even though Obama honors McCain for his heroic service to the American country during the Vietnam war (McCain is described as a 'hero', a 'patriot' and a 'honorable man'), he remains very critical of his political action. He also laments the entrenched status quo in Washington and McCain's loyal standing with George Bush's worn-out policies. Obama's attacks to the Republican party can be synthesized in four major lines of argumentation.

First of all, and quite unsurprisingly, he describes Republicans (and McCain as their representative) as the traditional conservative politicians who stubbornly stick to old and failed policies of the past and the broken politics in Washington. In Obama's words, 'John McCain refuses to learn from the failures of the Bush years' (20 March 2008), 'the other side [the Republican party] knows they have embraced yesterday's policies and so they will also embrace yesterday's tactics' (20 May 2008), and 'Washington remains trapped in an earlier era' (21 June 2008). Obama counteracts this by suggesting a fresher, younger and more dynamic leadership that is nicely echoed in his insistence on change and hope, two of the leitmotifs in his campaign. Change is the only possibility to overcome the crisis and it requires taking a new direction and heading towards a different destination. As Obama remarks, 'we can't steer ourselves out of this crisis by heading in the same, disastrous direction. We can't change direction with a new driver who wants to follow the same old map' (20 September 2008). This kind of criticism is obviously a reflection of the well-known, and to a certain extent simplistic, equation of conservatism with the past and progressive thought with the future, and their respective implications. However, Obama is wise and skillful in relying on and reinforcing this established dichotomy that inevitably attracts Democratic supporters and is appealing to young new voters. As reported in Keeter *et al.* (2008), there is a general trend among young voters to describe themselves as liberal and lean more and more towards the Democratic Party.

A case in point: the 2008 presidential election recorded a high number of voters between 18 and 29 years of age (66 per cent) voting for Obama.

Obama is also very critical of Republican policies that, on a large scale, encourage division among Americans and use religion to put people against each other. When he refers to the current Republican administration and their moral conduct, Obama talks about 'the same politics that seeks to divide us with false charges and meaningless labels' and the 'politics that uses religion as a wedge and patriotism as a bludgeon' (4 March 2008). Obama's Democratic orientation actually calls for inclusiveness and cooperative coexistence between different groups of people who do not typically share the same kind of interests, including people of different ethnicity, gender, social class, age and, last but not least, political leaning. Obama is very fond of addressing his audience as 'America', that is to say a nation united by a common history and the same aspirations. Criticizing Republican divisive policies and promoting political action that is aimed to unite people under the same proud flag is, in fact, another strategic move that is very likely to capture Independents and swing voters.

The third line of criticism targets Republican personality traits, such as greed and lack of responsibility, that constitute the prerequisite for questionable social action. Obama is resolute and quite harsh when he describes the Republican administration as 'the most fiscally irresponsible administration in modern times' (21 June 2008). As the analysis in the following sections will show, Obama reiterates the importance of both individual and social responsibility and he is in favor of a moral code that strengthens forms of socially oriented behavior. Closely connected to the lack of responsibility is the Republican tendency to divert people's attention from the real problems and distract them with a form of politics that is guided by sensationalism. As he points out when blaming McCain and his party, 'it's easy to get caught up in the distractions and the silliness and the tit-for-tat that consumes our politics; the bickering that none of us are immune to, and that trivializes the profound issues–two wars, an economy in recession, a planet in peril' (22 April 2008).

Lastly, another major target of Obama's criticism is the war in Iraq and the exorbitant human and economic costs that it has involved. Obama's fierce objection to the war in Iraq is summarized in one of his early speeches when he says 'John McCain won't be able to say that I ever supported this war in Iraq, because I opposed it from the beginning' (12 February 2008).

These lines of criticism have been teased apart for ease of explanation but they also happen to co-occur in the compressed space of one or two subsequent neutral paragraphs. Let us consider the following example:

(12) His [McCain's] plans for the future are nothing more than the failed policies of the past. And his plan to win in November appears to come from the very same playbook that his side has used time after time in election after election.

Yes, we know what's coming. We've seen it already. The same
names and labels they always pin on everyone who doesn't agree
with all their ideas. The same efforts to distract us from the issues
that affect our lives by pouncing on every gaffe and association
and fake controversy in the hope that the media will play along.
The attempts to play on our fears and exploit our differences to
turn us against each other for pure political gain – to slice and dice
this country into Red States and Blue States; blue-collar and white-
collar; white and black, and brown. (6 May 2008)

This passage gives an idea of how Obama frames his discourse when com-
plaining about McCain's suggested policies. The opponent is out of touch not
just for his nostalgic support of politically 'bad' practices that have already
been unsuccessfully tried out, but also in that he is not receptive to the real
needs of the American people. In Obama's words, McCain's politics does not
care about solving the problems that afflict American citizens. It rather creates
diversions that distract from the real issues. In line with this, McCain's conduct is metaphorically described as the one of a player who does not play by
the rules. The game metaphor is constant in Obama's description of McCain's
dealings in Washington and the suggestion holds the same across different
speeches: the game that Republicans keep on playing is not fair and it has
the sole objective of making the unfair players score new points. The excerpt
also alludes to the kind of divisions that McCain and his party outrageously
foster. They attempt to reduce the country to small groups of individuals with
competing interests. As recurrently formulated throughout the campaign,
McCain's tactic is to play on fears, doubts and divisions that divert people's
attention away from what really counts. The consequences of this unruly
game reach their climax in McCain's support of the war in Iraq, which Obama
defines in many neutral paragraphs as 'a war that should have never been
authorized and should have never been waged'. Obama is extremely critical
of McCain's siding with George Bush to finance the Iraq war and he makes
a point of his distance from that ill-thought decision. In a speech addressing
the topic 'the cost of war', Obama makes the following observation:

(13) Now, at that debate in Texas several weeks ago, Senator Clinton
attacked John McCain for supporting the policies that have led to
our enormous war costs. But her point would have been more com-
pelling had she not joined Senator McCain in making the tragically
ill-considered decision to vote for the Iraq war in the first place.

The truth is, this is all part of the reason I opposed this war from the
start. It's why I said back in 2002 that it could lead to an occupation
not just of undetermined length or undetermined consequences,
but of undetermined costs. It's why I've said this war should have
never been authorized and never been waged. (20 March 2008)

In these paragraphs Obama's words of complaint even extend to his Democratic competitor, Senator Hillary Clinton, since she also voted in favor of the war in Iraq. Obama signals his strong disapproval and points out how the costs (human and economic) of this unreasonable war are immeasurable.

To sum up, the image of McCain that comes out from the speeches is that of a man who is illogically bound to the past, cynical in his behavior, insensitive towards people's needs and, lastly, not true to his own words, as expressed in the paragraphs below:

> (14) And while I respect John McCain, it's not change when he offers four more years of Bush economic policies that have failed to create jobs at a living wage, or insure our workers, or help Americans afford the skyrocketing cost of college. That isn't change.
>
> Now, one place where Senator McCain used to offer change was on immigration. He was a champion of comprehensive reform, and I admired him for it. But when he was running for his party's nomination, he walked away from that commitment and he's said he wouldn't even support his own legislation if it came up for a vote.
>
> If we are going to solve the challenges we face, you need a President who will pursue genuine solutions day in and day out. And that is my commitment to you. (28 June 2008)

Obama reprimands McCain for having done nothing to create job opportunities, improve the health care or help people afford the high costs of education. Even though he made proposals for improving legislation on immigration, when the time came to act, he did not do anything. In the end, McCain appears as the man who doesn't play by the rules and cannot even keep his words. In brief, someone not to be trusted.

If we now consider textual organization, neutral paragraphs that present Obama's critique of Republican policies and behavior generally precede paragraphs that are classified as Contra SF. While this other type of paragraphs will be analyzed later, it is useful at this point to mention how this sequential pattern is by no means a matter of mere coincidence. Indeed, neutral paragraphs containing forms of criticism of the Republican political conduct are, so to say, the most natural way to introduce other textual units where Obama directly objects the value system that is at the base of the Republican worldview.

5.2.3   Communicating key notions

Neutral paragraphs also serve the purpose of presenting the general aim of Obama's campaign, change, with its corollary of hope and choice. As a key notion, the term *change* is repeated incessantly throughout the campaign and it is also alluded to via the use of metaphorical language, as in the following example:

(15) America, this is our moment. This is our time. Our time to turn the page on the policies of the past. Our time to bring new energy and new ideas to the challenges we face. Our time to offer a new direction for the country we love. (3 June 2008)

Here Obama addresses his country(wo)men with self-confident enthusiasm and a strong belief in the capacity of Americans to renew their nation. Metaphors help shape his line of reasoning. Politics is seen as a book and the need to bring about change is metaphorized as the turning of a page. In addition, the conventional journey metaphor is relied upon to indicate that politics should take a new path and politicians should lead the country in a new direction.

As mentioned before, the concept of change is one of the leitmotifs in the campaign and as such it occupies different types of paragraphs in relation to how it is expressed. When Obama simply talks about change as a basic necessity, as in the example above, his ideas are contained in neutral paragraphs. Conversely, when he explains how he would implement change in the lives of Americans, he typically does so in the space of so-called nurturant paragraphs, which will be discussed later.

Obama's message of change in the lives of Americans implies an optimistic belief in things getting better for ordinary people, coupled with the empowering feeling of actually choosing for one's own destiny. Accordingly, the three notions of change, choice and hope often co-occur in the same speech.

(16) That is the dream I am running to help restore in this election. If I get the chance, that is what I'll be talking about from now until November. That is the *choice* that I'll offer the American people – four more years of what we had for the last eight, or fundamental *change* in Washington.

People may be bitter about their leaders and the state of our politics, but beneath that, they are *hopeful* about what's possible in America. That's why they leave their homes on their day off, or their jobs after a long day of work, and travel – sometimes for miles, sometimes in the bitter cold – to attend a rally or a town hall meeting held by Senator Clinton, or Senator McCain, or myself. Because they believe that we can change things. Because they believe in that dream. (14 April 2008, my emphasis)

With their vote Americans can choose the way decisions will be taken in Washington in the coming four years. In Obama's words, people have the power to decide whether or not real change will eventually come to America. The same people also know, deep in their hearts, that they can hope for a better future. Their actions already prove that they believe in this possibility for change. To instill hope in the lives of Americans, Obama read-justs and rephrases his optimistic message throughout the whole campaign. The emotional resonance of the campaign is, after all, about hope. And one could also add, at this point, that the title of Obama's campaign book, *The Audacity of Hope* (2006), reinforces this idea. Hope, however, is a notion with an ephemeral nature, it is a concept that is more easily evoked than described. As a political theme it may result as quite insubstantial. This can explain the reason why it is only when the campaign odyssey has almost reached its zenith, that Obama eventually provides a definition of hope.

> (17) Ohio, *that's what hope is* – that thing inside us that insists, despite all evidence to the contrary, that something better is waiting around the bend; that insists there are better days ahead. If we're willing to work for it. If we're willing to shed our fears and our doubts. If we're willing to reach deep down inside ourselves when we're tired and come back fighting harder. (27 October 2008, my emphasis)

In this speech, which Obama delivered in Ohio one week before election day, the significance of hope is revealed to the fullest. Hope is described as a force that acts inside people's bodies and that one has the freedom to either follow or counteract. Following this force means abandoning one's fears and doubts and becoming stronger. In other words, people who are guided by hope will have the strength to face the crisis and realize the American Dream (or the 'American promise' as Obama likes calling it).

5.2.4 Expressing patriotism

A very proud American, Obama does not restrain himself from showing his patriotic feelings. These often find expression in neutral paragraphs where Obama describes his own personal story or that of his own parents. Let us consider a couple of examples.

> (18) I owe what I am to this country I love, and I will never forget it. Where else could a young man who grew up herding goats in Kenya get the chance to fulfill his dream of a college education? Where else could he marry a white girl from Kansas whose parents survived war and depression to find opportunity out west? Where else could they have a child who would one day have the chance to run for the highest office in the greatest nation the world has ever known? Where else, but in the United States of America? (4 March 2008)

In this passage Obama sketchily traces the life course of his nuclear fam-ily and celebrates America as the only country on earth where dreams can come true. America is described as the place where his Kenyan father could eventually obtain a university degree and marry a white woman from Kansas. It is also the place where Obama, the child of a mixed marriage between an African man and an ordinary American woman, could have a chance to run the presidential race. As reported in Obama's biographies (cf., for example, Thomas 2008), Obama's father came from Kenya to get his tertiary education in Hawaii, where, thanks to his merits, he could get his university degree free of charge. During his study, he met Ann, who would soon become his second wife and Obama's mother. After Barack was born, his father decided to pursue his education further and accepted an invitation from Harvard University, where he was granted full coverage of his tuition fees. Later on, after completing his Ph.D., he went back to Kenya to his former family and since then he has never returned, except for a brief visit when Barack was nine. America, however, remained for him that land of opportunity where he could get the degrees he had long aspired for.

On other occasions, Obama takes the space of a neutral paragraph to elaborate on his own upbringing and the way his personality has been shaped by different traditions.

(19) I am the son of a black man from Kenya and a white woman from Kansas. I was raised with the help of a white grandfather who survived a Depression to serve in Patton's Army during World War II and a white grandmother who worked on a bomber assembly line at Fort Leavenworth while he was overseas. I've gone to some of the best schools in America and lived in one of the world's poorest nations. I am married to a black American who carries within her the blood of slaves and slave owners – an inheritance we pass on to our two precious daughters. I have brothers, sisters, nieces, nephews, uncles and cousins, of every race and every hue, scattered across three continents, and for as long as I live, I will never forget that in no other country on Earth is my story even possible. (18 March 2008)

Obama is very grateful to his white American grandparents, who worked hard serving their country and took much care of him when he was a young boy. He also admits how his life was shaped by the contrasting experiences he went through spending part of his childhood in poor Indonesia and later attending some of the best schools in America (Occidental College in Los Angeles, Columbia University in New York and Harvard University). His 'blended' identity is reinvigorated through his marriage to a black woman who gave birth to their beloved daughters. Thus, in the end, Obama emerges as a sort of cosmopolitan, post-racial figure whose enlarged family extends beyond America's national borders to include three continents. Obama is able to blend the reality of his African heritage into the multicultural narrative of his American story that brings together white grandparents from Kansas, a white mother who studied in Hawaii and a stepfather from Indonesia. Obama's reiterated patriotic appeals (America is described as the only country on earth where a story like his is possible) probably worked well together with his post-racial profile to capture more of the white electorate. As observed in the literature, overt appeals to racial issues tend to dishearten white voters (see McCormick and Jones 1993), and for a candidate like Obama it could have been ineffectual to present himself more straightforwardly as a black Senator.

Obama's praising of America is so pervasive in his speeches that one starts wondering whether this move is actually intended to counterbalance doubts on his real place of belonging. After all, a man of three continents, as he defines himself, can well stand for American multiculturalism, but still needs to make it clear that America comes first. Thus, America is often glorified as the land of opportunity that pays back great potential and is justified in leading the world due to its superiority. Obama's story and that of his family is framed according to this celebratory vision of America.

(20) I know something about that dream [American dream]. I wasn't born into a lot of money. I was raised by a single mother with the help my grandparents, who grew up in small-town Kansas, went to school on the GI Bill, and bought their home through an FHA loan. My mother had to use food stamps at one point, but she still made sure that through scholarships, I got a chance to go to some of the best schools around, which helped me get into some of the best colleges around, which gave me loans that Michelle and I just finished paying not all that many years ago.

In other words, my story is a quintessentially American story. It's the same story that has made this country a beacon for the world – a story of struggle and sacrifice on the part of my forbearers and a story overcoming great odds. I carry that story with me each and every day, It's why I wake up every day and do this, and it's why I continue to hold such hope for the future of a country where the dreams of its people have always been possible. Thank you. (14 April 2008)

Obama's story is 'quintessentially American' because it appears as a more than prototypical 'from rags to riches narrative'. The story describes Obama as the son of a poor family who can raise his social status thanks to hard work and sacrifice and he does so to such an extent that he is able in the end to run for the American presidency. To give the American story an almost epic resonance, Obama reconstructs a personal chronicle that evokes the ups and downs of three generations, from his grandparents up to his marital status, and even alludes to a longer genealogy with the mention of 'forebears'. America is depicted as the country where a single mother with a low salary can send her children to some of the best schools on scholarships. It is the country where young men and women can get loans for a university education that can guarantee a good, well-paying job afterwards. It is also the place where an honorable man (Obama's grandparent) could go to college after returning from the Second World War and he and his wife could buy their first home with a loan from the government. In this personal story, everyone was given a chance to succeed and everyone could make it. Hardly anything could sound more American than this. Hardly anything could be more convincing of Obama's standing for and standing with America. This need to speak for America is also motivated by the frequent attacks of political opponents who like questioning Obama's patriotic feelings, as the passage below indicates:

(21) Finally, it is worth considering the meaning of patriotism because the question of who is – or is not – a patriot all too often poisons our political debates, in ways that divide us rather than bringing us together. I have come to know this from my own experience on the campaign trail. Throughout my life, I have always taken my deep and abiding love for this country as a given. It was how I was raised; it is what propelled me into public service; it is why I am running for President. And yet, at certain times over the last sixteen months, I have found, for the first time, my patriotism challenged – at times as a result of my own carelessness, more often as a result of the desire by some to score political points and raise fears about who I am and what I stand for.

So let me say at this at outset of my remarks. I will never question the patriotism of others in this campaign. And I will not stand idly by when I hear others question mine.

My concerns here aren't simply personal, however. After all, throughout our history, men and women of far greater stature and significance than me have had their patriotism questioned in the midst of momentous debates. Thomas Jefferson was accused by the Federalists of selling out to the French. The anti-Federalists were just as convinced that John Adams was in cahoots with the British and intent on restoring monarchal rule. Likewise, even our wisest Presidents have sought to justify questionable policies on the basis of patriotism. Adams' Alien and Sedition Act, Lincoln's suspension of habeas corpus, Roosevelt's internment of Japanese Americans – all were defended as expressions of patriotism, and those who disagreed with their policies were sometimes labeled as unpatriotic. (30 June 2008)

Obama presents himself as an American to the bone. His upbringing and the kind of ideals that have guided his life make him into a proud American. For Obama, it is crucial to show that political adversaries who question his patriotism are ungrounded in their criticism. Their sole objective is to 'strike more points' in the unfair game of political competition. The offense is so unreasonable that Obama feels it is necessary not just to deny it but to recall how American presidents of high stature were the target of similar misplaced accusations. As Obama seems to suggest, if we check historical records, the labels 'patriotic' and 'unpatriotic' refer to anything but clear and stable concepts. History can teach how being called a patriot or a traitor is often a matter of mere political convenience. If political behavior is subject to the judgments of biased commentators, what remains and really counts is the opinion of American citizens. They are the ones who can more reasonably speculate on the patriotism of their leaders, because they can see and evaluate political action beyond the petty bickering that poisons political rivalry. What these words suggest is that the electorate will decide whether or not Obama is a patriot.

5.2.5   Asking for commitment

To establish a strong American identity is a very important move for Obama. Once people start looking at him as their truly American leader, they can also feel inspired by his frequent requests for a commitment to hard work and community. Obama often asks the electorate to believe in America's capacity to survive the crisis and redo itself anew. As he points out, American history records a number of critical times, but it also reminds Americans of how they could cope with each and every one of those difficult moments. This point is illustrated in the following examples:

(22) So I know these are difficult days. But here's what I also know. I know we can steer ourselves out of this economic crisis. That's who we are. That's what we've always done as Americans. Our nation has faced difficult times before. And at each of those moments, we've risen to meet the challenge because we've never forgotten that fundamental truth – that here in America, our destiny is not written for us, but by us. (20 September 2008)

In this passage Obama incites his people to take the lead and drive the nation out of the economic crisis. In order to be persuasive he summons up a feeling of shared proud identity and historic infallibility. This all ties in convincingly with the final call for self-determination: since American people write their own destiny, they will decide what is going to happen. They won't be acted upon by others. The same message is expressed on different occasions by Obama. What changes is the number of details that he is able to compress into one or two paragraphs.

(23) I know these are difficult times. I know folks are worried. But I believe that we can steer ourselves out of this crisis because I believe in this country. Because this is the United States of America. This is a nation that has faced down war and depression; great challenges and great threats. And at each and every moment, we

have risen to meet these challenges – not as Democrats, not as Republicans, but as Americans. With resolve. With courage.

We have seen our share of hard times. The American story has never been about things coming easy – it's been about rising to the moment when the moment is hard; about rejecting panicked division for purposeful unity; about seeing a mountaintop from the deepest valley. That's why we remember that some of the most famous words ever spoken by an American came from a President who took office in a time of turmoil – "The only thing we have to fear is fear itself." (10 October 2008)

Here Obama manifests his firm belief in America's capacity to face the most threatening situations walking tall. He also reminds people that in order to face the crisis it is essential to stick together as one nation. Political divisions won't help solve American problems. And this is why, by implication, people should not follow McCain's preaching. In Obama's words, the American story has never been the story of 'things coming easy'. Therefore, again and again, people will have to make efforts and struggle together if they do not intend to break the line of so far unbeaten success against the most unfavorable conditions. This call for responsible action concludes with an almost solemn note. Obama quotes a very famous statement, 'the only thing we have to fear is fear itself', that President Franklin D. Roosevelt employed to inspire a nation at a time of war and disastrous depression. Obama also relies on a firm belief in American supremacy to induce people to take action and make a commitment to save their nation from the crisis.

> (24) America can meet this moment. We still have the most talented, most productive workers of any country on Earth. We're home to innovation and technology, colleges and universities that are the envy of the world. Some of the biggest ideas in history have come from our small businesses and research facilities. It won't be easy, but there's no reason we can't make this century another American century. (15 October 2008)

America's role as the leader in the global economy is celebrated to motivate people never to lose faith in their great nation. American workers are praised because they have the knack and an ethic of work that make them outcompete with the rest of the world. America is also magnified as the site of technological advancement and intellectual development. These words express strong patriotic sentiments and are likely to have touched the individual and collective sensibilities of many American voters. In Rowland's opinion (2010: 204), 'it was the urgency of the situation, the need for action to protect the American Dream, that made Obama's primary campaign so effective and that ultimately carried him to the presidency.'

5.2.6 Showing closeness to people

For Obama it is vital to show not just how much he loves and believes in America but also how close he is to the American people and the kind of everyday problems they have to cope with. As a way to show this closeness, Obama often recounts the stories of ordinary Americans. Here follows one example:

(25) I still remember the email that a woman named Robyn sent me after I met her in Ft. Lauderdale. Sometime after our event, her son nearly went into cardiac arrest, and was diagnosed with a heart condition that could only be treated with a procedure that cost tens of thousands of dollars. Her insurance company refused to pay, and their family just didn't have that kind of money.

In her email, Robyn wrote, "I ask only this of you – on the days where you feel so tired you can't think of uttering another word to the people, think of us. When those who oppose you have you down, reach deep and fight back harder". (27 October 2008)

Health care is one of the big issues of Obama's campaign and as such it appears in many of his speeches. As this excerpt shows, the topic can be addressed indirectly. This happens, for instance, when Obama recounts the story of a person who is suffering and cannot afford the necessary cure because of its high costs. In this case the message is made even more personal thanks to the final direct quote from the woman's words. This quote is particularly interesting since Obama's voice and that of an American citizen (the woman of the story) seem to echo each other. Throughout the campaign Obama is the one who keeps on asking people to be strong in the face of all adversities. In the quote, a woman who is suffering and does not resign asks Obama to do the same. The quote thus suggests an implicit identification between the candidate and the electorate.

The technique employed in the above quotation has been described by some scholars as a form of 'personification' (see Capone 2010): in order to talk about certain issues Obama narrates the stories of American people. It is an instance of personification in the sense that Obama communicates political ideas via personal stories that speak for them. To use a term that is dear to Bakhtin (1981), a harmonious 'polyphony' emerges once Obama's voice becomes the carrier of many other American voices. This process can be captured by the image of a ventriloquist (to which Capone 2010 refers), but it is possibly the one of a chorus that symbolizes Obama's rhetorical act at its best. To compare Obama's strategy to the job of a ventriloquist is a way to emphasize how giving voice to other voices reduces the distance between self and other (in this case the presidential candidate and his electorate). Instead, to think of Obama's voice on a par with other American voices, as in a chorus, is a way to empower the electorate by giving it not just audibility but visibility as well. Symbolically, the image of a chorus alludes to the American people standing on the podium next to Obama. A leading voice remains but, and most importantly, it is not expected to 'incorporate' all the others. Furthermore, the image of a chorus is more in line with Obama's insistence on communal effort and strong cooperative action.

For Obama, being close to people means talking to them, listening to their stories and sharing his own personal experience with that of others. In the course of the campaign, he meets many Americans and one way he shows how he treasures their exchanges is by reporting their conversations. This is illustrated in the excerpt below:

> (26) Over the course of this campaign, I've had the opportunity to visit schools and talk to teachers and students; paraprofessionals and support staff; college faculty and employees; public employees, nurses and health care workers all across this country. But so much of what informs my visits comes from an experience I had a few years ago at Dodge Elementary School in Chicago, not far from where you're assembled today.
>
> I asked a young teacher there what she saw as the biggest challenge facing her students. She gave me an answer I had never heard before. She talked about what she called "These Kids Syndrome" – the tendency to explain away the shortcomings and failures of our education system by saying "these kids can't learn" or "these kids don't want to learn" or "these kids are just too far behind." And after a while, "these kids" become somebody else's problem.
>
> And she looked at me and said, "When I hear that term, it drives me crazy. They're not 'these kids.' They're our kids. All of them." (13 July 2008)

Obama's visit to Dodge Elementary School in Chicago gives him the chance to reflect on his own experience in that place and to demonstrate how he cares for children's education and their future. By recounting the story of a young teacher who is employed at that school, Obama can make it clear how important it is that people take a commitment to solve American problems together. To foster divisions between 'first class' and 'second class' children won't lead the nation in the right direction. Obama suggests that the education system should be fixed and this should be done so that everyone can benefit from it. All children should be cared for and be given the opportunity to succeed.

The fact that Obama shows an inclination for listening to the stories of ordinary American citizens is significant and should be given special consideration because of its implications for our general discussion of nurturant morality (see Section 5.3). Representing oneself as a good listener, as Obama does, means constructing a public image that is coherent with a nurturant worldview. In the US, as in many other societies, the capacity to lead a discussion is viewed as a strength. By contrast, those who participate in a conversation mostly as silent listeners tend to be seen as weak. After all, the idea of winning or losing an argument is based on the metaphorical display of force. However, if people are guided by the desire to understand others' views and experiences, then a listening attitude is necessary. For Obama, to be a good listener is a way to show how he cares for other people. The image that Obama communicates (be it fabricated or a reflection of his own personality) is that of a politician who learns from people the causes of social distress and works for people to solve their agony and make America a better nation.

Obama also manifests his closeness to the American people when he seems to interpret and anticipate people's critical judgments and their whishes. In other words, Obama presents himself as the candidate who knows and understands how the people feel like at this critical moment in history. This is exemplified in the following paragraphs:

(27) The men and women I've met in small towns and big cities across this country see this election as a defining moment in our history. They understand what's at stake here because they're living it every day. And they are tired of being distracted by fake controversies. They are fed up with politicians trying to divide us for their own political gain. And I believe they'll see through the tactics that are used every year, in every election, to appeal to our fears, or our biases, or our differences – because they've never wanted or needed change as badly as they do now.

The people I've met during this campaign know that government cannot solve all of our problems, and they don't expect it to. They don't want our tax dollars wasted on programs that don't work or perks for special interests who don't work for us. They understand that we cannot stop every job from going overseas or build a wall around our economy, and they know that we shouldn't. (14 April 2008)

Obama is skillful in presenting his own ideas as if they were the ideas of American citizens. Thus, his understanding of the historical moment as defining, his aversion to the politicians who encourage division and controversy and his proposals to solve American problems by rationalizing the economy (taxes should not pay for programs that do not work for people) are described as if they were part of people's own belief system. Furthermore, change also comes out as an undeniable necessity. In this passage, Obama first flatters the audience (American people can see through the mischievous political tactics) and then turns the need for change into a sort of logical necessity (it is because people can see through the political tactics that they cannot but desire change as strongly as never before).

5.2.7   Introducing a topic

There is yet another general function that neutral paragraphs can perform: setting the scene for addressing a specific topic. Accordingly, in a speech that focuses on the economy, Obama introduces his proposals for fixing economic problems by providing a snapshot of the American economic situation:

> (28) Just today, we learned that 51,000 jobs were lost last month alone, the seventh straight month of job loss – now totaling over 460,000 jobs lost since the beginning of this year. This follows yesterday's news that in the last year, wages and benefits fell further behind inflation than at any time in over twenty-five years. Meanwhile, gas prices are out of control. Food prices are soaring. If you're lucky enough to have health care, your co pays, deductibles, and premiums are skyrocketing. College is becoming less affordable. And we've seen more foreclosures than at any time since the Great Depression. Back in the 1990s, your incomes grew by $6,000, and over the last several years, they've actually fallen by nearly $1,000. (1 August 2008)

Here Obama describes a situation of economic crisis with a shortage of jobs, rising living costs and unaffordable education. The fact that the passage is interspersed with numbers serves a clear purpose. Numbers make Obama's statements sound more realistic. They can capture the attention of his large audience and provide an image of objectivity.

5.2.8   Concluding remarks on neutral paragraphs

The discussion so far has illustrated how neutral paragraphs contribute to communicating different facets of the general electoral message. To sum up, we can say that neutral paragraphs serve seven major purposes:

(a)   Describing the unfolding of different phases in the election campaign.
(b)   Showing Obama's criticism of the Republican party, and of McCain in particular. The specific targets of criticisms are: (1) Republican reliance on old and failed policies of the past and on the broken politics in Washington; (2) Republican encouragement of divisions among Americans and their use of religion to put people against each other; (3) Republican greed and lack of responsibility as well as their tendency to divert people's attention from the real problems by distracting them with sensationalism; (4) Republican support of the war in Iraq with all its (human and economic) costs.
(c)   Expressing the overarching aim of Obama's campaign – change – and its corollary of hope and choice.
(d)   Showing Obama's strong patriotic feelings, mostly through the description of Obama's personal story and that of his family.

(e) Expressing Obama's requests to the Americans for renewed commitment to hard work and community.
(f) Communicating Obama's closeness to the American people. This is
achieved via: (1) recounting the stories of ordinary Americans; and
(2) showing Obama's capacity to read the minds of the American people
and understand their needs.
(g) Setting the scene for the discussion of a specific issue.

In terms of textual organization, neutral paragraphs generally crop up at
the beginning of a speech since they prepare the reader for the actual value-
laden discussion of political issues and policies. However, they can also
connect value-laden paragraphs and thus occur in other parts of a speech.

A concluding observation about neutral paragraphs regards their distribution across different speeches. As observed in Section 5.1, some variation
can be observed if one considers the ratio of neutral paragraphs to the total
number of paragraphs for each speech. In the corpus, neutral paragraphs
constitute roughly half of all paragraphs, but not every speech follows
this general pattern. In particular, there are five speeches where the ratio
of neutral paragraphs to total paragraphs is higher than 60 per cent (18
March 2008: 64.4 per cent; 20 March 2008: 64.7 per cent; 3 May 2008: 65.8
per cent; 30 June 2008: 77.1 per cent; 28 August 2008: 61.7 per cent). In
these rather long speeches (the one given on 28 August is the longest in the
corpus) Obama takes more time introducing the actual message to be conveyed, which results in a particularly high number of neutral paragraphs.
Conversely, there are six other speeches where the number of neutral paragraphs in relation to the whole number of paragraphs is lower than 40 per
cent (21 June 2008: 26.5 per cent; 13 July 2008: 34.8 per cent; 1 August
2008: 22.7 per cent; 12 September 2008: 28.6 per cent; 10 October 2008:
32.5 per cent; 15 October 2008: 38.63 per cent). Here, the expression of
values is more pervasive and neutral paragraphs are more interspersed with
other types of value-laden paragraphs.

5.3 Nurturant paragraphs

Lakoff's description of a nurturant moral worldview revolves around the
notion of nurturance. A nurturant family is one in which parents care, support and protect their children. It is a family in which parents and children
communicate openly, where cooperation is emphasized over competition,
where strength and discipline are not narrowly bound to individual efforts
but are realized thanks to the support and love of people who care for you.
In this type of family children are taught the importance of social responsibility so that they can learn how to become good nurturers and take care
of others. Children are also lovingly supported in the realization of their
own aspirations, since parents believe in their children's potential and want
them to be happy in their lives.

Accordingly, a nurturant moral worldview sets a number of moral priorities. In particular, it is a moral responsibility to help people in need. This implies personal sacrifice for others. In fact, strength is not discarded, but rather put at the service of nurturance. Being nurturers also requires taking care of oneself: securing one's living and maintaining one's health are prerequisites for being a good nurturer. Nurturant morality also makes the cultivation of social ties in communities into a moral necessity. Furthermore, it attributes great importance to establishing communion with the natural world and to cultivating one's own happiness. In relation to general prosperity, nurturant morality is in favor of a fair distribution of material objects.

Once nurturant morality is applied to the political context, what comes out is the image of a government who takes care of its citizens by providing each of them with the basics, namely food, shelter, education and health care. A nurturant government should provide protection and grant equal rights to everyone. It should also build infrastructures, create job opportunities and diminish the exploitation of the environment. Fairness, in this vision, should translate into higher taxes for the wealthiest. Foreign policy should be guided by the principle of building diplomatic alliances.

In Lakoff's view, Democratic candidates are inspired by a nurturant morality and they should explicitly address nurturant values if they intend to win election campaigns. The general expectation, therefore, is that Obama expressed NP values consistently throughout his speeches. As the following argumentation will explain, this expectation has been confirmed by the semantic analysis of 30 of Obama's electoral speeches.

As pointed out above, the analysis of the corpus has yielded a classification of each speech in relation to the different types of paragraphs it consists of. Findings in Table 5.1 show that, next to neutral paragraphs, nurturant paragraphs are those that take the largest share in the corpus: 40.2 per cent of all paragraphs are classified as nurturant. This fact is significant in light of our discussion of Obama's speeches and it draws our attention to the close connection between political siding (here Democratic) and political morality (here nurturant).

In contrast to neutral paragraphs, nurturant paragraphs are value-laden. They are paragraphs where at least one value is expressed that fits a nurturant moral worldview. Thus, in order for a paragraph to be classified as nurturant, it is necessary that it contains at least one linguistic expression that can be taken as the manifestation of a nurturant moral worldview (that is, a nurturant value).

After having analyzed the entire corpus, a large number of values could be identified that adhere to a nurturant moral view. The multitude of specific nurturant values that were observed in the corpus are connected to the more general NP values described in the methodology chapter. More precisely, it was possible to arrange the identified NP values according to eight general nurturant concepts (ordered according to their relative frequency of occurrence in the corpus): 'care' (32.1 per cent), 'we' (22.8 per cent), 'social rights' (20.8 per cent), 'fairness' (10.3 per cent), 'opportunity' (6.9 per cent), 'protection' (3.9 per cent), 'responsibility' (1.3 per cent) and 'freedom' (1.3 per cent).

Each of the eight NP concepts/values will be discussed in the following sections. As anticipated, each general concept/value subsumes a series of specific values. Indeed, the analysis revealed that Obama applies each of the general concepts to different domains and, in order to stay close to his words, it is important to show all the different domains. This is why for each NP concept/value a table will be provided that shows the different domains where the values are applied. For instance, in the case of 'care', the domains of application (that is, the specific NP values) include 'caring for the environment', 'caring for children', 'caring for workers' and so on. The overview of specific values given in the following sections shows which topics Obama frames in a NP worldview.

5.3.1 Care

The first concept, 'care', is not only the one that is most frequently addressed, but it is the most elaborate, since it can be further subdivided into 17 distinct NP values. Table 5.2 shows the number of occurrences in the corpus for each of the specific NP values that are grouped together under the umbrella term 'care'.[3]

In line with our predictions, a sentiment of care inspires the expression of a good range of nurturant values. As Table 5.2 shows, the value of care is used particularly for talking about the environment. Obama shows his engagement with the environment through statements like the following: 'I'll invest 150 billion dollars over the next decade in affordable, renewable sources of energy – wind power and solar power and the next generation of biofuels' (28 August 2008). Environmental and energy issues were indeed very prominent during the 2008 presidential campaign. As Bomberg and Super (2009) observe, this fact was totally unexpected. In previous American elections environmental and energy issues were scarcely discussed, and in the 2000 and 2004 presidential races they were almost absent. In contrast, in 2008 the environment turned into one of the major concerns of domestic policy and one of the main battlegrounds between Obama and McCain. Obama repeatedly signaled his distance from Bush's record on the environment, climate change and energy. He also markedly expressed his objection to McCain's support of nuclear power and offshore drilling for oil. Obama's suggested policies can be summed up as follows: (a) promoting an active government involved in energy and environmental protection, (b) supporting biofuels and scientific research in new forms of energy, (c) setting targets for renewables and (d) raising fuel economy standards. Interestingly enough, Obama's expression of care for the environment is often framed in terms of energy independence from the Middle East. This is an idea that

Table 5.2   'Care': list of NP values

NP values	No of occurrences
Caring for the environment	32
Supporting nurturant professions (teachers)	26
Caring for people	26
Supporting/investing in education	23
Caring for children	23
Help for the people in need	22
Caring for the troops/veterans	19
Caring for workers	17
Caring for one's family	11
Caring for the old	10
Supporting social services/work	7
Caring for families	6
Caring for future generations	6
Supporting state and local government	5
Caring for communities	2
Granting affordable housing	2
Prenatal care	1
Total	**239**

Obama conveys when he talks about the need to free America from 'oil addiction', as exemplified in the excerpt below:

(29) And if you want to take a permanent holiday from our oil addiction, we can finally get serious about energy independence and create five million new green jobs in the process – jobs that pay well and can't be outsourced. We'll do what I did when I went to Detroit and tell the automakers it's time they raised fuel mileage standards in this country. We'll make companies pay for the pollution they release into the air, we'll tax the record profits of the oil companies, and we'll use that money to invest in clean, affordable, renewable energy like solar power, and wind power, and biofuels. (3 May 2008)

Considering that oil dependence on the Middle East is the cause of constant conflicts in this 'hot' region of the world, setting a plan to reduce that dependence can be seen as a possible way out from wars and armed conflicts. Thus, the benefits of this plan would be two-fold. On the one hand, securing new sources of clean energy would have positive repercussions on the environment. On the other, it would redefine the nature of foreign policy after eight years of Republicans playing it tough with foreign enemies.

The value of care is also applied to the domain of education, which is another major concern in Obama's campaign. Obama promotes education through his insistence on the necessity to invest in this sector and to provide teachers with more support. He speaks in favor of the NP value of 'supporting/investing in education' when he says, for instance: 'we will begin changing the odds for our at-risk children by providing quality, affordable early childhood education for all our children' (13 July 2008). He is supportive of the NP value of 'supporting nurturant professions' when he makes statements of this tenor: 'As President, I will recruit an army of new teachers, pay them more, and give them more support' (27 October 2008). Obama's deep concern with the state of public and higher education is reflected in the range of measures that he proposes. They include investments in early childhood education, programs to increase pupils' literacy, numeracy and science proficiency, mentoring programs, afterschool and summer programs, tax credits to new teachers willing to work in lower-performing urban and rural schools, high-quality teachers in every classroom and more government funding for a high-quality education for all young people. This emphasis on education resonates well with the overall electoral message, the need to bring about change in America. Education gives people the essential intellectual tools and skills that can allow future generations to keep faith to the American promise of a good chance for everyone to succeed in the twenty-first century.[4]

On a more general level, Obama's words incite a caring attitude towards all people and, crucially, towards particular social categories such as workers, troops/veterans, the old and children. To take but one example, Obama's insistence on care as a foundational sentiment in one's life is nicely captured in his words, 'no matter what you do for living – I think we can all agree that raising our children and caring for our loved ones is the most important job we have' (10 July 2008). Obama's support also extends to all people in need, who should never be left alone. Not only does Obama's expression of care embrace the social groups one may think of as in need of assistance, but it even radiates to future generations, thus demonstrating the amplitude of his compassion. Caring for others is part of a philosophy where community prevails on individualism. For this reason, forms of social work are encouraged in the presidential narrative.

The family, itself a very important value in American politics, occupies an important position in Obama's rhetoric. When addressing this theme, Obama draws a distinction between the government's social responsibility to care for American families and American citizens' individual responsibility to care for their own families. Both aspects are fundamental in a democracy guided by responsible governance.

5.3.2   We

The second set of NP values consists of values that illustrate different facets of the general concept 'we'. These values are reported in Table 5.3:

Table 5.3   'We': list of NP values

NP values	No of occurrences
Cooperation	50
Unity (national & social)	43
Empowering people	26
Equality	26
Work for the good of others	11
Non confrontational diplomacy	7
Support of immigration	4
Respect of diversity	3
Acting for the common good	1
Total	**172**

The reason for choosing the cover term 'we' resides in its flexibility and inclusiveness. The label 'we' has been preferred to others that could have synthesized the range of values reported in Table 5.3 because it straightforwardly evokes a nurturant worldview and nicely captures the philosophy motivating each of these values. What all these values have in common is the belief that the American people should consider themselves as part of a social community where their action is not motivated by individualistic needs and personalism. To put it differently, these NP values are based on the understanding of community as the social space where people care about something larger than the self and have goals that transcend their individualities. Here people act so that everyone can benefit from their action and the community as an organism can develop and grow. Reasoning along similar lines, Crocker and Hughes (2009) have identified an 'ecosystem perspective' in Obama's campaign for the presidency. As they observe:

[...] we cannot know the inner workings of Obama's mind, but his speeches and actions suggest that at critical moments of the campaign, he viewed situations with an ecosystem perspective. [...] In biology, an ecosystem is a community of species together with its physical environment, considered as a unit. In a healthy ecosystem, the species fulfill each other's biological needs for nutriments, oxygen, carbon dioxide, light, and shade, etc., creating an often delicate balance of mutually interdependent life. Harm to one element of the ecosystem can negatively affect all species in the ecosystem. We draw on the biological notion of an ecosystem as a metaphor for a perspective on human relationships in which the self is seen as part of a larger whole, as part of a system of separate but interconnected individuals whose actions have consequences for others, with repercussions for the entire system, and ultimately affect the ability of everyone to satisfy their fundamental needs. [...] People with an ecosystem perspective see themselves as embedded within a larger context in which the relationship between the self and others is a nonzero-sum. The well-being of the system depends on the well-being of each of its parts, and harm to one part ripples through the system, ultimately affecting the self. (2009: 126)

As this passage explains, in order for an ecosystem to be healthy, each of its parts must be fit, since each of them essentially contributes to the overall well-being of the system. To look at society as an ecosystem requires understanding the lives of individuals as interconnected and interdependent in fundamental ways. In this view, someone's success can make society prosper and does not come at other people's expense (it is a nonzero-sum perspective). Furthermore, this perspective is based on and promotes collaboration, trust and honest relationships instead of competitiveness, mistrust and conflict. To lead a nation according to an ecosystem perspective implies giving the same importance to one's needs as to those of others and promoting a philosophy of life according to which people should take care of each other. In our discussion this perspective can be defined as nurturant.

If we now consider the individual NP values in Table 5.3, the way each of them highlights an aspect of nurturant morality should be clearer. The basic assumption that informs Obama's conceptualization of American society in terms of 'we' is that the American people are not and should never be divided by race, gender, age or social status, because all together they constitute one proud nation. This idea, and thus the emphasis on the NP value of 'unity', is communicated whenever Obama makes statements like the following: 'we are bringing together Democrats and Independents and Republicans; blacks and whites; Latinos and Asians; small states and big states; Red States and Blue States into a United States of America' (12 February 2008). Closely related to this is the idea that society should not promote any form of stigmatized contraposition of good vs. bad citizens, but rather fight any form of discrimination, since the Constitution and the Declaration of Independence make every citizen equal before the law. Diversity needs to be respected, as well as everyone's rights, especially immigrants' rights. Once this message is taken as the ideological baseline of the campaign, Obama can ask people to follow a nurturant code of behavior. This requires that people work together in the interest of a larger community; shared effort to reach a common goal should be a moral priority for the nation. Obama invokes the NP value of 'cooperation' when he addresses his audience using these and similar words: 'We owe our country a better future. And for all those who dream of that future tonight, I say – let us begin the work together. Let us unite in common effort to chart a new course for America' (3 June 2008). Furthermore, citizens are asked to put themselves at the service of others, because the only way for the country to prosper is to allow everyone to prosper. In this design, government cannot escape their moral responsibilities to treat people on an equal footing. In his speeches, Obama repeats how in a true democracy decisions should not be taken top-down, and in a situation of crisis real change can only come bottom-up ('empowering people'). Political leaders have a moral duty to listen to and be receptive of people's needs and their action cannot be driven by self-interest. In foreign policy, the government should be inspired by the same general logic and thus foster collaborative relations that are based on dialogue, tolerance and respect ('non confrontational diplomacy').

5.3.3   Social rights

The third set gathers values ('employment for everyone', 'education for everyone' and 'health care for everyone') that, on a general level, can also be said to be inspired by a sense of care but more specifically classify as expressions of basic social rights. These NP values are reported in Table 5.4.

At a time of economic crisis and social instability, Obama runs a campaign where he keeps on reassuring the American electorate that their most essential social rights (a decent job, affordable education and health care) will be set as a priority in his political agenda for renewal. In the course of the campaign, Obama promises American people to create millions of new, well-paying jobs that can give everyone a chance to pay for their bills and the skyrocketing prices of living. According to his proposals, new jobs will be created in different sectors (industry, public infrastructure, education) to save the economy from collapse and improve people's lives.

High-quality education for everyone is also among his major concerns. Education should not be the privilege of the happy few who can pay exorbitant sums of money for it. On the contrary, the government should work

Table 5.4   'Social rights': list of NP values

NP values	No of occurrences
Employment for everyone	60
Education for everyone	48
Health care for everyone	47
Total	**155**

hard so that children from low-income families can get good education and realize their potential. On a larger scale, this also fits with the nurturant value of 'granting everyone equal opportunities' (see Table 5.6).

Heated discussion on health care programs has inflamed political debates since ever. In 2008, health care is again a leading issue in the presidential race. Obama insists on everyone's right to receive the proper cure when sick and in need of assistance. He also makes clear that it is the government's responsibility to take care for each and every American citizen, irrespective of their income. The excerpt below is an example of how Obama expresses the NP value of 'health care for everyone':

(30) My health care plan will make sure insurance companies can't discriminate against those who are sick and need care most. If you have health insurance, the only thing that will change under my plan is that we will lower premiums. And if you don't have health insurance, you'll be able to get the same kind of health insurance that Members of Congress get for themselves. We'll invest in preventative care and new technology to finally lower the cost of health care for families, businesses, and the entire economy. That's the change we need. (10 October 2008)

5.3.4 Fairness

The fourth group of NP values is made up of moral priorities that respond to a logic of nurturant fairness. They are summarized in Table 5.5.

Obama's discussion of fairness revolves around taxes and money distribution. According to nurturant morality, taxes are the price of democracy. Paying taxes means securing a life where you can count on good government services and infrastructure. Taxes, therefore, should be looked at as something positive that can grant everyone a decent living. They should not be seen as a burden but as a way to guarantee the correct functioning of a democratic society. According to Lakoff (2004), Republican politicians have

Table 5.5 'Fairness': list of NP values

NP values	No of occurrences
Fair distribution of money/fair taxation	63
Regulated free market	8
Fair working conditions	2
Judicial fairness	2
Fairness: unspecified	2
Total	**77**

imposed a particular framing of taxes in the US. From the day George W. Bush took office, the term *tax relief* started circulating among politicians and it soon became a fixed phrase to refer to taxes in political discourse (see Chapter 3). This framing of taxes as an affliction made people suspicious of their actual contribution to general well-being and it also justified policies to cut down taxes for the rich. Since the wealthy, in the Republican worldview, create jobs, it makes sense to give them more money (that is, lower taxes) to create more jobs. In Lakoff's view (2004), Democratic leaders should reframe the concept of taxes and encourage policies that are in line with nurturant morality. During the 2008 election campaign, Obama is very critical of a tax system that impinges on the middle class and regular taxpayers but leaves the assets of CEOs, executives, lobbyists and corporations almost untouched. As he says,

> (31) It's time for something new. It's time to restore balance and fairness to our economy so it works for all Americans. That's why as President, I will put a middle class tax cut into the pockets of 95% of workers, provide relief to struggling homeowners, and eliminate income taxes for seniors making less than $50,000 a year. And I'll end tax breaks for companies that ship jobs overseas and give them to companies that create good jobs here at home. But you can't wait that long. You need immediate relief. (1 August 2008)

Obama is in favor of more taxes for the wealthy and an actual 'relief' for the people who earn less and are struggling in the economic crisis. This 'relief' should consist in 'tax cuts' for American working families who cannot cope with the crisis. It is real 'relief' because these people are seriously afflicted and the relief should come from the government, which has a moral responsibility to support people in need. On the contrary, people with top salaries do not need any relief from the government and they have a moral obligation to contribute to the general well-being of American society more than anyone else (that is, they must pay more taxes). This is an interesting example of reframing. In Obama's speeches, taxes are no longer conceptualized as an affliction, government ceases to be viewed as the villain who proposes them and there is no reason to see the rich as the ones in need to be relieved from an affliction. In 2008, the real affliction is an economic crisis that strongly affects the lives of ordinary American citizens. These people need to be relieved from a palpable affliction and the government can help in this. It can do so by implementing a fair tax system which requires the wealthiest to pay the highest taxes and introduces 'tax breaks/cuts' for middle class families, seniors and homeowners who have been seriously struck by the crisis.

As Lakoff explains, Republican politicians (who share a Strict Father moral worldview) are against any form of government's interference in people's life (minimal government intervention). Thus, they object to taxes (an affliction), social welfare transfers to the poor and trade barriers. In their view, government should not create any obstacle to a free market economy. For this reason, they are in favor of deregulation (that is, free trade policies) as a way to spur competitiveness and keep the economy on the roll. In opposition to this, Democratic (nurturant) politicians share the view that in order for the economy not to run wildly, the government should keep it under control by setting rules. In his campaign speeches, Obama insists on the necessity that fundamental values like fairness, accountability, honesty and responsibility to one another are respected. This means, among other things, that political leaders are called upon to stop the market from running wild by introducing new rules and regulations. As Obama affirms, 'I called for a new, 21st century regulatory framework to restore accountability, transparency and trust in our financial markets' (27 September 2008).

Fairness also means rewarding people for their hard work and promoting policies that avoid discrimination in the workplace. Finally, Obama shows his belief in 'judicial fairness' as he recounts his experience as a civil rights attorney when he tried to 'reform a criminal justice system that sent thirteen innocent people to death row' (3 June 2008).

5.3.5 Opportunity

The fifth set of NP values is captured by the notion of 'opportunity' and brings together two categories: 'opportunity for children' and 'opportunity for everyone', as illustrated in Table 5.6.

The concept of opportunity is consonant with a nurturant moral vision in that it emphasizes the importance of self-fulfillment. Government and political leaders have a moral responsibility to provide people with opportunities to realize their potential, prosper and be happy in their lives. During the electoral campaign, Obama makes it clear to his electorate how he will work to give everyone an opportunity to succeed. This is yet another expression of the American Dream: everyone should have a chance to see their dreams realized. Obama's major concern, in this respect, lies with the young generation, that of children. He spends many words to show how he cares for the future of children. As he claims, 'I've laid out an ambitious urban poverty plan that will help make sure no child begins the race of life behind

Table 5.6 'Opportunity': list of NP values

NP values	No of occurrences
Opportunity for children	35
Opportunity for everyone	17
Total	52

the starting line' (21 June 2008). Since children are the future of the nation, the nation should invest in them.

5.3.6   Protection

The sixth group brings together values that share a basic nurturant assumption: the government should provide 'protection' for their citizens. Protection can be manifested in different ways as expressed in Table 5.7.

Table 5.7   'Protection': list of NP values

NP values	No of occurrences
Investing in public infrastructure/urban development	15
Protection from nuclear, biological, cyber threats	7
No war	3
Safe housing for everyone	1
Control on gun ownership	1
Protection from crime	1
Protection from harm	1
Total	**29**

Protection is a form of care. When the American government makes sure to protect people from real and potential dangers, they show how they care for the American people and their lives. The concept of protection is often seen in conjunction with that of security, as if the two notions were interchangeable. However, according to a nurturant philosophy, protection is a prerequisite for security. People feel free from danger (that is, secure) because they know and feel that someone is protecting them. When politicians emphasize the need for more security, they implicitly speak of their nation as in a state of danger or threat. On the contrary, if political leaders frame their discourse in terms of government's efforts to protect citizens, what they talk about is a nation where people are not left on their own and can rely on government's help to face dangerous situations.

In the course of the 2008 campaign, proposals for investments in public infrastructure represent the form of protection that Obama addresses most frequently. The focus is on the need for government's intervention to fix 'crumbling' schools, roads and bridges that put the lives of millions of Americans in danger. The NP value of 'investing in public infrastructure/ urban development' is transmitted in passages like the following:

(32) And we won't just unlock the potential of our individual regions; we'll unlock the potential of all our regions by connecting them with a 21st century infrastructure. You know why this is so important. You see the traffic along I-95 in Miami. You see the

crumbling roads and bridges, the aging water and sewer pipes, the faltering electrical grids that cost us billions in blackouts, repairs, and travel delays. It's gotten so bad that the American Society of Civil Engineers gave our national infrastructure a "D." And it's no wonder – because we're spending less on our infrastructure than at any time in the modern era. (21 June 2008)

Obama's main message of protection is that of investing to rebuild a safer nation. This is perceived as an urgent priority. As Table 5.7 shows, Obama scarcely mentions other forms of protection ('no war', 'safe housing for everyone', 'control on gun ownership' and 'protection from harm'). Even the NP value of 'protection from nuclear, biological and cyber threats', which appears seven times in the corpus, occurs in only one speech that deals with that specific issue (that is, 16 July 2008).

5.3.7 Responsibility

The seventh set of NP values is encapsulated by the notion of 'responsibility' and illustrated in Table 5.8.

Table 5.8 'Responsibility': list of NP values

NP values	No of occurrences
Responsibility to one another	6
Fiscal responsibility	4
Total	10

So far, the concept of responsibility has been evoked with reference to the government's moral obligation to care for, protect and provide opportunities and the basics for a decent life to American citizens. Here, the concept refers to people's social and individual responsibility to act as good citizens who care for the common good. The kind of change that Obama advocates is that of 'a new politics – a politics that calls on our better angels instead of encouraging our worst instincts; one that reminds us of the obligations we have to ourselves and one another' (27 September 2008). Obama also calls for more responsibility on Wall Street and in Washington so that money is not wasted but spent wisely to the benefit of the whole community ('fiscal responsibility').

5.3.8 Freedom

The eighth and last set of NP values is one that, on the whole, is underrepresented in the corpus. It unites four individual manifestations of the broad concept 'freedom', as shown in Table 5.9.

Table 5.9 'Freedom': list of NP values

NP values	No of occurrences
Freedom: independence from non-renewable energy sources	7
Freedom: unspecified	1
Preservation of liberties	1
Right to abortion	1
Total	**10**

In Lakoff's view (2006), the concept of freedom has been since long appropriated by Republican politicians. Therefore, he suggests that Democrats should reclaim the meaning and significance of freedom in today's context. The present analysis reveals that the concept of freedom has not been sufficiently elaborated during the 2008 election campaign. Notwithstanding this lack of explicit elaboration of the Democratic idea of freedom, Obama, at least partly, refers to it when discussing certain environmental and foreign policy issues. Specifically, he alludes to the nation's need for freedom when dealing with the energy issue and claiming that the US should reduce their 'oil dependence' from the Middle East. Thus, the importance of national freedom surfaces in Obama's plans for energy renewal.

5.3.9   Strategies for presenting values

So far, the discussion has shed light on the type of nurturant values that enrich Obama's speeches and were fundamental for identifying nurturant paragraphs. The focus will now shift to the presentation of values in NP paragraphs. In particular, we will show how Obama adopts certain rhetorical strategies in his NP paragraphs that fit the general narrative structure of his campaign speeches.

Obama's rhetoric in NP paragraphs shares a few of the strategies previously observed in neutral paragraphs, while at the same time being uniquely characterized by some more. Starting with the elements that NP and N paragraphs have in common, the analysis reveals that Obama has a tendency to evoke NP values when he: (a) recounts his own personal story and that of his family, (b) tells the stories of ordinary American citizens and (c) appeals to patriotic feelings. The function of these rhetorical strategies, however, is distinct in different types of paragraphs. Thus, in neutral paragraphs, story-telling (recounting one's own personal story and that of one's family, reporting the stories of American citizens) and the related expression of patriotic feelings help Obama establish an emotional connection with the American electorate and construct his own identity (or public image) as that of a proud American citizen. On the contrary, in NP paragraphs,

Obama's inclination for story-telling and his attempts to inspire a sense of shared identity and spur the belief in the American Dream are essentially connected to the expression of nurturant values.

In NP paragraphs, Obama often talks about himself and his life experiences to create an image of himself that can be taken as a model of nurturance. Consider the following example:

(33) This is something of a homecoming for me. Because while I stand here today as a candidate for President of the United States, I will never forget that *the most important experience in my life* came when I was doing what you do each day – *working at the local level to bring about change in our communities.*

As some of you may know, after college, I went to work with a group of churches *as a community organizer in Chicago* – so *I could help lift up neighborhoods that were struggling* after the local steel plants closed. And it taught me a fundamental truth that I carry with me to this day – that in this country, *change comes not from the top-down, but from the bottom-up.* [...]

Now, let me be clear – *we must help tackle areas of concentrated poverty.* I say this not just as a former community organizer, but as *someone who was shaped in part by the economic inequality I saw as a college student* in cities like Los Angeles and New York. (21 June 2008, my emphasis)

In this passage, Obama evokes the NP values of 'work for the good of others', 'help for the people in need' and 'empowering people' as he describes his involvement with the local community in Chicago and alludes to the experiences that shaped his life as a college student. The value of 'work for the good of others' is expressed in the first paragraph, which connects Obama's work as a community organizer to people's activities in their own communities. The importance of helping people in need is shown in both the second and third paragraphs. In the second paragraph Obama describes how he could give his help to people who lost their jobs, while in the third paragraph he makes a moral statement ('we must help tackle areas of concentrated poverty'). The second paragraph also contains an expression, 'change comes from the bottom-up', that captures the nurturant idea of joint effort. The excerpt as a whole depicts Obama not just as a spokesman of nurturant values but also as a model of how to live by these values.

As previously observed for neutral paragraphs, Obama often talks about the life experiences of his own family. In nurturant paragraphs, mentioning his family means taking them as examples or clear referents for promoting values that are at the core of his campaign. The passage below gives an indication of this.

(34) And as someone who watched *his own mother spend the final months of her life arguing with insurance companies* because they claimed her cancer was a pre-existing condition and didn't want to pay for treatment, *I will stop insurance companies from discriminating against those who are sick and need care most.* (27 October 2008, my emphasis)

As Obama reports on the occasion of this and other speeches, his mother died of ovarian cancer at the age of 53 because her insurance company did not pay for additional treatments that could have prolonged her life. Obama shares with his audience this personal, and tragic, anecdote as a way to reinforce his political campaign message: health care is a social right that must be granted to every citizen.

If every American has a right to health care, each of them also has a right to get good education that can give them a chance to develop their potential and fulfill their dreams. In the following excerpt Obama takes himself and his wife Michelle as examples to transmit this idea.

(35) So I know that *the only reason Michelle and I are where we are today is because this country we love gave us the chance at an education.* And the reason I'm running for President is to give every single American that same chance; to give the young sisters out there born with a gift for invention the chance to become the next Orville and Wilbur Wright; to give the young boy out there who wants to create a life-saving cure the chance to become the next Jonas Salk; and to give the child out there whose imagination has been sparked by the wonders of the internet the chance to become the next Bill Gates. (9 September 2008, my emphasis)

Here Obama defines his success and that of his wife as dependent on the education they could get. Obama speaks in favor of good education for every American child and connects education to the opportunity for self-fulfillment. He also provides examples of people who relied on their intellectual abilities and intuitions to improve transportation (the aviation revolution pioneered by the Wright brothers), transform communication (the personal computer revolution lead by Bill Gates) and find a remedy against a frightening public health problem (Jonas Salk's discovery of the first polio vaccine). If good education stops being the privilege of wealthy people, then everyone can take these proudly American models as an incentive to make good use of their brilliant ideas and make society develop. Thus, according to the presidential message, to promote high-quality education for everyone is a way to give society the possibility to grow.

Besides recounting his truly American success story and depicting himself as a model of nurturance (one who has cared for people throughout his whole life), Obama also reports the sad stories of ordinary Americans to inspire nurturant feelings in the electorate and present himself as the nurturant candidate people can rely upon if they want to see the quality of their lives improve. The passage below illustrates how Obama employs this rhetorical strategy (that is, story-telling) to openly support nurturant values.

(36) The mother in Wisconsin who gave me a bracelet inscribed with the name of the son she lost in Iraq; the families who pray for their loved ones to come home; the heroes on their third and fourth and fifth tour of duty – they can't afford four more years of a war that should've never been authorized and never been waged. They can't afford four more years of our veterans returning to broken-down barracks and substandard care. They need us to end a war that isn't making us safer. *They need us to treat them with the care and respect they deserve.* That's why I'm running for President. (6 May 2008, my emphasis)

What makes this nurturant paragraph different from neutral paragraphs where Obama also reports the stories of ordinary Americans is the fact that here Obama offers a solution to the painful situations that make people grieve. In neutral paragraphs, Obama describes the kind of problems American people have to deal with in their everyday life by merely reporting their stories. In nurturant paragraphs, recounting people's stories is a way to introduce strategies of nurturant political intervention and invoke the need for a nurturant leadership. In the excerpt above, Obama takes the perspective of all those American families whose loved ones have been enrolled for the war in Iraq. His aim in doing so is two-fold. On the one hand, he criticizes that war and its proponents. On the other hand, as he deplores the human cost of the armed conflict, he can show how he shares the grief of millions of American families and how he would care for troops, veterans and their families as President of the US. Obama talks of American heroes who are sacrificing their lives for a war that should have never been fought and he laments the conditions of 'substandard care' that are reserved for them on their return after three or four tours of duty. Providing care for people who serve the nation is one among Obama's moral priorities. These people need to be rewarded not just with medals and honorary titles, but with the love and affection they deserve.

In addition to Obama's penchant for story-telling, his speeches also bear the traces of an election campaign that is unmistakably American. Not surprisingly, Obama's speeches invoke the best known of American mythical narratives – the American Dream – and they often look for consensus through appeals to shared identity and common history. This technique was previously observed in our discussion of neutral paragraphs and its presence was interpreted as a means to reinforce Obama's own American identity. The effect of Obama's appeals to patriotic feelings in nurturant paragraphs is different. Here, they establish an identification between American ideals and nurturant values. Obama is very astute in doing this since redefining

American values as nurturant ones means reinforcing his electoral message. While Democratic voters can be expected to support Obama because they share with him core nurturant values, Independents and swing voters are more likely to support Obama's nurturant values (and hence his cause) if they are presented as truly American values. Establishing connections between nurturant morality and the values that shape American identity is important for two reasons. It can help redefine American political rhetoric from a Democratic point of view and it can increase the number of Democratic voters. The following excerpts from Obama's campaign illustrate this point.

(37) *We could be fighting to put the American dream within reach for every American – by giving tax breaks to working families*, offering relief to struggling homeowners, reversing President Bush's cuts to the Manufacturing Extension Partnership, and protecting Social Security today, tomorrow, and forever. That's what we could be doing instead of fighting this war. (20 March 2008, my emphasis)

(38) *It's about who we are as Americans*. It's about whether this country, at this moment, will continue to stand by while the wealthy few prosper at the expense of the hardworking many, or *whether we'll stand up and reclaim the American dream for every American*. It's about whether we'll watch the Chinas and the Indias of the world move past us, or whether we'll decide that in the 21st century, the home of innovation, and discovery, and progress will still be the United States of America. (3 May 2008, my emphasis)

(39) I trust the American people to understand that it's not weakness, but *wisdom to talk not just to our friends, but our enemies – like Roosevelt did, and Kennedy did, and Truman did*. (6 May 2008, my emphasis)

In the first of these passages, Obama reclaims the American Dream for every single American. The Democratic frontrunner sets his proposals for future policies in opposition to those of his rival, the Republican John McCain. While McCain supports the kind of tax cuts for the wealthiest that were first introduced by George W. Bush, and keeps on financing the war in Iraq, Obama's major concerns are American 'working families' and 'struggling homeowners'. One of the objectives of Obama's campaign is making the American dream into a graspable reality for every American. One way to reach this objective is introducing a new tax system that makes the wealthiest pay the most. This responds to the logic of Democratic 'fair taxation'.

The second excerpt revolves around the American Dream as well, though with a different aim. Here Obama speaks in favor of the nurturant value 'opportunity for everyone', but he does so at the service of a capitalist market economy. Giving everyone a chance to succeed is presented as a necessity for a nation that does not intend to lose its leading position in the global market. Competition, especially that with China and India, is creating more and more pressure in the US. For this reason, Obama suggests that the country should invest more in its people by giving everyone the opportunity to succeed.

The third passage shows Obama's nurturant framing of foreign policy. Obama takes the example of former Democratic presidents Roosevelt, Kennedy and Truman to inspire the nation to change the nature of their political relations with 'friends' and 'enemies'. This statement contains an implicit critique of the Republican 'war on terror' and depicts a public image of Obama as the leader who sustains the nurturant value of 'non-confrontational diplomacy' and believes in the force of dialogue.

In addition to the rhetorical strategies that neutral and nurturant paragraphs have in common (crucially, story-telling and appealing to patriotism), there are a number of other strategies that more distinctively, though not exclusively, characterize nurturant paragraphs. These include the following: (a) comparison, (b) clustering, (c) personification, (d) metaphor, (e) NP reframing and (f) policy presentation. In the following discussion examples will be provided for each of the strategies.

Starting with the first strategy, comparison, the analysis of nurturant paragraphs reveals that Obama is able to establish connections between a Christian code of behavior and nurturant values. As a presidential candidate, Obama is critical of the tendency observed in former Democratic candidates to consider religion an inappropriate subject of political discourse and thus avoid conversation about it. In his view, it is because progressive secularists have long supported strategies of avoidance that religion has turned into a conservative prerogative. Obama tries to regain religion as a subject of progressive debate. He attempts to reclaim the religious voice of the American political Left. His view of religion as expressed in his political manifesto, *The Audacity of Hope* (2006), is actually in line with that of many liberal theorists. He recognizes the role of religion in public life and insists on the necessity to translate religious values into universal values that can be shared by a large number of people. Throughout the 2008 campaign, Obama's interpretation and adaptation of religious teachings for a pluralistic democracy surfaces in some of his speeches. Consider the following examples.

(40) That is our calling in this campaign. To reaffirm that fundamental belief – I am my brother's keeper, I am my sister's keeper – that *makes us one people, and one nation*. It's time to stand up and reach for what's possible, because together, people who love their country can change it. (12 February 2008, my emphasis)

In this passage Obama openly appeals to the nurturant value of 'unity' by transforming religious preaching into a moral code of conduct that many people can identify with, irrespective of their faith or even lack of it. The excerpt contains a quote from the Scriptures ('I am my brother's keeper', Genesis 4, 9) with a more than appropriate expansion ('I am my sister's keeper') that renders the whole message egalitarian. The significance of this quote lies in its universal appeal. Not only do different religions share a common belief in the importance of caring for each other, lots of non-religious people also consider caring for each other a social obligation. It is part of their code of behavior: helping and supporting each other is simply ethical. In Obama's message, caring for each other is what binds different people together in the same community. This is what makes them 'one people' and 'one nation'. As a result, care emerges as the value at the core of Obama's suggested moral vision. Caring necessarily implies to consider oneself and others as 'we', a community that 'rise and fall together' and that together can decide to change the course of events. Relying on the value of 'care', Obama can inspire a nation to think of themselves and act as 'one'. No doubt, this is a powerfully human message, going beyond any religious distinctions and with the potential to move a large number of voters.

To think of the nation as 'one' also means to believe in the importance of doing things together, in other words, cooperating. The excerpt below shows how Obama's call for the nurturant value of 'cooperation' is grounded in his religious faith as well as in his belief in the essential goodness of American people.

(41) But I have asserted a firm conviction – a conviction rooted in my faith in God and my faith in the American people – that *working together we can* move beyond some of our old racial wounds, and that in fact we have no choice if we are to continue on the path of a more perfect union. (18 March 2008, my emphasis)

The statement above belongs to one of the most quoted of Obama's 2008 campaign speeches, the 'A more perfect union' speech. This speech was delivered by Obama in Philadelphia Constitution Centre on 18 March 2008 in response to some of Reverend Wright's controversial remarks. Obama's first encounter with Reverend Wright goes back to the time when he joined the Trinity United Church of Christ on the South Side of Chicago in the 1980s. As Mansfield points outs (2011: xxi), this experience was crucial for Obama's life since it 'exposed [him] to a passionate Afrocentric theology and a Christian mandate for social action that permanently shaped his poli-tics.' Obama, however, soon realized that Trinity Church's Christianity was 'permeated by a defining, if understandable, spirit of anger: toward white America, toward a spirit of black suffering and toward a US government that consistently lived beneath the promise of her founding vision' (xxi). Such anger, which reinforced American racial divisions, putting black and white society against each other, was never consonant with Obama's own belief in the greatness of the American promise. The same anger to which Reverend

Wright had given voice in his sermons for so many years was exploited by the media during the 2008 election campaign to fuel a debate on Obama's politics of faith. However, if the media's rebroadcasting of Reverend Wright's provocative statements caused great controversy in American politics, it also offered Obama the great chance to deliver a masterful address. In 'A more perfect union', Obama could reinforce his message of unity and motivate people to cooperate and make America a better place for everyone. In this speech, Obama refers to his mixed ethnicity and unusual personal history to reclaim the idea that 'this nation is more than the sum of its parts – out of many we are truly one'. Being 'one', however, is not enough. This union can be made more perfect and that is what Obama asks the American people to do. Americans should work together, to 'move beyond racial wounds' and realize a more perfect union. This stands out as one of Obama's moral requests for 'cooperation' and it is framed in a language that goes beyond the specificities of religious affiliation.

While Obama's framing of religion for the political Left creates links between general religious values and the nurturant values of 'unity' and 'cooperation', his framing of the notion of 'freedom' suggests connections between American constitutional values and the nurturant concept of choice in relation to the right to an abortion. The example below is a case in point.

(42) Change isn't a President who thinks Roe vs. Wade is a flawed decision and whose party platform outlaws abortion, even in cases of rape and incest. Change is a President who will stand up for choice – who understands that five men on the Supreme Court don't know better than women and their doctors what's best for a woman's health. That's why I fought so hard in Illinois and in Washington to stop laws that would've restricted choice. That's why *I'm committed to appointing judges* who understand how law operates in our daily lives, judges *who will uphold the values at the core of our Constitution*. And that's why *I will never back down in defending a woman's right to choose*. (20 September 2008, my emphasis)

During his election campaign, Obama made strong statements endorsing women's right to abortion.[5] Obama's discussion of abortion is all framed in terms of granting women the freedom to choose. The Roe vs. Wade decision [410 U.S. 113, 1973], which Obama refers to in the passage above, represented a fundamental achievement in the long 'war' over abortion in the US. The Supreme Court decision in the Roe vs. Wade case legalized abortion nationwide. By recognizing the constitutional right to abortion, this decision emphasized women's freedom and right to bodily autonomy. In this speech, as well as on other public occasions, Obama does not refrain from showing his moral commitment to protecting women's right to choose. Choice is a value at the core of American Constitution. As such, choice, in

Obama's words, cannot be denied to American women when it comes to discuss the meaning of abortion.

The last three examples have illustrated how Obama conveys the nurturant values of 'unity', 'cooperation' and 'right to an abortion' utilizing the rhetorical strategy of comparison. Comparisons are drawn between nurturant values and Christian values as well as between nurturant values and American constitutional values. The following excerpt sheds light on another strategy that Obama frequently employs in his speeches, that of clustering. The term clustering in this study refers to the co-occurrence of diverse nurturant values in the dense space of one nurturant paragraph. An example of clustering is presented below:

(43) It's a dream shared in big cities and small towns; across races, regions and religions – that *if you work hard, you can support a family*; that *if you get sick, there will be health care you can afford*; that *you can retire with the dignity and security and respect that you have earned*; that *your kids can get a good education, and young people can go to college even if they're not rich.* That is our common hope. That is the American Dream. (12 February 2008, my emphasis)

In this paragraph Obama celebrates the American Dream and identifies it with a number of nurturant values that he intends to support with his plans and programs. These values include: 'caring for one's family', 'health care for everyone', 'caring for the old' and 'education for everyone'. They are the values that Obama communicates consistently in his campaign and that he often presents together as part of a political project. The advantage of presenting more nurturant values together is that of reinforcing his moral framing of issues. Since all these values are consistent with a nurturant moral vision, their co-occurrence makes the entire nurturant worldview more graspable for the electorate.

Another rhetorical strategy that Obama utilizes is that of personification. Considering that our discussion is centered on the expression of values, what we intend with personification is the attribution of certain nurturant values to a particular individual who turns, so to say, into the 'embodied' representation of the value(s) in question. An example of how Obama employs personification is given below.

(44) We've certainly had our differences over the last sixteen months. But as someone who's shared a stage with her many times, I can tell you that what gets Hillary Clinton up in the morning – even in the face of tough odds – is exactly what sent her and Bill Clinton to sign up for their first campaign in Texas all those years ago; what sent her to work at the Children's Defense Fund and made her fight for health care as First Lady; what led her to the United States Senate and fueled

her barrier-breaking campaign for the presidency – *an unyielding desire to improve the lives of ordinary Americans, no matter how difficult the fight may be.* (3 June 2008, my emphasis)

In this passage Obama praises his Democratic adversary, Hillary Clinton, and depicts her as the personification of the nurturant value of 'caring for people'. Hillary Clinton appears as the humanitarian, progressive politician who has put all her efforts into a fight to improve the life of American people. The battles she has fought demonstrate how deeply she cares for people and especially for those who need care the most.

The discussion above has also demonstrated how Obama likes drawing an image of himself that makes him into a model of nurturance. That is another instance of personification.

The strategy of personification is also used to provide models of nurturance among ordinary American citizens, as shown in the following paragraphs.

(45) And Ashley said that when she was nine years old, her mother got cancer. And because she had to miss days of work, she was let go and lost her health care. They had to file for bankruptcy, and that's when Ashley decided that *she had to do something to help her mom.*

She knew that food was one of their most expensive costs, and so Ashley convinced her mother that what she really liked and really wanted to eat more than anything else was mustard and relish sandwiches. Because that was the cheapest way to eat.[6]

She did this for a year until her mom got better, and she told everyone at the roundtable that the reason *she joined our campaign was so that she could help the millions of other children in the country who want and need to help their parents too.* (18 March 2008, my emphasis)

Telling the personal story of Ashley Baia, a 23-year-old campaign organizer, Obama makes her into a potential source of moral inspiration for Americans. Ashley personifies the nurturant value of 'caring for one's family'. She got to know about her mum's medical condition when she was young, and since then she did all she could to help her and make her sufferance more bearable. As Obama states, Ashley decided to participate in the campaign to support other people in the country who fight similar battles. Through Ashley's story Obama is able to convey an important message: caring for one's parents must be a moral priority for everyone.

Models of nurturance (Hillary Clinton, Barack Obama, Ashley Baia) are the most straightforward representations of personification. However, Obama also employs another technique to personify nurturance. He talks about the men and women he met during the campaign to give a body, so to say, to the recipients of care. This is another way to personify care. Here follows an example of it.

(46) There's nothing empty about the *call for help that came from the mother in San Antonio* who saw her mortgage double in two weeks and didn't know where her two-year olds would sleep at night when they were kicked out of their home. (4 March 2008, my emphasis)

The nurturant value that Obama communicates in this passage is that of 'help for the people in need'. In order to do so, he takes the example of a specific person, in a specific place and with specific problems. He tells the sad story of a mother who lives in San Antonio and can no longer pay the interest rates for her house. This story is likely to touch us through empathetic identification. Many voters who listen to it can readily identify with the poor mother in San Antonio, feel empathy for her and hence embrace Obama's political cause.

The next strategy we consider is metaphor. The relevance of metaphor for our discussion of political framing is the subject of the next chapter. Here, we just provide an example of a particular metaphor that was frequently used by Obama to invoke the value of 'supporting nurturant professions'.

(47) Change is giving every child a world-class education by *recruiting an army of new teachers with better pay and more support*; by promising four years of tuition to any American willing to serve their community and their country; by realizing that the best education starts with parents who turn off the TV, and take away the video games, and read to our children once in awhile. (20 May 2008, my emphasis)

The passage above contains a number of nurturant values: 'supporting nurturant professions (teachers)', 'education for everyone', 'supporting social work' and 'caring for one's family (children)'. In this respect, the paragraph provides an example of clustering. However, if we pay attention to how the first of these values is expressed, another strategy is revealed, metaphor. Obama uses a military metaphor to talk about the need for new teachers: an army of new teachers should be recruited. Obama's framing of this nurturant value is significant. It shows how important it is not just to nurture, but to nurture with strength. Obama seems to believe in the strength of nurturance. In his speeches, he often refers to people who fight to care for others. The personal story Obama crafts of himself is that of a man who has struggled and put his efforts at the service of others. Hillary Clinton and Ashley Baia are further examples of strong nurturers. Senator Edward Kennedy is yet another champion of the strength of nurturance. About him, Obama says: 'he has spent his life in service to this country [...] because he cares [...] about the causes of justice, and equality and opportunity. So many of us here have benefited in some way or another because of the *battles he's waged*, and some of us are here because of them. [...] we know *he is a fighter*' (20 May 2008, my emphasis). In Obama's public narrative, also teachers line up among the troops of nurturers. They are depicted as an army involved in a metaphorical war to improve education. According to the narrative, their battle won't be easy and it will require a lot of effort. Teachers are not the only ones involved in the fight for better education, but they are given the role of main characters. Thus, even though they won't fight alone, they will be the ones advancing in the front line. In Obama's story of hope, teachers are among the strong people who can bring forth change. They can do it by providing the kind of high-quality education the nation is waiting for.

Another strategy that features in nurturant paragraphs is NP reframing. This consists in Obama's ability to suggest a nurturant reframing of an idea that has already gained popularity in political language. Obama's reframing of taxes is a clear case in point. Consider the following passages from his speeches.

(48) I also have a health care plan that would save the average family $2,500 on their premiums and provide the uninsured with the same kind of health care Members of Congress give themselves. *That's real relief*, but we can only pay for this if we finally rollback the Bush *tax cuts* for the wealthiest 2% of Americans who don't need them and weren't even asking for them. (3 May 2008, my emphasis)

(49) *As we provide relief*, we must also be mindful of the swelling budget deficit. That is why I am proposing that we pay for this rebate by taxing the windfall profits of oil companies like Exxon Mobil – a company that announced yesterday that it made nearly $12 billion last quarter, more than any U.S. corporation has ever made in a single quarter. It's time we used some of their record profits to help you pay record prices. (1 August 2008, my emphasis)

As pointed out earlier (see Section 5.3.4), George W. Bush is responsible for the wide spread of the expression *tax relief* in political discourse. This phrase, which refers to a reduction in taxes for the wealthiest, indicates a framing of taxes as an affliction. As we know, Democrats, in principle, do not consider taxes as an affliction. One therefore might expect Democratic leaders to put forward a reframing of taxes that is in line with progressive ideas. Obama's lexical choices in his campaign speeches confirm this expectation. Obama shows a clear preference for the terms *tax cut* and *tax breaks* over *tax relief*. Used in combination with *tax*, the words *cut* and *break* suggest a factual interpretation. When we talk of a *tax break/cut* we describe a process whereby something is made smaller, reduced in its size or quantity. So, the expressions *tax break* and *tax cut* describe the process they refer to much more accurately than the emotionally loaded phrase *tax relief*. Thus, replacing *tax relief* with *tax break/cut* is an achievement in terms of reframing American public debate on taxes. But Obama doesn't stop there. The word *relief* is not ruled out of his discussion on taxes. American citizens who have been struck by the economic crisis need relief. They need someone to relieve them from their affliction and a government that cares for its people has the duty to do it. Obama's suggestion consists in giving relief to the people who are seriously afflicted by the economic crisis by making the wealthiest pay their fair share of taxes. The two passages above illustrate this strategy. In the first one Obama speaks in favor of the nurturant value 'health care for everyone' and suggests that health insurance could be guaranteed to all Americans by making the wealthiest pay higher taxes. This means that the value 'health care for everyone' is presented as dependent on the introduction of a new and fairer tax system ('fair taxation'). In the second passage quoted above, Obama is more specific about his concrete strategy for granting 'fair taxation' in the US and hence relief to the Americans who really need it. This time, oil companies are his target: their skyrocketing profits should be taxed more. This would help reducing the 'swelling budget deficit' and make the US a stronger nation.

Nurturant paragraphs also contain clear instances of strategic planning, which is arguably one of the most persuasive forms of policy presentation. As Lakoff (2004) observes, it is crucial for politicians to think strategically in terms of large moral goals that are inspired by a number of values. In his view, Republicans have already been successful in doing this, and Democrats would greatly benefit from finding their own ways to integrate different values in a coherent narrative that can function as a convincing political plan. More precisely, Lakoff refers to 'strategic initiatives', which he defines as 'plan[s] in which a change in one carefully chosen issue area has automatic effects over many, many, many other issue areas' (2004: 29). According to Lakoff, Democratic politicians tend not to think strategically. The only major exception that he comments upon is the New Apollo Initiative. This could be simply described as a massive investment in alternative energy; however, the initiative has a number of repercussions for many other areas as well, including employment, health care, clean air and water, habitat, global warming, foreign policy and third world development (2004: 31). If we now consider the way Obama often presents different nurturant values, we can see his attempts at presenting strategic plans that are intended to tackle a number of issues. The following passages illustrate that:

(50) We can *invest in* the types of *renewable energy* that won't just reduce our dependence on oil and save our planet, but *create up to five million new jobs* that can't be outsourced. (14 April 2008, my emphasis)

(51) We can build an American green energy sector by *investing in renewable energies* like wind power, solar power, and the next generation biofuels. And we can *create up to five million new green jobs* that pay well and can't be outsourced. That's what we can choose to do in this election. (1 August 2008, my emphasis)

In both of the above excerpts, Obama communicates his intention not just to promote green energy ('caring for the environment') and thus reduce American dependence on foreign oil, but also to create new job opportunities for Americans ('employment for everyone') in the process of achieving this goal.

Obama is well aware that many American people have lost their jobs and are in search of new opportunities. For this reason, the nurturant value of 'employment for everyone' is often presented as the most obvious result of different forms of political action. This can be observed in the following excerpt.

(52) We'll *invest* the other half of this $50 billion *in our national infrastructure* so we can *create new jobs* and save over one million jobs that are in danger of being cut. [...] We'll also *invest* some of this money *to repair our crumbling schools* – because that won't just help make sure our children are getting a world-class education, it will *spur job-growth* and boost our local economies. (1 August 2008, my emphasis)

Here, the presidential candidate is in favor of large investments in public infrastructure that can make people feel safer while at the same time preserving certain jobs from 'extinction' and reducing unemployment. Particular attention is reserved to the sector of education, where repairing unstable structures is presented as an advantage for children as well as for local economies.

Other forms of strategic planning establish a link between people's right to receive good education and the social duties citizens have towards their communities. Accordingly, the importance of affordable education that can give people a real chance to fulfill their potential and realize their dreams is skillfully connected to the nurturant value of 'supporting social work'. This strategic initiative is well illustrated in the following passages.

(53) That's why I'll make *college affordable with an annual $4,000 tax credit if you're willing to do community service*, or national service. We will invest in you, but we'll ask you to invest in your country. (12 February 2008, my emphasis)

(54) I will make *college affordable for every single American who has the talent and drive to go with an annual $4000 tax credit for anyone who commits to 100 hours of public service*. You invest in America, and America invests in you – that's how we'll make college affordable for every American. That's change. (12 September 2008, my emphasis)

As the quotes above indicate, Obama believes in the importance of committing oneself to social work to the point of making it into a prerequisite for having part of one's studies financed. Significantly enough, this strategic initiative is framed in terms of a peculiar commercial transaction: if the American people invest in their country by making it a better place for everyone, the government can invest in their people by giving them a chance at self-fulfillment. In other words, if you do something good for others, America can make something good for you and, in the end, everyone will gain from it. This can be taken as an open expression of Obama's support of a nurturant moral view.

5.3.10 Concluding remarks on nurturant paragraphs

To recapitulate, nurturant paragraphs are characterized by the occurrence of at least one NP value, and they are stylistically devised according to a range of recurrent rhetorical strategies that, for the sake of clarity, are summarized below:

(a) Story-telling (Obama telling: his own story, the story of his family, and the stories of American people)
(b) Appealing to patriotism (celebrating the American Dream)
(c) Comparison (drawing a comparison between NP values and Christian values, and between NP values and American Constitutional values)
(d) Clustering (grouping a few NP values together in one paragraph)
(e) Personification (presenting concrete models of nurturance)
(f) Metaphor (presenting a metaphorical understanding of NP values)
(g) Reframing (reconsidering certain basic concepts from a nurturant perspective)
(h) Policy presentation (proposing examples of strategic planning)

As far as the textual space occupied by nurturant paragraphs is concerned, one may observe that they are likely to occur in the central part of a speech and at the end of it. The concluding paragraphs of a speech that are marked as nurturant typically bring together a range of nurturant values that are expressed throughout the speech. In this respect, they have a distinctive summarizing function.

Nurturant paragraphs are consistently present in each of the speeches and their frequency gets higher starting with mid-June 2008. Significantly enough, this general trend mirrors the unfolding of two different phases in the campaign: the primary season and the general election. The frequency of nurturant paragraphs rises after the primary season is over and Obama has been elected the Democratic frontrunner. This means that the presence of nurturant paragraphs gets proportionally higher when Obama starts competing with the Republican nominee John McCain. Unsurprisingly, in this last phase of the election campaign, it is crucial for the Democratic candidate to mark the ideological distance from his opponent. The presence of nurturant paragraphs is significantly high (more than 50 per cent of all paragraphs) in three speeches: 1 July 2008 (60.9 per cent), 1 August 2008

(68.2 per cent) and 10 October 2008 (57.5 per cent). While the high frequency of nurturant paragraphs in the 1 July speech may be dependent in part on the type of audience that Obama directly addresses (the speech is delivered on the occasion of the 80th Convention of the American Federation of teachers), Obama's expression of nurturant values in the other two speeches (1 August and 10 October) is a stronger indication of his ideological stance and of his moral framing of the campaign narrative. The 1 August speech is centered on the economy and contains proposals to fix it that embrace a large number of nurturant values, including 'fair taxation', 'opportunities for everyone', 'help for the people in need', 'investing in public infrastructure', 'empowering people', 'caring for the environment', 'health care for everyone', 'education for everyone', 'employment for everyone', 'fiscal responsibility' and 'cooperation'. Similarly, the 10 October speech deals with the impending financial crisis and contains suggestions on how to cope with it that are in line with nurturant morality and emphasize the need to help those who need care the most.

The analysis shows that Obama's nurturant framing is pervasive in the corpus. As previously pointed out, next to neutral paragraphs, nurturant paragraphs are the most frequent. Furthermore, no instance was found of Obama's objecting to a nurturant view (there is no 'contra NP paragraph' in the whole corpus).

5.4   Contra Strict Father paragraphs

According to Lakoff's morality models, a SF world view is based on the general assumption that the world is a dangerous and threatening place and that people are born bad. Consequently, life is conceptualized as a constant struggle against all types of external and internal evils and other people are conceived chiefly as one's competitors, if not one's enemies. How is a person able to survive under such unsettling and menacing circumstances? Family plays a fundamental role in preparing people to face the world without falling. The construction of one's personality revolves around a clear morality figure, the father. Crucially, he is the one who has control over his family members. He decides what is right and what is wrong, and thus instills the good vs. bad dichotomy in his children. An authority, he sets rules and enforces obedience by the threat of punishment. In the micro-social context of one's family, children learn the importance of discipline for their lives. The notion of discipline entails obedience to and respect for authorities as well as the development of self-control to become self-reliant. This all contributes to the creation of moral strength, which is necessary for having authority over one's life and developing personal responsibility. People need to be strong in order to achieve success in the tough, competitive and hierarchical world. According to the SF view, wealth is an unquestionable sign of moral strength. In contrast, poverty is paired with immorality.

The application of SF morality to the domain of politics involves an emphasis on individual responsibility in opposition to nurturant social responsibility. This means that people are expected to be strong enough to care for themselves. Social programs are considered immoral because they support weak people who are not able to be self-sufficient. In line with the SF logic, these people should be punished by depriving them of any form of help. While weak people are doomed to poverty unless they become strong, morally strong citizens are rich thanks to their discipline. Good discipline makes them into ideal citizens who care for themselves and make society prosper with their wealth. For these reasons, they have a moral right to receive some compensation from the government, which can reward them by reducing their taxes. Strength also depends on people's competitive striving to accumulate more wealth than others, and people are believed to get the most out of this struggle if the government does not interfere. Stated differently, government regulation should be minimized to promote free competitiveness. Another facet of strength involves relations with foreign countries: supposed enemies should by fought against with strong military power.

As illustrated in Section 5.3, Obama's moral framing throughout the 2008 election campaign is consistently nurturant. This orientation is proved by the large number of nurturant paragraphs that have been identified in the corpus. There is yet an additional, though less direct, indication of Obama's leaning toward a NP type of morality. The corpus also presents some instances of contra SF paragraphs. Here, SF assumptions and values are openly addressed and criticized. Such a critique reinforces the nurturant political message and emphasizes the core aspects of ideological divergence between the Democratic and Republican candidates.

In comparison to neutral and nurturant paragraphs, contra SF paragraphs are far less frequent. Only 7.4 per cent of all paragraphs can be marked as contra SF and their distribution in the corpus indicates a progressive decrease starting from the end of June up to the end of October. In this time span, six speeches did not contain any contra SF paragraphs (30 June; 1 July; 10 July; 16 July; 9 September; 20 October), while in the preceding phase of the campaign (from February to the end of June) only two speeches didn't have any contra SF paragraphs (15 April; 6 May). This reduction in the frequency of contra SF paragraphs may be due to a range of factors. However, one aspect should not be underestimated: once the primary phase was over, it was vital for Obama to communicate a strong nurturant identity to his electorate. The words of the Democratic candidate should place him in blatant opposition to his Republican adversary. As the 'don't think of an elephant' principle suggests,[7] evoking the don'ts is not a strategy which is as effective as listing the dos. So, talking of NP values is a far better way to convey a nurturant message than criticizing the opposing moral view, especially at a time of direct confrontation between just two candidates.

Contra SF paragraphs are textual units where one or more SF values are criticized. For the purpose of the analysis, the different SF values that are the target of Obama's criticism have been arranged in five major groups. Each of these groups is identified by a term which refers to a specific SF interpretation of (political) reality. The five groups are labeled as follows: (1) 'moral order', (2) 'strength', (3) 'freedom', (4) 'hierarchy' and (5) 'self-discipline/self-reliance'. The frequency of these criticized SF concepts/values in the corpus is reflected by their numbering (group 1 is the most frequent whereas group 5 is the least frequent). Since each of these general notions could refer to different facets of Republican ideology, it is important to explain which aspects are included in the individual definitions.

The notion of 'moral order' is used in this analysis to indicate two SF assumptions that Obama lambastes. The first one, and by far the one that he addresses mostly, is the idea that the rich are worthier than the poor and therefore deserve more. This idea reverberates in the Republican proposals for the distribution of public money that Obama rejects. Obama laments that Republican politicians put 'Wall Street before Main Street'. In detail, he attacks the Republican belief in the government having a moral responsibility to support oil and drug lobbyists, big corporations and banks, as well as safeguarding the interests of big companies and CEOs instead of caring for the needs of ordinary American people. Obama is also harsh in his attacks on Republican 'tax relief' for the wealthiest. The other aspect of the Republican 'moral order' assumption with which Obama disagrees is the idea that man is superior to nature and therefore has control over the environment and can exploit it for his own profit. Obama is very critical of American oil dependence and of the Republican refusal to look for alternative energy.

Similarly to the notion of 'moral order', the concept/value of 'strength' also consists of two components. 'Strength' is a SF value that Obama besets when it involves either lack of nurturance or the actual display of force. He is against 'strength' when it implies the following: (a) not caring for the most basic social rights, including education, health care, employment and pensions; (b) not caring for public services and infrastructures such as schools, hospitals and roads; and (c) not caring for future generations. In addition to this, Obama speaks against SF manifestations of 'strength' that involve Republican support of the so-called 'war on terror' and tough warfare in general, and Republican inclination for confrontational diplomacy and tough talk with adversaries.

As previously observed, freedom is a concept that has been largely framed by Republican politicians over the last decades (Lakoff 2006). The SF interpretation of 'freedom' that Obama rejects is that which justifies the economy to run wildly. In particular, he is against unregulated labor markets, delocalization, unregulated free market economy and the privatization of social security.

The label 'hierarchy' is closely related to authority. Obama opposes this SF value when he talks against the Republican tendency to emphasize the contrast between who is up (the people in Washington) and who is down (ordinary American citizens) and the general Republican attitude to be removed from people, who are excluded from any process of decision making. Furthermore, the Democratic candidate objects to the SF gender 'hierarchy'.

As stated above, 'self-reliance' is the result of 'self-discipline'. These SF values are encapsulated by the Bootstrap principle, according to which 'with enough self-discipline, everyone can pull himself or herself up by the bootstraps' (Lakoff and The Rockridge Institute 2006: 43) and therefore doesn't need any form of help from the government. Since Obama believes in the social responsibility of the government towards their citizens, he openly complains about the Bootstrap principle.

Having explained the specific meanings of the general SF concepts/values ('moral order', 'strength', 'freedom', 'hierarchy', 'self-discipline/self-reliance') that were identified in the contra SF paragraphs, we can now consider their actual frequency in this type of paragraphs. Table 5.10 below provides an overview of that.[8]

As Table 5.10 suggests, Obama is particularly harsh in his criticism of the SF moral justification for giving more to the ones who have the most ('moral order: distribution of wealth') and punishing the weak ('strength: lack of nurturance'). These ideas contrast with Obama's nurturant conception of fairness, according to which the rich should give more back to society than the poor, and with the nurturant principle of nurturance, which extends to the entire society and does not discriminate between people who are worthy of help and those who are not. With respect to foreign affairs, the discussion of nurturant paragraphs has also illustrated how Obama favors dialog and the strengthening of diplomatic alliances. In line with this, in contra SF paragraphs he condemns the ideology which sustains the war in Iraq and is in favor of new forms of armed conflict ('strength: display of force').

Table 5.10 List of SF values in contra SF paragraphs

SF values criticized	No of occurrences
Moral order: distribution of wealth	56
Moral order: dominance over nature	3
Strength: lack of nurturance	34
Strength: display of force	17
Freedom: unregulated free market	16
Hierarchy	9
Self-discipline/Self-reliance	5
Total	**140**

He also strongly disapproves of the SF belief that American government should in no way meddle in people's lives ('freedom'). Furthermore, as a reflection of his emphasis throughout the campaign on fostering cooperation among citizens and advocating social and national unity in different domains of American public life, Obama looks with disapproval at authoritarian forms of political behavior which reduce the role of American people in political decisions ('hierarchy'). As far as environmental issues are concerned, Obama's political message is framed almost entirely in positive terms. In a good number of nurturant paragraphs, he refers to the need to care for the environment with new investments in green energy. Having set this as a 'moral' priority in his agenda, Obama is scant in his direct accusations of Republican policies that rely on the exploitation of the environment ('moral order: dominance on nature'). Lastly, the SF value of 'self-discipline/ self-reliance', as encapsulated in the Bootstrap principle, is frowned upon on a few occasions by the Democratic candidate.

If we now consider how Obama verbalizes his criticism of SF values, three main strategies can be observed: accumulation, story-telling and irony. Starting with the first one, accumulation refers to the build-up of closely related facets of SF ideology that Obama disapproves in the textual space of a contra SF paragraph. The excerpt below illustrates this common strategy.

(55) And if I am your nominee, my opponent will not be able to say that I voted for the war in Iraq; or that I gave George Bush the benefit of the doubt on Iran; or that I support the Bush-Cheney policy of not talking to leaders we don't like. And he will not be able to say that I wavered on something as fundamental as whether or not it's ok for America to use torture – because it is never ok. That is the choice in this election. (5 February 2008)

In this passage, Obama clarifies his position concerning American support for wars in the Middle East by spelling out his distance from the decisions of the Republican political leaders McCain and George Bush. He also expresses his disapproval of policies that hinder dialogue with some foreign leaders. Furthermore, he points out how torture can never be used as a form of punishment because it is not to be used under any circumstances. As a textual unit, this contra SF paragraph condenses Obama's disapproval of SF interpretations of the concept/value of 'strength'. More specifically, Obama's words undermine the promotion of 'strength' involving the use of brutal force as in war and torture. They also discredit 'strength' as it finds expression in forms of confrontational diplomacy. The discussion of nurturant paragraphs has already explained how Obama's framing of 'strength' is guided by a nurturant world view that puts it at the service of nurturance. The strength to be nurturers reverberates as one of the moral values that are at the base of the moral edifice Obama constructs throughout the election campaign.

On other occasions, Obama's political (moral) message is phrased in ways that disqualify a SF framing of 'strength' which involves letting people on their own to solve their problems. Consider the contra SF paragraph below.

(56) It's not change when he offers four more years of Bush economic policies that have failed to create well-paying jobs, or insure our workers, or help Americans afford the skyrocketing cost of college – policies that have lowered the real incomes of the average American family, widened the gap between Wall Street and Main Street, and left our children with a mountain of debt. (3 June 2008)

Here, as in the previous example, one can observe the use of accumulation for rendering the expressed ideas more persuasive. Obama complains about the government's lack of nurturance toward its citizens as it appears in those policies that ignore people's right to have a decent job, to rely on health insurance that can pay when they get sick and to receive good education that can give them a chance to succeed in life. This lack of nurturance, which derives from a SF belief in 'strength' has important consequences in Obama's presidential narrative. It widens the gap between the people in power (Wall Street) and ordinary people (Main Street). Moreover, it inflicts suffering on future generations by postponing problems (crucially, fixing the economy) that should be solved in the present.

In other contra SF paragraphs, Obama speaks against the solutions to American economic problems that his Republican adversaries propose. The passage below can be taken as a case in point.

(57) And it's the same course that offers the same tired answer to workers without health care and families without homes; to students in debt and children who go to bed hungry in the richest nation on Earth – four more years of tax breaks for the biggest corporations and the wealthiest few who don't need them and aren't even asking for them. It's a course that further divides Wall Street from Main Street; where struggling families are told to pull themselves up by their bootstraps because there's nothing government can do or should do – and so we should give more to those with the most and let the chips fall where they may. (4 March 2008)

The Republican answer to the everyday concerns of many American citizens relies on the SF values of 'moral order' and 'self-reliance'. These values are closely related to the SF framing of 'strength' that Obama despises. Given the SF assumption that wealth is a sign of moral strength, morally strong people (the rich) should be rewarded, whereas morally weak people (the poor) should be punished. The moral reward comes in the form of tax breaks, while the punishment consists in letting people face their economic problems on their own. In the contra SF paragraph quoted above, which also works via accumulation, Obama opposes the SF logic of reward vs. punishment for deciding about people's individual contribution to the general well-being of the nation (that is, the amount of taxes to be paid by every citizen) and about the use of public money for the well-being of all citizens (that is, government's role in granting health care, education and minimal wages for everyone). Expected outcomes of the SF reward principle are also under attack in this paragraph. According to the SF view, giving more to the wealthiest means giving more to everyone because morally strong people can make the whole country prosper with their wealth. Obama criticizes this assumption by drawing on the idiomatic phrase 'let the chips fall where they may'.

To sum up, the strategy of accumulation is employed in contra SF paragraphs to express Obama's disapproval of Republican suggested policies that are inspired by closely related SF values or by different aspects of just one SF value. This strategy is very similar to that of clustering, which was commented upon in the discussion of nurturant paragraphs. The fine distinction that makes the two strategies distinct is their respective range of issues. Clustering is more inclusive than accumulation: it brings together more values. Furthermore, clustering relies on a richer internal diversification in comparison to accumulation: with clustering it is never the case that just one value is evoked and elaborated.

As already pointed out, one of Obama's favorite ways of communicating with his electorate is via story-telling. Since stories have a direct impact on listeners and guarantee for emotional involvement, they indisputably represent an excellent strategy to gain the support of voters. Obama likes telling stories about himself and 'real' American people. But what is the function of stories in different types of paragraphs? The stories that he tells in neutral paragraphs serve the mere purpose of establishing a link with his listeners. The stories to be found in nurturant paragraphs aim to convey NP values in a convincing manner. The stories told in contra SF paragraphs are intended to make the criticism of certain SF values particularly vivid. In order to appreciate the strategic use of story-telling in contra SF paragraphs, we can consider the passage reported below.

(58) But I will never walk away from the larger point that I was trying to make. For the last several decades, people in small towns and cities and rural areas all across this country have seen *globalization change the rules of the game on them. When I began my career as an organizer* on the South Side of Chicago, *I saw what happens when the local steel mill shuts its doors and moves overseas.* You don't just lose the jobs in the mill, you start losing jobs and businesses throughout the community. The streets are emptier. The schools suffer.

I saw it during my campaign for the Senate in Illinois when *I'd talk to union guys* who had worked at the local Maytag plant for twenty, thirty years before being laid off at fifty-five years old when it picked up and moved to Mexico; and they had no idea what they're going to do without the paycheck or the pension that they counted on. *One man* didn't even know if he'd be able to afford the liver transplant his son needed now that his health care was gone. (14 April 2008, my emphasis)

Here Obama blames an economy that prospers to the detriment of people. In particular, he points his finger at the typical SF framing of 'freedom' as applied to free market economy in the era of globalization. What he condemns is the 'immorality' of many American businesses who moved overseas or to other parts of the continent (Mexico) to maximize their profits, and in so doing left many American workers without a job. In order to make his 'moral' message more striking, Obama adopts a well-established strategy, story-telling. First, he talks about his own experience as a community organizer on the South Side of Chicago. As he refers, during this period, he could observe the impoverishment of entire communities as the result of business delocalization. This is one story. Then, he mentions his encounters with union guys during his campaign for the Senate in Illinois. At that time, he heard the tragic reports of middle-aged people losing their jobs and pensions. This is the second story he tells. But Obama doesn't stop here. He elaborates on the second story by presenting the case of a man who lost his job and cannot afford health care for his family any longer. In this third story the Democratic candidate implicitly shows his blame for a SF understanding of 'strength' that limits government's social responsibility towards American people just to cases of natural disasters (earthquakes, floods and so on). The public image of Obama that gets constructed through these stories is that of an eyewitness who knows from experience (because he saw things and talked to people) what happens when the economy is stripped of too many rules. This all contributes to making Obama's harsh criticism of applying SF ideology to the economy more reliable.

In contra SF paragraphs targeting the SF values of 'freedom' and 'strength' (that is, lack of nurturance) the technique of story-telling is often used. As illustrated above, in these types of paragraphs Obama tells the sad stories of people left without a job because of companies moving to more profitable lands. He also tells the stories of many people across the country who need support from the government. The two excerpts below provide further examples.

(59) We're here because of the more than one hundred workers in Logansport, Indiana who just found out that their company has decided to move its entire factory to Taiwan. We're here because of the young man I met in Youngsville, North Carolina who almost lost his home because he has three children with cystic fibrosis and couldn't pay their medical bills; who still doesn't have health insurance for himself or his wife

and lives in fear that a single illness could cost them everything. (22 April 2008)

(60) And that's what you need now more than ever. Because for eight long years, Washington hasn't been working for ordinary Americans. And few have been hit harder than Latinos and African Americans. You know what I'm talking about. You know folks like Felicitas and Francisco, a couple I met in Las Vegas who were tricked into buying a home they couldn't afford. You know about the families all across this country who are out of work, or uninsured, or struggling to pay rising costs for everything from a tank of gas to a bag of groceries. And that's why you know that we need change in this country. (28 June 2008)

In addition to the strategy of accumulation and that of story-telling, in contra SF paragraphs Obama employs irony to talk about his political adversary McCain and attack his value system. Consider the following examples.

(61) Now, I don't believe that Senator McCain doesn't care what's going on in the lives of Americans. I just think he doesn't know. Why else would he define middle-class as someone making under five million dollars a year? How else could he propose hundreds of billions in tax breaks for big corporations and oil companies but not one penny of tax relief to more than one hundred million Americans? How else could he offer a health care plan that would actually tax people's benefits, or an education plan that would do nothing to help families pay for college, or a plan that would privatize Social Security and gamble your retirement? (28 August 2008)

(62) Now I do want to be fair. Senator McCain is offering some tax cuts. He'd spend nearly $2 trillion over a decade in tax breaks for corporations. He would continue the Bush tax cuts for the wealthiest Americans. His plan gives more than a half million dollars in tax cuts for households making over $2.8 million. That's right – $2.8 million. Now I know that Senator McCain has said that only those making over $5 million a year are rich, so maybe he thinks that folks making $2.8 million are middle class. (12 September 2008)

In the first of the paragraphs above, Obama makes his point through a series of questions based on the same unsustainable assumption: McCain is not aware of the real problems American people have to face (that is, the rising costs of taxes for the middle class, the extremely high costs of education and health care). Here lies the irony. Since no one can believe McCain doesn't know anything about these problems, it follows that McCain simply doesn't care about the lives of Americans. In the second passage, the irony revolves around McCain's intended recipients of tax cuts. While no one can deny that McCain is offering some tax cuts, it is self-evident that he is not suggesting the middle class should pay less. It is actually the understanding of middle class that is derided. In both cases, what is under attack is the SF belief in moral order, according to which the rich deserve more than the poor.

The discussion so far has provided a good deal of evidence that Obama's framing of issues throughout the 2008 election campaign is chiefly nurturant. NP values clearly emerge in NP paragraphs and a nurturant ideology motivates contra SF paragraphs as well. In the whole corpus only one instance of a SF paragraph was identified, which is reported below.

> (63) The people I've met in small towns and big cities across this country understand that *government can't solve all our problems* – and we don't expect it to. We believe in *hard work*. We believe in *personal responsibility and self-reliance*. (6 May 2008, my emphasis)

In this passage, Obama evokes the SF belief that government is not there to help people in all situations. Since the government cannot be taken as the panacea for every problem, people need to work hard, take personal responsibilities and be self-reliant. This is a strong message that does not allow much space for either empathy or nurturance. What is significant, however, is that this isolated example of SF framing is followed by a paragraph that immediately reduces the impact of the SF message.

> (64) *But we also believe that we have a larger responsibility to one another as Americans* – that America is a place – that America is the place – where you can make it if you try. That no matter how much money you start with or where you come from or who your parents are, opportunity is yours if you're willing to reach for it and work for it. It's the idea that while there are few guarantees in life, you should be able to count on a job that pays the bills; health care for when you need it; a pension for when you retire; an education for your children that will allow them to fulfill their God-given potential. That's the America we believe in. That's the America I know. (6 May 2008, my emphasis)

Here, Obama's call for personal responsibility expands to a more inclusive demand for social responsibility. People should care for one another and the government should care for all of them by granting employment, education and health care.

5.5 Mixed paragraphs

In addition to neutral, NP, SF and CSF paragraphs, the corpus also presents some instances of mixed paragraphs: textual units that bring together criticism of SF values and praise of opposing NP values (that is, contra SF + NP paragraphs). The presence of mixed paragraphs in the corpus is, however, very limited: their frequency is 2.4 per cent.

These paragraphs chiefly involve an ideological contrast in the framing of three basic notions: 'economic fairness', 'community' and 'social nurturance'. When they deal with 'economic fairness', the clash is between the SF belief in the rich deserving more than the poor and the NP assumption that the wealthy are the ones who should give most to society. The actual matter of debate is the proper (that is, morally justified) amount of taxes every citizen should pay. The clash is, therefore, between what we have defined as SF 'moral order' and NP 'fair taxation'. Here follow two examples of it.

(65) That's why, while Senator McCain wants to continue the Bush tax cuts for the wealthiest Americans who don't need them and didn't ask for them, I'll pass a tax cut of up to $1,000 per working family. (10 July 2008)

(66) He wants to give more tax cuts to Fortune 500 CEOs. I want to give 95 percent of working Americans the tax relief they deserve. (15 October 2008)

These paragraphs show how Republican and Democratic suggested policies and the moral systems underlying them are far apart from each other.

When mixed paragraphs draw an image of 'community', a marked ideological distance between a SF and a NP conception of it emerges. The SF interpretation of 'community' resides in strong individualism and clear hierarchical relations. In contrast, the NP view of community relies on dialogue, exchange and cooperation between members of the same social group. The SF values of 'moral order', 'strength' and 'hierarchy' are therefore set in opposition to the NP values of 'national unity', 'social unity', 'empowering people' and 'non-confrontational diplomacy'. Consider the example below.

(67) It's a game where trade deals like NAFTA ship jobs overseas and force parents to compete with their teenagers to work for minimum wage at Wal-Mart. That's what happens when the American worker doesn't have a voice at the negotiating table, when leaders change their positions on trade with the politics of the moment, and that's why we need a President who will listen to Main Street – not just Wall Street; a President who will stand with workers not just when it's easy, but when it's hard. (12 February 2008)

In this paragraph Obama describes the consequences of applying an SF ideology to politics and the advantages of embracing a NP worldview, which is presented as a solution to current afflictions of many Americans.

Mixed paragraphs dealing with 'social nurturance' consist in the juxtaposition between the SF ideas that people should help themselves and the government should support the strong and the NP consideration of the government's moral responsibility to care for each and every citizen. Thus, these paragraphs express the contrast between the SF values of 'strength' and 'moral order' and the NP value of 'caring for people'.

> (68) Now my opponent wants to have a debate about change, and that's a debate that I welcome. Because the choice in this election is very simple. If you are better off than you were eight years ago and you want four more years of a President who puts the special interests and the biggest corporations first, then vote for John McCain. If you believe it's time for fundamental change in Washington and a President who puts the middle class first, then we will win this election in November, and we will change this country for our children and our grandchildren. That's the choice in this election. That's why I'm running for President of the United States. (12 September 2008)

The passage above contains one of the leitmotifs of the campaign, change. Change consists in rejecting Republican policies that favor special interests and corporations, and putting the interests of American people and future generations first.

6
Values and Metaphors in Obama's Speeches

This chapter discusses the presence of metaphorical expressions in Obama's 2008 electoral speeches. Since moral values are at the core of the investigation carried out in this book, the chapter explores in particular the relation between metaphors and values. The analysis revolves around the identification of values that are communicated using metaphorical language. More precisely, the discussion sheds light on the values that are evoked by metaphors as well as on the type and range of metaphors that are associated with specific values.

6.1 Metaphors in the corpus: an introduction

As pointed out earlier in our discussion of the literature dealing with conceptual metaphors in political discourse (see Chapter 3), some of the studies that are inspired by Lakoff's morality models (that is, Cienki 2004, 2005a) take as a general assumption that specific moral metaphors should be searched for in order to prove a politician's NP or SF ideological leaning. Accordingly, for his analyses Cienki (2004, 2005a) relies on two lists of metaphors that Lakoff (1996) provides and that, in the intentions of their deviser, describe and define the NP and SF idealized cognitive models of political morality.

In Cienki (2004), the presence of metaphorical expressions that are seen to reflect central NP/SF morality metaphors in a corpus of political language is directly correlated to either a NP or a SF framing of campaign discourse by the Democrat Al Gore and the Republican George W. Bush. In addition to considering metaphorical expressions (at or below the sentence level) that can be taken as a direct reflection of central SF and NP metaphors, Cienki (2004) also looks for metaphorical and non-metaphorical entailments of these metaphors. His study shows that while the total amount of metaphorical language that directly reflects SF and NP metaphors is very small, metaphorical and non-metaphorical logical entailments of SF and NP metaphors, on the whole, are used much more often by both candidates.

In a companion study, Cienki (2005a) motivates the overall small number of NP metaphorical expressions found in his data in terms of a structural unbalance between central SF and NP metaphors. The findings and general assumptions that inform and support Cienki's investigations (2004, 2005a) have already been looked at with a critical eye in Chapter 3. Suffice it to say here that our study moves in a different direction.

In contrast to Cienki's analyses, the present investigation is not guided by the general hypothesis that central SF and NP metaphors, which are used by Lakoff to explain the contrasting SF and NP morality models, should find a direct mirroring in the metaphorical language used by Republican and Democratic politicians. As discussed in Chapter 5, the starting point of this book is the identification of NP and/or SF values in a corpus of presidential speeches. Moreover, the analysis is not limited to the linguistic expressions that directly evoke values consonant with a specific moral worldview (either SF or NP). Instead, it also takes into account potential criticism towards values that cohere with a particular moral view (see CSF paragraphs). In the analyzed speeches, the linguistic manifestation of moral values is widespread, while not occupying the entire textual space. According to the presence, absence or criticism of NP and SF moral values, individual paragraphs (the textual units of the semantic analysis) have been labeled as follows: N, NP, SF, CSF and NP+CSF. Having identified values and classified paragraphs (see Chapter 5), the analysis now focuses on the actual use of language in value-laden textual units. More specifically, attention is given to the presence of metaphors in the paragraphs in which moral values are expressed. Which are the metaphors Obama relies upon in his articulate narrative when he, more or less explicitly, invokes moral values? Is the language used to talk about moral values intrinsically metaphorical? Are moral values expressed via specific moral metaphors? The discussion which follows aims to provide adequate answers to these and similar questions that one may ask concerning the relation between morality and metaphoricity in political speeches.

6.2   Metaphors in value-laden paragraphs

Given our general assumption that investigating metaphoricity in relation to Lakoff's models of political morality involves focusing on moral values and observing whether or not they are expressed metaphorically, the analysis of metaphors was necessarily restricted to value-laden paragraphs. All these paragraphs (NP, SF, CSF, CSF+NP) were searched for metaphorical expressions (see Appendix 1). No metaphor was found in the only SF paragraph present in the corpus. The other types of paragraphs (NP, CSF, CSF+NP) contain instances of metaphors with some variability (see Appendix 2 for an overview of the distribution of metaphors across individual speeches). It was also observed that metaphorical expressions are not always employed to introduce or define a particular value. Some metaphors just occur in a value-laden paragraph without having any direct relation to the value or values conveyed in that paragraph. This made it necessary to draw a finer distinction between the metaphors that are linked to values and the ones that are not. The frequency of value-laden paragraphs containing metaphors and values expressed metaphorically is reported in Table 6.1.

The columns in Table 6.1 display the number of paragraphs, the number of paragraphs with metaphors and the number of paragraphs with values expressed metaphorically. This shows the relation of metaphors to the expression of values. In particular, the right-most column summarizes those paragraphs where a metaphor is used to express a value.

As Table 6.1 indicates, in the case of NP paragraphs, 59.5 per cent of them contain metaphors, with the remaining 40.5 per cent being literal. A similar distribution of metaphors can be found in CSF paragraphs: metaphors occur in 65.8 per cent of them. As for mixed paragraphs, they are overall more metaphorical than the other types of paragraphs considered. Metaphorical expressions feature in 73 per cent of CSF+NP paragraphs. This general presence of metaphors is, however, not so much of a surprise since metaphorical expressions are expected to be found regularly in political discourse. As discussed in Chapter 3, the language of politics abounds with metaphors.

What is more significant for our discussion is to notice the frequency with which values are conveyed using metaphors. Table 6.1 also accounts for that. As the numbers indicate, in 44.6 per cent of all NP paragraphs values are communicated with the help of metaphors. Clearly, this also means that in 55.4 per cent of NP paragraphs values are expressed literally. In this respect, the findings show how Obama frequently employs literality as a means to transmit his nurturant message to the electorate. The situation is very similar in CSF paragraphs. Here, 41.8 per cent of all paragraphs contain values that are linked to metaphors. Only in the case of mixed paragraphs, which are overall more metaphorical, is the tendency to use metaphors when presenting values more marked. 61.5 per cent of CSF+NP paragraphs contain values that are metaphorically expressed.

Table 6.1 Metaphors in value-laden paragraphs

Paragraph types	No of paragraphs	No of paragraphs with metaphors	No of paragraphs with values metaphorically expressed
NP	430	256 (59.5%)	192 (44.6%)
CSF	79	52 (65.8%)	33 (41.8%)
CSF+NP	26	19 (73%)	16 (61.5%)

Considering that Obama communicates his moral values using both literal and metaphorical means, the question arises of which values are conveyed via metaphors and which particular metaphors are relied upon to achieve that aim. But before delving into these matters, an example is provided that shows how literal expressions can be used in the electoral narrative to evoke values. Consider the passage below.

(69)   You can make this election about how we're going to *make health care affordable for that family* in North Carolina; how we're going *to help those families* sitting around the kitchen table tonight pay their bills and stay in their homes. (22 April 2008, my emphasis)

In excerpt (69) Obama talks about the NP values of 'employment for everyone' and 'caring for people' and he uses literal language to communicate his nurturant message. While literality appears as a recurrent strategy, the use of metaphorical language allows for detailed interpretations and it is thus the subject of the next section.

6.3   Metaphorical values

As pointed out when presenting the different types of paragraphs, a good number of distinct values have been singled out in the corpus. Their significance in terms of Obama's moral message to the American electoral body has already been discussed above. Here, the analytical focus rests on the level of expression of the whole group of identified values. The semantic analysis conducted on value-laden paragraphs reveals two important facts. Literal language is used to evoke each and every of the values. Some of the values are also expressed via metaphorical language use. Tables 6.2 and 6.3 provide an overview of the values that, besides being communicated literally, also appear in the corpus as metaphorically transmitted.

Before commenting on the results reported in Tables 6.2 and 6.3, a brief methodological explanation is deemed helpful. Table 6.2 accounts for the metaphorical occurrence of all NP values in the corpus. This means that it considers NP values occurring in both NP and CSF+NP paragraphs. By analogy, Table 6.3 provides numerical details about the CSF values that were found in both CSF and CSF+NP paragraphs. Another methodological concern regards the frequency of values in the corpus. At this point, the reader is reminded that, as pointed out in the methodology section, a moral value is only counted once in a paragraph, even if it is instantiated more often in that same paragraph. Therefore, the figures for 'total number of paragraphs with values' shown in Tables 6.2 and 6.3 also represent the total number of values found in the corpus.

In Tables 6.2 and 6.3 a few data are highlighted in bold. This indicates that the frequency with which certain values are metaphorically conveyed

Table 6.2 Metaphorical NP values

Values	Total no of paragraphs with values	No of paragraphs with values metaphorically expressed
Fairness: fair taxation/distribution of money	63	**47**
Social rights: employment for everyone	60	15
We: cooperation	50	**21**
Social rights: education for everyone	48	7
Social rights: health care for everyone	47	9
We: unity	43	**18**
Opportunity: opportunity for children	35	**16**
Care: caring for the environment	32	3
Care: caring for people	26	**13**
Care: supporting nurturant professions	26	**12**
We: empowering people	26	**11**
We: equality	26	8
Care: caring for children	23	8
Care: investing in education	23	5
Care: help for people in need	22	**16**
Care: caring for troops/veterans	19	4
Opportunity: opportunity for everyone	17	**17**
Protection: investing in infrastructure/ urban development	15	4
Care: caring for the old	10	3
Freedom: independence from non-renewable energy sources	7	7
Protection: protection from nuclear, biological, cyber threats	7	**4**
We: non-confrontational diplomacy	7	1
Responsibility: responsibility to one another	6	2
Care: caring for future generations	6	1
Care: caring for families	6	1
We: support of immigration	4	1
Fairness: unspecified	2	1
Freedom: unspecified	1	1
Protection: protection from crime	1	1
Protection: protection from harm	1	1
Freedom: right to abortion	1	1

Table 6.3   Metaphorical CSF values

Values	Total no of paragraphs with values	No of paragraphs with values metaphorically expressed
Moral order: distribution of wealth	56	29
Strength: lack of nurturance	34	5
Strength: display of force	17	1
Freedom	16	5
Hierarchy	9	5
Self-discipline/self-reliance	5	4

is significant. Accordingly, we will start our exploration of metaphorical language use by taking a closer look at the values that are more frequently expressed via metaphor.

6.4   Using metaphorical fixed phrases

A first observation regarding the metaphorical expression of values in the corpus concerns the strategic use of fixed phrases to communicate a specific value. This rhetorical strategy is based on the repeated use of a typically short combination of words in association to a value. The repetition of the same phrase in semantically related contexts turns the phrase into a sort of refrain or catchphrase that allows for an immediate connection to the message behind it, that is, the value it evokes. The use of metaphorical fixed phrases was observed in relation to three values in particular: 'fairness' (as in 'fair taxation/distribution of money'), 'care' (as in 'supporting nurturant professions (teachers)') and 'we' (as in 'empowering people' and 'self-discipline/self-reliance'). For each of the four values comments and examples are presented below.

6.4.1   Fairness: fair taxation/distribution of money

The NP value of 'fairness' as 'fair taxation' and 'fair distribution of money' is metaphorically conveyed in the corpus, relying almost entirely on three metaphorical compounds: *tax break*, *tax cut* and *tax relief*. The same expressions are also used in CSF paragraphs, where the value criticized is that of 'moral order: distribution of wealth'.

The nominal combinations *tax break* and *tax cut* presuppose that taxes are physical entities whose size can be reduced at one's will. Taxes are like objects that can be handled and acted upon, and the president together with the government can decide what to do with them. This metaphorical conceptualization of taxes as objects implies a form of reification. Talking of *tax breaks/cuts* instead of using the vaguer phrase *reduction in taxes* makes the idea that is expressed particularly tangible. The compound is not simply shorter. It evokes a type of image, that of something being cut/broken, which is at the same time common and concrete. For these reasons, we can expect that the metaphorical rendering of the concept is effective.

The nominal phrase *tax break* is used with a double function. On the one hand, Obama specifies his intention to provide tax breaks to certain groups of people. On the other hand, he also states his will to stop giving tax breaks to other types of benefit receivers. So, the contrast that one can observe across the speeches is between Obama's proposal to give tax breaks to: (a) working families, (b) companies that create good jobs in America, and (c) the middle class, and his equally strong commitment to end tax breaks for: (a) corporations, (b) companies that ship American jobs overseas, and (c) oil companies that are doing better than ever. The metaphorical compound *tax break*, which is the most recurrent in the corpus, is employed to provide a full coverage of Obama's suggested interventions concerning taxes for the American people.

In contrast to *tax break*, the use of the phrase *tax cut* is more limited in scope. It occurs with a specification of its intended beneficiaries only. In this case, Obama talks of (a) a middle class tax cut, (b) putting a tax cut into the pockets of working people/workers and (c) a tax cut for working women. Another difference between *tax break* and *tax cut* consists in the syntactical rendering of the concept. The verbal expression *break taxes* is not used in English, whereas one can refer to the need to *cut taxes*. Accordingly, Obama also talks about the importance of *cutting taxes* for middle class families, senior citizens, struggling homeowners and, more generally, for 95 per cent of all working families.

In addition to the phrases *tax break* and *tax cut*, Obama also perpetuates the worn-out usage of the expression *tax relief*, one that was greatly exploited at the time of the last Bush administration. As mentioned previously (see Chapters 3 and 5), the metaphorical concept of 'tax relief' involves a conceptualization of taxes as an affliction, and therefore calls for a strong emotional reaction. The idea is that taxes are bad, or anyway make you feel bad, and people should not pay them. Obama is skillful in using the old phrase but giving it new significance and powerful reverberation. At a time of economic and financial crisis like the one that America and consequently the world dramatically faced in 2008, people were hungry for a message of recovery. In this respect, the concept of relief could be instrumental in transmitting the possibility to get over the bad situation. Thus, the old phrase *tax relief* was not discarded. It was rather re-contextualized. Again, as already observed for *tax break* and *tax cut*, Obama emphasizes that those who need relief are (a) struggling homeowners, (b) families who are struggling in this economy, (c) middle-class families and (d) the people who actually need it. Obama defines a clear ideological distance from the Republicans and what they did in the past by making it very explicit that what he proposes is not just relief but 'real relief'. This implies that any other form of tax relief the political opponents may talk (or have talked) about already is not to be taken seriously. It is fake relief because it suggests relieving someone who is not in a state of economical (and thus emotional) affliction.

To conclude, Obama metaphorically communicates the value of 'fairness as fair taxation and fair distribution of money' by relying on a very restricted array of lexical resources. He uses the three metaphorical constructions *tax break, tax cut* and *tax relief* followed by their intended recipients. The message is therefore very straightforward. A more elaborate metaphorical conceptualization occurs only when the metaphors of affliction and that of reification are mingled with a liquid metaphor. This is shown below:

(70)   Main Street needs *[tax] relief* and you need it now. We won't grow government – we'll work within the Small Business Administration *to keep folks afloat*, while providing *tax cuts to lift the tide*. (10 October 2008, my emphasis)

In this passage, pathos is achieved via the combination of different metaphorical concepts. The usual metaphors of TAXES ARE AN AFFLICTION and TAXES ARE OBJECTS are reinforced by the additional metaphor SURVIVING IS REMAINING ON TOP OF WATER. By using these metaphors, Obama can communicate that the people who will benefit from the suggested reductions in taxes are those Americans who are not just in a difficult situation but, and much more dramatically, in a life-threatening condition. Implementing the proposed measures on taxes means saving the lives of many American people. It is not simply a matter of making their lives easier.

6.4.2   Care: Supporting nurturant professions (teachers)

The value of 'supporting nurturant professions' is metaphorically conveyed in the corpus by relying on one specific military metaphor. According to the metaphor, teachers are soldiers and the government is in charge of recruiting them for the battle to provide children with better education. The metaphorical linguistic expression Obama relies upon to express this idea is that of *recruiting an army of new teachers*. This occurs in different speeches, as exemplified below.

(71)   That means investing in early childhood education. It means that we need to recruit *an army of new teachers* by not just talking about how great teachers are, but rewarding them for their greatness with better pay and more support. (3 May 2008, my emphasis)

(72)   Change is giving every child a world-class education by recruiting *an army of new teachers* with better pay and more support [...]. (20 May 2008, my emphasis)

(73) And maybe if he spent some time in the schools of South Carolina or St. Paul or where he spoke tonight in New Orleans, he'd understand that we can't afford to leave the money behind for No Child Left Behind; that we owe it to our children to invest in early childhood education; to recruit *an army of new teachers* and give them better pay and more support; [...]. (3 June 2008, my emphasis)

(74) We can invest in early childhood education, recruit *an army of qualified teachers* with better pay and more support, and finally make college affordable by offering an annual $4,000 tax credit in exchange for community or national service. (1 August 2008, my emphasis)

(75) I'll recruit *an army of new teachers*, and pay them higher salaries and give them more support. (28 August 2008, my emphasis)

(76) We need a new vision for a 21st century education – one [...]; where we're recruiting, retaining, and rewarding *an army of new teachers*, and students are excited to learn because they're attending schools of the future [...]. (9 September 2008, my emphasis)

(77) I'll invest in early childhood education, and recruit *an army of new teachers* to our schools, and provide a $4,000 tuition tax credit to help make college affordable for any middle class student who's willing to serve their community or their country. (20 September 2008, my emphasis)

(78) And now is the time to finally meet our moral obligation to provide every child a world-class education, because it will take nothing less to compete in the global economy. I'll recruit *an army of new teachers*, and pay them higher salaries and give them more support. (27 September 2008, my emphasis)

(79) It is time to provide every American with a world-class education. That means investing in early childhood education. That means recruiting *an army of new teachers*, and paying them better, and giving them more support in exchange for higher standards and more accountability. (10 October 2008; 15 October 2008; 20 October 2008, my emphasis)

(80) As President, I will invest in early childhood education, recruit *an army of new teachers*, pay them more, and give them more support. (27 October 2008, my emphasis)

What is important to emphasize here is the fact that a central NP value is communicated using a metaphor that alludes to military force. The usual association of the term *army* with tours of duty in far away countries is overturned and the result is powerful. It is as if he is saying that the type of army America is in need of does a different job: no killing and destruction, but the cultivation of people's potentials. The message is as strong as its wording. Teachers need to be strong, because if they are true to their duty, they will provide children with the necessary tools to succeed in their lives. Considering the significance of teachers' work for American society (as well as any society), it is the government's responsibility to 'give them better pay and more support'.

6.4.3 We: empowering people

The concept of 'empowering people' is rendered through the metaphorical expression *from the bottom up*, which rests on the traditional cultural notion of the Great Chain of Being. According to this metaphorical system, humans as well as animals and other organisms are ordered in hierarchies. In this metaphorical Chain, which is aligned vertically, the less powerful occupy the lower positions. This is why giving power to the ones who have fewer privileges means to start by considering the bottom and then moving upwards from there. Let us have a look at the following examples:

(81) This is the new American majority. This is what change looks like when it happens *from the bottom up*. And in this election, your voices will be heard. (12 February 2008, my emphasis)

(82) Because in my two decades of public service to this country, I have seen time and time again that real change doesn't begin in the halls of Washington, but on the streets of America. It doesn't happen from the top-down, it happens *from the bottom-up*. (22 April 2008, my emphasis)

(83) Because that's how we've always changed this country – not from the top-down, but *from the bottom-up*. (6 May 2008, my emphasis)

(84) But understand – while the change we seek will require major investments by a more accountable government, it will not come from government alone. Washington can't solve all our problems. The statehouse can't solve all our problems. City Hall can't solve all our problems. It goes back to what I learned as a community organizer all those years ago – that change in this country comes not from the top-down, but *from the bottom up*. (21 June 2008, my emphasis)

(85) As I've said many times, I believe that change comes not from the top-down, but *from the bottom-up*, and few are closer to the people than our churches, synagogues, temples, and mosques. (1 July 2008, my emphasis)

(86) This is the change we need – the kind of *bottom up growth* and innovation that will advance the American economy by advancing the dreams of all Americans. (27 September 2008, my emphasis)

(87) We need policies that grow our economy *from the bottom-up*, so that every American, everywhere, has the chance to get ahead. Not just the person who owns the factory, but the men and women who work on its floor. (15 October 2008, my emphasis)

(88)   That's how we make sure businesses have customers that can afford their products and services. That's how we've always grown the American economy – *from the bottom-up*. (27 October 2008, my emphasis)

(89)   In one week, we can choose an economy that rewards work and creates new jobs and fuels prosperity *from the bottom-up*. (27 October 2008, my emphasis)

As the passages above suggest, the campaign is aimed at bringing about change that will not happen because people in power decide for it. Ordinary people are empowered by being given a chance to decide the future of the country. Here lies the contrast that is encapsulated in the phrase *not from the top down but from the bottom up*.

6.4.4   Self-discipline/self-reliance

Obama's attacks on the SF value of 'self-discipline/self-reliance' are verbalized through the well-known and typically American metaphorical idiom *pull oneself up by one's own bootstraps*. According to the definition provided in the Oxford English Dictionary, the phrase means 'to raise or better oneself by one's own unaided efforts'. Stated differently, the idiom refers to someone's ability to get out of a difficult situation by relying on their own efforts. Clearly enough, the difficulty lies in the fact that no one can realistically lift themselves off the ground by pulling their laces. The task is simply impossible.

The 'bootstrap narrative' is discussed by politicians on both sides since the idea of taking responsibility for oneself and hence being independent is an important part of what defines an American. However, one can observe remarkable differences in the use of the idiom. While conservatives are supportive of the idea that everyone should succeed through their individual efforts alone, liberals believe that the government should provide some help. Accordingly, Democrats often complain about how difficult it is to pull yourself up by your own bootstraps, especially if you don't have any boots. As the examples below suggest, Obama confirms the typical Democratic attitude.

(90)   It's a course that further divides Wall Street from Main Street; where struggling families are told to *pull themselves up by their bootstraps* because there's nothing government can do or should do – and so we should give more to those with the most and let the chips fall where they may. (4 March 2008, my emphasis)

(91)   Ronald Reagan called this trickle-down economics. George Bush called it the Ownership Society. But what it really means is that you're on your own. If your premiums or your tuition is rising faster than you can afford, you're on your own. If you're that

Maytag worker who just lost his pension, tough luck. If you're a child born into poverty, you'll just have to *pull yourself up by your own bootstraps*. (14 April 2008, my emphasis)

(92)   For over two decades, he's subscribed to that old, discredited Republican philosophy – give more and more to those with the most and hope that prosperity trickles down to everyone else. In Washington, they call this the Ownership Society, but what it really means is – you're on your own. Out of work? Tough luck. No health care? The market will fix it. Born into poverty? *Pull yourself up by your own bootstraps* – even if you don't have boots. You're on your own. (28 August 2008, my emphasis)

Each of the above passages shows Obama's disapproval of the philosophy that lies behind the metaphorical idiom *pull oneself up by one's own bootstraps*.

6.5   Fight as a source domain for different values

As pointed out in Chapter 3, the notion of fight lies at the core of a SF worldview. According to this view, life is difficult and everyone is on their own. Therefore, succeeding in one's life is very often a matter of fighting against multiple adversities. It is the fight of the individual against everyone else. The concept of fight as such is not excluded from the NP *Weltanschauung*, but here it receives a different framing. As the NP conceptualization of reality suggests, the fight is fought for others so that everyone can enjoy a better life. It is not a fight for personal achievement, but one that is aimed at social advancement. The idealized and prototypical image of the nurturer encompasses sacrifice in the name of general well-being. In a nutshell, a fight in the NP worldview is at the service of nurturance and the ideal nurturer is strong in his/her capacities to help and support other people.

Significantly, the term *fight* features frequently in Obama's electoral narrative. In a way, he likes depicting himself as the 'Robin Hood' of twenty-first century America. The concept of fight is presented as part of Obama's own American upbringing and it is associated with certain phases in his career. In particular, he mentions frequently his fights as a community organizer when he worked on the South Side of Chicago to help people have a more decent life. In the present of the electoral campaign, Obama's fights are also set in opposition to the military expeditions that cause millions of Americans to put their lives at unnecessary risk.

The idea that life is a fight is deeply engrained in Obama's view of the world. Undeniably, a strongly nationalistic component goes with it. His fights also speak of the American struggle to realize one's dreams and reach clear and tangible objectives. Along these lines, he shows his caring affection for the young generations and their right to be granted opportunities. At the same time, and no less importantly, his words of nurturance address many other Americans: the ones with no job, no health coverage and poor education; those facing unbearable situations; and the people who just cannot do it without some form of help. In this respect, Obama's fight is the struggle to help less gifted or less fortunate people have a decent life. His enemies are entities like joblessness and poverty and the expected gains of his fight are social goals like better education, extended health care coverage and good employment. This form of care emerges as a moral duty that everyone should have towards their fellow men.

The passages reported below indicate the goals towards which Obama's fights are directed. The headings represent the values and examples are given for each of them.

'Social rights: employment/education/health care for everyone'

(93)   And the volunteers looked out that window, and they decided that night to keep going – to keep organizing, keep *fighting for better schools, and better jobs, and better health care.* And so did I. (5 February 2008, my emphasis)

(94)   I know this because I *fought* on the streets of Chicago as a community organizer *to bring jobs to the jobless in the shadow of a shuttered steel plant.* (12 February 2008, my emphasis)

(95)   Instead of fighting this war, we could be *fighting to make universal health care a reality* in this country. We could be *fighting for the young woman* who works the night shift after a full day of college and still can't afford medicine for a sister who's ill. (20 March 2008, my emphasis)

(96)   Instead of fighting this war, we could be *fighting to give every American a quality education.* We could be *fighting for the young men and women* all across this country who dream big dreams but aren't getting the kind of education they need to reach for those dreams. (20 March 2008, my emphasis)

(97)   In spite of this absence of leadership from Washington, I have seen a new generation of Americans begin to take up the call. I meet them everywhere I go, young people involved in the project of American renewal; not only those who have signed up to fight for our country in distant lands, but those who are *fighting for a better America here at home, by teaching in underserved schools, or caring for the sick in understaffed hospitals, or promoting more sustainable energy policies in their local communities.* (30 June 2008, my emphasis)

(98)   And we should extend expiring unemployment benefits to those Americans who've lost their jobs and can't find new ones. I've been *fighting for this plan* for months. (10 October 2008, my emphasis)

'Care: caring for people'

(99)   And so while I will always listen to you, and be honest with you, and *fight for you* every single day for the next four years, I will

also ask you to be a part of the change that we need. (22 April 2008, my emphasis)

(100)   In her thirty-five years of public service, Senator Hillary Rodham Clinton has never given up on her *fight for the American people*, and tonight I congratulate her on her victory in Kentucky. (20 May 2008, my emphasis)

(101)   [...] an unyielding desire to improve the lives of ordinary Americans, no matter how difficult the *fight* may be. (3 June 2008, my emphasis)

(102)   We need a President who will *fight for the middle class every single day*, and that's exactly what I'll do when I'm President of the United States. (27 September 2008, my emphasis)

(103)   We have given Treasury a broad menu of options that should be pursued. But we should not put taxpayer money at unnecessary risk. Taxpayers should not have all the downside without any of the upside. *That's a principle that I've fought for*, that's a principle that I'll maintain, and that's a principle that I'll stand up for as President. (10 October 2008, my emphasis)

'Care: help for the people in need'

(104)   And that's why I've proposed real [tax]relief for struggling homeowners and a trust fund to provide affordable housing. And let me say this – if George Bush carries out his threat to veto the housing bill – a bill that would provide critical resources to help you solve the foreclosure crisis in your towns and cities – I will *fight to* overturn his veto and *make sure you have the support you need*. (21 June 2008, my emphasis)

(105)   So, yes we need to *fight poverty*. (21 June 2008, my emphasis)

(106)   Look, we must act quickly to end this housing crisis. That's why last March, I was calling for us to help innocent home buyers. And that's why I *fought* to make sure the recent rescue package gives Treasury the responsibility and authority to help homeowners avoid foreclosure. (20 October 2008, my emphasis)

'Care: caring for children'

(107)   And I know these kids. I began my career over two decades ago in communities on Chicago's South Side. And I worked with parents and teachers and local leaders *to fight for their future*. (13 July 2008, my emphasis)

'Care: caring for troops/veterans'

(108)   And I will have a simple principle for veterans sleeping on our streets: zero tolerance. I've *fought for this* in the Senate, and as President I'll expand housing vouchers, and launch a new

supportive services housing program to prevent at-risk veterans and their families from sliding into homelessness. (15 April 2008, my emphasis)

'Care: supporting/investing in education'

(109) That's what we need to be doing – because America isn't a country that accepts second place. When I'm President, we'll *fight* to make sure we're once again first in the world when it comes to high school graduation rates. (9 September 2008, my emphasis)

'We: equality'

(110) I've *fought* in the courts as a civil rights lawyer *to make sure people weren't denied their rights* because of what they looked like or where they came from. [...] I've *fought* in the legislature *to take power away from lobbyists*. (12 February 2008, my emphasis)

'Protection: investing in public infrastructure; protection from crime'

(111) Instead of fighting this war, we could be *fighting to rebuild our roads and bridges*. (20 March 2008, my emphasis)
(112) Yes, we need to *fight crime*. (21 June 2008, my emphasis)

'Freedom: right to abortion'

(113) Change isn't a President who thinks Roe vs. Wade is a flawed decision and whose party platform outlaws abortion, even in cases of rape and incest. Change is a President who will stand up for choice – who understands that five men on the Supreme Court don't know better than women and their doctors what's best for a woman's health. That's why I *fought* so hard in Illinois and in Washington to stop laws that would've restricted choice. (20 September 2008, my emphasis)

Various

(114) This election is our chance to reclaim our future – to end the fight in Iraq and take up the *fight for good jobs and universal health care*. To end the fight in Iraq and take up *the fight for a world-class education and retirement security*. To end the fight in Iraq and take up the *fight for opportunity, and equality*, and *prosperity* here at home. (20 March 2008, my emphasis)

This plethora of examples shows how Obama uses the term *fight* to communicate his nurturant message.

6.6   Values relying on the general source domains of motion, orientation, construction and a few others

As is well known, at least since the publication of Lakoff and Johnson's book (1980) onwards, the LIFE IS A JOURNEY metaphor is one of the most basic and hence pervasive of our metaphorical conceptualizations of reality. Similarly to life, every event and action that involves a temporal unfolding is subject to a metaphorical understanding in terms of motion along a path. Accordingly, election campaigns are conceived as metaphorical journeys marked by a clear itinerary (from the start of the electoral competition to the final election), distinct phases (for example, American primaries and general election), specific travelers (political adversaries), *ad hoc* equipment (for example, political speeches), obstacles (for example, attacks from the competitors) and so on. The source domain of MOTION inspires different metaphorical linguistic expressions that are used by Obama to talk about NP values. Most significantly, even though not exclusively, MOTION is the source domain for metaphors relating to the values of 'we: cooperation', 'we: unity' and 'opportunity: opportunity for children/opportunity for everyone'. Another feature that the identified motion metaphors have in common is the directionality of movement. Most of the time, motion is forward. Alternatively, motion is directed upwards. In both cases, motion has positive connotations of progress and improvement.

In addition to motion, general orientation and the related binaries of up/down, back/front and in/out also characterize a good number of our metaphorical concepts since they rely on basic image schemas. In Obama's speeches, the category of orientational metaphors brings together a large array of metaphorical concepts referring to values. What is striking about these metaphors, is the fact that Obama's metaphorical verbalizations indicate a preference for upwards orientation. The type of orientational metaphors he relies upon more recurrently for evoking NP values are GOOD IS UP and MORE IS UP, as well as the related SOCIAL STATUS IS UP and SUCCESS IS UP. The upward orientation conveyed by Obama's metaphorical expressions brings positive connotations to his electoral message. It contributes to generating an impression of optimism and positive action.

A third category of metaphorical source domains that accounts for a good number of metaphorical values is that of CONSTRUCTION. In the examples reported in the following sections(6.6.1–6.6.4), construction appears as a source domain along with the already mentioned domains of MOTION and upwards orientation (UP) for describing specific NP values. The discussion on specific building metaphors will be expanded in Section 6.7.

6.6.1   We: cooperation

Obama employs four different metaphorical concepts for presenting the value of cooperation: MOTION, SAILING, CONSTRUCTION and LIGHT/DARKNESS.

However, only one of them takes the lion's share. This is the metaphorical conceptualization of COOPERATION AS MOTION TOGETHER ALONG A PATH. This idea is verbally rendered in different ways, each of them highlighting a peculiar component of the general metaphorical message. Here follows a representative selection of these related metaphorical linguistic expressions that describe cooperation in terms of MOTION:

(115)   [...] working together we can *move beyond* some of our old racial wounds. (18 March 2008, my emphasis)

(116)   That's what is happening in America – *our journey* may be long, our work will be great, but we know in our hearts we are ready for change, we are ready to come together, and in this election, we are ready to believe again. (20 May 2008, my emphasis)

(117)   Let us unite in common effort *to chart a new course* for America. (3 June 2008, my emphasis)

(118)   America will invest in you, you'll invest in America, and together, we'll *move this country forward* (1 August 2008, my emphasis). You invest in America, America invests in you, and together, *we'll move this country forward*. (20 September 2008; 10 October 2008; 15 October 2008; 27 October 2008, my emphasis)

(119)   America, we cannot *turn back*. Not with so much work to be done. Not with so many children to educate, and so many veterans to care for. [...] We cannot *walk alone*. [...] At this moment, in this election, we must pledge once more to *march into the future*. (28 August 2008, my emphasis)

(120)   And I hope you'll join me. I hope you'll *walk with me* so that we can turn the page on the failed policies of the past. (20 September 2008, my emphasis)

In example (115) cooperation is identified with a type of motion than can bring some positive change to American society, namely abolish racial inequalities and divisions. In (116) Obama uses the conventional journey metaphor to incite the American people to act together, follow their hearts and bring about change. Excerpt (117) reveals that cooperation is fundamental for deciding about the future of the country. Only together people can draw a new map and assign to America a desired course to take and follow. Example (118) brings together two sentences expressing the same ideas and both constructed around the rhetorical figure of chiasmus. They contain a plea for common action and shared effort that is built around the idea of reciprocation. Again, to do things together for the country, and hence for the common good, equals moving the country forward. In passage (119), the type of motion, directionality and participants' active involvement are all specified. Cooperating means walking forward as a group and the seriousness of the goal(s) to achieve is revealed by the fact that by the end the walk turns into a march, a term that evokes the American marches for civil rights. In example (120), the plurality of subjects implied by the idea of cooperation is not conveyed directly by means of the personal pronoun *we*. Here, Obama asks the American people to join him in a shared walk that will bring some change to the metaphorical book representing American history. In order to be able to write a new chapter in the book, Americans cannot but walk together.

Another conceptualization of cooperation relies on a specific sailing metaphor. This is used only twice and it appears in the excerpts reported below:

(121)   The fact is, the challenges we face today – from saving our planet to ending poverty – are simply too big for government to solve alone. *We need all hands on deck.* (1 July 2008, my emphasis)

(122)   It will take an *all-hands-on-deck effort* from America – effort from our scientists and entrepreneurs; from businesses and from every American citizen. (5 August 2008, my emphasis)

The expression *all hands on deck* is used in English to indicate that everyone's help is needed to face a situation. It also involves that there is a lot of work to be done and not so much time to do it. Obama relies on this sailing metaphor to render the urgency with which the American people are called upon to cooperate.

In addition to being metaphorically expressed as motion and strategic movement on a boat, cooperation is also metaphorical building. Consider the passages below:

(123)   I ask you to believe – to believe in yourselves, in each other, and in *the future we can build together*. (15 October 2008; 20 October 2008, my emphasis)

(124)   [...] we can *come together and build an America* that gives every child, everywhere the opportunity to live their dreams. (5 February 2008, my emphasis)

(125)   That's the proud tradition our cities uphold. That's the story our cities have helped write. And if you're willing to work with me and *fight with me* and stand with me this fall, then I promise you this – we will not only rebuild and renew our American cities, north and south, east and west, but you and I – together – *will rebuild* and renew *the promise of America*. (21 June 2008, my emphasis)

In the first of the examples above (123), cooperating means building something together and the object of construction is something so immaterial as the future. This is a type of metaphor that, similarly to the ones implied by the compounds *tax break* and *tax cut*, adds concreteness to the electoral message and makes the concept of cooperation factual. In the second example (124), cooperation is expressed again with motion and the metaphorical construction of the country. In the third example (125), Obama seems to play on the polysemous meaning of construction by drawing a comparison between the literal construction of American cities and the metaphorical construction of the American promise. The promise of America, an alternative phrasing for the American Dream, can only be achieved if people work together for that particular objective and this joint effort takes the shape of a metaphorical building. Furthermore, in the third excerpt (125), the building metaphor is interwoven with another metaphorical concept. Besides being described as a form of physical construction, cooperation is seen as a type of fight. As explained earlier, FIGHT is a source domain on which Obama often relies to evoke NP values.

In order for people to come together and do things together, they need to be spurred by an optimistic message that reinforces trust in each other and confidence in themselves. Obama appears to motivate people to shared effort for a common and higher purpose by evoking the archetypal metaphors of light and darkness with their intrinsic positive and negative connotations. Osborn (1967) explains that lightness and darkness work as archetypal metaphors. While light relates to survival, sight and warmth, darkness relates to fear of the unknown, vulnerability and cold. Osborn takes the example of former British Prime Minister Winston Churchill, who made frequent use of light and darkness metaphors, to make the point that, in moments of crisis

> the speaker must turn to the ancient archetypal verities, to the cycle of light and darkness, to the cycle of life and death and birth again … and find them all unchanged, all still appealing symbolically to the human heart and thus reassuring one that man himself, despite all the surface turbulence, remains after all man. (1967: 339)

The paragraph below illustrates how light and darkness metaphors were used by Obama in his speeches.

(126)   We can do this if we come together; if we have confidence in ourselves and each other; if we *look beyond the darkness of the day to the bright light of hope that lies ahead*. Together, we can change this country and change this world. (10 October 2008, my emphasis)

Cooperating is linked to the metaphorical idea of shifting our gaze from the darkness of the present towards the light of hope of the future that is in front of us if we decide to stand for the Democratic candidate. In this last example the value of cooperation is elaborated in relation to the specific attitude that it requires. Cooperation calls for the type of optimism that allows one to see a bright light notwithstanding the gloomy surroundings.

6.6.2   We: unity

The value of 'unity' is conveyed via a few metaphorical conceptualizations. Here we will consider the most significant of them. The most recurrent way of presenting the value of 'unity' is based on the primary conceptual metaphors GOOD IS UP and BAD IS DOWN, which are encapsulated in the clause 'we rise and fall as one nation' and its variant 'we rise and fall together'. Consider the following examples.

(127)   We believe that we *rise or fall as one nation, as one people* (4 March 2008, my emphasis).

(128)   All of this is possible, but it's just a list of policies until you decide that it's time to make the Washington we have look like the America we know – one where the future is not determined by those with money and influence; where common sense and honesty are cherished values; where we are stronger than that which divides us because we realize that in the end, we *rise or fall as one nation – as one people*. (3 May 2008, my emphasis)

(129)   Because we are all Americans. Todos somos Americanos. And in this country, *we rise and fall together*. (28 June 2008, my emphasis)

(130)   In the end, though, the conversation we're having isn't just about policies and plans. It's also about our most fundamental values – that when you work hard, you should be paid fairly and be able to retire with dignity; that *we rise and fall together* – and there are no second class citizens in our workplaces; that both work and family should be part of the American Dream. (10 July 2008, my emphasis)

(131)   That's the promise of America – the idea that we are responsible for ourselves, but that *we also rise or fall as one nation*; the fundamental belief that I am my brother's keeper; I am my sister's keeper. (28 August 2008, my emphasis)

(132)   Because if we've learned anything from this economic crisis, it's that we're all connected; we're all in this together; and *we will rise or fall as one nation – as one people*. (15 October 2008, my emphasis)

The use of the metaphorical expressions *rising* and *falling* in connection to the value of 'unity' to communicate that either the whole nation is good or bad, is an idea that is not completely new to American election campaigns. Indeed, Obama's sentence 'we believe that we rise or fall as one nation, as one people' very closely resembles Franklin Roosevelt's words in his second inaugural address: 'In every land there are always at work forces that drive men apart and forces that draw men together. In our personal ambitions we are individualists. But in our seeking for economic and political progress as a nation, *we all go up, or else we all go down, as one people*' (Franklin D. Roosevelt,

Inaugural Address, 20 January 1937, my emphasis). To inspire a nation at a time of destabilizing economic crisis, Obama draws his imagery from Roosevelt's rhetoric of the New Deal.

In order to emphasize the importance of unity, Obama uses another metaphorical concept that already belongs to a tradition of presidential discourse. In this case, the concept of unity is linked to one of the most common metaphors in political language, A NATION IS A HOUSE. The excerpts below represent an exemplification of this.

> (133) […] we stood on the steps of the Old State Capitol to reaffirm a truth that was spoken there so many generations ago – that *a house divided cannot stand*; that we are more than a collection of Red States and Blue States; we are, and always will be, the United States of America. (5 February 2008, my emphasis)
>
> (134) We are the hope of the future; the answer to the cynics who tell us *our house must stand divided*; that we cannot come together; that we cannot remake. (5 February 2008, my emphasis)

The sentence 'a house divided cannot stand' is a slight variation of US President Abraham Lincoln's famous line 'A house divided against itself cannot stand'. After Lincoln, this sentence was also used by Dwight Eisenhower in a speech he gave to the Illinois State Republican Convention after he was nominated as the candidate for the United States Senate (see Gill and Whedbee 1997: 170).

Another interesting instantiation of Obama's recourse to metaphor for invoking unity regards the conceptualization of unity as physical connection. This is expressed in the examples that follow:

> (135) Passions fly on immigration, but I don't know anyone who benefits when a mother is separated from her infant child or an employer undercuts American wages by hiring illegal workers. This too is part of America's promise – the promise of a democracy where we can find the strength and grace *to bridge divides and unite in common effort*. (28 August 2008, my emphasis)
>
> (136) Yes, we can argue and debate our positions passionately, but at this defining moment, all of us must summon the strength and grace *to bridge our differences and unite in common effort* – black, white, Latino, Asian, Native American; Democrat and Republican, young and old, rich and poor, gay and straight, disabled or not. (27 October 2008, my emphasis)

As the passages above suggest, unity can be achieved through the construction of metaphorical bridges that do away with social, racial and ethnic divisions.

6.6.3   Opportunity: opportunity for children, opportunity for everyone

The value of 'opportunity for children' is conveyed relying on a limited set of conventional metaphors, most of them having either FORWARD MOTION or UPWARDS ORIENTATION as their general source domains. When the metaphorical concept draws on the notion of movement, opportunity equals progress. Consider the examples provided below:

(137)   [...] we may not look the same and we may not have come from the same place, but we all want to *move in the same direction – towards a better future for our children and our grandchildren.* (18 March 2008; 6 May 2008, my emphasis)

(138)   The children of America are not those kids, they are our kids, and we will *not let them fall behind* in a 21st century economy. (18 March 2008, my emphasis)

(139)   That is why I've laid out an ambitious urban poverty plan that will help make sure *no child begins the race of life behind the starting line.* (21 June 2008, my emphasis)

(140)   Now it's our turn. It's our turn to make those sacrifices so the next generation doesn't have to. Our turn to *open the doors of opportunity* that our daughters and granddaughters will one day *walk through.* (20 September 2008, my emphasis)

Example (137) is the most straightforward: if Americans intend to provide opportunities for their children they need to move in the same direction. By doing so, they will create a future for the next generations. In (138) the subjects of the metaphorical motion are children themselves and the role of their symbolic parental figures is that of helping them to move on. Example (139) is based on the LIFE IS A RACE metaphor and refers to the parental role of the government in making sure that no one is left behind. In (140), the role of the older generation is that of removing barriers so as to allow free motion forward to the generations to come.

In addition to being expressed as forward motion, 'opportunity' is also depicted as upward motion. This is exemplified in the passages that follow:

(141)   [the legacy of discrimination ... must be addressed] ...; by providing this generation with *ladders of opportunity* that were unavailable for previous generations. (18 March 2008, my emphasis)

(142)   When we transform our energy policy and *lift our children out of poverty*, it will be because she worked to help make it happen. (3 June 2008, my emphasis)

(143)   These are the changes and reforms we need. A new era of responsibility and accountability on Wall Street and in Washington.

Common-sense regulations to prevent a crisis like this from ever happening again. Investments in the technology and innovation that will restore prosperity and lead to new jobs and a new economy for the 21st century. *Bottom-up growth that gives every American a fair shot at the American dream.* (10 October 2008, my emphasis)

The metaphorical expression *ladders of opportunity* in example (141) relies on the well-known metaphorical notion of the social climb as an indication of achievement. The motion upwards that is allowed by the ladder stands for the value of 'opportunity'. Providing opportunity also involves improving the lives of children and in excerpt (142) this is communicated via the conventional metaphor GOOD IS UP, as lexicalized in *lift*. In example (143), the motion upwards refers to the general economic resurgence of the nation and it is presented as a prerequisite for 'opportunity'. In addition, 'opportunity' is also metaphorically expressed in the idiomatic phrase *fair shot.*

Especially when it refers to everyone, the value of 'opportunity' is measured in terms of relative distance from ego. This means that providing real opportunity for people is expressed metaphorically by the idea that something is placed within reach and hence is graspable. Consider the examples below:

(144)   But my family gave me love, they gave me education, and most of all they gave me hope – hope that in America, *no dream is beyond our grasp* if we reach for it, and fight for it, and work for it. (12 February 2008, my emphasis)

(145)   And we can do something more. We can *tear down the barriers that keep the American dream out of reach* for so many Americans. (28 June 2008, my emphasis)

(146)   So for many families, these anxieties are getting worse, not better. People are starting to lose faith in the American dream, which is the idea that if you work hard, you can build a better life not just for yourselves but for your children and grandchildren. A lot of people feel *like that dream is slipping further out of reach.* (1 August 2008, my emphasis)

Excerpts (144), (145) and (146) elaborate the idea of the American Dream, which in itself stands for the opportunity granted to everyone who is ready to invest one's energies for getting it. The dream is reified. It is the object one needs to reach and grasp with one's hands. Reaching the dream is not easy and the difficulty involved in the action is conveyed by distinct metaphors. In (144) the activity calls for a fight. In (145) the object is kept under custody behind barriers that need to be broken down. In (146) the object is not in a fixed position, but is progressively moving away.

6.6.4   Care: help for the people in need

One way to communicate the value of 'care' as 'help for the people in need' is via the source domain of MOTION UPWARDS. As the passages below indicate, the value is mostly lexicalized in the verbal phrase *lift up*.

(147)   The man I met more than twenty years ago is a man who helped introduce me to my Christian faith, a man who spoke to me about our obligations to love one another; to care for the sick and *lift up the poor*. (18 March 2008, my emphasis)

(148)   As some of you may know, after college, I went to work with a group of churches as a community organizer in Chicago – so I could help *lift up neighborhoods* that were struggling after the local steel plants closed. (21 June 2008, my emphasis)

(149)   I'm thinking of [...] and so many other mayors across this country, who are finding new ways to *lift up their communities*. (21 June 2008, my emphasis)

(150)   Finally, we've got to do more to *help folks at the bottom of the ladder climb* into the middle class. (10 July 2008, my emphasis)

The nurturer appears as the person whose moral duty consists in making people feel better and thus allowing for their metaphorical rise, their motion from a lower to a higher position.

6.7   Metaphorical (re)building and repairing

As pointed out above, the source domain of CONSTRUCTION is useful for presenting certain facets of 'cooperation'. However, metaphorical building is not exclusive to this value. Obama's metaphorical worldview consists of many abstract entities that are to be built and many others that need to be fixed. The notions of (re)constructing and repairing evoked by terms like *(re)build* and *fix* contribute to create an impression of concreteness, dynamism and novelty. They entail the presence of a constructor or repairer, of someone who can make things with physical work and is capable of mending them if they fall apart. Obama's narrative abounds with metaphorical objects that he suggests should be (re)constructed. They include the economy, the green energy sector, diplomatic partnerships, the middle class and the capacity to deal with nuclear, biological and cyber threats.

This process of reification also involves other entities that are depicted as broken, including the public education system, the health care system, and the promises and failures of No Child left Behind. Here follow some examples:

'Care: investing in education'

(151)   They [the people I've met during this campaign] believe we can train our workers for those new jobs, and keep the most

productive workforce, the most competitive workforce in the world if we *fix our public education system* by investing in what works and finding out what doesn't; [...]. (14 April 2008, my emphasis)

(152) We need to focus on *fixing* and improving *our public schools*; not throwing our hands up and walking away from them. (13 July 2008, my emphasis)

'Care: caring for children'

(153) And unlike Senator McCain, I'll make sure every working woman has the chance to not just get by, but get ahead – to save, invest, *build a nest egg*, and provide a better life for their children. (10 July 2008, my emphasis)

(154) Bringing about that future begins with *fixing the broken promises of No Child Left Behind*. Now, I believe that the goals of this law – educating every child with an excellent teacher, closing the achievement gap, ensuring more accountability and higher standards – were right. (13 July 2008, my emphasis)

(155) We must *fix the failures of No Child Left Behind*. [...] But Democrats have to realize that *fixing No Child Left Behind* is not enough to prepare our children for a global economy. (9 September 2008, my emphasis)

'Care: help for the people in need'

(156) But now we need a rescue plan for the middle class. If we're going to *rebuild this economy* from the bottom up, it has to start on Main Street – not just the big banks on Wall Street. (15 October 2008, my emphasis)

(157) The rescue plan that passed Congress was a necessary first step to easing this credit crisis, but if we're going to *rebuild this economy* from the bottom up, we need an immediate rescue plan for the middle-class – and that's what I'll offer as President of the United States. (20 October 2008, my emphasis)

'Care: caring for people'

(158) If we're going to *rebuild this economy* from the bottom up, it has to start with our small businesses on Main Street – not just the big banks on Wall Street. (10 October 2008, my emphasis)

'Care: caring for the environment'

(159) We can *build an American green energy sector* by investing in renewable energies like wind power, solar power, and the next generation biofuels. (1 August 2008, my emphasis)

'We: non-confrontational diplomacy'

(160)   I will *build new partnerships* to defeat the threats of the 21st century: terrorism and nuclear proliferation; poverty and genocide; climate change and disease. (28 August 2008, my emphasis)

'Protection: protection from nuclear, biological and cyber threats'

(161)   Today, we will focus on nuclear, biological, and cyber threats – three 21st century threats that have been neglected for the last eight years. It's time to break out of Washington's conventional thinking that has failed to keep pace with unconventional threats. In doing so, we'll better ensure the safety of the American people, while *building our capacity* to deal with other challenges – from public health to privacy. (16 July 2008, my emphasis)

(162)   We need to prevent terrorists or spies from hacking into our national security networks. We need to *build the capacity* to identify, isolate, and respond to any cyber-attack. (16 July 2008, my emphasis)

'Social rights: employment for everyone, health care for everyone'

(163)   Finally, change means *building an economy* that rewards work, creates jobs you can raise a family on [...]. (20 September 2008, my emphasis)

(164)   That's why I'm going to stop giving tax breaks to companies that ship jobs overseas, and start *rebuilding the middle class* by helping companies create jobs here in Ohio. (10 October 2008, my emphasis)

(165)   If I am President, I will finally *fix our broken health care system*. (10 October 2008; 20 October 2008, my emphasis)

6.8   Concluding remarks on values and metaphors

The analysis presented in this chapter has shown that while metaphors inhabit the textual space of Obama's political speeches, the expression of moral values is not necessarily metaphorical. Indeed, a general tendency has been observed for moral values to be communicated using literal language. This indicates that the language Obama uses to promote nurturant values and to downplay Strict Father values is not intrinsically metaphorical.

After having proved that no binding links exist between values and metaphors, it is also worth noticing how certain values lend themselves more easily to a metaphorical conceptualization. These include, in particular, the NP values of 'fair taxation/distribution of money', 'cooperation', 'unity', 'opportunity for children', 'caring for people', 'supporting nurturant professions', 'empowering people', 'help for the people in need', 'opportunity for everyone' and 'protection' as well as the criticized SF values of 'distribution of wealth', 'hierarchy' and 'self-discipline/self-reliance'.

Another significant observation concerning metaphoricity in relation to the expression of values has to do with the type of metaphors that are used and the strategies employed. Obama often communicates key values via metaphorical fixed phrases. In detail, he shows lexical preferences for the metaphorical compounds *tax break* and *tax cut*, the metaphorical nominal phrase *army of teachers*, the metaphorical adverbial *from the bottom up* and the metaphorical idiomatic expression *pull oneself up by the bootstraps*. Each of these phrases is used for evoking a specific moral value and it works via a metaphorical understanding of that concept. Thus, the notion of 'fair distribution of money/taxation' is presented metaphorically in terms of reduction of a physical object (*tax break/cut*), that is to say it relies on a process of reification. The concept of 'supporting nurturant professions' is conveyed through a military metaphor that suggests a conceptualization of teachers as soldiers (*army of teachers*). The idea of 'empowering people' is rendered trough a metaphorical understanding of empowerment as motion upwards (*from the bottom up*). Finally, criticism of the SF value of 'self-discipline/self-reliance' is obtained relying on a lexicalized metaphorical phrase (*pull oneself up by the bootstraps*).

The presence of military metaphors to talk about values is arguably the most striking feature that characterizes Obama's rhetoric. In addition to the military metaphor that uniquely marks the value of 'supporting nurturant professions (teachers)', a lexicon that is metaphorically belligerent is used to describe a range of nurturant values. The concept of a metaphorical fight for care is endorsed recurrently in Obama's speeches. The Democratic candidate draws an image of himself as a fighter ready to use his strength for improving education and health care, providing employment, helping and protecting citizens, granting people equal rights and opportunities and addressing the needs of children and veterans. Such metaphorical language usage calls for an understanding of strength as a quality that is at the service of nurturance. To phrase it differently, Obama's words celebrate the strength to be nurturers.

We conclude with a remark regarding the presence of other general metaphors for presenting values. The analysis of the corpus reveals that Obama is rather conventional in his usage of metaphors for discussing values. The source domains in terms of which metaphorical values are described can be grouped into three major semantic categories: MOTION, ORIENTATION and CONSTRUCTION. None of them gives rise to a metaphorical interpretation of values that is idiosyncratic. They rather determine the occurrence of a good range of metaphorical expressions that are well entrenched in the English language (that is, *fix the education system, build an economy, lift up the poor*). Overall, this underlines the fact that, in Obama's speeches, metaphors do not play a decisive role in the expression of values. Furthermore, these findings demonstrate that a testing of Lakoff's models needs to go beyond an investigation of metaphorical language.

7
Values and Lexical Preferences in Obama's Speeches

The analysis presented in this chapter focuses on the lexicon of Obama's speeches in his 2008 election campaign with the aim of shedding light on: (a) the role of highly frequent lexical items that Obama uses to express his political message to the American electorate, and (b) the relation between lexemes and Obama's political moral framing according to either a NP or a SF worldview.

Wordsmith 4 was used for data analysis. The first step involved searching for highly frequent content words. These were extracted from the automatically generated Wordlist of lexical items in the corpus. To single out collocational patterns and to check for Obama's framing of individual words, the concordances of lexical items were then taken into consideration.

Furthermore, this chapter also discusses the frequency and contextual use of words that in previous studies were associated with either the SF or the NP models (Ahrens 2009, 2011, Ahrens and Yat Mei Lee 2009). This comparison shows that, in contrast to previous research, considering the actual use of words in context is essential for assigning words to either a SF or a NP model of political framing.

7.1 Obama's lexical preferences

The selection and combination of words is very important for every politician addressing an audience, but it becomes crucial for American leaders of political parties when they run their race for the presidency. As mentioned in Chapter 2, presidential candidates can rely on the collaboration of communication experts. These professionals prepare the drafts of electoral speeches with great care, relying on their personal knowledge of the candidate. Indeed, speeches need to speak the mind and the heart of the person who delivers them. Obama's speeches conform to this American rhetorical tradition. They are tailored to suit his personality and to tell the story he wants to share with the American people. The words of his speeches fabricate his public image in a way which is consonant with the personality of

Obama as an American politician. Starting from these assumptions, we can expect that Obama's lexical preferences reveal interesting facets of his own story.

In order to explore Obama's political message more closely, the lexical analysis started by identifying the 100 most frequent content words he used in his speeches. The complete list of these highly frequent words can be found in Appendix 3. This list was obtained by filtering out the first 100 content words from a prearranged lexical set that was organized by frequency and included all the words in the corpus. Even though the definition of a content word may appear rather straightforward, it is important to specify which words were not taken into account to generate the pool of highly frequent lexical items: determiners (articles, demonstratives, possessives, distributives, wh-words, quantifiers), pronouns, prepositions, conjunctions, modal verbs, auxiliaries and proper nouns. In addition to this, another methodological criterion was applied, lemmatization. This means that for each of the identified highly frequent content words, frequency also includes the inflected forms found in the corpus (for example, *care, cares, cared, caring*). Furthermore, in cases of verb/noun conversion (for example, *work, change, help*) the count is inclusive of all nominal and verbal inflected forms.

Based on these criteria, the 30 most frequent content words are reported in Table 7.1.

Table 7.1   List of the 30 most frequent content words in the corpus

Lexemes	No of occurrences
American	386
make	349
America	299
year	292
work	285
need	281
country	275
change	275
time	272
job	258
tax	237
people	210
new	209
children	203
know	201
come	191

(*continued*)

Table 7.1   Continued

Lexemes	No of occurrences
good	187
get	185
family	177
president	175
help	175
go	174
say	170
want	169
give	158
pay	158
economy	157
now	155
state	153
take	151

A first observation regarding the words reported in Table 7.1 has to do with the fact that they appear to fit at least three distinct types of functions: provide context, describe content and stimulate appeal. Considering the relatively high number of words involved in this discussion, each of the three categories is discussed below in a separate sub-section.

7.1.1   Words providing context

This first category consists of words that set the context in that they provide details concerning the specificities of place, time and people. These are terms such as *America, country* and *state*, which provide Obama's story with clear territorial boundaries; *now, time,* and *year*, which refer to the present of the election campaign; *President*, which gives a name to the hero of the narrative; and *American* and *people*, which designate the other major participants in the story.

Unsurprisingly, the word *country* typically collocates with *this* and *our* to designate America, and the most frequent clusters[1] where the word is used are *in this country* and *across this country*. In Obama's speeches, *country* and *America* define one and the same concept: the nation of the American people. The word *state*, on the other hand, has more specific referents that include, for instance, the state of Florida, the state of California and the state of Maryland. Thus, the word *state* is used to indicate the place where a speech is delivered and metonymically it refers to the people who live there.

The term *now* communicates the urgency of Obama's message, as clearly signaled by its frequent occurrence in combination with *right* to form the phrase *right now* and the clauses *(right) now we need* and *(right) now is the time*. This works very well together with the frequent collocates *this time* and *this year* and the expression *it's time to*. To quote one of Martin Luther King's memorable speeches, it is the 'fierce urgency of now' that Obama emphasizes throughout his campaign. What he asks his fellow countrymen to do is to put their efforts together and write a new chapter in the history of America.

The word *President* projects Obama in his future role of political leader of the country. That's why the term is used almost exclusively to talk about this specific scenario in expressions such as *as President, when I'm President, if I'm elected President* and *I'll be the President*, where Obama gives his electorate good reasons to cast the ballot for him. While the word *President* profiles Obama, the term *American* is used in the combinations *American people, every American* and *American workers*. The word *American* is chiefly associated with the nominal concept of Americans to refer to Obama's addressees. Two remarkable exceptions are represented by the phrases *the American Dream* and *the American story*. Both of them indicate the specificity of American political discourse and, more broadly, of American culture. They encapsulate the cultural belief that everyone can do it, if they work for it, and the related assumption that, as Obama says, 'the American story has never been about things coming easy' (10 October 2008; 27 October 2008), which reinforces the idea that people need to work hard if they intend to achieve anything.

As just mentioned, the term *people* is chiefly used in the phrase *the American people*. Besides being American, *people* are qualified as *young* and *working*. Interestingly, the word is also employed to convey a message of inclusivity as expressed in the phrases *one people* and *people of all faiths*, as well as in the binominals *people in small towns and big cities* and *people of every creed and color*. Furthermore, the term *people* can signal Obama's closeness to Americans. This happens when he makes his story personal and says 'the people I've met (during this campaign)' (14 April 2008).

7.1.2   Words describing content(s)

This second category defines the content(s) of the election campaign. In other words, it brings together the terms that designate the general topics addressed on these political occasions. Words pertaining to this group include *job, tax, economy, children* and *family*. While these are the issues that are usually addressed by every politician, their framing in the context of the campaign is significant.

In his speeches Obama uses the word *job* to describe a sad scenario of *job losses* and of jobs disappearing overseas. This allows him to emphasize the necessity to spur *job growth* and *job creation* so that every person can have work that pays their bills.

As pointed out earlier in our discussion, the term *tax* is used in the compounds *tax break, tax cut* and *tax relief* to suggest that people with a lower income should pay fewer taxes, whereas the wealthiest Americans have the moral responsibility to pay the largest amount of taxes.

When referring to the present state of the American *economy*, Obama uses expressions such as *in turmoil, in serious trouble, fragile, broken* and *to be fixed*, which depict a scenario of chaos, danger and destruction and, therefore, call for immediate intervention. In addition to suggesting that the economy should go *in a new direction* and *change*, Obama also describes the type of action that should be taken and he proposes ways to transform the economy. In detail, in order to *save the economy, put it back on track* and *make it grow*, Obama says it is necessary to *strengthen* and *(re)build* it. Significantly, the creation of a new economy entails a clearly stated ideological orientation. Obama talks of a new economy that *grows from the bottom-up, works for all Americans* and *honors the dignity of work*. He also refers to the importance of making *the global economy work for working Americans*. A key phrase in the campaign is the following: 'Change is building an economy that rewards not just wealth, but the work and workers who created it' (3 June 2008).

When talking about *children*, who are described as *our children*, and so the children of the American country, the discussion revolves around education. Children need to get good quality education, they cannot stay any longer in *crumbling schools* that are *stealing their future*, and they need an *army of new teachers* who are better trained and can give them more opportunities. The government can help in this, but parents should do their part too. They should *spend more time with our children, help our children with their homework* and *switch off the TV and read to them*. Children should get a *world-class education* because they need to be *prepared to compete in a global economy*. Obama appeals to a feeling of proud nationalism when he compares *our children* with *the children in Beijing/Bangalore/China/India/Berlin* to suggest that American children must be better than the children who live in other parts of the world. American children cannot come second. This is the clear message with which no American is expected to disagree. Besides education, other concerns regard health and protection. The government takes on the social responsibility to *provide more children with health insurance* and *leave our children a planet that is safer*.

The word *family* is used to designate, on a general level, *American families* or, more specifically, *working families* and *average families* who have to face difficult times. Obama also refers to his own family, who taught him *important lessons* and *gave him love*.

7.1.3   Words searching for appeal

The third of the categories unites terms that are expected to exert some form of appeal on the electorate. These are words that the candidate uses to communicate a distinctive ethos and produce certain emotional responses (pathos). Under the label of appeal we can put words such as *change, need, new, help, make, know, work, come, say* and *pay*. These words speak of the candidate's positioning towards issues and of his moral standing. They say something about his commitment and his attitude towards Americans.

Unsurprisingly, the word *change* is among the ten most frequent words in the corpus (see Appendix 3). Change was indeed a key concept during Obama's 2008 election campaign. Back then, TV and radio commentators spent a lot of time reminding the entire world that Obama's campaign was all about change. The concept was celebrated as a sort of panacea for twenty-first century American politics. Notwithstanding its bare simplicity (or maybe because of it), the word *change* became extremely powerful. Nobody could really think of Obama without connecting him to the idea of change. Before the primary season started, 'change we can believe in' was the undisputable motto for the Democratic Senator (see Obama for America 2008). After that, the motto was replaced with a new one 'change we need'. The corpus confirms that the two words *change* and *need* are mostly used in combination. Change is what the American people need because of what has happened during the eight years of the Bush administration. Change is needed because the lives of many Americans have been transformed for the worse, and this has affected people to such an extent that they cannot bear it any longer. As Obama says, people are *hungry for change*, they desperately *seek for* it, *call for* it and *stand for* it. So, the time is ripe for something new to come and Obama offers America this much needed transformation. He promises to change Washington, the country and the world. One might wonder why Obama decided to introduce a second motto about change in his campaign. It is very likely that the new motto, 'change we need', was not intended to replace the previous one, but rather to implement it. At a time when the competition became more intense and the Republican adversary McCain also started talking about bringing change to America, it was important for Obama to say more about this term or actually make clear that it was not just an empty word. This is why Obama doesn't only speak of *change* but, more significantly, refers to *real change*, as if implying that what McCain proposes has nothing to do with it. What is also interesting to observe, is that Obama takes great care providing clear definitions of the concept of change. Throughout the selected speeches, it was possible to find a number of statements describing the actual conceptualization, so to say, of change. Table 7.2 is meant to provide an overview of these explanations. The table also shows how the concept of change is appearing in different values.

As Table 7.2 shows, the word *change* is a vehicle to transmit important messages. The word is used to convey some of the key values on which Obama's campaign is based. Interestingly, the urge to define this concept becomes stronger starting from August 2008, when the direct confrontation with McCain started.

The leitmotif of change is partly reinforced by the use of the adjective *new* to suggest the need to take a *new direction* or a *new course*. Thus, *change* and *new* jointly indicate the beginning of a new phase in American politics and in the lives of American people. But the word *new* is used for other purposes too. In particular, *new* is employed to convey the concept of increase, or, in other words, the idea that more of something is necessary. To this aim, *new* appears very frequently in combination with *jobs* and *teachers*. Obama offers *new jobs* (especially green jobs) and *new teachers* to the Americans.

208

Table 7.2 Definitions of change in value-laden paragraphs

Speech	Definition of change	Value
20 May 2008	**Change is a tax code** that rewards work instead of wealth by cutting taxes for middle-class families, and senior citizens, and **struggling homeowners**; a tax code that rewards businesses that create good jobs here in America instead of the corporations that ship them overseas.	Fairness: fair distribution of money/fair taxation
	Change is a health care plan that guarantees insurance to every American who wants; that brings down premiums for every family who needs it; that stops insurance companies from discriminating and denying coverage to those who need it most.	Social rights: health care for everyone
	Change is an energy policy that doesn't rely on buddying up to the Saudi Royal Family and then begging them for oil – an energy policy that puts a price on pollution and makes the oil companies invest their record profits in clean, renewable sources of energy that will create five million new jobs and leave our children a safer planet.	Care: caring for the environment Social rights: employment for everyone Care: caring for children
	Change is giving every child a world-class education by **recruiting an army of new teachers** with better pay and more support [...]	Chance: opportunity for children Care: Supporting nurturant professions
	Change is ending a war that we never should've started and finishing a war against Al Qaeda in Afghanistan that we never should've ignored. **Change is facing the threats of the twenty-first century** not with bluster, or fear-mongering, or tough talk, but with tough diplomacy, and strong alliances, and confidence in the ideals that have made this nation the last, best hope of Earth. That is the legacy of Roosevelt, and Truman, and Kennedy.	We: non-confrontational diplomacy
3 June 2008	**Change is a foreign policy that doesn't begin and end with a war** that should've never been authorized and never been waged.	Strength: display of force[2]
	Change is realizing that meeting today's threats requires not just our firepower, but **the power of our diplomacy** [...]	We: non-confrontational diplomacy
	Change is building an economy that rewards not just wealth, but **the work and workers who created it.**	Care: caring for people

(continued)

Table 7.2 Continued

Speech	Definition of change	Value
28 August 2008	**Change means a tax code** that doesn't reward the lobbyists who wrote it, but the American workers and small businesses who deserve it.	Fairness: fair distribution of money/fair taxation
12 September 2008	It's time for change. And let me tell you exactly what that change will look like. **Change means a tax code** that doesn't reward the lobbyists who wrote it, but the American workers and seniors and small businesses who deserve it.	Fairness: fair distribution of money/fair taxation
20 September 2008	**Change is** finally **closing that pay gap.** It's unacceptable that women in this country are losing thousands of dollars each year – money you could use for gas or groceries or college tuition.	We: equality
	Change isn't a President who thinks Roe vs. Wade is a flawed decision and whose party platform outlaws abortion, even in cases of rape and incest. **Change is a President who will stand up for choice** – who understands that five men on the Supreme Court don't know better than women and their doctors what's best for a woman's health.	Freedom: right to abortion
	Change means refusing to accept an America where staying home with a new baby is treated as an unpaid vacation, and **taking time off to take a sick parent to the hospital is a fireable offense. Change means making sure people have paid sick days and tax credits to help with childcare,** and expanding the Family and Medical Leave Act to help millions of people care for their kids and their parents and participate in school activities like parent-teacher conferences and assemblies.	Care: caring for children Care: caring for one's family Social rights: health care for everyone
	Change means keeping the promise of affordable, accessible health care for every single American.	Social rights: health care for everyone
	Change means having a Vice President who's spent his career working to improve women's lives.	Care: caring for women
	Finally, **change means building an economy that rewards work** [...]	Care: caring for workers
27 September 2008	**Change means a tax code** that doesn't reward the lobbyists who wrote it, but the American workers and small businesses who deserve it.	Fairness: fair distribution of money/fair taxation

The word *help* embraces some aspects of Obama's nurturant attitude. In the speeches, he presents a whole plethora of needy subjects who will receive his support. Obama's help is first and foremost addressed to *hard-working families* who are *struggling* in the economic crisis and find it hard to make ends meet. So, he proposes to help families *refinance their mortgage, stay in their homes, pay for college, cope with multiple tours (of duty)*. His help then extends to other social categories such as *workers, students, children, innocent homebuyers and struggling homeowners, the middle class*, and *folks at the bottom of the ladder*. He also stretches out his helping hand to *small businesses, local communities, states and local governments*. More inclusively, his help seems to overcome any form of division when he claims that it needs to be directed to *others, our fellow citizens* and *people of all faiths*.

The term *make* is used consistently in the verbal phrase *make sure* to shed light on important aspects of Obama's public image. The frequent use of *make sure* helps in drawing an image of Obama as a scrupulous, assuring and caring politician. He appears as the one who doesn't let things just happen. On the contrary, he is the conscientious and principled person who checks back on things to be certain all is moving in the right direction. The most obvious response to this is trust. So, the recurrent use of *make sure* in the speeches can be expected to generate some form of bonding between Obama and his electorate. The corpus provides multiple examples of Obama's caring attitude. Here follows a small selection of them: 'we need to make sure that veterans have the same opportunities that my grandfather had' (15 April 2008), 'we'll make sure American workers and American companies can thrive in a 21ˢᵗ century economy' (5 August 2008), 'we'll make sure you can afford a college education' (28 August 2008), 'I'll make sure the minimum wage rises each year to keep up with rising costs' (10 July 2008), 'I will make certain those companies stop discriminating against those who are sick and need care the most' (28 August 2008), 'we'll make sure these cars are built not in Japan, not in China, but right here in the United States of America' (5 August 2008), 'I'll make sure every working woman has the chance to not just get by, but get ahead' (10 July 2008), 'to make sure all our kids have that chance' (13 July 2008), 'we can make sure that the millions of Latinos who are uninsured get the same health care that I get' (28 June 2008), 'we need to make sure that every child, everywhere gets a world-class education' (3 May 2008) and 'we will make sure you can afford your tuition' (10 October 2008).

The mental verb *know* is mostly used with the first person singular and plural pronouns. Obama and his fellow Americans are depicted as knowledgeable people who share a very practical form of wisdom. According to the narrative, they know that the situation they are facing is difficult, but they also know how they can steer themselves out of it. The election offers a real chance for immediate relief. The American people are also depicted as being aware that the road to change won't be easy and that it will take more than one election to fix all of America's problems.

The word *work* occurs in the corpus to express different ideas. On the one hand, *work* is connected to the possibility of changing the country and moving in a new direction. In this case, the usual formula prescribes that Americans must *work together* to achieve that goal. On other occasions, Obama emphasizes the value of *hard work* and the American belief that if you work hard and make sacrifices, you can have a better future and realize your dreams. Alternatively, work is presented as a basic human right. This is why, as he says, people *willing to work* should be given a job, and work should be justly rewarded.

In relation to the verb *come*, the most significant combination found in the corpus is *come together*. Obama invites people to *come together* as one nation to solve *monumental problems* and challenges – *a falling economy, two wars, a chronic health care crisis, a potentially devastating climate change, a crumbling education* and increasing unemployment. When Obama asks people to come together, he formulates a message of unity against all forms of racial, ethnic, social and religious division. Whites, Blacks, Latinos, Asians, immigrants, rich and poor, old and young, parents and educators, people of all faiths and citizens all across America are invited to *come together*. Obama's words also encourage people to do things together. Thus, the phrase *come together* functions as a call for cooperation to build a new and stronger America, a country that is more prosperous and more just. It is only by coming together that people can change America.

Similarly to *new*, the adjective *good* collocates preferably with *jobs*, especially in the clause *create good jobs*, which is used to invoke Obama's commitment to create good, well-paying jobs in America. In line with this, the inflected form *better* occurs in the following collocations: *better pay, better future* and *better life*. While *good* and *better* define opportunities that are open to American citizens if they vote for Obama, the superlative form *best* is used together with *schools* to refer to the institutions that Obama (and his sister) attended. Here, Obama says something of himself by publicly referring to the schools where he graduated. In this respect, he shares his personal story with the electorate. At the same time, he emphasizes the importance of high-level education for individual achievement.

A significant use of the verb *say* involves the creation of a hypothetical dialogue between Americans and McCain. In this illusionary conversation, the American people address their interlocutor in a deprecatory manner by saying *not this time, not this year, eight is enough*, or *enough is enough*. In this way, Obama's accusations of eight years of unscrupulous Republican leadership turns into the blame from all Americans who want *no more of the same*.

Obama uses the verb *pay* positively to indicate that the American people should be the receivers of money. Accordingly, he refers to the need to create *jobs that pay well*, to provide teachers with *better pay*, and to guarantee *equal pay* for women. When Obama alludes to these measures, his focus is solely on beneficiaries (workers, teachers, women). The only concrete payers he identifies are corporations that will have to *pay for their pollution*. Conversely, in the scenario that depicts the Americans as the givers of money, the image that is drawn is one of affliction. Families can't pay for the rising costs of everything and students can't pay for their tuition. These are the real problems that the government should solve.

7.1.4   Further considerations on highly frequent words

The highly frequent words that have not been discussed in the preceding subsections (that is, *get, go, want, give* and *take*) do not show any clear pattern that would allow them to fit one of the three identified categories (context, content(s) and appeal). These words do not mark Obama's election campaign speeches in any distinctive way.

In addition to the 30 most frequent words reported in Table 7.1, there is another highly frequent word (see Appendix 3) that requires some discussion. It is the verb *stand*. When this verb occurs in the speeches, it does not solely refer to the literal meaning of 'supporting oneself on the feet in an erect position'. The verb is also used in the phrasal verb construction *stand with* to convey the metaphorical meaning of 'taking someone's side and giving them support'. The related phrasal verb *stand up* is also present in the corpus and its metaphorical sense is exploited consistently. More than expressing the rise to an erect position, *stand up* signifies a symbolic act of protest and dissent. By employing *stand up*, Obama incites Americans to take action and make change happen. This strategic use of the verb is particularly evident in the paragraphs where he conveys moral values. Table 7.3 provides a number of examples in value-laden paragraphs.

Table 7.3   *Standing* as a symbolic action in value-laden paragraphs

Speech	Symbolic expression	Value
5 February 2008	Their voices echoed from the hills of New Hampshire to the deserts of Nevada, where teachers and cooks and kitchen workers **stood up** to say that maybe Washington doesn't have to be run by lobbyists anymore.	We: unity
	We need you to **stand with** us, and work with us, and help us prove that together, ordinary people can still do extraordinary things.	We: cooperation
12 February 2008	It's time to **stand up** and reach for what's possible, because together, people who love their country can change it.	We: unity

(*continued*)

Table 7.3 Continued

Speech	Symbolic expression	Value
	It's a game where trade deals like NAFTA ship jobs overseas and force parents to compete with their teenagers to work for minimum wage at Wal-Mart. That's what happens when the American worker doesn't have a voice at the negotiating table, when leaders change their positions on trade with the politics of the moment, and that's why we need a President who will listen to Main Street – not just Wall Street; a President who will **stand with** workers not just when it's easy, but when it's hard.	Care: caring for workers
3 May 2008	It's about whether this country, at this moment, will continue to stand by while the wealthy few prosper at the expense of the hardworking many, or whether we'll **stand up** and reclaim the American dream for every American.	Chance: opportunity for everyone
6 May 2008	I trust the American people to realize that while we don't need big government, we do need a government that **stands up** for families who are being tricked out of their homes by Wall Street predators; a government that **stands up** for the middle-class by giving them a tax break [...]	Care: caring for families Fairness: fair distribution of money/fair taxation
	The college student I met in Iowa who works the night shift after a full day of class and still can't pay the medical bills for a sister who's ill – she can't afford four more years of a health care plan that only takes care of the healthy and the wealthy; that allows insurance companies to discriminate and deny coverage to those Americans who need it most. She needs us to **stand up** to those insurance companies and pass a plan that lowers every family's premiums and gives every uninsured American the same kind of coverage that Members of Congress give themselves.	Social rights: health care for everyone
1 July 2008	And my Council for Faith-Based and Neighborhood Partnerships will also have a broader role – it will help set our national agenda. Because if we are going to do something about the injustice of millions of children living in extreme poverty, we need interfaith coalitions like the Let Justice Roll campaign **standing up** for the powerless.	Care: caring for children
10 July 2008	That's why I **stood up** for equal pay in the Illinois State Senate, and helped pass a law to give 330,000 more women protection from paycheck discrimination. That's why I've been fighting to pass legislation in the Senate, so that employers don't get away with shortchanging hardworking women.	We: equality

(continued)

214

Table 7.3 Continued

Speech	Symbolic expression	Value
	And that's why I'll continue to **stand up** for equal pay as President. Senator McCain won't – and that's a real difference in this election.	
	It means **standing up** for paid leave – so I'll invest $1.5 billion to help create paid leave systems across America – and I'll require employers to provide all their workers with at least seven paid sick days a year. Senator McCain has no clear plan to expand paid leave and sick leave – and that's a real difference in this election.	Care: caring for families
	Unlike Senator McCain, I'll work as a partner with our unions, because we know that when it comes to **standing up** for women's rights in the workplace, our unions are second to none – and it's time we start giving them the support they deserve.	We: equality
13 July 2008	And if you **stand up** with me these next four months; if you march with me and knock on doors and make phone calls and register voters, and talk to your friends and co-workers and neighbors; then I promise you this: we will win this election; we will change education in this country; and we will bring about a better future for our children and for this country we love.	Chance: opportunity for children Care: supporting/ investing in education
28 August 2008	You don't defeat a terrorist network that operates in eighty countries by occupying Iraq. You don't protect Israel and deter Iran just by talking tough in Washington. You can't truly **stand up for** Georgia when you've strained our oldest alliances. If John McCain wants to follow George Bush with more tough talk and bad strategy, that is his choice – but it is not the change we need.	Strength: display of force
12 September 2008	To pay for these tax cuts, I'll **stand up** to special interest carve-outs, close corporate loopholes and off-shore tax havens, and ask the wealthiest Americans to give back a portion of the Bush tax cuts.	Fairness: fair taxation/ distribution of money
27 September 2008	Well North Carolina, I know what we need to do. We need to stop giving those tax cuts to corporations and CEOs on Wall Street, and start **standing up** for families out on Main Street.	Fairness: fair distribution of money/fair taxation
10 October 2008	But we should not put taxpayer money at unnecessary risk. Taxpayers should not have all the downside without any of the upside. That's a principle that I've fought for, that's a principle that I'll maintain, and that's a principle that I'll **stand up** for as President.	Care: caring for people

(continued)

Table 7.3 Continued

Speech	Symbolic expression	Value
20 October 2008	And if you **stand with** me, I promise you – we will win Florida, we will win this election, and then you and I – together – will change this country and change this world. Thank you, God bless you, and may God bless America.	We: unity

As Table 7.3 shows, the verb 'stand up' often occurs with a concomitant expression of values. This suggests that the word is used strategically to reinforce Obama's moral message.

7.2 Obama's lexical choices and Lakoff's models

Among the studies that have applied Lakoff's models to the analysis of American political language, just a few focused specifically on the lexicon (Ahrens 2006, 2011, Ahrens and Yat Mei Lee 2009). They investigated terms that can be associated to either the SF or the NP models. For these studies, lists of words were established and searched for in different corpora (see Chapter 3).

In this chapter, the same pool of lexical items is considered, and these items are taken as a starting point to find out their actual meaning and framing in context. For the purpose of the lexical analysis in this book, the words in Ahrens (2006, 2011) and Ahrens and Yat Mei Lee (2009) are classified in three sets. The first set of words consists of gender and family terms that can be related to Lakoff's models. The second set brings together NP lexemes. The third set is made up of SF words.

7.2.1 Gender and family words

The group of gender and family words is based on Ahrens (2006) and consists of the following words (in alphabetical order): *father, humankind, man, mankind, mother, parent* and *woman*. The search also took into account the inflected forms of each of the nouns. Words that associate more closely to a SF worldview include *man* and *father*, whereas terms that are more in line with a NP moral framing are *woman, mother* and *parent*. In line with results in Ahrens (2006), the general terms *mankind* and *humankind* are expected to be outdated and therefore rarely used. Table 7.4 reports the frequency for each of the selected words.

As Table 7.4 shows, *woman* is used more often than *man*; *mother* occurs more frequently than *father*; and the frequency of *parent* is higher than that of *mother* and significantly higher than that of *father*. Table 7.4 also illustrates that the use of *mankind* and *humankind* is irrelevant. On a general level, these findings allude to the fact that the language of Obama's speeches is more female- than male-oriented, at least as far as the subjects of his discourse are

Table 7.4   Frequency of gender and family terms in the corpus

Gender/family terms	No of occurrences
woman	127
man	90
parent	50
mother	27
father	17
mankind	1
humankind	1
Total	**313**

concerned. It is a fact that he talks more about women and mothers than about men and fathers. Another observation regards the attribution of family roles. The corpus reveals an absolute preference for gender-neutral family roles. Most of all, he refers to parents. These lexical preferences appear more in line with a NP worldview than with a SF vision.

The question now remains of how each of these words is framed in the corpus. Starting with *woman*, Obama uses this word to generate a precise image of women's role and positioning in contemporary American society. First of all, he talks about tough, hardworking women who struggle daily because of the impending economic crisis and ongoing gender discrimination. He tells the stories of women who do more than one job, but cannot afford to pay for the rising costs of life. He denounces the unfairness with which women are still treated today when it comes to their pay. The women he talks about are strong and do a lot, but society is not fair and lets them down. Then there are a few female figures who emerge as role models for society at large. In particular, Obama appears to celebrate (almost glorify) his mother and grandmother, as well as his political competitor Hillary Clinton. Consider the following examples:

(166)   But I think we're up for the challenge. We always have been. That's why I'm standing here today. Because of what my mother and grandmother did for me – because of their hard work and sacrifice and unflagging love. That's why all of us are here today – because of the women who came before us. Women who reached for the ballot and raised families and traveled those lonely roads to be the first ones in those boardrooms and courtrooms and battlefields and factory floors. Women like my friend Hillary Clinton who put those 18 million cracks in that glass ceiling so that my daughters – and all our sons and daughters – could dream a little bigger and reach a little higher. (20 September 2008)

(167) That is particularly true for the candidate who has traveled further on this journey than anyone else. Senator Hillary Clinton has made history in this campaign not just because she's a woman who has done what no woman has done before, but because she's a leader who inspires millions of Americans with her strength, her courage, and her commitment to the causes that brought us here tonight. (3 June 2008)

Obama describes women who work hard both in and out of their families. They are women who are ready to face great challenges and can do it with courage and enthusiasm. His strong women also include the ones who wear uniforms and do their service in the battlefields. When he refers to them, Obama typically uses the binominal construction *the men and women*. This phrase, however, is not employed exclusively to indicate the people who fight in a war. The expression *men and women* is also used as an inclusive form of address that refers to the American people.

The main referents of the term *man* are ordinary American citizens who risk losing their job or have lost it already. They are also young Americans who fight wars in distant lands. Other men who occur in the speeches are Obama's father, his grandfather, Reverend Wright and his competitor McCain. In its plural form, *men* occurs 66 per cent of the times in the expression *men and women*. The corpus contains only one instance of *men* used to refer to all people. This occurrence, however, is not representative of Obama's lexicon, since it is part of a quote from the Declaration of Independence.

The term *parent* is used mostly in the plural form (*parents*) and when it occurs in the singular it has a general collective meaning. When talking of *parents*, Obama takes two different perspectives: that of the relation between parents and their young children and the one between grown-up sons and daughters and their elderly parents. As he describes the first scenario, he emphasizes how parents face the difficult job of raising their children and he encourages them to spend more time with their young ones. He also reminds parents about the importance of getting involved in the education of their children and participating in parent–teacher conferences. Furthermore, he refers to their moral responsibility to think of their children's future and work hard so that future generations can have a better life. With reference to the second scenario, he is not less firm in his words that speak of children's moral responsibility to care for their ailing parents. In both cases, the caring parents he talks about are working parents whose obligations do not make it easy for them to find enough time to spend with their families. The framing of the term *parent* also reflects typical aspects of American political discourse. Accordingly, Obama likes repeating that opportunity is there for everyone who is willing to work for it. So, it doesn't matter who your parents are. Lastly, but not less importantly, Obama shows his concerns for families with a single parent. The fact that he cherishes these untraditional families is confirmed by his own story. He often refers to his single mother, who was able to raise him and his sister with love.

The term *mother* is used almost exclusively in the singular form. Unsurprisingly, its most frequent referent is Obama's own mother (60 per cent). She is described as the caring, hardworking parent and the one who died of ovarian cancer because she couldn't afford the cost of her illness. In addition to his mother, Obama also talks of other working mothers who have to fight with insurance companies and do not have health coverage. So the framing of this word is either personal or triggered by Obama's personal story.

Similarly to the word *mother*, *father* is also chiefly employed in the singular. The referents of this term are: (a) Obama's father, who was attracted by America and saw it as a beacon of hope, as the place to look for a college degree, (b) Obama himself as the father of two young daughters, (c) Obama's father-in-law, a city worker who worked hard to support his family, notwithstanding his illness, and (d) an American father who goes to work before dawn.

Obama's framing of the terms *mother* and *father* does not allow for a clear association between gender and the roles of either carer or provider. However, the female protagonists of Obama's speeches are more likely to be depicted equally as carers and providers, whereas the male counterparts tend to appear more as providers than carers.

7.2.2   Potential NP words

Moving now to the second group of lexical items that are related to Lakoff's models, this contains words that are connected to NP morality. The list of lexemes is drawn from Ahrens and Yat Mei Lee (2009) and Ahrens (2011), and consists of the following terms (in alphabetical order): *aid, anguish, attend, attention, care, empathy, feeling, nourish, nourishment, nurturance, provide, share, sympathy, sorrow, tend, treatment* and *understand*. Table 7.5 illustrates the frequency of these words in the corpus.

Table 7.5 shows that some of the listed NP words are absent in the corpus, that is, *anguish, empathy, nourish, nourishment, nurturance, sorrow* and *tend*.

Unsurprisingly, *care*, the NP word par excellence, is the one that Obama uses the most. *Care* features very often in the collocation *health care* (66.4 per cent) as Obama describes a situation where many people live without health care since they cannot afford its rising costs. To change that, Obama proposes to make health care affordable and available to every American. In addition to *health care*, the corpus also presents other semantically related compounds, such as *health care plan, health care system, health care policy, child care assistance* and *preventive care*. As pointed out in the semantic analysis of Obama's NP values (see Chapter 5), the concept of care is ubiquitous in his speeches. The word *care* itself is used to refer to the need to *provide people with care, care for veterans and troops, care for one's own family, care for elderly parents, care for the sick, care for loved ones* and *care for our citizens*.

Table 7.5 Frequency of potential NP terms in the corpus

NP terms	No of occurrences
care	146
provide	68
understand	47
share	22
attend	10
attention	6
feeling	6
treatment	6
aid	3
sympathy	1
anguish	0
empathy	0
nourish	0
nourishment	0
nurturance	0
sorrow	0
tend	0
Total	315

The basic semantic roles allowed by the verb *provide* are provider, goods/ services and recipient. In the speeches, the implied provider is the government, which makes a commitment to give things to the American people. The beneficiaries of governmental prodigality are families, children and students, workers, homeowners, the sick and the old. According to the electoral narrative, the range of goods and services that will be provided is big, but some of them are more salient. The focus is indeed on education, health care, tax relief and tax credits for struggling people, jobs, ladders of opportunity, and, more broadly, care. Obama is also specific when he commits to *provide workers with paid leave, provide automatic retirement saving accounts, provide affordable housing, provide resources to help people solve the foreclosure crisis*, and *provide more counseling and services to families*. Sometimes (7 per cent), *provide* is used as a synonym for *support*. In these cases, the actual providers are American people who provide for their families.

The most frequent subjects of the verb *understand* are Obama himself (*I*) and the American people (addressed as *they* or directly as *you*). While Obama understands that people are disappointed and hurt, the Americans understand what is at stake in this election (the future of the country). They also understand that government can't solve all the problems. So, the verb *understand* contributes to creating a public image of the Democratic candidate as empathetic and close to his people and their sufferance. Moreover, the use of *understand* makes it appear as a very natural and rational thing that people will vote for him. It is as if he were saying that Americans are aware that this is the only viable option. In addition, by portraying people as conscious of the government's limitations, Obama reduces his own responsibility in implementing new policies. Interestingly, the negative form of the verb is only used in association with the Republican adversary. In contrast to American greatest leaders who *have always understood*, McCain appears as the person who *doesn't understand*. In detail, McCain doesn't understand: what Americans need, the kind of change that people are looking for, the real problems that American citizens face, that America can't afford for four more years of addiction to oil from dictators, and that success depends on education.

The word *share* contributes to creating a feeling of nationalism. The protagonists of Obama's speeches share beliefs, ideas, principles, a common destiny and common hopes. In brief, they share an American identity and the American Dream. The word *share* is also used to encourage economic fairness. This is manifest in the expression *shared prosperity*. When the word *share* is used as a noun, its connotations are typically negative, as in the phrases *our share of mistakes, our share of difficult and uncertain days* and *our share of hard times*. There is just one exception. Obama evokes the nurturant value of fairness when he talks of *our fair share* referring to taxes.

The word *attend* is used with reference to education (*attending college/ schools*) and to the role of parents in caring for their children (*attending parent–teacher conferences*).

The term *attention* doesn't describe the engagement of the government and the targets of its future action. Conversely, *attention* is either distracted or not given. Due to political anger, attention is distracted from solving real problems. Also the crisis is not given enough attention.

Feeling is used to illustrate the psychological state of Americans. The type of feeling described in the speeches is one of anxiety, uncertainty and concern.

The word *treatment* is used in relation to health and medicine to express the need for affordable medical treatments for all American citizens and better treatments for the troops.

The sole occurrence of *aid* is in collocation with *financial* and it has *education* as its target.

Lastly, *sympathy* is present only once in the corpus and it appears in the plural form when Obama makes the following ironic comment on McCain:

> (168)   And just the other day, Senator McCain traveled to Iowa to express his *sympathies* for the victims of the recent flooding. I'm sure they appreciated the sentiment, but they probably would have appreciated it more if he hadn't voted against funding for levees and flood control programs, which he seems to consider pork. (21 June 2008, my emphasis)

This discussion has illustrated how words that have been associated with a NP worldview are used in Obama's speeches. A few comments can be made in this respect. A first general observation has to do with the presence of potential NP words in the corpus. The analysis has revealed that the occurrence of these words might depend on the actual size of the corpus. While large corpora are more likely to contain all of these words, in small corpora only some of them may be present. Secondly, the mere occurrence of these words does not necessarily involve a NP framing of political reality. In the corpus, the terms *care, provide, understand* and *treatment* are chiefly used to convey a nurturant message, whereas some of the terms previously considered to be NP words, that is, *share, attend, attention, feeling, aid* and *sympathy*, do not appear to contribute to Obama's framing of NP values. The word *care* appears as the main linguistic vehicle of the NP attitude that Obama expresses. It is significant to observe that *care* is used in collocations (for example, *health care plan, health care policy, child care assistance, preventive care*) that communicate Obama's intention to help people who suffer by introducing new policies. Similarly to *care*, the term *provide* also contributes to creating a NP image of the government as a provider of (health) care, education, jobs and tax relief for the people who need it. The word *understand* is crucial for transmitting yet another facet of Obama's nurturant message. It emphasizes the importance of mutual support by depicting Obama as empathetic and close to Americans, and the American people as aware of the difficulties that their future leader will have to face.

Having observed the use in context of potential NP words in Obama's speeches, we can now proceed to consider potential SF words.

7.2.3 Potential SF words

The third lexical group contains words that are connected to SF morality. The list of words is derived from Ahrens and Yat Mei Lee (2009) and Ahrens (2011) and consists of the following terms (in alphabetical order): *authority, authorization, authorize, control, decision, determine, direct, dominance, dominate, force, forcefulness, intensity, order, potency, power, right, strength* and *strengthen*. Table 7.6 gives an overview of the frequency of occurrence of each of these SF lexemes in the corpus.

As Table 7.6 indicates, a few of these words never occur in Obama's speeches. They include *authorization, dominance, forcefulness, intensity* and *potency*.

A first general consideration regards the actual status of potential SF words in the corpus. The semantic analysis of Obama's speeches has already revealed that his framing of political issues is consistently nurturant (see Chapter 5). Considering this finding, it is now interesting to observe how words that have been classified as in line with SF morality are used in context.

Starting with the most frequent among the potential SF words, a few comments can be made. After checking for the actual usage of the word *right* in

Table 7.6   Frequency of potential SF terms in the corpus

SF terms	No of occurrences
right	103
power	37
strength	14
strengthen	13
decision	11
force	11
determine	10
authorize	7
direct	7
control	6
authority	3
dominate	3
order	2
authorization	0
dominance	0
forcefulness	0
intensity	0
potency	0
Total	**227**

Obama's speeches, it is possible to state that the word is used half the time as an adverb in the temporal expression *right now* and in the locative *right here* that indicate two fundamental proximal deictic categories of Obama's narrative. *Right* is also employed, though less frequently (15 per cent), as an adjective (for example, *right thing/course/investment/path/goals*) and in the verbal phrase *be right*. The phrase *right and left* occurs only three times. The NP framing of *right* becomes evident when the word is used as a noun (25 per cent), in both the singular and plural forms. Coherently to this framing, Obama refers to: *the right to vote, the right to a quality education, women's right to choose (for abortion), the right to make sure that people's tax dollars are protected, the right to be disappointed and angry with leaders* and *the right to pursue one's individual dreams*. When the noun is used in the plural, the recurrent expressions are: *fundamental rights of our troops, people's rights, women's rights (in the workplace), workers' rights, God-given, inalienable rights, full rights as citizens of the United States* and also, more specifically, *civil rights laws, civil rights movement* and *march for civil rights*.

The framing of the word *power* is distinctively nurturant. This term occurs recurrently (38 per cent) in collocation with wind (*wind power*) and solar (*solar power*) to indicate Obama's will to invest in renewable energy sources and keep the planet greener and safer. In a related vein, he also employs the phrase *new power sources* to emphasize the positive aspects of alternative energy. Still conveying the same idea, *power* is used in its verbal meaning in the expression *power homes (and businesses) using solar panels and wind turbines*. The compound *nuclear power*, on the other hand, is employed only three times, when Obama suggests that safer ways should be found to harness nuclear power. In addition to the forms of concrete power that depend on physical resources, other more abstract types of power are invoked in the speeches. Here, the most relevant are mentioned: *the power of our diplomacy, the power of our ideals, the power to change the country, our power to remake the world as it should be*. There are also forms of power that should be dismantled or taken away: for example that of lobbyists.

The word *strength* is associated mostly with economy (37 per cent) to profile a truly American nurturant vision of society. Here follow a few examples:

(169)   We measure *the strength of our economy* not by the number of billionaires we have or the profits of the Fortune 500, but by whether someone with a good idea can take a risk and start a new business, or whether the waitress who lives on tips can take a day off to look after a sick kid without losing her job – an economy that honors the dignity of work. (28 August 2008, my emphasis)

(170)   We have a different way of measuring the fundamentals of our economy. We know that the fundamentals that we use to measure *economic strength* are whether we are living up to that fundamental promise that has made this country great – that America is a place where you can make it if you try; that everyone should have the chance to live their dreams. (27 September 2008, my emphasis)

Evoking the NP value of unity and the American promise of democracy, Obama also talks of 'the strength and grace to bridge divides and unite in common effort' (28 August 2008). Moreover, *strength* is considered in the sphere of morality proper. This happens, for instance, when Obama states that 'faith and values can be a source of strength in our lives' (1 July 2008). No less importantly, his foreign politics appears to be guided by the principle according to which leaders should rely on *the strength of diplomacy*.

The word *strengthen* is used to convey different responsibilities of the government towards American citizens, especially with regard to protection. Obama suggests that America should *strengthen defense* against terrorist attacks, but also *strengthen cities* (meaning infrastructure), *strengthen mass transit, strengthen and protect Social Security* and *strengthen oversight* (meaning control on expenditure). Obama also proposes to *strengthen the economy* with a rescue plan for the middle class.

The word *decision* is used with a negative connotation to indicate bad decisions that have already been taken by political actors and whose effects are felt and seen in the present situation. They include the *ill-considered decisions* made by Senator McCain in relation to foreign and domestic policy (the war in Iraq, gender discrimination), as well as *shameful decisions* of the Bush administration (especially those concerning wounded warriors' right to register), *irresponsible decisions* in Wall Street and *dangerous decisions* by greedy executives. Only twice is the word *decision* used with a future orientation to indicate the decisions that American citizens will make in November and the importance of the decisions that leaders will make about education.

The term *force* doesn't display a clear pattern of usage. However, through this word Obama sometimes criticizes a condition where, due to the current legislation, people are restricted in their freedom to act, remaining limited in their potential (for example, *teachers are forced to teach to the test*).

In the case of the word *determine*, the actors of future determination include the presidential election, which will determine the new course of the nation, and future decisions of American political leaders, the government and academia. The implication is that what is going to come (if Americans vote for Obama) will be different from what used to be in the past. Democrats will determine a new course.

The word *authorize* occurs exclusively in the fixed phrase *should've never been authorized*, which refers to the war in Iraq.

Obama shows a preference to use *direct* when he refers to foreign policy and emphasizes the relevance of diplomatic relations. The expressions found in the corpus are *direct diplomacy* and *direct diplomatic attention*.

The word *control* portrays a contrast between the current lack of control on foreign crises and on rising prices, and the promise of future control on energy, infrastructure, markets and the environment.

In the speeches, the Treasury is given *authority* to help homeowners avoid foreclosure. The word *authority* only occurs in this association.

Finally, in relation to the word *dominate*, the type of domination to which Obama alludes is the one enacted by special interests and lobbyists on Washington. Being *dominated*, the government doesn't work for people.

As this analysis has shown, potential SF words can be used for the opposite aim of reinforcing a political message that is framed according to a NP worldview. In the corpus, the words *right, power, strength, strengthen* and *authority* seem to fit this general purpose. While implicitly evoking a SF perspective on political reality, these words are grounded in a nurturant narrative and used to reinforce NP values. This fact can even make one wonder whether the presence of potential SF words in the speeches responds to a political strategy. By alluding to a lexicon of strength that is typically Republican while supporting nurturant ideas, these terms can be expected to attract the attention, if not the sympathy, of more voters. On a more specific level, these words cohere with Obama's celebration of the strength to be nurturers. They contribute to shaping the idea that care, empathy and nurturance require strength at the service of others.

8
Conclusion

Within the vast area of linguistic investigation in the field of research on political language and cognition, this book has explored specific facets of language use in the context of US electoral politics. It has provided a linguistic application of Lakoff's (1996) SF and NP models of political morality to the analysis of a number of speeches made by Barack Obama during his first run for the American Presidency in 2008. More specifically, the analytical chapters have tested the usefulness of Lakoff's models for understanding American political language, especially at crucial times such as during a presidential election campaign.

As Chapters 2 and 3 have illustrated, the linguistic exploration carried out in the book has been grounded in a tradition of research that includes the study of political language in the US, cognitive approaches to the analysis of political discourse, and previous linguistic applications of Lakoff's models. Indeed, the results and the methodology adopted in the studies that first applied parts of Lakoff's models have been an incentive for proposing a new application of the models that moves in a different direction.

This book has critically reconsidered the major assumptions that motivated this previous research and it has provided a new methodology for putting Lakoff's models to the test. The approach that has been adopted here emphasizes the centrality of moral values for testing the models. Accordingly, the semantic analysis has involved the identification of moral values in a corpus of carefully selected speeches from Obama's election campaign in 2008: the one that made him not only the president of the US, but also a world celebrity. In addition to providing details on the full range of values that were found in the corpus, the analysis has also considered some of the discursive strategies employed to convey them.

The major finding of this semantic analysis is that Obama consistently frames political issues in line with nurturant values (see Chapter 5). Different results of the analysis confirm Obama's overall NP perspective on political reality. A first clear indication of that is shown by the number of NP paragraphs that have been identified in the corpus. As discussed in Chapter 5, after neutral paragraphs, nurturant paragraphs appear as the most frequent ones in the speeches (40.2 per cent). Obama's preference for NP values is further confirmed by the presence of CSF and NP+CFS paragraphs, in which he criticizes some of the beliefs that are at the core of SF ideology. His criticism of SF values is coherent with the NP ideology that shines through each and every one of his electoral speeches. The analysis has also shown that the expression of Obama's nurturant message is very articulate. This aspect is conveyed by the range of NP values that have been identified. The large number of distinct NP values have been arranged into general categories ('care', 'we', 'social rights', 'fairness', 'opportunity', 'protection', 'responsibility' and 'freedom'), which illustrate Obama's major concerns throughout the campaign and allude to the policies he proposed for improving the lives of American citizens.

The analysis of values has also revealed that Obama has a preference for the rhetorical strategy of story-telling. On a general level, the use of story-telling appears to be very well suited to the purpose of gaining the electorate's favor. Stories shorten the distance between Obama and his listeners and by being personal they naturally call for engagement. Obama relies heavily on stories to construct his public image. The electoral narrative abounds with stories that are about Obama himself, the members of his extended family and, more generally, American citizens. The way Obama talks about himself and his upbringing is aimed at instilling a feeling of trust in the electorate. His success appears to be linked to a strong work ethic, and his work as a community organizer on the South Side of Chicago ties in very nicely with his suggested political agenda of helping and supporting the American people who have been deeply struck by the economic crisis. While these types of stories are chiefly characterized by an ethical appeal, the stories that feature Obama's family members as their protagonists mostly rely upon pathos. This effect is achieved by establishing similarities between the difficulties faced by his family and the hardships experienced by ordinary Americans in their everyday lives. In addition to this, Obama also recounts the stories of suffering and courage of many compatriots in order to communicate to his potential voters that he is aware of their problems and willing to solve them.

Closely related to the use of stories is the celebration of the American Dream. Obama presents himself as the embodiment of this strongly held patriotic belief, and he encourages the American people not to lose their faith in the possibility of realizing their dreams. By consistently evoking the logic of the American Dream, Obama is able to link himself to a tradition of American presidential rhetoric that relies on the most basic of the American myths and has the potential to encourage the nation at times of pressing economic crises.

After having disclosed the type of values evoked by Obama, their frequency in the corpus and the range of rhetorical strategies used to convey them, the analysis has shifted to consider how values are linguistically encoded (see Chapter 6). In particular, the investigation has focused on the role of literal and metaphorical language for the expression of moral values. Surprisingly, findings reveal that values are mostly encoded using literal language. This is an important result that points to the need to reconsider the actual role of metaphor when analyzing SF and NP values in political language. Having established that the communication of values does not necessarily involve the use of metaphorical language, it was interesting to observe which metaphors were used by Obama to transmit his nurturant message by means of values. The analysis has thus concentrated on values that are metaphorically expressed and the aim has been to identify the metaphorical source domains. This metaphorical exploration has brought to the fore certain patterns of usage. When talking metaphorically about values, Obama appears to draw upon a limited set of source domains, which basically include motion, orientation and construction. His discourse about values also involves forms of metaphorical reification. The identification of these source domains allows for important considerations. While Obama's metaphorical expression of values cannot be expected to arouse powerful reactions in his addressees, it contributes significantly to the shaping of his public image. Values that are expressed metaphorically are not likely to gain the attention of Obama's potential voters because they represent conventional ways of expressing certain ideas in English (for example, *fix the education system, lift up the poor, build an economy*). In other words, they are expressions that are well entrenched in the English language and, thus, can be expected to go unnoticed. However, the occurrence of these metaphorical expressions in the electoral narrative helps to create an image of the Democratic candidate as a person who is concrete, active, positive and oriented towards progress. As a result, the combination of these conventional metaphorical expressions generates a strong image that is likely to be subtly persuasive.

In addition to this, what seems to be intriguingly striking about the NP values that are expressed metaphorically is that many of them are verbalized using the term *fight*. Obama's oratory is characterized by the presence of many metaphorical fights. He presents himself as the nurturant politician who is ready and willing to fight to improve the lives of the American people. More precisely, Obama draws an image of himself as a fighter ready to use his strength for improving education and health care, providing employment, helping and protecting citizens, granting people equal rights and opportunities and addressing the needs of children and veterans. The metaphorical fights Obama talks about in his speeches contribute to shaping a portrait of the Democratic candidate as a strong nurturer. In other words, they celebrate the strength to be nurturers.

A third important component of the semantic analysis has involved exploring how specific lexical items are used in context and what their contribution is to the overall political message of Obama's electoral campaign (see Chapter 7). The type of words that have been considered include highly frequent lexical items, gender and family terms, potential NP words, and potential SF words. The analysis of this highly frequent vocabulary has shown that content words help to provide the basic spatio-temporal coordinates (those of the here and now) and are embedded in a discourse that is distinctively nurturant.

More significantly, findings for gender and family terms in the corpus allow us to locate Obama's speeches within a tradition of recent political rhetoric in the US. His preference for the term *parent* over both *father* and *mother* is partly in line with a general trend of gender-neutral attribution of family roles that has been observed in modern American political language (see Chapter 3). Furthermore, the use of *parent* can be taken to be coherent with a moral worldview that doesn't assign to either father or mother a special status in the family. Lexical searches have additionally shown that the word *woman* is used more than *man* and that, in contrast to previous findings for American politicians (see Chapter 3), the role of women emerging from the speeches is not confined to that of nurturers. Women are seen as both nurturers and providers. Obama talks about tough, hardworking women who struggle daily because of the impending economic crisis and gender discrimination.

The analysis of potential NP and SF words used in context has also revealed other important facts. In particular, the investigation of potential NP words has demonstrated that they can also be employed neutrally to communicate a message that is deprived of any specific ideological orientation. This indicates how words that have been associated to a particular worldview in previous research are not necessarily bound to that. On the other hand, the exploration of potential SF words has made clear that they can also be used to convey a nurturant message. In other terms, the analysis has proved that words that are expected to fit one of the two morality models can be used for the opposite aim. This is exactly what happens in the case of potential SF terms, such as *power*, *strength* and *strengthen*, that Obama uses to talk about NP values. This last finding is particularly significant because it connects with Obama's recurrent references to his metaphorical fights. In this sense, the use of potential SF terminology for transmitting a nurturant moral view reinforces Obama's ideal of the strength to be nurturers.

To conclude, the different linguistic analyses discussed in this book have confirmed the fact that in order to apply Lakoff's models to the analysis of political language, it is necessary to conduct a semantic analysis that takes into consideration how discourse is morally framed by politicians. Because it is values which occupy a central role in Lakoff's models, the analysis needs to consider the type of values evoked by a politician. The presence or absence of certain values can reliably indicate the moral worldview that a politician communicates to his audience in his public deliveries. Conversely, no direct correlation can be established between the use of specific metaphors and a politician's moral framing of issues. Metaphors are secondary to the expression of values and values are often conveyed using literal language. All together, these findings prove the hypothesis raised in the introduction: that Obama as a Democratic politician has consistently relied upon a NP worldview to create his political persona during the 2008 election campaign.

The book has also shown that it is not possible to assume that certain words stand unambiguously for a specific moral framing. Only the actual usage of words in context can reveal whether or not these words are supportive of a particular worldview. Thus, for instance, the presence of the term *strength* in a political speech cannot be taken *prima facie* as an indication of a SF framing of discourse. On the contrary, the word *strength* can be used strategically to sustain a logic of nurturance. The fact that Obama uses words and metaphors that can allude to a SF framing of political reality is very unlikely to be purely accidental. Instead, it can be interpreted in light of his wish to appeal to as many voters as possible and, in particular, to attract the sympathies of so-called swing voters.

All the observations that emerged from the analyses presented in the book provide insights for understanding the unprecedented success of the 44th American president, the first African American to rise to the highest office in the history of US democracy.

Appendix 1: Metaphorical Expressions in Value-laden Paragraphs

The tables below are aimed to show the amount of metaphorical language that is present in NP, CSF and mixed paragraphs. To help the reader navigate through the data, a brief introduction is provided here. The reader should be aware that:

- Each table is organized according to the different speeches, and the examples of metaphorical language are given in the context of the paragraphs where they appear. Instances of metaphorical language use are printed in bold. Note that only the relevant portions of the paragraphs are reported.
- It can happen that different metaphorical expressions are used within one paragraph. In this case, each of the metaphorical expressions is highlighted separately.
- While each of the selected passages might, in principle, convey a particular NP value or criticize a specific SF value, this type of information is not provided in the table. The last column in each table is meant to only indicate values that are metaphorically expressed. If metaphors in a passage do not express a value, this is marked by a dash.
- If there are more metaphorical expressions in an excerpt, those that refer to a value are marked with a symbol in brackets. Different symbols are used to disambiguate multiple values and their metaphorical expressions.

Metaphorical expressions in NP paragraphs

Speech	Metaphorical expressions per paragraph	Value metaphorically expressed
5 February 2008	[...] we stood on the steps of the Old State Capitol to reaffirm a truth that was spoken there so many generations ago – that **a house divided cannot stand**; that we are more than a collection of Red States and Blue States; we are, and always will be, the United States of America	We: unity
	Their voices echoed from the hills of New Hampshire to the deserts of Nevada, where teachers and cooks and kitchen workers stood up to say that maybe **Washington doesn't have to be run** by lobbyists anymore.	–
	They reached the coast of South Carolina when people said that maybe we don't have to be divided by race and region and gender; that **crumbling schools are stealing the future of black children and white children** [...]	–
	[...] that we can come together and **build an America** that gives every child, everywhere the opportunity to live their dreams.	We: cooperation
	I'll be the President who ends the **tax breaks** (*) to companies that ship our jobs overseas and start **putting them in the pockets of working Americans** (*) who deserve it. And **struggling homeowners**. And seniors who should retire with dignity and respect.	Fairness: fair taxation/ distribution of money (*) –
	And we will harness the ingenuity of farmers and scientists and entrepreneurs to **free this nation from the tyranny of oil** once and for all.	Freedom: inde-pendence from non-renewable energy sources
	So tonight I want to speak directly to all those Americans who have yet to join this movement but still **hunger for change** – we need you.	–
	I was a young organizer then, intent on **fighting joblessness and poverty** on the South Side [...]	Social rights: employment for everyone
	And the volunteers looked out that window, and they decided that night to keep going – to keep organizing, keep **fighting for better schools, and better jobs, and better health care**. And so did I.	Social rights: education, employment, health care for everyone
	We are the hope of the woman who hears that her city will not be rebuilt; that she cannot reclaim **the life that was swept away** in a terrible storm.	–

(*continued*)

232

Continued

Speech	Metaphorical expressions per paragraph	Value metaphorically expressed
	We are the hope of the future; the answer to the cynics who tell us **our house must stand divided**; that we cannot come together; that we cannot remake this world as it should be.	We: unity
12 February 2008	This is the new American majority. This is what change looks like when it happens **from the bottom up**. And in this election, your voices will be heard.	We: empowering people
	It's the dream of the father who goes to work before dawn and lies awake at night wondering how he's going to pay the bills. He needs us to restore fairness to our economy by **putting a tax cut into the pockets of working people, and seniors, and struggling homeowners.**	Fairness: fair taxation/distribution of money
	But my family gave me love, they gave me education, and most of all they gave me hope – hope that in America, **no dream is beyond our grasp** if we reach for it, and **fight for it**, and work for it.	Chance: opportunity for everyone
	I know this because I **fought** on the streets of Chicago as a community organizer **to bring jobs to the jobless in the shadow of a shuttered steel plant.**	Social rights: employment for everyone
	I've **fought** in the courts as a civil rights lawyer **to make sure people weren't denied their rights** because of what they looked like or where they came from.	We: equality
	I've **fought** in the legislature **to take power away from lobbyists.**	We: equality
	The voices of the American people have carried us **a great distance on this improbable journey**, but we have **much further to go**.	–
	[...]; it's the same message we had when we **were up**, and when **were down**; [...]	–
	[...]; that our **destiny will not be written** for us, but by us;[...]	–
	[...]; and that we can cast off our doubts and fears and cynicism because our **dream will not be deferred**; [...]	–
4 March 2008	We believe that **we rise or fall as one nation – as one people.**	We: unity

(continued)

Continued

Speech	Metaphorical expressions per paragraph	Value metaphorically expressed
18 March 2008	This was one of the tasks we set forth at the beginning of this campaign – to **continue the long march** of those who came before us, **a march for a more just** (*), **more equal** (#), **more free** (|), **more caring** (+) **and more prosperous America** (!).	Fairness: unspecified (*) We: equality (#) Freedom: unspecified (|) Care: caring for people (+) Chance: opportunity for everyone (!)
	I chose to **run for the presidency** at this moment in history because I believe [...]	–
	[...] we may not look the same and we may not have come from the same place, but we all want to **move in the same direction – towards a better future for our children and our grandchildren.**	Chance: opportunity for children
	Throughout the first year of this campaign, against all predictions to the contrary, we saw how **hungry** the American people were **for this message of unity.**	–
	Despite the temptation to **view my candidacy through a purely racial lens,** we **won commanding victories** in states with some of the whitest populations in the country.	–
	In South Carolina, where the Confederate Flag still flies, we **built a powerful coalition** of African Americans and white Americans.	–
	The man I met more than twenty years ago is a man who helped introduce me to my Christian faith, a man who spoke to me about our obligations to love one another; to care for the sick and **lift up the poor.**	Care: help for the people in need
	But I have asserted a firm conviction – **a conviction rooted** in my faith in God and my faith in the American people [...]	–
	[...] that working together we can **move beyond some of our old racial wounds** (*), and that in fact we have no choice if we are to **continue on the path** (#) of a more perfect union.	We: equality (*); We: cooperation (#)
	For the African-American community, that path means **embracing the burdens of our past** without becoming **victims of our past.**	–
	It means continuing to insist on a full measure of justice in every aspect of American life. But it also means **binding our particular grievances – for better health care, and better schools, and better jobs** – to the larger aspirations of all Americans [...]	Social rights: education, employment, health care for everyone

Continued

Speech	Metaphorical expressions per paragraph	Value metaphorically expressed
	And it means taking full responsibility for our own lives – by demanding more from our fathers, and spending more time with our children, and reading to them, and teaching them that while **they may face challenges and discrimination** in their own lives, **they must never succumb to despair or cynicism**; they must always believe that **they can write their own destiny**.	–
	[...] – a country that has made it possible for one of his own members **to run for the highest office** in the land [...]	–
	[...] and [a country that has made it possible to] **build a coalition** of white and black; Latino and Asian, rich and poor, young and old – [...]	We: unity
	[as if this country] is still irrevocably **bound to a tragic past**.	–
	In the white community, **the path to a more perfect union** means acknowledging that what ails the African-American community does not just exist in the minds of black people [...]	We: unity
	[the legacy of discrimination ... must be addressed]...; **by providing this generation with ladders of opportunity** that were unavailable for previous generations.	Chance: opportunity for children
	This time we want to talk about the **crumbling schools that are stealing the future** of black children and white children and Asian children and Hispanic children and Native American children. [...]	–
	The children of America are not those kids, they are our kids, and we will **not let them fall behind** in a 21st century economy.	Chance: opportunity for children
20 March 2008	Instead of fighting this war, we could be **fighting for the people of West Virginia**. For what folks in this state have been spending on the Iraq war, we could be giving health care to nearly 450,000 of your neighbors, hiring nearly 30,000 new elementary school teachers, and making college more affordable for over 300,000 students.	–
	We could be **fighting to put the American dream within reach** for every American [...]	Chance: opportunity for everyone
	[...] – by giving **tax breaks to working families**, offering [tax]relief to struggling homeowners [...]	Fairness: fair taxation/distribution of money

(*continued*)

Continued

Speech	Metaphorical expressions per paragraph	Value metaphorically expressed
	Instead of fighting this war, we could be **fighting to make universal health care a reality** in this country. We could be **fighting for the young woman** who works the night shift after a full day of college and still can't afford medicine for a sister who's ill.	Social rights: health care for everyone
	Instead of fighting this war, we could be **fighting to give every American a quality education**. We could be **fighting for the young men and women** all across this country who dream big dreams but aren't getting the kind of education they need to reach for those dreams.	Social rights: education for everyone
	Instead of fighting this war, we could be **fighting to rebuild our roads and bridges**.	Protection: investing in public infrastructure
	I've proposed a fund that would do just that and generate nearly two million new jobs – many in the construction industry that's been **hard hit by our housing crisis**.	–
	Instead of fighting this war, we could be **freeing ourselves from the tyranny of oil** [...]	Freedom: independence from non-renewable energy sources
	We'll have to give veterans the health care and disability benefits they deserve, the support they need, and the respect they've earned. This is an **obligation I have fought to uphold** on the Senate Veterans' Affairs Committee by joining Jay Rockefeller to expand educational opportunities for our veterans.	Care: caring for veterans
	This election is our chance to reclaim our future – to end the fight in Iraq and take up the **fight for good jobs (*) and universal health care (#)**. To end the fight in Iraq and take up **the fight for a world-class education (|) and retirement security (+)**. To end the fight in Iraq and take up the **fight for opportunity (!)**, and **equality (\\)**, and **prosperity (^)** here at home.	Social rights: employment for everyone (*); health care for everyone (#); education for everyone (|) Care: caring for the old (+) Chance: opportunity for everyone (!) We: equality (\\) Care: caring for people (^)

(continued)

Continued

Speech	Metaphorical expressions per paragraph	Value metaphorically expressed
14 April 2008	**Years of pain** on Main Street **have finally trickled up** to Wall Street **and sent us** hurtling toward recession, reminding us that we're all connected – that we can't prosper as a nation where a few people are doing well and everyone else is **struggling**.	–
	They [the people I've met during this campaign] believe it's time we provided **real relief** to the victims of this housing crisis; that we help families refinance their mortgage so they can stay in their homes; that we start giving **tax relief to the people who actually need it – middle-class families, and seniors, and struggling homeowners**.	Fairness: fair distribution of money/fair taxation
	They believe that we can and should make the global economy work for working Americans; that we might not be able to stop every job from going overseas, but we certainly can **stop giving tax breaks to companies** who send them their [sic.] and **start giving tax breaks to companies** who create good jobs right here in America.	Fairness: fair distribution of money/fair taxation
	They believe we can train our workers for those new jobs, and keep the most productive workforce the most competitive workforce in the world if **we fix our public education system** by investing in what works and finding out what doesn't; [...]	Care: investing in education
15 April 2008	I led a bipartisan effort to improve outpatient facilities, slash red tape, and reform the disability process – because **recovering troops should go to the front of the line, and they shouldn't have to fight to get there.**	Care: caring for the troops/veterans
	I'm tired of hearing stories about vets **navigating a broken VBA bureaucracy**. We need to hire additional workers, and create an electronic system that is fully linked up to military records and the VA's health network.	–
	And I will have a simple principle for veterans sleeping on our streets: zero tolerance. I've **fought for this** in the Senate, and as President I'll expand housing vouchers, and launch a new supportive services housing program to **prevent** at-risk **veterans and their families from sliding into homelessness**.	Care: caring for the troops/ veterans
	It's time to make sure that every veteran has the support they need to get an education that **puts them on a pathway to their dreams**.	Care: caring for the troops/ veterans
22 April 2008	And so while I will always listen to you, and be honest with you, and **fight for you** every single day for the next four years, I will also ask you to be a part of the change that we need.	Care: caring for people

(*continued*)

Continued

Speech	Metaphorical expressions per paragraph	Value metaphorically expressed
	Because in my two decades of public service to this country, I have seen time and time again that real change doesn't begin in the halls of Washington, but on the streets of America. It **doesn't happen from the top-down, it happens from the bottom-up.**	We: empowering people
	You can make this election about how we plan to leave our children and all children a planet that's safer and a world that still sees **America** the same way my father saw it from across the ocean – **as a beacon** of all that is good and all that is possible for all mankind.	–
3 May 2008	It's about whether we'll watch the Chinas and the Indias of the world **move past us**, or whether we'll decide that in the 21st century, the home of innovation, and discovery, and progress will still be the United States of America.	–
	We can **provide [tax] relief** (*) that's more than a holiday **to families who are struggling in this economy.** I'm the only candidate who's proposed a genuine middle-class **tax cut** (*) that's paid for in part by closing corporate loopholes and shutting down tax havens.	Fairness: fair distribution of money/fair taxation (*) –
	It would save nearly every working family $1,000, eliminate income taxes for seniors making under $50,000, and provide a mortgage tax credit to **struggling homeowners** that would cover ten percent of their mortgage interest payment every year.	–
	That's **real relief**, but we can only pay for this if we finally **rollback the Bush tax cuts** for the wealthiest 2% of Americans who don't need them and weren't even asking for them.	Fairness: fair distribution of money/fair taxation
	We may not be able to **bring back all the jobs** that we've **lost** to trade, but we can create tomorrow's jobs in this country.	Social rights: employment for everyone
	There's absolutely no reason we should be giving **tax breaks** to corporations who ship jobs overseas. When I'm President, I will eliminate those **tax breaks** and give them to companies who create good jobs right here in America.	Fairness: fair taxation/distribution of money
	That's why I'm proposing a National Infrastructure Reinvestment Bank that will invest $60 billion over ten years and generate nearly two million new jobs – many of them in the construction industry that's been **hard hit by this housing crisis.**	–

(continued)

238

Speech	Metaphorical expressions per paragraph	Value metaphorically expressed
	And if [you] want to take a **permanent holiday from our oil addiction**, we can finally get serious about energy independence and create five million new green jobs in the process – jobs that pay well and can't be outsourced.	Freedom: independence from non-renewable energy sources
	That means investing in early childhood education. It means that we need to **recruit an army of new teachers** by not just talking about how great teachers are, but rewarding them for their greatness with better pay and more support.	Care: supporting nurturant professions (teachers)
	All of this is possible, but it's just a list of policies until you decide that it's time to make the Washington we have look like the America we know – one where the future is not determined by those with money and influence; where common sense and honesty are cherished values; where we are stronger than that which divides us because we realize that in the end, we **rise or fall as one nation – as one people.**	We: unity
6 May 2008	More importantly, because of you, we have seen that it's possible to overcome the politics of division and distraction; that it's possible to overcome the same old negative **attacks** that are always about **scoring points** and never about solving our problems. We've seen that the American people aren't looking for more **spin** or more **gimmicks**, but honest answers about the challenges we face. That's what you've accomplished in this campaign, and that's how we'll change this country together.	–
	They need us to end a war that isn't making us safer. They need us to treat them with the care and respect they deserve. That's why **I'm running for President.**	–
	Because that's how we've always changed this country – **not from the top-down, but from the bottom-up (*)**; when you – the American people – decide that **the stakes are too high** and the challenges are too great.	We: empowering people (*) —
	I trust the American people to realize that while we don't need big government, we do need a government that stands up for families who are being tricked out of their homes by Wall Street predators; a government that stands up for the middle-class by **giving them a tax break** [...]	Fairness: fair taxation/distribution of money
	We may not look the same or come from the same place, but we want to **move in the same direction – towards a better future for our children and our grandchildren.**	Chance: opportunity for children

Continued

Speech	Metaphorical expressions per paragraph	Value metaphorically expressed
	That's why I'm in this **race**. I love this country too much to see it divided and distracted at this moment in history.	–
	So don't ever forget that this election is not about me, or any candidate. Don't ever forget that this campaign is about you – about your hopes, about your dreams, about your struggles, about **securing your portion of the American Dream.**	Chance: opportunity for everyone
20 May 2008	You know, there is **a spirit that brought us here** tonight – a spirit of change, and hope, and possibility.	–
	You spoke of a future where the politics we have in Washington finally reflect the values we hold as Americans – the values you live by here in Iowa: common sense and honesty; generosity and compassion; decency and responsibility. These values don't belong to one class or one region or even one party – they are the **values that bind us together** as one country.	We: unity
	That is the country I saw in the faces of crowds that would stretch far into the horizon of our heartland – faces of every color, of every age – faces I see here tonight. You are Democrats who are tired of being divided; Republicans who no longer recognize the **party that runs** Washington; Independents who are **hungry for change.**	–
	The **road here has been long**, and that is partly because we've **traveled** it with one of the most formidable candidates to ever **run** for this office.	–
	In her thirty-five years of public service, Senator Hillary Rodham Clinton has never given up on her **fight for the American people**, and tonight I congratulate her on her victory in Kentucky.	Care: caring for people
	We have had our disagreements during this campaign, but we all admire her courage, her commitment and her perseverance. No matter how this primary ends, Senator Clinton has **shattered myths** and **broken barriers** and changed the America in which my daughters and yours will come of age.	Chance: opportunity for children
	Some may see the millions upon millions of votes cast for each of us as evidence that our party is divided, but I see it as proof that we have never been more energized and **united in our desire to take this country in a new direction.**	We: unity
	More than anything, we need this unity and this energy in the months to come, because while **our primary has been long and hard-fought**, the **hardest and most important part of our journey still lies ahead.**	–

240

Speech	Metaphorical expressions per paragraph	Value metaphorically expressed
	Change is a tax code that rewards work instead of wealth by **cutting taxes for middle-class families (*)**, and senior citizens, and **struggling homeowners** [...]	Fairness: fair taxation/ distribution of money (*) −
	Change is giving every child a world-class education by **recruiting an army of new teachers** with better pay and more support [...]	Care: supporting nurturant profession (teachers)
	That's what is happening in America – **our journey** may be long, our work will be great, but we know in our hearts we are ready for change, we are ready to come together, and in this election, we are ready to believe again.	We: cooperation
3 June 2008	We've certainly had our differences over the last sixteen months. But as someone who's shared a stage with her many times, I can tell you that what gets Hillary Clinton up in the morning – even in the face of **tough odds** – is exactly what sent her and Bill Clinton to sign up for their first campaign in Texas all those years ago;	−
	[...] what sent her to work at the Children's Defense Fund and made her **fight for health care** as First Lady; [...] And you can rest assured that when we finally **win the battle for universal health care** in this country, she will be central to that victory.	Social rights: health care for everyone
	[...] what led her to the United States Senate and **fueled her barrier-breaking campaign** for the presidency [...]	−
	[...] an unyielding desire to improve the lives of ordinary Americans, no matter how difficult the **fight** may be.	Care: caring for people
	When we transform our energy policy and **lift our children out of poverty**, it will be because she worked to help make it happen.	Chance: opportunity for children
	Let us **unite in common effort to chart a new course** for America.	We: cooperation
	And maybe if he spent some time in the schools of South Carolina or St. Paul or where he spoke tonight in New Orleans, he'd understand that we can't afford to **leave the money behind for No Child Left Behind (*)**; that we owe it to our children to invest in early childhood education; to **recruit an army of new teachers (#)** and give them better pay and more support; [...]	Care: caring for children (*); Care: supporting nurturant professions (teachers) (#)

Continued

Speech	Metaphorical expressions per paragraph	Value metaphorically expressed
	I've **walked arm-in-arm** with community leaders on the South Side of Chicago and watched tensions fade as black, white, and Latino fought together for good jobs and good schools.	–
	And I've worked with friends in the other party to provide more children with health insurance and **more working families with a tax break** [...]	Fairness: fair taxation/distribution of money
	So it has been for every generation that **faced down** the greatest challenges and **the most improbable odds** to leave their children a world that's better, and kinder, and more just.	–
	The journey will be difficult. The **road** will be long. I face this challenge with profound humility, and knowledge of my own limitations.	–
21 June 2008	As some of you may know, after college, I went to work with a group of churches as a community organizer in Chicago – so I could help **lift up neighborhoods (*)that were struggling** after the local steel plants closed.	Care: help for the people in need (*) –
	Now, despite the absence of leadership in Washington, we're **actually seeing a rebirth in many places**.	–
	I'm thinking of [...] and so many other mayors across this country, who are finding new ways to **lift up their communities**.	Care: help for the people in need
	But you shouldn't be succeeding despite Washington – you should be succeeding **with a hand from Washington**. Neglect is not a policy for America's metropolitan areas. It's time City Hall had someone in the White House you could count on the way so many Americans count on you.	Care: help for the people in need
	That is why I've laid out an ambitious urban poverty plan that will help make sure **no child begins the race of life behind the starting line**; and create public-private business incubators to open up economic opportunity. That's why I'll fully fund the COPS program, restore funding for the Community Development Block Grant program, and recruit more teachers to our cities, and pay them more, and give them more support.	Chance: opportunity for children
	And that's why I've proposed **real [tax]relief (*) for struggling homeowners** and a trust fund to provide affordable housing. And let me say this – if George Bush carries out his threat to veto the housing bill – a bill that would provide critical resources to help you solve the foreclosure crisis in your towns and cities – I will **fight (*)** to overturn his veto and make sure you have the support you need.	Care: help for the people in need (*) –

242

Speech	Metaphorical expressions per paragraph	Value metaphorically expressed
	So, yes we need to **fight poverty**.	Care: help for the people in need
	Yes, we need to **fight crime**.	Protection from crime
	Yes, we need to **strengthen our cities**. But we also need to stop seeing our cities as the problem and start seeing them as the solution. Because **strong cities are the building blocks of strong regions**, and strong regions are essential for a strong America. That is the new metropolitan reality and we need a new strategy that reflects it – a strategy that's about South Florida as much as Miami; that's about Mesa and Scottsdale as much as Phoenix; that's about Stamford and Northern New Jersey as much as New York City. As President, I'll work with you to develop this kind of strategy and I'll appoint the first White House Director of Urban Policy to help make it a reality.	Protection: investing in urban development
	And we won't just **unlock the potential of our individual regions**; we'll **unlock the potential of all our regions** by connecting them with a 21st century infrastructure.	Protection: investing in public infrastructure
	Let's invest that money in a world-class transit system. Let's recommit federal dollars to **strengthen mass transit** and reform our tax code to give folks a reason to take the bus instead of driving to work – because investing in mass transit helps make metro areas more livable and can **help our regional economies grow**.	Protection: investing in public infrastructure
	But understand – while the change we seek will require major investments by a more accountable government, it will not come from government alone. Washington can't solve all our problems. The statehouse can't solve all our problems. City Hall can't solve all our problems. It goes back to what I learned as a community organizer all those years ago – that change in this country **comes not from the top-down, but from the bottom up**.	We: empowering people
	That's the proud tradition our cities uphold. That's the story our cities have helped write. And if you're willing to work with me and **fight with me** and **stand with me** this fall, then I promise you this – we will not only rebuild and renew our American cities, north and south, east and west, **but you and I – together – will rebuild** and renew **the promise of America**.	We: cooperation

(*continued*)

Continued

Speech	Metaphorical expressions per paragraph	Value metaphorically expressed
28 June 2008	You know, being here today is a reminder of why I'm in this **race**. Because the reason I'm **running for President** is to do what you do each day in your communities – help make a difference in the lives of ordinary Americans.	–
	We need immigration reform that will secure our borders, and punish employers who exploit immigrant labor; reform that finally brings the 12 million people who are here illegally **out of the shadows** by requiring them to **take steps** to become legal citizens. We must assert our values and reconcile our principles as a nation of immigrants and a nation of laws. That is a priority I will pursue from my very first day.	We: support of immigration
	And we can do something more. We can **tear down the barriers that keep the American dream out of reach** for so many Americans.	Chance: opportunity for everyone
	Like the **waves of immigrants** that came before them and the Hispanic Americans like Ken Salazar whose families have been here for generations, the recent arrival of Latino immigrants will only enrich our country.	–
	Because America can only prosper when all Americans prosper – brown, black, white, Asian, and Native American. That's the idea that lies **at the heart of my campaign**, and that's the idea that will lie **at the heart of my presidency**.	–
	Because we are all Americans. Todos somos Americanos. And in this country, we **rise and fall together**.	We: unity
30 June 2008	We reflect on these questions as well because we are in the midst of a presidential election, perhaps the most consequential in generations; a **contest** that will determine the **course of this nation** for years, perhaps decades, to come.	–
	In spite of this absence of leadership from Washington, I have seen a new generation of Americans begin to take up the call. I meet them everywhere I go, young people involved in the project of American renewal; not only those who have signed up to fight for our country in distant lands, but those who are **fighting for a better America here at home, by teaching in underserved schools (*), or caring for the sick in understaffed hospitals (#), or promoting more sustainable energy policies in their local communities (|)**.	Social rights: education for everyone (*), health care for everyone (#); Care: caring for the environment (|)

(*continued*)

Continued

Speech	Metaphorical expressions per paragraph	Value metaphorically expressed
	When we **pile up mountains of debt** for the next generation to absorb, or put off changes to our energy policies, knowing full well the potential consequences of inaction, we are **placing our short-term interests ahead** of the nation's long-term well-being.	–
	When we fail to educate effectively millions of our children so that they might compete in a global economy, or we fail to invest in the basic scientific research that has driven innovation in this country, we risk **leaving behind an America** that has **fallen in the ranks of the world**. Just as patriotism involves each of us making a commitment to this nation that extends beyond our own immediate self-interest, so must that commitment extends beyond our own time here on earth.	–
	That is the **community we strive to build** – one in which we trust in this sometimes messy democracy of ours, one in which we continue to insist that there is nothing we cannot do when we put our mind to it, one in which we see **ourselves as part of a larger story**, our own **fates wrapped up in the fates** of those who share allegiance to America's happy and singular creed.	We: unity
1 July 2008	As I've said many times, I believe that change comes **not from the top-down, but from the bottom-up**, and few are closer to the people than our churches, synagogues, temples, and mosques.	We: empowering people
	The fact is, the challenges we face today – from saving our planet to ending poverty – are simply too big for government to solve alone. **We need all hands on deck.**	We: cooperation
	I'm not saying that faith-based groups are an alternative to government or secular nonprofits. And I'm not saying that they're somehow better at **lifting people up**.	–
10 July 2008	We take it for granted that women are the **backbone of our families**, but we too often ignore the fact that women are also the **backbone of our middle class**. And we won't truly have an economy that puts the needs of the middle class first until we ensure that when it comes to pay and benefits at work, women are treated like the equal partners they are.	–

(continued)

Continued

Speech	Metaphorical expressions per paragraph	Value metaphorically expressed
	That's why I stood up for equal pay in the Illinois State Senate, and helped pass a law to give 330,000 more women **protection from paycheck discrimination.** That's why I've been **fighting to pass legislation** in the Senate, so that employers don't get away with shortchanging hardworking women.	We: (gender) equality
	Finally, we've got to do more to **help folks at the bottom of the ladder climb** into the middle class.	Care: help for the people in need
	And I'll expand the Earned Income Tax Credit so that no one working fulltime winds up living in poverty. That's what I did in the state senate, bringing together Democrats and Republicans to provide more than $100 million in **tax relief (*) for struggling families** across Illinois.	Fairness: fair distribution of money/fair taxation (*) –
	Unlike Senator McCain, I'll make sure the minimum wage **rises** each year to keep up with **rising costs** – it'll be $9.50 by 2011, giving 8 million women a well-deserved **raise.**	–
	And unlike Senator McCain, I'll make sure every working woman has the chance to not just get by, but **get ahead (*)** – to save, invest, **build a nest egg (#)**, and provide a better life for their children.	We: (gender) equality (*) Care: caring for children (#)
	These are the real differences in this election. And my policies add up to **real relief** for working women. Here in Virginia alone, 2 million working women will get a $500 **tax cut** [...]	Fairness: fair taxation/ distribution of money
	In the end, though, the conversation we're having isn't just about policies and plans. It's also about our most fundamental values – that when you work hard, you should be paid fairly and be able to retire with dignity; that **we rise and fall together** – and there are no second class citizens in our workplaces; that both work and family should be part of the American Dream.	We: unity
	As hard as it is for me to be away from my own daughters so much, that's what I think about when I have the chance to tuck them in at night. How I want my daughters – and all our daughters – to have no limits on their dreams, no obstacles to their achievement, **no opportunities beyond their reach.**	Chance: opportunity for children

(continued)

Continued

Speech	Metaphorical expressions per paragraph	Value metaphorically expressed
13 July 2008	Bringing about that future begins with **fixing the broken promises of No Child Left Behind**. Now, I believe that the goals of this law – educating every child with an excellent teacher, closing the achievement gap, ensuring more accountability and higher standards – were right.	Care: caring for children
	But promising all this while **leaving** the resources **behind** is wrong. Labeling a school and its students as failures one day and then abandoning them the next is wrong.	–
	We must **fix the failures of No Child Left Behind** by providing the funding that was promised, giving states the resources they need, and finally meeting our commitment to special education.	Care: caring for children
	In fact, his only proposal seems to be **recycling tired rhetoric** about vouchers and school choice.	–
	We need to focus on **fixing** and improving **our public schools**; not throwing our hands up and walking away from them.	Care: supporting/investing in education
	Real change is finally giving our kids everything they need to have **a fighting chance** in today's world.	Chance: opportunity for children
	And together, we will begin **changing the odds for our at-risk children** by providing quality, affordable early childhood education for all our children.	Care: caring for children
	To address the **dropout crisis that condemns so many futures**, we'll intervene much earlier in a child's education – because the forces that lead a high school student to drop out start well before the ninth grade.	–
	And I know these kids. I began my career over two decades ago in communities on Chicago's South Side. And I worked with parents and teachers and local leaders **to fight for their future**. We set up after school programs and protested outside government offices so that we could get those who had dropped out into alternative schools. And in time, we **changed the odds for our children.**	Care: caring for children
	That's why I'm **running for President**, AFT. To make sure all our kids have that chance. But I need your help to get there. From your earliest days in Chicago, you've stood up for change – when minorities weren't allowed full union membership; when **parents fought to integrate our schools**; when it was time to take the march for civil rights to Washington, you stood up.	–

Continued

Speech	Metaphorical expressions per paragraph	Value metaphorically expressed
16 July 2008	Today, we will focus on nuclear, biological, and cyber threats – three 21st century threats that have been neglected for the last eight years. It's time to **break out of Washington's conventional thinking** that has failed to **keep pace with** unconventional **threats**. In doing so, we'll better ensure the safety of the American people, while **building our capacity** to deal with other challenges – from public health to privacy.	Protection: protection from nuclear, bio- logical, cyber threats
	As President, I will launch an effort across our government to **stay ahead of this threat.**	Protection: protection from nuclear, biological, cyber threats
	Just as we **step up our ability to prevent an attack,** we must also **bolster our capacity to protect against** – and respond to – the threats that may come.	Protection: protection from nuclear, biological, cyber threats
	As President, I'll make **cyber security the top priority** that it should be in the 21st century.	–
	We need to prevent terrorists or spies from hacking into our national security networks. We need to **build the capacity to identify, isolate, and respond to any cyber-attack.**	Protection: protection from nuclear, biological, cyber threats
	In the Cold War, we didn't defeat the Soviets just because of the strength of our arms – we also did it because **at the dawn of the atomic age** and the onset of the space race, the smartest scientists and most innovative workforce was here in America.	–
	The same holds true for our security. If we're not investing in math and science education, **our nation will fall behind**.	Care: supporting/ investing in education
	That is the **task that lies before us**. We must never **let down our guard**, nor suffer another failure of imagination. It's time for sustained and aggressive action – to take the offense against new dangers abroad, while **shoring up our defenses** at home.	Protection: protection from harm

(continued)

Continued

Speech	Metaphorical expressions per paragraph	Value metaphorically expressed
1 August 2008	So for many families, these anxieties are getting worse, not better. People are starting to lose faith in the American dream, which is the idea that if you work hard, you can build a better life not just for yourselves but for your children and grandchildren. A lot of people feel like **that dream is slipping further out of reach (*)**. That's why I'm **running for President** of the United States – because America is supposed to be the place where you can make it if you try.	Chance: opportunity for everyone (*) –
	It's time for something new. It's time to restore balance and fairness to our economy so it works for all Americans. That's why as President, I will put a middle class **tax cut into the pockets (*)** of 95% of workers, provide [tax]relief (*)to struggling homeowners, and eliminate income taxes for seniors making less than $50,000 a year. And I'll end **tax breaks (*)** for companies that ship jobs overseas and give them to companies that create good jobs here at home. But you can't wait that long. You need immediate [tax] relief (*).	Fairness: fair distribution of money/fair taxation (*) –
	Now, I've already called for a **stimulus package** on two different occasions this year, and much of what I've proposed has passed in Congress. These efforts have made some difference. But with **job losses mounting, prices rising, increased turbulence in our financial system**, and a **growing credit crunch**, we need to do more.	–
	I discussed these issues with my **top economic advisers** at a meeting on Monday and we agreed that the main risk we face today is doing too little in the face of our **growing economic troubles**.	–
	That's why today, I'm announcing a two-part emergency plan to **help struggling families make ends meet** and **get our economy back on track**.	–
	As we provide [tax] **relief (*)**, we must also be mindful of the **swelling budget deficit**. That is why I am proposing that we pay for this rebate by taxing the windfall profits of oil companies like Exxon Mobil – a company that announced yesterday that it made nearly $12 billion last quarter, more than any U.S. corporation has ever made in a single quarter. It's time we used some of their record profits to help you pay record prices.	Fairness: fair distribution of money/fair taxation (*) –

(continued)

Continued

Speech	Metaphorical expressions per paragraph	Value metaphorically expressed
	The second part of my plan is a $50 billion stimulus to help jump-start job creation and help local **communities that are struggling** due to our **economic downturn.**	–
	By offering $25 billion to state governments, we can help ensure that they don't have to let workers go or **freeze their salaries** or **raise property taxes** on families who are hurting.	–
	And we can also help ensure that they continue providing foreclosure counseling and other services to help families stay in their homes in areas that have been **hard-hit by our housing crisis.**	–
	We'll invest the other half of this $50 billion in our national infrastructure so we can create new jobs and **save over one million jobs that are in danger of being cut (*)**. With construction costs **rising,** the Highway Trust Fund is facing a deficit for the first time ever [...] We'll also invest some of this money to repair our **crumbling schools** – because that won't just help make sure our children are getting a world-class education, it will **spur job-growth** (*)and **boost our local economies.**	Social rights: employment for everyone (*) –
	Well, I do not believe that giving $4 billion in new **tax cuts** to oil companies – including $1.2 billion to Exxon-Mobil alone – will create any jobs or save you any money. Instead, I believe America is at its strongest when our **economy is growing from the bottom-up.** If we want relief for families, we should give **[tax]relief** to families.	Fairness: fair distribution of money/fair taxation
	But we have to do more than just provide **short-term [tax] relief.** We have to secure our long-term prosperity [...]	Care: caring for people
	I'm **running** for President because I believe we can **seize our own economic destiny.**	–
	We can choose to go another four years without truly solving our energy crisis; or we can make America energy independent so we're less **vulnerable to oil price shocks** and $4 a gallon gas.	Freedom: independence from non-renewable energy sources
	We can **build an American green energy sector** by investing in renewable energies like wind power, solar power, and the next generation biofuels.	Care: caring for the environment
	We can choose to go another four years with the same **reckless fiscal policies** that have **busted our budget, wreaked havoc in our economy,** and **mortgaged** our children's future on a **mountain of debt;** or we can restore fiscal responsibility in Washington [...]	–

Continued

Speech	Metaphorical expressions per paragraph	Value metaphorically expressed
	We can go another four years with a **broken health care system**; or we can say that if we're spending more money on health care per capita than any other nation on earth, we shouldn't have 47 million people without health care.	–
	We shouldn't have families going bankrupt just because they got sick. We shouldn't have businesses **struggling to stay afloat** because they can't afford **rising health care costs**.	–
	We can choose to **stay mired in the same education debate** that's **consumed Washington** for decades, or we can provide every child with a quality education so they have the skills to succeed in our global economy.	–
	We can invest in early childhood education, **recruit an army of qualified teachers** with better pay and more support, and finally make college affordable by offering an annual $4,000 tax credit in exchange for community or national service.	Care: Supporting nurturant professions (teachers)
	America will invest in you, you'll invest in America, and together, we'll **move this country forward**.	We: cooperation
	These are the choices we face in November. And yet, instead of talking about these real choices, my opponent is **running an increasingly negative campaign** that's distorting my record and using the same old Washington **political attacks** that are trotted out every four years.	–
	And you deserve real solutions to our economic problems – solutions that will help ensure that here in this country, **opportunity is open to anyone** who's willing to work for it.	Chance: opportunity for everyone
5 August 2008	Now, we know our families need immediate **relief from high gas prices** – **relief** to the mother who's cutting down on groceries because of gas prices, or the man I met in Pennsylvania who lost his job and can't even afford to drive around and look for a new one.	Care: help for the people in need
	And if I'm elected President, unlike Senator McCain, I won't be giving **tax breaks** (*) to oil companies that are doing better than ever while you're **struggling** more than ever.	Fairness: fair taxation/distribution of money (*)
		–

(continued)

Continued

Speech	Metaphorical expressions per paragraph	Value metaphorically expressed
	And in the short-term, as we **transition to renewable energy**, we can and should increase our domestic production of oil and natural gas.	Care: caring for the environment
	But the truth is, neither of these **steps** will seriously reduce our energy dependence in the long-term. We simply cannot pretend, as Senator McCain does, that we can **drill our way out of this problem** (*). Breaking our **oil addiction** (*) will take nothing less than a complete transformation of our economy.	– Freedom: independence from non-renewable energy sources (*)
	It will take an **all-hands-on-deck effort** from America – effort from our scientists and entrepreneurs; from businesses and from every American citizen.	We: cooperation
	So if I am President, I will immediately **direct the full resources** of the federal government and the full energy of the private sector **to a single, overarching goal** – in ten years, we will eliminate the need for oil from the entire Middle East and Venezuela.	Freedom: independence from non-renewable sources of energy
	To do this, we'll invest $150 billion over the next decade and leverage billions more in private capital to harness American energy and create five million new American jobs – jobs that pay well and won't be outsourced, good **union jobs that lift up** our families and revitalize our communities.	–
	The state of California has implemented such a successful efficiency strategy that while **electricity consumption grew** 60% in this country over the last three decades, it didn't **grow** at all in California. There is no reason we can't do the same thing all across America.	–
	Or we can choose another future. In just a few years, we can watch cars that run on plug-in batteries come off our assembly lines. We can see shuttered **factories open their doors to manufacturers** that sell wind turbines and solar panels that will power our homes and our businesses.	–
28 August 2008	We **measure progress** by how many people can find a job that pays the mortgage; whether you can put a little extra money away at the end of each month so you can someday watch your child receive her college diploma.	–

(continued)

252

Speech	Metaphorical expressions per paragraph	Value metaphorically expressed
	We **measure progress** in the 23 million new jobs that were created when Bill Clinton was President – when the average American family saw its income go **up** $7,500 instead of **down** $2,000 like it has under George Bush.	–
	We **measure the strength of our economy** not by the number of billionaires we have or the profits of the Fortune 500, but by whether someone with a good idea can take a risk and start a new business, or whether the waitress who lives on tips can take a day off to look after a sick kid without losing her job – an economy that honors the dignity of work.	–
	She's the one who put off buying a new car or a new dress for herself so that I could have a better life. She [Obama's mother] **poured everything she had into me.**	Care: caring for children
	It's a promise that says the market should reward drive and innovation and **generate growth** [...]	–
	[...] but that businesses should live up to their responsibilities to create American jobs, look out for American workers, and **play by the rules of the road**.	Responsibility to one another
	That's the promise of America – the idea that we are responsible for ourselves, but that we also **rise or fall as one nation**; the fundamental belief that I am my brother's keeper; I am my sister's keeper.	We: unity
	Unlike John McCain, I will stop giving **tax breaks** to corporations that ship jobs overseas, and I will start giving them to companies that create good jobs right here in America.	Fairness: fair taxation/dis-tribution of money
	I **will cut taxes – cut taxes** – for 95% of all working families. Because in an economy like this, the last thing we should do is **raise taxes** on the middle-class.	Fairness: fair tax-ation/distribu-tion of money
	Now is the time to finally meet our moral obligation to provide every child a world-class education, because it will take nothing less to compete in the global economy. Michelle and I are only here tonight because we were given a chance at an education. And I will not **settle for an America where some kids don't have that chance**. I'll invest in early childhood education.	Chance: opportunity for children
	I'll **recruit an army of new teachers**, and pay them higher salaries and give them more support.	Care: support-ing nurturant professions (teachers)

Continued

Speech	Metaphorical expressions per paragraph	Value metaphorically expressed
	Now is the time to change our bankruptcy laws, so that your pensions are **protected ahead of** CEO bonuses; and the time to protect Social Security for future generations.	Care: caring for the old
	And Democrats, we must also admit that fulfilling America's promise will require more than just money. It will require a renewed sense of responsibility from each of us to recover what John F. Kennedy called our "intellectual and moral strength." Yes, government must lead on energy independence, but each of us must do our part to make our homes and businesses more efficient. Yes, we must provide **more ladders to success** for young men who fall into lives of crime and despair.	Chance: opportunity for everyone
	I will end this war in Iraq responsibly, and finish the fight against al Qaeda and the Taliban in Afghanistan. I will **rebuild our military** to meet future conflicts.	–
	But I will also renew the tough, direct diplomacy that can prevent Iran from obtaining nuclear weapons and curb Russian aggression. I will **build new partnerships to defeat the threats** of the 21st century: terrorism and nuclear proliferation; poverty and genocide; climate change and disease.	We: non confrontational diplomacy
	We may not agree on abortion, but surely we can agree on reducing the number of unwanted pregnancies in this country. The reality of gun ownership may be different for hunters in rural Ohio than for those **plagued by gang-violence** in Cleveland, but don't tell me we can't uphold the Second Amendment while keeping AK-47s out of the hands of criminals.	–
	Passions fly on immigration, but I don't know anyone who benefits when a mother is separated from her infant child or an employer undercuts American wages by hiring illegal workers. This too is part of America's promise – the promise of a democracy where we can find **the strength and grace to bridge divides and unite in common effort.**	We: unity
	I believe that as hard as it will be, the **change** we need **is coming.**	–
	I've seen it [change] in Illinois, when we provided health care to more children and **moved more families from welfare to work.**	Social rights: employment for everyone

(continued)

254

Continued

(*continued*)

Continued

Speech	Metaphorical expressions per paragraph	Value metaphorically expressed
	If we want to see middle class incomes **rising** like they did in the 1990s, we can't afford a future where so many Americans are priced out of college [...]	–
	That's why last November, I proposed an education agenda that **moves beyond** party and ideology and focuses instead on what will make the most difference in a child's life.	–
	My plan calls for giving every child a world-class education from the day they're born until the day they graduate from college.[...] And it's a plan that will finally **put a college degree within reach for anyone** who wants one [...]	Social rights: education for everyone
	Of course, we also have to **fix the broken promises of No Child Left Behind.**	Care: caring for children
	We must **fix the failures of No Child Left Behind**. [...]But Democrats have to realize that **fixing No Child Left Behind** is not enough to prepare our children for a global economy.	Care: caring for children
	We need a new vision for a 21st century education – one [...] ; where we're recruiting, retaining, and rewarding **an army of new teachers**, and students are excited to learn because they're attending schools of the future [...]	Care: supporting nurturant professions (teachers)
	That's what we need to be doing – because America isn't a country that accepts second place. When I'm President, we'll **fight** to make sure we're once again first in the world when it comes to high school graduation rates. We'll **push** our kids to study harder and aim **higher**. [...] And we'll also set a goal of increasing the number of high school students taking college-level or AP courses by 50 percent in the coming years.	Care: supporting/ investing in education
	This fund will invest in schools like the Austin Polytechnical Academy, which is located in a part of Chicago that's been **hard hit by the decline** in manufacturing over the past few decades.	–
	Thanks to partnerships with a number of companies, a curriculum that prepares students for a career in engineering, and a requirement that students graduate with at least two industry certifications, Austin Polytech is **bringing hope back** to the community.	–

(*continued*)

Continued

Speech	Metaphorical expressions per paragraph	Value metaphorically expressed
	Giving our parents real choices about where to send their kids to school also means showing the same kind of leadership at the national level that I did in Illinois when I passed a law to double the number of charter schools in Chicago.	–
	Charter schools that are successful will get the support they need to **grow**.	–
	As we **bring our school system into the 21st century**, we also have to **bring our schools** into the 21st century.	Care: supporting/ investing in education
	Because while technology has transformed just about every aspect of our lives – from the way we travel to the way we communicate to the way we look after our health – one of the places where we've failed to **seize its full potential** is in the classroom.	–
	That's why last year, I proposed a new Service Scholarship program that will recruit **top talent** into the profession, and place these new teachers in overcrowded districts and **struggling rural towns**, or hard-to-staff subjects like special education in schools across the nation.	–
	But we can help parents do a better job. That's why I'll create a parent report card that will show you whether your **kid is on the path to college**.	–
	We'll help schools post student progress reports online so you can get a regular update on what kind of grades your child is getting on tests and quizzes from week to week. If your **kid is falling behind**, or playing hooky, or **isn't on track** to go to college or compete for that good paying job, it will be up to you to do something about it.	–
	So I know that the only reason Michelle and I are where we are today is because this country we love gave us the chance at an education. And the reason I'm **running for President** is to give every single American that same chance [...]	–
12 September 2008	Take a close look at the **tax cuts** I'm proposing and the special interest giveaways that my opponent is proposing, because that will tell you everything you need to know about who we're going to put first as President.	Fairness: fair taxation/ distribution of money

(*continued*)

Continued

Speech	Metaphorical expressions per paragraph	Value metaphorically expressed
	I will **cut taxes** – **cut taxes** – for 95 percent of all working Americans.	Fairness: fair taxation/ distribution of money
	I will **ease the burden** (*) on **struggling homeowners** through a universal homeowner's tax credit.	Fairness: fair taxation/ distribution of money (*) –
	My opponent has voted for those **tax breaks**, and he'll continue them as President. I will end **tax breaks** for companies that ship jobs overseas, and start investing in American jobs and workers.	Fairness: fair taxation/ distribution of money
	To pay for these **tax cuts**, I'll stand up to special interest carve-outs, close corporate loopholes and offshore tax havens, and ask the wealthiest Americans to give back a portion of the Bush **tax cuts**.	Fairness: fair taxation/ distribution of money
	It's time for folks like me who make over $250,000 to pay our fair share to **keep the American promise alive for our children and grandchildren**.	Care: caring for future generations
	And under my plan, middle class families will get three times as much **[tax] relief** as Senator McCain is offering.	Fairness: fair taxation/ distribution of money
20 September 2008	Growing up, I saw my mother **struggle** to put herself through school and raise me and my sister on her own.	–
	I think women like her [Obama's mother] who work hard and **pour** everything they've got **into their kids** (*) should be able to pay the bills and **get ahead** (#) for a change – that's why I'm **running for President**.	Care: caring for children (*); We: (gender) equality (#)
	I saw my grandmother, who helped raise me, **work her way up from the secretarial pool to middle management** at a bank.	–
	But I also saw her **hit a glass ceiling**, as men no more qualified than she was **moved up** the corporate ladder **ahead of her**. I think women like her should be paid fairly and have the same chance to succeed as everyone else – that's why I'm **running** for President.	–

258

Continued

Speech	Metaphorical expressions per paragraph	Value metaphorically expressed
	I've seen my wife, Michelle, **the rock** of the Obama family, juggling work and parenting with more skill and grace than anyone I know. But I've seen how it's torn at her. How sometimes, when she's with the girls, she's worrying about work – and when she's at work, she's worrying about the girls.	–
	It's a feeling I share every day – especially these days, when I'm away so much, out **on the campaign trail**. And I think it should be a little easier for parents in this country to raise their kids and do their jobs – that's why I'm **running for President**.	–
	First, we have to make sure that whatever plan our government comes up with works not just for Wall Street, but for Main Street. We have to make sure it helps folks cope with **rising prices**, and **sparks job creation**, and helps homeowners stay in their homes.	–
	Change is finally **closing that pay gap**. It's unacceptable that women in this country are losing thousands of dollars each year – money you could use for gas or groceries or college tuition. This isn't just an economic issue for millions of American families – it's about our most fundamental values as a nation: that we treat people fairly, that we reward hard work, and there are no second class citizens in our workplaces. That's why I helped pass a law in Illinois to give 330,000 more women **protection from paycheck discrimination**.	We: (gender) equality
	Change isn't a President who thinks Roe vs. Wade is a flawed decision and whose party platform outlaws abortion, even in cases of rape and incest. Change is a President who will stand up for choice – who understands that five men on the Supreme Court don't know better than women and their doctors what's best for a woman's health. That's why I **fought** so hard in Illinois and in Washington to stop laws that would've restricted choice.	Freedom: right to abortion
	So I'm proud to **have him** [Joe Biden] **by my side** in this campaign.	–

(continued)

Continued

Speech	Metaphorical expressions per paragraph	Value metaphorically expressed
	Finally, change means **building an economy that rewards work, creates jobs you can raise a family on** (*), and gives each of us the chance **to get ahead** (#).	Social rights: employment for everyone (*); Chance: opportunity for everyone (#)
	I'll invest in early childhood education, and **recruit an army of new teachers** to our schools, and provide a \$4,000 tuition tax credit to help make college affordable for any middle class student who's willing to serve their community or their country.	Care: supporting nurturant professions (teachers)
	You invest in America, America invests in you, and together, **we'll move this country forward**.	We: cooperation
	He wants to give **tax breaks** to oil companies and companies that ship jobs overseas – I want to give a **tax break** to 95% of all working families and create jobs here at home by investing in renewable energy.	Fairness: fair taxation/distribution of money
	And don't be fooled by the tired old **attacks** my opponent is launching.	–
	In fact, I offer three times the **tax relief for middle-class families** as Senator McCain does – because in an economy like this, the last thing we should do is **raise taxes** on the middle-class.	Fairness: fair distribution of money/fair taxation
	So let's be clear, when I'm President, we're not going to **gamble** with Social Security. We're not going to **gamble** with your ability to retire with dignity after a lifetime of hard work. We're going to **strengthen and protect Social Security** so it's a safety net our families can count on – today, tomorrow and always.	Care: caring for the old
	Women like my friend Hillary Clinton who **put those 18 million cracks in that glass ceiling** (*) so that my daughters – and all our sons and daughters – could **dream a little bigger** and **reach a little higher** (#).	We: (gender) equality (*); Chance: opportunity for children (#)
	Now it's our turn. It's our turn to make those sacrifices so the next generation doesn't have to. Our turn to **open the doors of opportunity** that our daughters and granddaughters will one day **walk through**.	Chance: opportunity for children
	That's what I think about whenever I get the chance to tuck my girls in at night. How I want them – and all our daughters – to have no limits on their dreams, no obstacles to their achievement, **no goals beyond their reach**.	Chance: opportunity for children

(*continued*)

Continued

Speech	Metaphorical expressions per paragraph	Value metaphorically expressed
	And I hope you'll join me. I hope you'll **walk with me** so that we can **turn the page on the failed policies** of the past.	We: cooperation
27 September 2008	Well North Carolina, I know what we need to do. We need to stop giving those **tax cuts** to corporations and CEOs on Wall Street, and start standing up for families out on Main Street. We need to **turn the page on the failed policies** of the last eight years, and finally put working people first.	Fairness: fair distribution of money/fair taxation
	That's why I'm **running for President** of the United States.	–
	We don't need any more **out-of-touch**, on-your-own **leadership** in Washington.	–
	We need a President who knows that America's strength and leadership abroad depends on the **strength of our economy** at home.	–
	We need a President who will **fight** for the middle class every single day, and that's exactly what I'll do when I'm President of the U nited States.	Care: caring for people
	First, we need to set up an independent board, selected by Democrats and Republicans, to provide oversight and accountability for how and where this money is spent at **every step of the way**.	–
	Second, if American taxpayers are financing this solution, you should be treated like investors. That means that Wall Street and Washington should give you every penny of your money back once this **economy recovers**.	–
	Third, we cannot and will not simply bailout Wall Street without helping the millions of innocent **homeowners who are struggling** to stay in their homes.	–
	They deserve a plan too. And Washington needs to feel the same sense of urgency in passing an economic stimulus plan for working families – a plan that would help folks cope with **rising food and gas prices**, save one million jobs by rebuilding our schools and roads, and help states and cities avoid budget cuts and tax increases.	–

(*continued*)

Continued

Speech	Metaphorical expressions per paragraph	Value metaphorically expressed
	I believe that our **free market has been the engine of America's great progress.**	–
	It's a market that has created a prosperity that is the envy of the world, and rewarded the innovators and risk-takers who have made **America a beacon** of science, and technology, and discovery.	–
	Change means a tax code that doesn't reward the lobbyists who wrote it, but the American workers and small businesses who deserve it. I will stop giving **tax breaks** to corporations that ship jobs overseas, and I will start giving them to companies that create good jobs right here in America [...]	Fairness: fair distribution of money/fair taxation
	In fact, I offer three times the **tax relief for middle-class families** as Senator McCain does – because in an economy like this, the last thing we should do is **raise taxes** on the middle-class.	Fairness: fair distribution of money/fair taxation
	And now is the time to finally meet our moral obligation to provide every child a world-class education, because it will take nothing less to compete in the global economy. I'll **recruit an army of new teachers**, and pay them **higher** salaries and give them more support.	Care: supporting nurturant professions (teachers)
	This is the change we need – the kind of **bottom up growth and innovation** that will advance the American economy by advancing the dreams of all Americans.	We: empowering people
	I know that we'll have to overcome our doubts and divisions and the determined opposition of powerful special interests before we can truly reform a **broken economy** and advance opportunity.	–
	But if you want real change – if you want an economy that rewards work, and that works for Main Street and Wall Street; if you want **tax relief for the middle class** and millions of new jobs; if you want health care you can afford and education that helps your kids compete; then I ask you to knock on some doors, make some calls, talk to your neighbors, and give me your vote on November 4th.	Fairness: fair taxation/ distribution of money

(continued)

Continued

Speech	Metaphorical expressions per paragraph	Value metaphorically expressed
10 October 2008	The American people aren't looking for someone who can **divide this country** – they're looking for someone who will lead it. We're in a serious crisis – now, more than ever, it is time to **put country ahead of politics (*)**.	– Care: caring for people (*)
	At first, he said this spending would come from the **rescue package** that already passed. But the **rescue package** included taxpayer protections that prevent exactly this kind of scheme.	–
	We are not going to solve the immediate crisis by **going back** and changing the law we passed last week to **push forward a plan** that would take months to implement.	–
	So I have a different view from Senator McCain. Yes, we need to help innocent homebuyers. That's why I insisted that the **rescue package** give the Treasury authority to buy and rework mortgages. We have given Treasury a broad menu of options that should be pursued. But we should not put taxpayer money at unnecessary risk. Taxpayers should not have all **the downside without any of the upside. That's a principle that I've fought for (*)**, that's a principle that I'll maintain, and that's a principle that I'll stand up for as President. That's the choice in this election.	– – Care: caring for people (*)
	I repeat: we must do more to help innocent home-buyers. [...]It means giving taxpayers a share of the benefit when our **housing market recovers**. And it means **cracking down on predatory lenders** by treating mortgage fraud like the crime that it is.	–
	Now let's be clear Ohio: the **rescue plan** that passed Congress last week isn't the end of what we need to do **to strengthen this economy**. It's only the beginning. Now we need to pass a **rescue plan for the middle-class that will provide every family immediate relief (*)** to cope with **rising food and gas prices**, save one million jobs by rebuilding our schools and roads, and help states and cities avoid budget cuts and tax increases. And we should extend expiring unemployment benefits to those Americans who've lost their jobs and can't find new ones. I've been **fighting for this plan** (#)for months.	– Care: caring for families (*); – Social rights: employment for everyone (#)

(*continued*)

Continued

Speech	Metaphorical expressions per paragraph	Value metaphorically expressed
	If we're going to **rebuild this economy from the bottom up**, it has to start with our small businesses on Main Street – not just the big banks on Wall Street.	Care: caring for people
	Small businesses employ half of the workers in the private sector in this country, and account for the majority of the **job growth**. But we also know that a **credit crunch** has **dried up** capital and put these jobs at risk [...]	–
	That's why we need a **Small Business Rescue Plan** – so that we're **extending our hand** (*)to the shops and restaurants; the start-ups and small firms that create jobs and **make our economy grow**.	Care: help for the people in need (*) \n –
	Main Street needs relief and you need it now. We won't grow government – we'll work within the Small Business Administration **to keep folks afloat** (*), while providing **tax cuts to lift the tide** (#). It's what we did after 9/11, and we were able to get low cost loans out to tens of thousands of small businesses. That's **one of the many steps** (*) we can and should take to help stop job losses and turn this economy around.	Care: help for the people in need (*); Fairness: fair taxation/ distribution of money (#)
	By temporarily eliminating fees for borrowers and lenders, we can **unlock the credit** that small firms need **to move forward**, pay their workers, and **grow their business**.	–
	Just as we make lending more available, we need **to relieve the tax burden** on small businesses to help create jobs.	Fairness: fair taxation/ distribution of money
	Because it's time to protect the jobs we have and to create the jobs of tomorrow by **unlocking the drive, and ingenuity, and innovation** of the American people.	Social rights: employment for everyone
	I have a different set of priorities. I'll give a **middle-class tax cut** to 95% of all workers. And if you make less than $250,000 a year – which includes 98 percent of small business owners – you won't see your taxes increase one single dime. [...] Because in an economy like this, the last thing we should do is **raise taxes on the middle-class**.	Fairness: fair taxation/ distribution of money

Continued

Speech	Metaphorical expressions per paragraph	Value metaphorically expressed
	Wages are **flat-lining**.	–
	But it doesn't have to be this way. That's why I'm going to stop giving **tax breaks (*)** to companies that ship jobs overseas, and start **rebuilding the middle class by helping companies create jobs here in Ohio (#)**.	Fairness: fair taxation/distribution of money (*); Social rights: employment for everyone (#)
	If I am President, I will finally **fix our broken health care system**.	Social rights: health care for everyone
	This issue is personal for me. My mother died of ovarian cancer at the age of 53, and I'll never forget how she spent the final months of her life lying in a hospital bed, **fighting with her insurance company** because they claimed that her cancer was a pre-existing condition and didn't want to pay for treatment.	–
	It is time to provide every American with a world-class education. That means investing in early child-hood education. That means **recruiting an army of new teachers**, and paying them better, and giving them more support in exchange for higher stand-ards and more accountability.	Care: supporting nurturant professions (teachers)
	You invest in America, America will invest in you, and together, we will **move this country forward**.	We: cooperation
	These are the changes and reforms we need. A new era of responsibility and accountability on Wall Street and in Washington. Common-sense regulations to prevent a crisis like this from ever happening again. Investments in the technology and innovation that will restore prosperity and lead to new jobs and a new economy for the 21st century. **Bottom-up growth that gives every American a fair shot at the American dream.**	Chance: opportunity for children
	Together, we cannot fail. Not now. Not when we have a crisis to solve and an **economy to save**.	–
	Together, we can overcome the **broken policies** and **divided politics** of the last eight years. Together, we can renew an **economy that** rewards work and **rebuilds** the middle class.	–

(*continued*)

Continued

Speech	Metaphorical expressions per paragraph	Value metaphorically expressed
	We can do this if we come together; if we have confidence in ourselves and each other; if we **look beyond the darkness of the day to the bright light of hope that lies ahead**. Together, we can change this country and change this world.	We: cooperation
15 October 2008	It is time to **turn the page on eight years of economic policies** that put Wall Street before Main Street but ended up **hurting** both.	–
	We need policies that **grow our economy from the bottom-up** (*), so that **every American**, everywhere, **has the chance to get ahead** (#). Not just the person who owns the factory, but the men and women who work on its floor.	We: empowering people (*); Chance: opportunity for everyone (#)
	Because if we've learned anything from this economic crisis, it's that we're all connected; we're all in this together; and we will **rise or fall as one nation** – as one people.	We: unity
	The **rescue plan** that passed the Congress was a necessary **first step** to easing this credit crisis. It's also important that we continue to work with governments around the globe to confront what is truly a global crisis.	–
	But now we need a **rescue plan** (*) for the middle class. If we're going to **rebuild this economy from the bottom up** (*), it has to start on Main Street – not just the big banks on Wall Street.	Care: help for the people in need (*)
	That's why I've outlined **several steps** (*) that we have to take right now **to help folks who are struggling**.	–
	First, we've got to act now to create good paying jobs. We've already lost three-quarters of a million jobs this year, and some experts say **unemployment may rise** to 8% by the end of next year.	–
	Second, we need to help small businesses **get back on their feet**.	–
	To fuel the real engine of job creation in this country, I'll eliminate all capital gains taxes on investments in small businesses and start-up companies, and provide an additional tax incentive through next year to encourage new small business investment.	Social rights: employment fir everyone

(continued)

Continued

Speech	Metaphorical expressions per paragraph	Value metaphorically expressed
	Third, we need to provide [tax] **relief** (*) for home-owners who are watching their home values **decline while property taxes go up**.	Care: help for the people in need (*) –
	The Treasury must use the authority it's been granted and **move aggressively to help people** avoid foreclosure and stay in their homes.	Care: help for the people in need
	For those responsible homeowners in danger of losing their homes, I've proposed a three-month moratorium on foreclosures so that we **give people the breathing room** they need **to get back on their feet**.	Care: help for the people in need
	Finally, we've got to help **states and local govern-ments that have been squeezed**. This is a part of this crisis that hasn't gotten enough attention.	–
	If Washington keeps **pushing the burden on to states and cities and towns**, you might be forced **to raise new revenue** through cuts in services or increases in taxes.	–
	We will also **save one million jobs** (*) by creating a Jobs and Growth Fund that will provide money to states and local communities so they can **move forward** with projects that put people to work rebuilding and repairing our roads, our bridges, and our schools.	Social rights: employment for everyone (*) –
	We also need a new lending facility that **reaches out to states and localities** – we can't **extend a hand** to banks on Wall Street without **reaching out to Main Street** (*) so states can make payroll and deliver ser-vices. That's why I'm **running for President** of the United States.	Care: help for the people in need (*) –
	I have a different set of priorities. I'll give **a middle-class tax cut** to 95% of all workers. And if you make less than $250,000 a year – which includes 98 percent of small business owners – you won't see your taxes increase one single dime. Not your payroll taxes, not your income taxes, not your capital gains taxes – nothing.	Fairness: fair taxation/ distribution of money
	Because in an economy like this, the last thing we should do is **raise taxes on the middle-class**.	Fairness: fair taxation/ distribution of money

(continued)

Continued

Speech	Metaphorical expressions per paragraph	Value metaphorically expressed
	We know that it's time to create the good-paying jobs of tomorrow. That's why I'm going to **stop giving tax breaks** (*) to companies that ship jobs overseas, and start **rebuilding the middle class** (#)by helping companies create jobs here in America.	Fairness: fair taxation (*); Social rights: employment for everyone (#)
	If I am President, I will finally **fix our broken health care system**.	Social rights: health care for everyone
	It is time to provide every American with a world-class education. That means investing in early childhood education. That means **recruiting an army of new teachers**, and paying them better, and giving them more support in exchange for higher standards and more accountability.	Care: supporting nurturant professions (teachers)
	Senator McCain's **top economic advisor** actually said the other day that they have no plan to invest in college affordability because we can't have a giveaway to every special interest. [...]	–
	That's why I'll make this deal with you: if you commit to serving your community or your country, we will make sure you can afford your tuition. You invest in America, America will invest in you, and together, we will **move this country forward.**	We: cooperation
	These are the changes and reforms we need. A new era of responsibility and accountability on Wall Street and in Washington. Common-sense regulations to prevent a crisis like this from ever happening again. Investments in the technology and innovation that will restore prosperity and lead to new jobs and a new economy for the 21st century. **Bottom-up growth that gives every American a fair shot** at the American dream. And above all confidence – confidence in America, confidence in our economy, and confidence in ourselves.	Chance: opportunity for everyone
	This is one of those moments. I realize you're cynical and fed up with politics. I understand that you're disappointed and even angry with your leaders. You have every right to be. But despite all of this, I ask of you what's been asked of the American people in times of trial and turmoil throughout our history. I ask you to believe – to believe in yourselves, in each other, and in **the future we can build together.**	We: cooperation

(continued)

Continued

Speech	Metaphorical expressions per paragraph	Value metaphorically expressed
	Together, we cannot fail. Not now. Not when we have a crisis to solve and an **economy to save**.	–
	If you want the next four years looking like the last eight, then I am not your candidate. But if you want real change – if you want an economy that rewards work, and that works for Main Street and Wall Street; if you want **tax relief** for the middle class and millions of new jobs; [...] then I ask you to knock on some doors, make some calls, talk to your neighbors, and give me your vote on November 4th.	Fairness: fair taxation/ distribution of money
20 October 2008	The **rescue plan** that passed Congress was a necessary **first step** to easing this credit crisis, but if we're going to **rebuild this economy from the bottom up (*)**, we need an immediate **rescue plan for the middle-class (*)** – and that's what I'll offer as President of the United States.	– Care: help for the people in need (*)
	Last week, I laid out a plan that will **jumpstart job creation (*)**, **provide relief to families (#)**, and **rebuild our financial system (#)**.	Social rights: employment for everyone (*); Fairness: fair distribution of money, fair taxation (#)
	It's a plan that will also help **struggling homeowners** stay in their homes – something that's particularly important here in Florida, where foreclosures are up 30% over the last year.	–
	Look, we must act quickly to end this housing crisis. That's why last March, I was calling for us to help innocent home buyers. And that's why I **fought** to make sure the recent **rescue package** gives Treasury the responsibility and authority to help homeowners avoid foreclosure.	Care: help for the people in need
	But we should not put your tax dollars at unnecessary risk. We should not let banks and lenders **off the hook** when it was their greed and irresponsibility that got us into this mess.	–
	If the American people are going to put up $700 billion **to rescue our financial institutions**, we should make sure those institutions are doing their part for the American people.	–

(*continued*)

Continued

Speech	Metaphorical expressions per paragraph	Value metaphorically expressed
	Now, we've also put in place long-term measures to restore our credit markets and help families refinance their mortgages, but until those measures start working, we need to help homeowners stay in their homes, and that's what this **foreclosure freeze** will do.	–
	And while we're at it, there's **another step we can take to help innocent homeowners** that won't cost taxpayers a dime.	Care: help for the people in need
	We have to help the hardworking families who are living in those homes with **shrinking paychecks** and **rising costs**.	–
	It's true that I want to roll back the Bush **tax cuts** (*) on the wealthiest Americans and **go back to the rate** they paid under Bill Clinton. John McCain calls that socialism.	Fairness: fair taxation/ distribution of money (*) –
	To create more American jobs, I've proposed a tax credit for each new employee that companies hire here in the United States over the next two years. And I'll stop giving **tax breaks** to companies that ship jobs overseas and invest in companies that create good jobs right here in Florida.	Fairness: fair taxation/ distribution of money
	I'll help small businesses **get back on their feet** by eliminating capital gains taxes and giving them emergency loans to keep their **doors open** and hire workers.	–
	And I will create a Jobs and Growth fund to help states and local governments **save one million jobs** (*) and pay for health care and education without having to **raise your taxes**.	Social rights: employment for everyone (*) –
	If I am President, I will finally **fix the problems in our health care system** that we've been talking.	Social rights: health care for everyone
	It is time to provide every American with a world-class education. That means investing in early childhood education. That means **recruiting an army of new teachers**, and paying them better, and giving them more support in exchange for higher standards and more accountability.	Care: supporting nurturant professions (teachers)

(continued)

270

Speech	Metaphorical expressions per paragraph	Value metaphorically expressed
	My opponent's **top economic advisor** actually said that they have no plan to invest in college afford-ability because we can't have a giveaway to every special interest.	–
	You invest in America, America will invest in you, and together, we will **move this country forward**.	We: cooperation
	At a defining moment like this, we don't have the luxury of relying on the same **political games** and the same **political tactics** that are used every election to divide us from one another and make us afraid of one another.	–
	I ask you to believe – to believe in yourselves, in each other, and in **the future we can build together**.	We: cooperation
	Together, we cannot fail. Not now. Not when we have a crisis to solve and an **economy to save**.	–
	If you want the next four years looking like the last eight, then I am not your candidate. But if you want real change – if you want an economy that rewards work, and that works for Main Street and Wall Street; if you want **tax relief** for the middle class and millions of new jobs [...]	Fairness: fair taxation/ distribution of money
27 October 2008	In one week, you can choose policies that invest in our middle-class, create new jobs, and **grow this economy from the bottom-up** so that everyone has a chance to succeed; from the CEO to the secretary and the janitor; from the factory owner to the men and women who work on its floor.	Chance: opportunity for everyone
	And I was convinced that when we come together, **our voices are more powerful** (*) than the most entrenched lobbyists, or the most vicious **political attacks**, or the full force of a status quo in Washington that wants to keep things just the way they are.	We: coopera-tion (*) –
	I know these are difficult times for America. But I also know that we have faced difficult times before. The American story has never been about things coming easy – it's been about **rising to the moment when the moment was hard**.	–

(*continued*)

Continued

Speech	Metaphorical expressions per paragraph	Value metaphorically expressed
	It's about **seeing the highest mountaintop from the deepest of valleys**.	–
	It's about rejecting fear and division for unity of purpose. That's how we've overcome war and depression. That's how we've **won great struggles** for civil rights and women's rights and worker's rights.	–
	And that's how we'll **emerge from this crisis stronger** and more prosperous than we were before – as one nation; as one people.	–
	Now, I don't believe that government can or should try to solve all our problems. I know you don't either. But I do believe that government should do that which we cannot do for ourselves – protect us from harm and provide a decent education for our children; invest in new roads and new science and technology. It should reward drive and innovation and **growth in the free market**, but it should also make sure businesses live up to their responsibility to create American jobs, and look out for American workers, and **play by the rules of the road** (*).	– Fairness: fair taxation/ distribution of money (*)
	It should ensure **a shot at success** not only for those with money and power and influence, but for every single American who's willing to work.	Chance: opportunities for everyone
	That's how we make sure businesses have customers that can afford their products and services. That's how we've always **grown the American economy – from the bottom-up.** John McCain calls this socialism. I call it opportunity, and there is nothing more American than that.	We: empowering people
	We don't have to choose between allowing our **financial system to collapse** and spending billions of taxpayer dollars to bail out Wall Street banks. As President, I will ensure that the **financial rescue plan** helps stop foreclosures and protects your money instead of enriching CEOs.	–

(continued)

272

Continued

Speech	Metaphorical expressions per paragraph	Value metaphorically expressed
	The choice in this election isn't between **tax cuts** and no **tax cuts**. It's about whether you believe we should only reward wealth, or whether we should also reward the work and workers who create it. I will give a **tax break** to 95% of Americans who work every day and get taxes taken out of their paychecks every week. I'll eliminate income taxes for seniors making under $50,000 and **give homeowners and working parents more of a break**. [...] No matter what Senator McCain may claim, here are the facts – if you make under $250,000, you will not see your taxes increase by a single dime – not your income taxes, not your payroll taxes, not your capital gains taxes. Nothing. Because the last thing we should do in this economy is **raise taxes** on the middle-class.	Fairness: fair taxation/ distribution of money
	When it comes to jobs, the choice in this election is not between **putting up a wall around America** or allowing every job to disappear overseas.	–
	The truth is, we won't be able to **bring back every job** (*) that we've lost, but that doesn't mean we should follow John McCain's plan to keep giving **tax breaks** (#) to corporations that **send American jobs** (*) overseas.	Social rights: employment for everyone (*); Fairness: fair taxation/ distribution of money (#)
	As President, I will invest in early childhood education, **recruit an army of new teachers,** pay them more, and give them more support.	Care: supporting nurturant professions (teachers)
	You invest in America, America will invest in you, and together, we will **move this country forward**.	We: cooperation
	But as I've said from the day we **began this journey** all those months ago, the change we need isn't just about new programs and policies.	–
	It's about a new politics – **a politics that calls on our better angels** instead of encouraging our worst instincts; one that reminds us of the obligations we have to ourselves and one another.	Responsibility: responsibility to one another

(*continued*)

Continued

Speech	Metaphorical expressions per paragraph	Value metaphorically expressed
	Yes, government must lead the way on energy independence, but each of us must do our part to make our homes and our businesses more efficient. Yes, we must provide more **ladders to success** for young men who fall into lives of crime and despair.	Chance: opportunity for everyone
	Yes, we can argue and debate our positions passionately, but at this defining moment, all of us must summon the strength and grace **to bridge our differences and unite in common effort** – black, white, Latino, Asian, Native American; Democrat and Republican, young and old, rich and poor, gay and straight, disabled or not.	We: unity
	Hope! That's what kept some of our parents and grandparents going when times were tough. [...]It's what led immigrants from distant lands to come to these shores **against great odds** and **carve a new life** for their families in America; what led those who couldn't vote to march and organize and stand for freedom; that led them to cry out, "It may look **dark** tonight, but if I hold on to hope, tomorrow will be **brighter**."	–
	In one week, we can choose an economy that rewards work and creates new jobs and fuels prosperity **from the bottom-up**.	We: empowering people
	That's **what's at stake**. That's what we're **fighting for**. And if in this last week, you will knock on some doors for me, and make some calls for me, and talk to your neighbors, and convince your friends; if you will stand with me, and **fight with me (*)**, and give me your vote, then I promise you this – we will not just win Ohio, we will not just win this election, but together, we will change this country and we will change the world. Thank you, God bless you, and may God bless America.	– We: cooperation (*)

274

Metaphorical expressions in CSF paragraphs

Speech	Metaphorical expressions per paragraph	Value metaphorically expressed
5 February 2008	What began as a whisper in Springfield soon carried across the corn fields of Iowa, where farmers and factory workers; students and seniors stood up in numbers we've never seen. They stood up to say that maybe this year, we don't have to settle for a **politics where scoring points** is more important than solving problems.	Strength: display of force
	It's different not because of me, but because of you. Because you are tired of being disappointed and tired of being **let down (*)**. You're tired of hearing promises made and plans proposed in the **heat of a campaign** only to have nothing change when everyone goes back to Washington. Because the lobbyists just write another check. Or because politicians start worrying about how they'll win the next election instead of why they should. Or because they focus on **who's up and who's down** (*) instead of who matters.	Hierarchy (*) –
	The Republicans **running for President** have already **tied themselves to the past.**	–
	They speak of a hundred year war in Iraq and billions more on **tax breaks (*)** for the wealthiest few who don't need them and didn't ask for them – **tax breaks (*)** that mortgage our children's future on a **mountain of debt** at a time when there are families who can't pay their medical bills and students who can't pay their tuition.	Moral order: distribution of wealth (*) –
12 February 2008	We know it takes more than one night – or even one election – to overcome decades of money and the influence; bitter partisanship and petty bickering that's **shut you out, let you down** and told you **to settle.**	Hierarchy
	It's a **game** where lobbyists write check after check and Exxon turns record profits, while you pay the price at the pump, and our planet is put at risk. That's what happens when lobbyists set the agenda, and that's why they won't **drown out your voices** (*) anymore when I am President of the United States of America.	– Hierarchy (*)
	George Bush won't be on the ballot this November, but his war and his **tax cuts** for the wealthy will.	Moral order: distribution of wealth

(*continued*)

Continued

Speech	Metaphorical expressions per paragraph	Value metaphorically expressed
	If we had **chosen a different path, the right path**, we could have finished the job in Afghanistan, and put more resources into the fight against bin Laden; and instead of spending hundreds of billions of dollars in Baghdad, we could have put that money into our schools and hospitals, our road and bridges – and that's what the American people need us to do right now.	–
	We can't keep spending money that we don't have in a war that we shouldn't have fought. We can't keep mortgaging our children's future on **a mountain of debt**. We can't keep driving a wider and wider gap between the few who are rich and the rest who **struggle to keep pace**. It's time **to turn the page**.	–
4 March 2008	It's the **same course** that threatens a century of war in Iraq – a third and fourth and fifth tour of duty for brave troops who've done all we've asked them to, even while we ask little and expect nothing Iof the Iraqi government whose job it is to put their country back together. **A course** where we spend billions of dollars a week that could be used to rebuild our roads and our schools; to care for our veterans and send our children to college.	–
	It's the **same course** that continues to **divide** and isolate **America** from the world by substituting bluster and bullying for direct diplomacy – by ignoring our allies and refusing to talk to our enemies even though Presidents from Kennedy to Reagan have done just that; because strong countries and strong leaders aren't afraid to tell hard truths to petty dictators.	–
	And it's the **same course** that offers the same tired answer to workers without health care and families without homes; to students in debt and children who go to bed hungry in the richest nation on Earth – four more years of **tax breaks** (*) for the biggest corporations and the wealthiest few who don't need them and aren't even asking for them.	– Moral order: distribution of wealth (*)

(continued)

Continued

Speech	Metaphorical expressions per paragraph	Value metaphorically expressed
	It's **a course** that further divides Wall Street from Main Street; where **struggling families** are told to **pull themselves up by their bootstraps** (#) because there's nothing government can do or should do – and so we should give more to those with the most and **let the chips fall** (|)where they may.	– – Self-discipline/ Self-reliance (#); Moral order: distribution of wealth (|)
18 March 2008	Just as black anger often proved counterproductive, so have these white resentments distracted attention from the real culprits of the **middle class squeeze** – a corporate culture rife with inside dealing, questionable accounting practices, and short-term greed; a Washington dominated by lobbyists and special interests; economic policies that favor the few over the many. And yet, to wish away the resentments of white Americans, to label them as misguided or even racist, without recognizing they are grounded in legitimate concerns – this too **widens the racial divide**, and blocks the **path to understanding**.	–
20 March 2008	What no one disputes is that President Bush has done what no other President has ever done, and given **tax cuts** to the rich in a time of war. John McCain once opposed these **tax cuts** – he rightly called them unfair and fiscally irresponsible. But now he has done an about face and wants to make them permanent, just like he wants a permanent occupation in Iraq.	Moral order: distribution of wealth
	That's an outcome America can't afford. Because of the Bush-McCain policies, our debt has **ballooned**. This is creating problems in our **fragile economy**.	–
	And that kind of debt also **places an unfair burden on our children** and grandchildren, who will have to repay it.	Strength: lack of nurturance
14 April 2008	But I will never **walk away from the larger point** that I was trying to make. For the last several decades, people in small towns and cities and rural areas all across this country have seen globalization change the **rules of the game** (*) on them.	– Freedom: unregulated free market (*)

(*continued*)

Continued

Speech	Metaphorical expressions per paragraph	Value metaphorically expressed
	There's no plan to address the **downside of globalization**. We don't do anything about the **skyrocketing cost** of health care or college or those disappearing pensions.	–
	Instead of **fighting** to replace jobs that aren't coming back, Washington ends up **fighting over the latest distraction** of the week.	Strength: lack of nurturance
	And after years and years and years of this, a lot of people in this country have become cynical about what government can do to improve their lives. They are angry and frustrated with their leaders for not listening to them; for **not fighting** for them; for not always telling them the truth. And yes, they are bitter about that.	Strength: lack of nurturance
	Ronald Reagan called this **trickle-down economics**. George Bush called it the Ownership Society. But what it really means is that you're on your own. If your premiums or your tuition is **rising** faster than you can afford, you're on your own. If you're that Maytag worker who just lost his pension, tough luck. If you're a child born into poverty, you'll just have to **pull yourself up by your own bootstraps (*)**.	– – Self-discipline/ self reliance (*)
	He's promising to make permanent the Bush **tax breaks for the wealthiest** few who didn't need them and didn't ask for them – **tax breaks** that are so irresponsible that John McCain himself once said they offended his conscience.	Moral order: distribution of wealth
	He's promising four more years of an Administration that will **push for** the privatization of Social Security – a plan that would **gamble away (*)** people's retirement on the stock market; a plan that was already rejected by Democrats and Republicans under George Bush.	– Freedom: unregulated free market (*)
	He's promising four more years of policies that won't guarantee health insurance for working Americans; that won't **bring down the rising cost** of college tuition; that won't do a thing for the Americans who are living in those communities where the **jobs have left** and the factories have **shut their doors**.	–

(*continued*)

Continued

Speech	Metaphorical expressions per paragraph	Value metaphorically expressed
22 April 2008	John McCain said that George Bush's economic policies have led to "great progress" over the last seven years, and so he's promising four more years of **tax cuts** for CEOs and corporations who didn't need them and weren't asking for them; tax cuts that he once voted against because he said they "offended his conscience."	Moral order: distribution of wealth
	Well they [tax cuts] may have stopped offending John McCain's conscience **somewhere along the road to the White House**, but George Bush's economic policies still offend ours. Because I don't think that the 232,000 Americans who've lost their jobs this year are seeing the great progress that John McCain has seen. I don't think the millions of Americans losing their homes have seen that progress. I don't think the families without health care and the workers without pensions have seen that progress. And if we continue **down the same reckless path**, I don't think that future generations who'll be **saddled with debt** will see these as years of progress.	–
20 May 2008	But this year's Republican primary was a **contest** to see which candidate could out-Bush the other, and that is the **contest John McCain won**.	–
	The Bush **tax cuts** for the wealthiest 2% of Americans that once bothered Senator McCain's conscience are now his only economic policy. The Bush health care plan that only helps those who are already healthy and wealthy is now John McCain's answer to the 47 million Americans without insurance and the millions more who can't pay their medical bills. The Bush Iraq policy that asks everything of our troops and nothing of Iraqi politicians is John McCain's policy too, and so is the fear of tough and aggressive diplomacy that has left this country more isolated and less secure than at any time in recent history.	Moral order: distribution of wealth
	The lobbyists who ruled George Bush's Washington are now **running John McCain's campaign**, and they actually had the nerve to say that the American people won't care about this.	–

(continued)

279

Continued

Speech	Metaphorical expressions per paragraph	Value metaphorically expressed
3 June 2008	It's not change when he offers four more years of Bush economic policies that have failed to create well-paying jobs, or insure our workers, or help Americans afford the **skyrocketing cost of college** – policies that have lowered the real incomes of the average American family, widened the gap between Wall Street and Main Street, and left our children with a **mountain of debt.**	–
	John McCain has spent a lot of time talking about trips to Iraq in the last few weeks, but maybe if he spent some time taking trips to the **cities and towns that have been hardest hit by this economy** – cities in Michigan, and Ohio, and right here in Minnesota – he'd understand the kind of change that people are looking for.	–
21 June 2008	And it's precisely because you're **on the front lines** in our communities that you know what happens when Washington fails to do its job. It may be easy for some in Washington to **remain out of touch** (*) with the consequences of the decisions that are made there – but not you.	– Hierarchy (*)
	You know what happens when Washington succumbs to petty partisanship and fails to pass comprehensive immigration reform – because it's your communities that are forced to **take immigration enforcement into their own hands**, your cities' **services that are stretched**, and your neighborhoods that are seeing **rising cultural and economic tensions.**	–
	You know what happens when Washington listens to big oil and gas companies and blocks real energy reform – because it's **your budgets that are being pinched by high energy costs**, and your schools that are cutting back on textbooks to keep their buses running; it's the lots in your towns and cities that are brownfields.	–
	At a time when you're facing budget deficits and looking to Washington for the support you need, he isn't proposing a strategy for America's cities. Instead, he's calling for nearly $2 trillion in **tax breaks for big corporations and the wealthiest** Americans – and yet he's actually opposed more funding for the COPS program and the Community Development Block Grant program.	Moral order: distribution of wealth

(continued)

Continued

Speech	Metaphorical expressions per paragraph	Value metaphorically expressed
21 June 2008	And that's what you need now more than ever. Because for eight long years, Washington hasn't been working for ordinary Americans. And few have been **hit harder** than Latinos and African Americans.	–
1 August 2008	In recent years, we have relearned the essential truth that in the long run, we cannot have a **thriving Wall Street** and a **struggling Main Street**. When **wages are flat, prices are rising,** and more **Americans are mired in debt,** the economy as a whole **suffers**. When a reckless few **game the system,** as we've seen in this housing crisis, millions suffer and we're all affected.	–
	When special interests **put their thumb on the scale, and distort the free market,** the people who compete by the rules come in last.	Freedom: unregulated free market
	And when our government fails to meet its obligation – to provide sensible oversight and stand on the side of working people and invest in their future – America **pays a heavy price**.	–
	Now my opponent has a very different economic philosophy. He's proposing to **cut the gasoline tax** paid by the oil companies and trust that they will pass on the savings in the form of lower prices at the pump. It's a plan that strips $9 billion from our highway construction funds, which means we will lose over 300,000 construction jobs. And he's also proposing **tax cuts** for corporations and the wealthiest Americans in the hope that a little bit of it will **trickle down** to you.	Moral order: distribution of wealth
28 August 2008	Now, I don't believe that Senator McCain doesn't care what's going on in the lives of Americans. I just think he doesn't know. Why else would he define middle-class as someone making under five million dollars a year? How else could he propose hundreds of billions in **tax breaks** (*)for big corporations and oil companies but not one penny of **tax relief** (*) to more than one hundred million Americans? How else could he offer a health care plan that would actually tax people's benefits, or an education plan that would do nothing to help families pay for college, or a plan that would privatize Social Security and **gamble your retirement** (#)?	Moral order: distribution of wealth (*) Strength: lack of nurturance (#)

(*continued*)

Continued

Speech	Metaphorical expressions per paragraph	Value metaphorically expressed
	For over two decades, he's subscribed to that old, discredited Republican philosophy – give more and more to those with the most and hope that **prosperity trickles down** (*) to everyone else. In Washington, they call this the Ownership Society, but what it really means is – you're on your own. Out of work? Tough luck. No health care? The market will fix it. Born into poverty? **Pull yourself up by your own bootstraps (#)** – even if you don't have boots. You're on your own.	Moral order: distribution of wealth (*) Self-discipline/ Self-reliance (#)
	Washington's been talking about our **oil addiction** for the last thirty years, and John McCain has been there for twenty-six of them. In that time, he's said no to higher fuel-efficiency standards for cars, no to investments in renewable energy, no to renewable fuels. And today, we import triple the amount of oil as the day that Senator McCain took office.	–
12 September 2008	That's what Senator McCain is offering. More of the discredited theory that if you **shower benefits on big corporations**, special interests and the wealthiest of the wealthy, it will all come **trickling down** to the middle class. Well, Dover, how much of that has **trickled down** to you? How much has **trickled down** to the Americans who have lost their jobs and their homes? How much has **trickled down** to the family that can't afford to pay next month's bills or the kids who can't afford college? We've tried this for eight years, and we can't afford to keep trying it for another four.	Moral order: distribution of wealth
	We can't afford to keep spending $10 billion a month in Iraq while the Iraqi government **sits on a surplus**. We can't afford more of the same **addiction to oil**. More of the same health care policy that only works for the healthy and wealthy. More of the same Washington lobbyists who run John McCain's campaign. More of the same Bush-Rove-McCain politics that tries to distract you from policies that are destroying the middle class.	–
	We've tried that way. It won't work. And yet Senator McCain stubbornly **holds to it**. The only change he offers is completing the Bush agenda. Privatizing your Social Security. Taxing your health benefits.	–
	And another $200 billion of budget-busting **tax breaks for corporations** like Exxon-Mobil that have just turned in the greatest profits in history, while you can barely afford to fill up a tank of gas.	Moral order: distribution of wealth

(*continued*)

Continued

Speech	Metaphorical expressions per paragraph	Value metaphorically expressed
	Now I do want to be fair. Senator McCain is offering some **tax cuts**. He'd spend nearly $2 trillion over a decade in **tax breaks** for corporations. He would continue the Bush **tax cuts** for the wealthiest Americans. His plan gives more than a half million dollars in tax cuts for households making over $2.8 million.	Moral order: distribution of wealth
	We cannot afford four more years of **out of touch**, on your own, **leadership** in the White House.	Self-reliance
	John McCain likes **to rail against the Washington herd**, but the truth is, when it comes to the issues that really matter in your lives, he's been **running in that herd** for 26 years, and they've **run this economy into a ditch**.	–
27 September 2008	We talked about the economy for forty minutes, and not once did Senator McCain talk about the **struggles** that middle class families are facing every day right here in North Carolina and around the country.	–
	He **defended his plan** to give $300 billion in **tax cuts** (*) to corporations and the wealthiest Americans, but he had nothing to say about the fact that wages have **flatlined** and jobs are being shipped overseas.	– / Moral order: distribution of wealth (*) / –
	The truth is, when my opponent first reacted to this crisis by saying that the fundamentals of our economy are strong, he didn't just make a mistake. He revealed an **out-of-touch philosophy** he's followed for decades in Washington – the idea that if we give more and more to those with the most, prosperity will **trickle down** (*) to everyone else; the idea that no harm will be done if we let lobbyists **shred consumer protections** (#) and **fight against every regulation** (#) as unwise or unnecessary.	– / Moral order: distribution of wealth (*); Freedom: unregulated free market (#)
	But I am **running for President** because we simply cannot afford four more years of an economic philosophy that works for Wall Street instead of Main Street, and ends up devastating both.	–
10 October 2008	We can't afford four more years of the economic theory that says we should give more and more to those with the most and hope that **prosperity trickles down** (*) to everyone else. We can't afford four more years of less regulation so that no one in Washington is watching anyone on Wall Street. We've seen **where that's led us and we're not going back**.	Moral order: distribution of wealth (*) / –

(continued)

Continued

Speech	Metaphorical expressions per paragraph	Value metaphorically expressed
15 October 2008	He wants an energy policy that gives billions to the oil companies, an education policy that **leaves our children behind**, and a war in Iraq that's costing us $10 billion a month while the Iraqi government **sits on a surplus** – a war that you and I know must end.	–
27 October 2008	In one week, you **can turn the page** on policies that have put the greed and irresponsibility of Wall Street before the hard work and sacrifice of folks on Main Street.	–
	At a moment like this, the last thing we can afford is four more years of the tired, old theory that says we should give more to billionaires and big corporations and hope that prosperity **trickles down** to everyone else.	Moral order: distribution of wealth
	The last thing we can afford is four more years where no one in Washington is watching anyone on Wall Street because politicians and lobbyists **killed common-sense regulations.** Those are the theories that got us into this mess.	Freedom
	But when it comes to the economy – when it comes to the central issue of this election – the plain truth is that John McCain has stood with this President **every step of the way**.	–
	Voting for the Bush **tax cuts** for the wealthy that he once opposed. Voting for the Bush budgets that spent us into debt. Calling for less regulation twenty-one times just this year. Those are the facts.	Moral order: distribution of wealth
	It's not change when John McCain wants to give a $700,000 **tax cut** to the average Fortune 500 CEO. It's not change when he wants to give $200 billion to the biggest corporations or $4 billion to the oil companies or $300 billion to the same Wall Street banks that got us into this mess. It's not change when he comes up with a tax plan that doesn't give **a penny of relief** to more than 100 million middle-class Americans. That's not change.	Moral order: distribution of wealth
	Part of the reason this economic crisis occurred is because we have been living through an era of profound irresponsibility. On Wall Street, easy money and an ethic of "what's good for me is good enough" **blinded** greedy executives to the danger in the decisions they were making.	–
	In Washington, politicians spent money they didn't have and allowed lobbyists to set the agenda. They **scored political points** instead of solving our problems, and even after the greatest attack on American soil since Pearl Harbor, all we were asked to do by our President was to go out and shop.	–

284

Metaphorical expressions in mixed paragraphs (CSF+NP)

Speech	Metaphorical expressions per paragraph	Value metaphorically expressed
12 February 2008	**It's a game** where trade deals like NAFTA ship jobs overseas and force parents to compete with their teenagers to work for minimum wage at Wal-Mart. That's what happens when the American worker doesn't have a voice at the negotiating table, when leaders change their positions on trade with the politics of the moment, and that's why we need a President who will listen to Main Street – not just Wall Street; a President who will stand with workers not just when it's easy, but when it's hard.	–
	It's a game where Democrats and Republicans fail to come together year after year after year, while another mother goes without health care for her sick child. That's why we have to put an end to the division and distraction in Washington, so that we can unite this nation around a common purpose, a higher purpose.	–
4 March 2008	It is with that hope that we began **this unlikely journey** – the hope that if we could go block by block, city by city, state by state and **build a movement** that spanned race and region; party and gender; if we could give young people a reason to vote and the young at heart a reason to believe again; if we could inspire a nation to come together again, then we could **turn the page on the politics that's shut us out, let us down**, and told us **to settle** (*).	– – – Hierarchy (*)
	We could **write a new chapter in the American story.**	–
6 May 2008	The woman I met in Indiana who just lost her job, and her pension, and her insurance when the plant where she worked at her entire life closed down – she can't afford four more years of **tax breaks** (*) for corporations like the one that shipped her job overseas. She needs us to give **tax breaks** (*) to companies that create good jobs here in America. She can't afford four more years of **tax breaks** (*) for CEOs like the one who walked away from her company with a multi-million dollar bonus. She needs **middle-class tax relief** (#) that will help her pay the **skyrocketing price** of groceries, and gas, and college tuition. That's why I'm **running for President**.	Moral order: distribution of money (*); Fairness: fair distribution of money/ taxation (#) – –

(continued)

Continued

Speech	Metaphorical expressions per paragraph	Value metaphorically expressed
	The man I met in Pennsylvania who lost his job but can't even afford the gas to drive around and look for a new one – he can't afford four more years of an energy policy written by the oil companies and for the oil companies; a policy that's not only keeping gas at record prices, but funding both sides of the war on terror and destroying our planet in the process. He doesn't need four more years of Washington policies that sound good, but don't solve the problem. He needs us to **take a permanent holiday from our oil addiction** by making the automakers raise their fuel standards, corporations pay for their pollution, and oil companies invest their record profits in a clean energy future. That's the change we need.	Freedom: independence from non-renewable energy sources
20 May 2008	You spoke of an America where working families don't have to file for bankruptcy just because a child gets sick; where they don't lose their home because some **predatory lender** tricks them out of it; where they don't have to **sit on the sidelines of the global economy** because they couldn't afford the cost of a college education. You spoke of an America where our parents and grandparents don't spend their retirement in poverty because some CEO **dumped their pension** (*) – an America where we don't just value wealth, but the work and the workers who create it.	– – Strength: lack of nurturance (*)
	You spoke of an America where we don't send our sons and daughters on tour after tour of duty to a war that has cost us thousands of lives and billions of dollars but has not made us safer. You spoke of an America where we match the might of our military with the strength of our diplomacy and the power of our ideals – **a nation that is still the beacon** of all that is good and all that is possible for humankind.	–

(*continued*)

Continued

Speech	Metaphorical expressions per paragraph	Value metaphorically expressed
3 June 2008	Change is building an economy that rewards not just wealth, but the work and workers who created it. It's understanding that the **struggles** facing working families can't be solved by spending billions of dollars on more **tax breaks** (*) for big corporations and wealthy CEOs, but by giving a **the middle-class a tax break** (#), and investing in our crumbling infrastructure, and transforming how we use energy, and improving our schools, and renewing our commitment to science and innovation. It's understanding that fiscal responsibility and shared prosperity can go **hand-in-hand**, as they did when Bill Clinton was President.	– Moral order: distribution of wealth (*); Fairness: fair taxation (#) –
10 July 2008	That's why, while Senator McCain wants to continue the Bush **tax cuts** (*) for the wealthiest Americans who don't need them and didn't ask for them, I'll pass a **tax cut** (#) of up to $1,000 per working family.	Moral order: distribution of wealth (*) Fairness: fair taxation (#)
12 September 2008	I think we need to encourage growth. Senator McCain thinks we need to give $200 billion a year in **tax breaks** (*) for corporations, but not a single new **tax break** (*) for small businesses – even though small businesses are the source of 80 percent of the new jobs in our economy. I will eliminate capital gains taxes for the small businesses and start-ups that will create the high-tech, high-wage jobs of tomorrow, and help them afford health insurance for their employees. That's how America is going to compete. That's how we're going **to build the middle class** (#). That's change.	Moral order: distribution of wealth (*) Care: caring for people (#)
	Apparently, Senator McCain doesn't think it's enough that your health premiums have doubled, he thinks you should have to pay taxes on them too. That's a $3.6 trillion tax increase on middle class families. That will eventually leave tens of millions of you paying **higher taxes**. That's his idea of change.	Moral order: distribution of wealth
27 September 2008	They said they wanted to **let the market** (*) run free but they let it **run wild**, and in doing so, they **trampled our core values** of fairness, balance, and responsibility to one another.	Freedom: unregulated free market (*) –

Continued

Speech	Metaphorical expressions per paragraph	Value metaphorically expressed
10 October 2008	It is time to **turn the page** on eight years of economic policies that put Wall Street before Main Street but ended up hurting both. We need policies that **grow our economy from the bottom-up** (*), so that **every American, everywhere has the chance to get ahead** (#). Not just corporate CEOs, but their secretaries too. Not just the person who owns the factory, but the men and women who work on its floor. Because if we've learned anything from this economic crisis, it's that we're all connected; we're all in this together; and we will **rise or fall as one nation – as one people** (|).	– We: empowering people (*); Chance: opportunity for everyone (#); We: unity (|)
	Bottom-up growth also depends on a tax code that doesn't just work for the folks at the **top**. You've heard a lot about taxes in this campaign. Well, here's the truth – my opponent and I are both offering **tax cuts** (*). The difference is, he wants to give $200 billion in **tax cuts** (*) to the biggest corporations in America, and he wants to give the average Fortune 500 CEO a $700,000 **tax cut** (*). But he gives nothing at all to over 100 million Americans.	– – Moral order: distribution of wealth (*)
15 October 2008	He wants to keep giving **tax cuts** (*)to corporations that ship your jobs overseas. I want to give **tax breaks** (#) to companies that create jobs right here in America.	Moral order: distribution of wealth (*); Fairness: fair taxation (#)
	He wants to give more **tax cuts** (*) to Fortune 500 CEOs. I want to give 95 percent of working Americans the **tax relief** (#) they deserve.	Moral order: distribution of wealth (*); Fairness: fair taxation (#)
	Bottom-up growth depends on a tax code that doesn't just work for the folks at the **top**. You've heard a lot about taxes in this campaign. Well, here's the truth – my opponent and I are both offering **tax cuts**. The difference is, he wants to give $200 billion in **tax cuts** (*) to the biggest corporations in America, and he wants to give the average Fortune 500 CEO a $700,000 tax cut. But he gives nothing at all to over 100 million Americans.	– – – Moral order: distribution of wealth (*)

(*continued*)

Continued

Speech	Metaphorical expressions per paragraph	Value metaphorically expressed
20 October 2008	We have tried it John McCain's way. We have tried it George Bush's way. It hasn't worked. It's time for something new. It is time to **turn the page** on eight years of economic policies that put Wall Street before Main Street but ended up hurting both. We need policies **that grow our economy from the bottom-up (*)**, so that every American, everywhere, has **the chance to get ahead (#)**. Not just the person who owns the factory, but the men and women who work on its floor. Because if we've learned anything from this economic crisis, it's that we're all connected; we're all in this together; and we will **rise or fall as one nation – as one people (|)**.	– We: empowering people (*); Chance: opportunity for everyone (#); We: unity (|)
	That starts with **tax relief**. There's been a lot of talk about taxes in this campaign. And the truth is, my opponent and I are both proposing **tax cuts**. The difference is, he wants to give a $700,000 **tax cut (*)** to Fortune 500 CEOs. I want to put a $1,000 **tax cut in the pockets of 95% of American workers (#)**. That's right – 95%. My opponent doesn't want you to know this, but under my plan, tax rates will actually be less than they were under Ronald Reagan.	– Moral order: distribution of wealth (*); Fairness: fair taxation (#)

Appendix 2: Frequency of Metaphorical Expressions in Value-laden Paragraphs

Frequency of metaphorical expressions in NP paragraphs

Speech	No. of paragraphs	No. of para-graphs with metaphors	No. of paragraphs with metaphorical values
5 February 2008	12	9	7
12 February 2008	11	5	4
4 March 2008	12	1	1
18 March 2008	19	8	7
20 March 2008	10	8	7
14 April 2008	7	4	3
15 April 2008	9	3	3
22 April 2008	8	2	1
3 May 2008	12	8	6
6 May 2008	11	7	4
20 May 2008	12	8	6
3 June 2008	7	6	4
21 June 2008	18	9	9
28 June 2008	7	5	3
30 June 2008	9	4	2
1 July 2008	9	3	2
10 July 2008	19	9	7
13 July 2008	14	7	6
16 July 2008	11	7	6
1 August 2008	15	13	9
5 August 2008	11	6	4
28 August 2008	27	14	12
9 September 2008	24	15	6
12 September 2008	12	7	7
20 September 2008	19	15	11
27 September 2008	17	12	7

(*continued*)

Continued

Speech	No. of paragraphs	No. of para- graphs with metaphors	No. of paragraphs with metaphorical values
10 October 2008	23	15	12
15 October 2008	22	17	14
20 October 2008	23	16	12
27 October 2008	20	13	10
Total	430	256	192

Frequency of metaphorical expressions in CSF paragraphs

Speech	No. of paragraphs	No. of para- graphs with metaphors	No. of paragraphs with metaphorical values
5 February 2008	4	3	3
12 February 2008	5	5	3
4 March 2008	3	3	1
18 March 2008	2	1	0
20 March 2008	2	2	2
14 April 2008	10	7	6
22 April 2008	7	2	1
3 May 2008	2	0	0
20 May 2008	1	1	1
3 June 2008	4	2	0
21 June 2008	7	4	2
28 June 2008	1	1	0
13 July 2008	1	0	0
1 August 2008	2	2	2
5 August 2008	1	0	0
28 August 2008	4	3	2
12 September 2008	5	5	4
20 September 2008	3	0	0
27 September 2008	7	4	2
10 October 2008	2	1	1
15 October 2008	1	1	0
27 October 2008	5	5	3
Total	79	52	33

Frequency of metaphorical expressions in CSF+NP paragraphs

Speech	No. of paragraphs	No. of paragraphs with metaphors	No. of paragraphs with metaphori- cal values
12 February 2008	3	2	0
4 March 2008	1	1	1
6 May 2008	3	2	2
20 May 2008	2	2	1
3 June 2008	4	1	1
10 July 2008	1	1	1
12 September 2008	3	2	2
27 September 2008	1	1	1
10 October 2008	2	2	2
15 October 2008	4	3	3
20 October 2008	2	2	2
Total	26	19	16

Appendix 3: Highly Frequent Words in the Corpus

List of the 100 most frequent content words in the corpus

Lexemes	Frequency
American	386
make	349
America	299
year	292
work	285
need	281
country	275
change	275
time	272
job	258
tax	237
people	210
new	209
children	203
know	201
come	191
good	187
get	185
family	177
president	175
help	175
go	174
say	170
want	169
give	158
pay	158
economy	157
now	155
state	153
take	151

(*continued*)

Continued

Lexemes	Frequency
care	146
war	137
senator	135
school	132
woman	127
here	127
health	126
together	122
day	121
education	119
world	112
policy	112
keep	110
plan	108
future	107
election	105
nation	102
street	103
home	103
see	103
unite	97
life	96
campaign	96
college	96
company	95
create	94
right	93
promise	93
afford	92
invest	92
worker	91
man	90
run	90
stand	89
cost	89
class	87
start	87

(*continued*)

Continued

Lexemes	Frequency
face	86
hard	86
high	84
government	83
way	82
put	81
end	78
energy	77
teacher	77
century	76
hope	76
moment	76
business	74
middle	74
crisis	73
today	72
think	72
mean	71
money	70
provide	68
challenge	68
economic	67
politics	67
small	67
great	66
lose	65
oil	64
young	61
chance	61
support	61
wall	58
white	58
kid	57

Notes

2 Political Discourse in the US

1. The reader should be reminded that Aristotle drew a distinction between logic and informal logic, and the latter was taken as the basis for logos (rational argumentation) (see Ross 1924).
2. All the excerpts from Obama's speeches that are provided as examples are numbered consecutively from here onwards.
3. Obama's speeches will be quoted by the date of the selected speech and the year.
4. Religious bigotry was used repeatedly as a weapon to delegitimize Obama in the course of his 2008 election campaign. Obama was the target of many harsh attacks on the grounds of his dubious religious background. His biological father was raised as a Muslim, his mother was an atheist who graduated in anthropology, his Indonesian stepfather was not deeply religious and the white grandparents who raised him were religious skeptics. Obama himself converted to Christianity only late in his life. These were taken by conservatives as sufficient facts to cast doubts on Obama's faith. The media also played a big role in making people confused about Obama's religious life. Thus, even though Obama made public affirmations of faith, many of them went unreported (see Mansfield 2011).
5. The State of the Union address is a genre that has received much attention because of its considerable influence on the media. This type of speech is broadcast live on major TV and radio channels and is discussed largely in the media in the days following its public delivery. Presidents deliver a State of the Union address at the beginning of every calendar year to inform about their accomplishments to date and to put forth their agenda for the upcoming months.
6. Lim's observation concerning the tendency of recent presidential rhetoric to sound anti-intellectual is not confirmed by the data analyzed in this book. As a matter of fact, both the mental verb *know* and the causal conjunction *because* have a high ranking among frequent lexical items in the corpus under investigation. *Know* is among the 100 most frequent terms and *because* is even among the 40 most frequent ones.
7. In the corpus of Obama's electoral speeches analyzed in this book, the inclusive pronouns *we*, *our* and *us* show a total of 2591 occurrences in contrast to *you* and *your* with 811 hits, *their* and *them* with 860, and *I*, *me* and *my* with 1253.
8. Since the publication of Tulis's highly influential book (1987), the notion of 'rhetorical presidency' has been commonly used to define the behavior of modern presidents from Theodore Roosevelt onwards. In the two decades following the publication of his book, Tulis's theory has been the subject of a lively debate among a number of scholars (see, for example, Hart 1987, Jamieson 1988, Ryan 1988, 1995, Campbell and Jamieson 1990, Stuckey 1991, Ellis 1998, Dorsey 2002). With the only exception of Zarefsky (2002), however, the majority of scholarship on the presidency tends to agree with Tulis's opinion that the 'rhetorical presidency' is a modern phenomenon starting in the early years of the twentieth century. A more recent voice of dissent comes from Medhurst (2008) and the contributors to his volume. Mostly reasoning from the perspective of

communication studies, these scholars have examined the speeches of 11 less-researched nineteenth-century presidents and come to the conclusion that, though using slightly different strategies, they can likewise be called 'rhetorical presidents'.

9. In February 2008, Michelle Obama, speaking in Milwaukee (Wisconsin), said: 'for the first time in my adult life I am proud of my country because it feels like hope is finally making a comeback'. Later on, in Madison, she reinforced that message by saying: 'For the first time in my adult lifetime, I'm really proud of my country, and not just because Barack has done well, but because I think people are hungry for change'. These statements generated a lot of criticism on the part of Republicans, who, taking the messages literally, could not understand why a woman of her age had never been proud of her country before then.

3   Cognition and Politics

1. The expression 'essentially contested concepts' was first introduced by W. B. Gallie (1956) to describe concepts such as 'democracy', 'conservatism', 'art' and many others that are expected to cause some form of contest or conflict when used by different social, cultural and linguistic groups. In his study, Gallie provided a normative framework for evaluating the contestedness of contested concepts that, besides raising a lot of interest, has generated a multitude of critiques and controversies among social and political scientists. In line with prototype theory, Lakoff's interpretation of contested concepts is based on the general assumption that 'contested concepts have uncontested cores – central meanings that almost everyone agrees on. The contested parts are left unspecified, blanks to be filled in by deep frames and metaphors' (2006: 14).

2. The role of metaphor in defining morality was first described in Johnson (1993).

3. What Lakoff admittedly does is to establish and present a ranking for the importance of the notions which characterize each of the two morality models he describes.

4. The moral accounting metaphor was first discussed in Johnson (1993). In Lakoff's work (1996), the use of this metaphor for explaining morality sticks out due to the cultural specificity of the notion of accounting. Considering that at the core of this notion lies the 'universal' (or at least more generalizable) idea that human interactions are characterized by a need to establish a balance between what is given and what is obtained, one could suggest the conceptual metaphor MORALITY IS BALANCE as a more culturally neutral way of describing the process of human interaction and its results.

5. Even though Lakoff does not present metaphors according to the usual 'X is Y' formula, the values and concepts he describes (strength, authority, order and so on) are to be taken as the source domains in terms of which SF morality is defined. Some of them (boundary, essence, purity) are themselves based on other conceptual metaphors. The same observation holds true for metaphors defining NP morality.

6. The formula 'Target domain as Source domain' is sometimes used instead of the more common 'Target domain is Source domain' without any theoretical distinction intended.

7. On a related note, the importance of finding words that by provoking emotional reactions can convey a successful message is one of the major concerns of Luntz (2007), an American political consultant and pollster. Luntz's expertise

lies in the identification of words that can shape public opinion and direct people's preferences towards a particular candidate. A supporter of the Republican cause, Luntz is the mind behind the introduction of certain expressions such as *death tax* (to replace the more neutral terms *inheritance tax, estate tax*), *energy exploration* (for *oil drilling*) and *tax relief* (for *tax cuts*) in political and public discourse.

8. More recently, studies in cognitive linguistics have shifted towards an interpretation of cognition as closely connected to culture (see, for example, Kövecses 2005, Sharifian 2011).

9. The institute closed in April 2008 but a large amount of the materials it produced up until then is now part of a virtual archive and freely available online (see http://www.cognitivepolicyworks.com/resource-center/rockridge-institute/).

10. This idea was first discussed in Lakoff and Johnson (1999, ch. 25), where the authors suggest a metaphorical interpretation of evolution as the survival of the best-nurtured.

11. The Gaia hypothesis was first put forward in the early 1970s as an alternative to deterministic theories of evolution. Initially received with skepticism by the scientific community, Gaia theory has been adopted as a model in the disciplines of physics, biology and, more recently, also philosophy and politics. Gaia theory 'sees the evolution of the species of living organisms so closely coupled with the evolution of their physical and chemical environment that together they constitute a single and indivisible evolutionary process' (Lovelock 1986: 25; see also Lovelock 1988). In other words, the Gaian paradigm sees the Earth as alive and its physical and biological processes as inextricably bound to form a self-regulating system.

12. The reader is invited to consult Harvey (2007) for a well-informed historical account of the use of the human body as a political metaphor for understanding society, and Musolff (2010) for a thorough investigation of the nation as a body metaphor in National Socialist racist ideology.

13. In a comparable fashion, Thornborrow (1993) has reported on the metaphors of 'security' used in British and French political discourse during the Cold War and post-Cold War periods.

14. Only British and Irish politicians seem to contradict this tendency towards homogenization.

15. Cienki (2004, 2005a,b) defines entailments as both metaphorical and literal expressions that logically follow from the SF and NP models. More accurately, he states: 'an entailment should be understood here as a logical consequence of a conceptual metaphor. [...] entailments can also be utterances which reflect the logic or principles behind a metaphor, but are not themselves metaphorical expressions' (2004: 416). Thus, for Cienki, SF and NP entailments are logical consequences of the metaphors defining SF and NP morality. As the following discussion will clarify, entailments play a significant role in Cienki's analysis. Conversely, entailments will not be part of the analysis conducted in the present study.

16. Quite significantly, if we compare how often the two candidates used these words, there are striking differences concerning the terms *teacher* and *man*. Gore uses the word *teacher*, which describes a prototypically nurturant profession, twice as often than Bush. Conversely, Bush shows a marked preference over Gore for the word *man*, which appears as more in line with a conservative view of gender roles in society.

17. As Ahrens explains 'Title IX prohibits institutions that receive federal funding from practicing gender discrimination in educational programs and activities' (2006: 321).
18. The expression 'family values' also features in the title of one of the chapters in *The Political Mind* (2008), where the family models and their implications for moral politics are discussed. Similarly, Chapter 6 of *Thinking Points* (Lakoff and The Rockridge Institute 2006) concerns 'fundamental values' for Republicans and Democrats in line with their SF and NP moral inclination.

4   Methodology and Introduction to the Analysis

1. This fact probably explains why previous research did not venture out on this terrain.

5   The Expression of Values in Obama's Speeches

1. The expression 'value-laden' refers to paragraphs that evoke (positively or negatively) either NP or SF values.
2. This is a general observation concerning the presence of the journey metaphor in neutral paragraphs. A more detailed account of metaphorical expressions will only be provided for value-laden paragraphs in Chapter 6.
3. These numbers refer to the occurrence of individual NP values both in nurturant paragraphs and in nurturant + contra strict father paragraphs. The same holds true for the other sets of NP values.
4. Scholars working in the framework of critical pedagogy lament Obama's instrumental and ideological use of education. In their view, Obama reduces education to training by putting it at the service of a capitalist market philosophy. Instead of emphasizing the importance of education as a means to make young people into autonomous and critically engaged social agents, Obama's view conflates education with the idea of creating a trained workforce, with work-related knowledge and skills, to compete in a global economy (see Giroux 2009).
5. This statement refers to the whole election campaign, which stretched well beyond the period considered in this study.
6. This paragraph was classified as neutral and it is included in the discussion of nurturant morality for ease of exposition.
7. Lakoff uses the expression 'don't think of an elephant' as a title in one of his books to make the point that if a person is told not to think about something, he/she inevitably thinks about it. So, if someone tells you not to think of an elephant, you will think of it nevertheless.
8. The numbers reported in Table 5.10 refer to the occurrence of individual SF values both in contra SF paragraphs and in nurturant + contra SF paragraphs.

7   Values and Lexical Preferences in Obama's Speeches

1. Clusters were calculated automatically by Wordsmith 4 according to the following parameters: a horizon of five words left and right of the search term, a default cluster length of three words, and a minimum frequency of five times in the corpus.
2. This is a SF value that Obama criticizes.

Bibliography

Ahrens, K. (2006) 'Using a small corpus to test linguistic hypotheses: Evaluating 'people' in the State of the Union Addresses', *Computational Linguistics and Chinese Language Processing*, 11 (4), 377–92.

Ahrens, K. (ed.) (2009) *Politics, Gender and Conceptual Metaphors* (Basingstoke: Palgrave Macmillan).

Ahrens, K. (2011) 'Examining conceptual metaphor models through lexical frequency patterns: A case study of U.S. presidential speeches'. In S. Handl and H. J. Schmid (eds), *Windows to the Mind: Metaphor, Metonymy and Conceptual Blending* (Berlin/New York: Mouton De Gruyter), pp. 167–84.

Ahrens, K. and S. Yat Mei Lee (2009) 'Gender versus politics: When conceptual models collide in the US Senate'. In K. Ahrens (ed.), *Politics, Gender and Conceptual Metaphors* (Basingstoke: Palgrave Macmillan), pp. 62–82.

Akrivoulis, D. E. (2008) 'The ways of stargazing: Newtonian metaphoricity in American foreign policy'. In T. Carver and J. Pikalo (eds), *Political Language and Metaphor. Interpreting and Changing the World* (London/New York: Routledge), pp. 15–27.

Alim, S. H. and G. Smitherman (2012) *Articulate While Black. Barack Obama, Language, and Race in the U.S.* (New York: Oxford University Press).

Atkinson, J. M. (1984) *Our Masters's Voices: The Language and Body Language of Politics* (London: Methuen).

Baker, W. (2005) *America's Crisis of Values: Reality and Perception* (Princeton, NJ: Princeton University Press).

Bakhtin, M. (1981) *The Dialogic Imagination* (trans. C. Emerson, M. Holquist) (Austin, TX: University of Texas Press).

Bakhtin, M. (1990) 'The problem of speech genres' (trans. V.W. McGee). In P. Bizzel and B. Herzberg (eds), *The Rhetorical Tradition: Readings from Classical Times to the Present* (Boston, MA: Bedford), pp. 944–63.

Bates, B. R. (2004) 'Audiences, metaphors, and the Persian Gulf War', *Communications Studies*, 55 (3), 447–63.

Beard, A. (2000) *The Language of Politics* (London/New York: Routledge).

Beer, F. A. and C. De Landtsheer (eds) (2004) *Metaphorical World Politics* (East Lansing, MI: Michigan State University Press).

Benoit, W. L., Blaney, J. R. and P. M. Pier (1998) *Campaign '96: A Functional Analysis of Acclaiming, Attacking and Defending* (Westport, CT: Praeger).

Bhatia, A. (2008) 'Discursive illusions in the American National Strategy for Combating Terrorism', *Journal of Language and Politics*, 7 (2), 201–27.

Billig, M. and K. Macmillan (2005) 'Metaphor, idiom and ideology: The search for "no smoking guns" across time', *Discourse & Society*, 16 (4), 459–80.

Bitzer, L. F. (1968) 'The rhetorical situation', *Philosophy and Rhetoric*, 1, 1–14.

Bomberg, E. and B. Super (2009) 'The 2008 US presidential election: Obama and the environment', *Environmental Politics*, 18 (3), 424–430.

Bowman, C. D. (2010) 'The myth of a non-polarized America', *The Hedgehog Review*, Fall, 65–77.

Browne, S. H. (2003) *Jefferson's Call for Nationhood. The First Inaugural Address* (College Station, TX: Texas A&M University Press).

Bybee, J. L. (1985) *Morphology: An Inquiry into the Relation between Meaning and Form* (Amsterdam/Philadelphia: Benjamins).

Burnes, S. (2011) 'Metaphors in press reports of elections: Obama walked on water, but Musharraf was beaten by a knockout', *Journal of Pragmatics*, 43, 2160–75.

Campbell, K. K. and K. Jamieson (1990) *Deeds Done in Words: Presidential Rhetoric and the Genre of Governance* (Chicago, IL: University of Chicago Press).

Campbell, K. K. and K. Jamieson (1995) 'Form and genre in rhetorical criticism: an introduction'. In C. R. Burgchardt (ed.) *Readings in Rhetorical Criticism* (State College, PA: Strata), pp. 394–411.

Cameron, L. and A. Deignan (2003) 'Combining large and small corpora to investigate tuning devices around metaphor in spoken discourse', *Metaphor and Symbol*, 18 (3), 149–60.

Cameron, L. and R. Maslen (eds) (2010) *Metaphor Analysis: Research Practice in Applied Linguistics, Social Sciences and the Humanities* (London: Equinox).

Capone, A. (2010) 'Barack Obama's South Carolina speech', *Journal of Pragmatics*, 42, 2964–77.

Carver, T. and J. Pikalo (2008) *Political Language and Metaphor. Interpreting and Changing the World* (London/New York: Routledge).

Charteris-Black, J. (2004) *Corpus Approaches to Critical Metaphor Analysis* (Basingstoke: Palgrave Macmillan).

Charteris-Black, J. (2005) *Politicians and Rhetoric. The Persuasive Power of Metaphor* (Basingstoke: Palgrave Macmillan).

Charteris-Black, J. (2006) 'Britain as a container: immigration metaphors in the 2005 election campaign', *Discourse & Society*, 17 (5), 563–81.

Charteris-Black, J. (2013) *Analysing Political Speeches: Rhetoric, Discourse and Metaphor* (Basingstoke: Palgrave Macmillan).

Chilton, P. A. (1987) 'Cooperation and non-cooperation: Ethical and political aspects of pragmatics', *Language and Communication*, 7 (3), 221–39.

Chilton, P. A. (1990) 'Politeness, politics and diplomacy', *Discourse and Society*, 1 (2), 201–24.

Chilton, P. A. (1996) *Security Metaphors. Cold War Discourse from Containment to Common House* (New York/Bern/Frankfurt am Main: Peter Lang).

Chilton, P. A. and M. Ilyn (1993) 'Metaphor in political discourse: The case of the "Common European House"', *Discourse & Society*, 4 (1), 7–31.

Chilton, P. A. and C. Schäffner (eds) (2002) *Politics as Text and Talk: Analytic Approaches to Political Discourse* (Amsterdam/Philadelphia: Benjamins).

Cienki, A. (2004) 'Bush's and Gore's language and gestures in the 2000 US presidential debate: A test case for two models of metaphor', *Journal of Language and Politics*, 3, 409–40.

Cienki, A. (2005a) 'Metaphor in the "Strict Father" and "Nurturant Parent" cognitive models: Theoretical issues raised in an empirical study', *Cognitive Linguistics*, 16 (2), 279–312.

Cienki, A. (2005b) 'The metaphorical use of family terms versus other nouns in political debates', *Information Design Journal + Document Design*, 13 (1), 27–39.

Cienki, A. (2008) 'Frames, idealized cognitive models and domains'. In D. Geeraerts and H. Cuyckens (eds), *The Oxford Handbook of Cognitive Linguistics* (Oxford: Oxford University Press), pp. 170–87.

Clausner, T. C. and W. Croft (1997) 'Productivity and schematicity in metaphor', *Cognitive Science*, 21 (3), 247–82.

Copeland, C. C. (2009) 'God-talk in the age of Obama: Theology and religious political engagement', *Denver University Law Review*, 86, 663–91.

Corcoran, P. (1979) *Political Language and Rhetoric* (Queensland: University of Queensland Press).

Crocker, J. and S. B. Hughes (2009) 'Ecosystem perspective and Barack Obama's campaign for the presidency', *Du Bois Review*, 6 (1), 125–36.

Damasio, A. (2000) *Descartes' Error. Emotion, Reason and the Human Brain* (New York: Quill).

Dayan, D. and E. Katz (1992) *Media Events. The Live Broadcasting of History* (Cambridge, MA: Harvard University Press).

Davis, N. and R. V. Robinson (1996) 'Religious orthodoxy in American society: The myth of a monolithic camp', *Journal for the Scientific Study of Religion*, 35 (3), 229–45.

De Landtsheer, C. (1994) 'The language of prosperity and crisis: A case study in political semantics', *Politics and the Individual*, 4, 63–85. ·

De Landtsheer, C. and I. De Vrij (2004) 'Talking about Srebrenica: Dutch elites and Dutchbat. How metaphors change during crisis'. In F. Beer and C. De Landtsheer (eds), *Metaphorical World Politics* (East Lansing, MI. Michigan State University Press), pp. 163–89.

De Sola Pool, I. (1956) 'Variety and Repetition in Political Language'. In H. Eulau, S. Eldersfeld and M. Janowitz (eds), *Political Behavior: A Reader in Theory and Research* (Glencoe, IL: The Free Press), pp. 217–31.

Deignan, A. (2005) *Metaphor and Corpus Linguistics* (Amsterdam/Philadelphia: Benjamins).

Denton, R. E. and G. C. Woodward (1998) *Political Communication in America*, 3rd edn (Westport, CT: Praeger).

Dickinson, E. (1924) *The Complete Poems of Emily Dickinson* (Boston, MA: Little Brown) (accessed online: www.bartleby.com/113/).

DiMaggio, P., Evans, J. and B. Bryson (1996) 'Have Americans' social attitudes become more polarize', *American Journal of Sociology*, 102 (3), 690–755.

Dirven, R., Frank, R. and C. Ilie (eds) (2001) *Language and Ideology. Vol. II: Descriptive Cognitive Approaches* (Amsterdam/Philadelphia: Benjamins).

Dorsey, L. G. (ed.) (2002) *The Presidency and Rhetorical Leadership* (College Station, TX: Texas A&M University).

Duman, S. and M. A. Locher (2008) '"So let's talk. Let's chat. Let's start a dialog": An analysis of the conversation metaphor employed in Clinton's and Obama's YouTube campaign clips", *Multilingua*, 27, 193–230.

Ellis, R. J. (ed.) (1998) *Speaking to the People. The Rhetorical Presidency in Historical Perspective* (Amherst, MA: University of Massachusetts Press).

Fairclough, N. (1989) *Language and Power* (London: Longman).

Fairclough, N. (1995) *Critical Discourse Analysis* (London: Longman).

Fairclough, N. and R. Wodak (1997) 'Critical discourse analysis'. In T. A. van Dijk (ed.), *Discourse Studies: A Multidisciplinary Introduction. Vol.2. Discourse as Social Interaction* (London: Sage), pp. 258–84.

Faucheux, R. (1994) 'The Message', *Campaigns and Elections*, May, 46–9.

Ferrari, F. (2007) 'Metaphor at work in the analysis of political discourse: Investigating a "preventive war" persuasion strategy', *Discourse & Society*, 18 (5), 603–25.

Fields, W. (1996) *Union of Words. A History of Presidential Eloquence* (New York: Free Press).

Fillmore, C. (1961) *Indirect Object Constructions in English and the Ordering of Transformations* (The Hague: Mouton).

Fillmore, C. (1968) 'The case for case'. In E. Bach and R. T. Harms (eds), *Universals in Linguistic Theory* (New York: Holt, Reinhart & Winston), pp. 1–88.

Fillmore, C. (1971) 'Verbs of judging: an exercise in semantic description'. In C. Fillmore and T. Langendoen (eds), *Studies in Linguistic Semantics* (New York: Holt, Reinhart & Winston), pp. 273–89.

Fillmore, C. (1975) 'An alternative to checklist theories of meaning'. In *Proceedings of the First Annual Meeting of the Berkeley Linguistics Society* (Amsterdam: North Holland) 1, pp. 123–31.

Fillmore, C. (1977) 'Topics in lexical semantics'. In R. Cole (ed.), *Current Issues in Linguistic Theory* (Bloomington, IN: Indiana University Press), pp. 76–138.

Fillmore, C. (1982) 'Frame semantics'. In Linguistic Society of Korea (ed.), *Linguistics in the Morning Calm* (Seoul: Hanshin Publishing), pp. 111–37.

Fillmore, C. (1985) 'Frames and the semantics of understanding', *Quaderni di Semantica*, 6, 222–54.

Fillmore, C. (1986) '"U"-semantics, second round', *Quaderni di semantica*, 7, 49–58.

Fillmore, C. (1987) 'A private history of the concept "frame"'. In R. Dirven and G. Radden (eds), *Concepts of Case* (Tübingen: Gunter Narr Verlag), pp. 28–36.

Fiorina, M., Abrams, S. J. and J. C. Pope (2005) *Culture War? The Myth of a Polarized America* (New York: Pearson Longman).

Flowerdew J. and S. Leong (2007) 'Metaphors in the discursive construction of patriotism: The case of Hong Kong's constitutional reform debate', *Discourse & Society*, 18 (3), 278–94.

Friedenberg, R. V. (2002) *Notable Speeches in Contemporary Presidential Campaigns* (Westport, CT: Praeger).

Gallie, W. B. (1956) 'Essentially contested concepts'. In *Proceedings of the Philosophical Society 56* (London: Harrisons and Sons), pp. 167–98.

Geeraerts, D. and S. Grondelaers (2003) 'Looking back at anger: Cultural traditions and metaphorical patterns'. In J. R. Taylor and R. E. MacLaury (eds), *Language and the Cognitive Construal of the World* (Berlin/New York: Mouton De Gruyter), pp. 153–79.

Gelderman, C. (1997) *All the Presidents' Words: The Bully Pulpit and the Creation of the Virtual Presidency* (New York: Walker and Company).

Gibbs, R. W. (1999) 'Taking metaphor out of our heads and putting it into the cultural world'. In R. W. Gibbs and G. J. Steen (eds), *Metaphor in Cognitive Linguistics* (Amsterdam/Philadelphia: Benjamins), pp. 145–66.

Gill, A. M. and K. Whedbee (1997) 'Rhetoric'. In T. A. Van Dijk (ed.), *Discourse Studies: A Multidisciplinary Introduction. Vol. 1. Discourse as Structure and Process* (London: Sage), pp. 157–84.

Giroux, H. A. (2009) 'Obama's dilemma: Postpartisan politics and the crisis of American education', *Harvard Educational Review*, 79 (2), 250–66.

Givón, T. (2005) *Context as Other Minds: The Pragmatics of Sociality, Cognition and Communication* (Amsterdam/Philadelphia: Benjamins).

Glynn, D. and K. Fisher (eds) (2010) *Quantitative Methods in Cognitive Semantics: Corpus-Driven Approaches* (Berlin/New York: De Gruyter).

Goatly, A. (2007) *Washing the Brain – Metaphor and Hidden Ideology* (Amsterdam/Philadelphia: Benjamins).

Hart, R. P. (1984) *Verbal Style and the Presidency: A Computer-based Analysis* (Orlando: Academic Press).

Hart, R. P. (1987) *The Sound of Leadership: Presidential Communication in the Modern Age* (Chicago, IL: University of Chicago Press).

Hart, R. P. (2000) *Campaign Talk: Why Elections are Good for Us* (Princeton, NJ: Princeton University Press).

Harvey, A. D. (2007) *Body Politic: Political Metaphor and Political Violence* (Newcastle: Cambridge Scholars Publishing).

Hobbes, T. (1988 [1651]) *Leviathan*, edited with an introduction by C.B. Macpherson (Harmondsworth: Penguin Books).

Hobbs, P. (2008) 'Surging ahead to a new way forward: the metaphorical foreshadowing of a policy shift', *Discourse & Communication*, 2 (1), 29–56.

Hodgkinson, G. and C. M. Leland (1999) 'Metaphors in the 1996 presidential debates: An analysis of themes'. In L. Lee Kaid and D. G. Bystrom (eds), *The Electronic Election: Perspectives on the 1996 Campaign Communication* (New Jersey/London: Lawrence and Erlbaum Associates), pp. 149–162.

Holmes, J. and M. Stubbe (2003) *Power and Politeness in the Workplace: A Sociolinguistic Analysis of Talk at Work* (London: Pearson).

Hume, D. (1740 [1969]) *A Treatise of Human Nature* (Harmondsworth: Penguin).

Hunter, J. D. (1991) *Culture Wars: The Struggle to Define America* (New York: Basic Books).

Hunter, J. D. and A. Wolfe (eds) (2006) *Is There a Culture War? A Dialogue on Values and American Public Life* (Washington, D.C.: Pew Research Center: Brookings Institution Press).

James, H. (1998) 'The question of our speech'. In P. A. Walker (ed.), *Henry James on Culture* (Lincoln, NE: Nebraska University Press), pp. 42–57.

Jamieson, K. H. (1988) *Eloquence in an Electronic Age: The Transformation of Political Speech Making* (New York: Oxford University Press).

Jansen, S. C. and D. Sabo (1994) 'The sport/war metaphor: Hegemonic masculinity, the Persian Gulf War and the New World Order', *Sociology of Sport Journal*, 11 (1), 1–17.

Johnson, M. (1990) *The Body in the Mind: The Bodily Basis of Meaning, Imagination and Reason* (Chicago, IL: Chicago University Press).

Johnson, M. (1993) *Moral Imagination: Implications of Cognitive Science for Ethics* (Chicago, IL: University of Chicago Press).

Johnson, M. (2007) *The Meaning of the Body: Aesthetics of Human Understanding* (Chicago, IL: University of Chicago Press).

Keech, W. R. and D. R. Matthews (1976) *The Party's Choice* (Washington, DC: Brookings Institution).

Keeter, S., Horowitz, J. and A. Tyson (2008) 'Young voters in the 2008 election', *Pew Research Centre for the People and the Press* [online], 12 November, available at: http://pewresearch.org/pubs/1031/young-voters-in-the-2008-election.

Kelley, C. E. (2001) *The Rhetoric of First Lady Hillary Rodham Clinton. Crisis Management Discourse* (Westport, CT: Praeger).

Kendall, K. E. (2000) *Communication in the Presidential Primaries: Candidates and the Media 1912–2000* (Westport, CT: Praeger).

Kernell, S. (1993) *Going Public. New Strategies of Presidential Leadership*, 2nd edn (Washington, DC: Congressional Quarterly Press).

Kiewe, A. (ed.) (1994) *The Modern Presidency and Crisis Rhetoric* (Westport, CT: Praeger).

Kövecses, Z. (2002) *Metaphor: A Practical Introduction* (Oxford: Oxford University Press).

Kövecses, Z. (2005) *Metaphor in Culture: Universality and Variation* (Cambridge: Cambridge University Press).

Koller, V. (2004) *Metaphor and Gender in Business Media Discourse: A Critical Cognitive Study* (Basingstoke: Palgrave Macmillan).

Kress, G. and B. Hodge (1993) *Language as Ideology*, 2nd edn (London/New York: Routledge).

Lakoff, G. (1987) *Women, Fire and Dangerous Things. What Categories Reveal about the Mind* (Chicago/London: University of Chicago Press).

Lakoff, G. (1991) 'The metaphor system used to justify war in the Gulf', *Journal of Urban and Cultural Studies*, 2 (1), 59–72.

304   *Bibliography*

Lakoff, G. (1996) *Moral Politics: How Liberals and Conservatives Think* (Chicago, IL: University of Chicago Press).
Lakoff, G. (2004) *Don't Think of an Elephant. Know Your Values and Frame the Debate* (White River Junction, Vermont: Chelsea Green Publishing).
Lakoff, G. (2006) *Whose Freedom? The Battle over America's Most Important Ideas* (New York: Farrar, Straus and Giroux).
Lakoff, G. (2008) *The Political Mind* (New York: Penguin).
Lakoff, G. and The Rockridge Institute (2006) *Thinking Points: Communicating Our American Values and Vision* (New York: Farrar, Straus and Giroux).
Lakoff, G. and M. Johnson (1980) *Metaphors We Live By* (Chicago, IL: University of Chicago Press).
Lakoff, G. and M. Johnson (1999) *Philosophy in the Flesh. The Embodied Mind and Its Challenge to Western Thought* (New York: Basic Books).
Langacker, R. (1987) *Foundations of Cognitive Grammar: Vol. I. Theoretical Prerequisites* (Stanford, CA: Stanford University Press).
Lasswell, H. (1949) 'Style in the language of politics'. In H. D. Lasswell and N. Leites (eds), *The Language of Politics: Studies of Quantitative Semantics* (Cambridge, MA: MIT Press), pp. 20–37.
Lehrman, R. (2010) *The Political Speechwriter's Companion. A Guide for Writers and Speakers* (Washington, DC: CQ Press).
Lim, E. T. (2002) 'Five trends in presidential rhetoric: An analysis of rhetoric from George Washington to Bill Clinton', *Presidential Studies Quarterly*, 32 (2), 328–66.
Lovelock, J. (1986) 'Gaia: The world as living organism', *New Scientist*, 18/12/1986, 25–8.
Lovelock, J. (1988) *The Ages of Gaia* (Oxford: Oxford University Press).
Luntz, F. I. (2007) *Words that Work: It's Not What You Say, It's What People Hear* (New York: Hyperion).
Lu, L. W. and K. Ahrens (2008) 'Ideological influence on BUILDING metaphors in Taiwanese presidential speeches', *Language & Society*, 19 (3), 383–408.
Mansfield, S. (2011) *The Faith of Barack Obama* (Nashville, TN: Thomas Nelson).
Marcus, G. E. (2002) *The Sentimental Citizen: Emotion in Democratic Politics* (University Park: Pennsylvania State University Press).
McCormick, J. and C. E. Jones (1993) 'The conceptualization of deracialization: Thinking through the dilemma'. In G. A. Persons (ed.), *Dilemma of Black Politics: Issues of Leadership and Strategy* (New York: Harper Collins College), pp. 66–84.
McEntee-Atalianis, L. J. (2011) 'The role of metaphor in shaping the identity and agenda of the United Nations: The imagining of an international community and international threat', *Discourse & Communication*, 5 (4), 393–412.
McKinney, M. S. and M. C. Banwart (eds) (2011) *Communication in the 2008 U.S. Election. Digital Natives Elect a President* (New York/Bern/Frankfurt am Main: Peter Lang).
Medhurst, M. J. (ed.) (2008) *Before the Rhetorical Presidency* (College Station: Texas A&M University).
Metcalf, A. (2004) *Presidential Voices. Speaking Styles from George Washington to George W. Bush* (Boston, MA: Houghton Mifflin).
Mieder, W. (2009) *Yes We Can. Barack Obama's Proverbial Rhetoric* (New York/Bern/ Frankfurt am Main: Peter Lang).
Miller, E. F. (1979) 'Metaphor and political knowledge', *The American Political Science Review*, 73 (1), 155–70.
Morgan, P. (2001) 'The semantics of an impeachment: meanings and models in a political conflict'. In R. Dirven, R. Frank and C. Ilie (eds), *Language and Ideology. Vol. II: Descriptive Cognitive Approaches* (Amsterdam/Philadelphia: Benjamins), pp. 77–105.

Musolff, A. (2000a) 'Political imagery of Europe: A *House* without *Exit Doors?*', *Journal of Multilingual and Multicultural Development*, 21 (3), 216–29.

Musolff, A. (2000b) 'Maritime journey metaphors in British and German public discourse: Transport vessels of international communication?', *German as a Foreign Language*, 3 (internet journal, cf. URL: http://www.gfl.journals.com)

Musolff, A. (2003) 'Ideological functions of metaphor: The conceptual metaphors of *health* and *illness* in public discourse'. In R. Dirven, R. Frank and M. Pütz (eds), *Cognitive Models in Language and Thought. Ideology, Metaphors and Meanings* (Berlin/New York: Mouton de Gruyter), pp. 327–52.

Musolff, A. (2004) *Metaphor and Political Discourse. Analogical Reasoning in Debates about Europe* (Basingstoke: Palgrave Macmillan).

Musolff, A. (2010) *Metaphor, Nation and the Holocaust: The Concept of the Body Politic* (London/New York: Routledge).

Musolff, A., Kleinke, S., Kövecses, Z. and V. Szelid (2012) *Cognition and Culture. The Role of Metaphor and Metonymy* (Budapest: Eötvös University Press).

Newton-Small, J. (2008) 'How Obama writes his speeches', *Time*, 28 August 2008.

Obama, B. (2006) *The Audacity of Hope* (New York: Vintage Books).

Obama for America (2008) *Change We Can Believe In. Barack Obama's Plan to Renew America's Promise* (New York: Three Rivers Press).

Osborn, M. (1967) 'Archetypal metaphor in rhetoric: the light-dark family', *Quarterly Journal of Speech*, 53 (2), 115–26.

Oxford English Dictionary Online, https://sslvpn.univr.it/,DanaInfo=www.oed.com+ (last accessed 1 May 2014).

Parker, A. (2008) 'What would Obama say?', *The New York Times*, 20 January 2008.

Patent, J. and G. Lakoff (2006) 'Conceptual levels: Bringing it home to values', The Rockridge Institute.

Perloff, R. M. (1998) *Political Communication. Politics, Press, and Public in America* (Mahwah, NJ: Lawrence Erlbaum Associates).

Philp, C. 'Profile: Barack Obama's speechwriter Jon Favreau', *The Sunday Times*, 19 January 2009.

Pikalo, J. (2008) 'Mechanical metaphors in politics'. In T. Carver and J. Pikalo (eds), *Political Language and Metaphor. Interpreting and Changing the World* (London/New York: Routledge), pp. 41–54.

Pilkington, E. (2009) 'Obama inauguration: Words of history ... crafted by 27-year-old in Starbucks', *Guardian.co.uk.*, 20 January 2009.

Pragglejaz Group (2007) 'MIP: A method for identifying metaphorically used words in discourse', *Metaphor and Symbol*, 22, 1–39.

Quinn, N.(1991) 'The cultural basis of metaphor'. In J. W. Fernandez (ed.), *Beyond Metaphor: The Theory of Tropes in Anthropology* (Stanford, CA: Stanford University Press), pp. 56–93.

Quinn, N. and D. Holland (1987) 'Culture and cognition'. In D. Holland and N. Quinn (eds), *Cultural Models in Language and Thought* (Cambridge: Cambridge University Press), pp. 3–40.

Remnick, D. (2010) *The Bridge. The Life and Rise of Barack Obama* (New York: Knopf).

Ritter, K. and M. J. Medhurst (eds) (2003) *Presidential Speechwriting. From the New Deal to the Reagan Revolution and Beyond* (College Station, TX: Texas A&M University Press).

Ryan, H. (1988) *Franklin D. Roosevelt's Rhetorical Presidency* (New York: Greenwood Press).

Ryan, H. (1995) *US Presidents as Orators: A Bio-Critical Source Book* (Westport, CT: Greenwood Press).

Ryfe, D. M. (1999) 'Franklin Roosevelt and the fireside chats', *Journal of Communication*, 49 (4), 80–103.

Rohrer, T. (1995) 'The metaphorical logic of (political) rape: The new wor(l)d order', *Metaphor and Symbolic Activity*, 10 (2), 115–37.

Rosch, E. (1975) 'Cognitive representations of semantic categories', *Journal of Experimental Psychology: General*, 104, 192–233.

Rosch, E. (1977) 'Human categorization'. In N. Warren (ed.), *Studies in Cross-linguistic Psychology* (London: Academic Press), pp. 1–49.

Rosch, E. (1978) 'Principles of categorization'. In B. Lloyd and E. Rosch (eds), *Cognition and Categorization* (Hillsdale, NJ: Erlbaum), pp. 27–48.

Rosch, E. and C. Mervis (1975) 'Family resemblances: Studies in the internal structure of categories', *Cognitive Psychology*, 7, 573–605.

Ross, W. D. (ed.) (1924) *The Works of Aristotle*, Vol XI, *Rhetorica* (trans. W. Rhys Roberts) (London: Oxford University Press).

Rowland, R. C. (2010) 'The fierce urgency of now: Barack Obama and the 2008 presidential election', *American Behavioral Scientist*, 54 (3), 203–21.

Sandikcioglu, E. (2000) 'More metaphorical warfare in the Gulf: Orientalist frames in news coverage'. In A. Barcelona Sanchez (ed.), *Metaphor and Metonymy at the Crossroads: A Cognitive Perspective* (Berlin/New York: Mouton de Gruyter), pp. 299–320.

Santa Ana, O. (1999) 'Like an animal I was treated: Anti-immigrant metaphor in US public discourse', *Discourse & Society*, 10 (2), 191–224.

Savoy, J. (2010) 'Lexical analysis of US political speeches', *Journal of Quantitative Linguistics*, 17 (2), 123–141.

Schäffner, C. (1996) 'Building a European house? Or at two speeds into a dead end? Metaphors in the debate on a united Europe'. In A. Musolff, C. Schäffner, and M. Townson (eds), *Conceiving of Europe: Unity in Diversity* (Aldershot: Dartmouth Publishers), pp. 31–59.

Schäffner, C. (2004) 'Political discourse analysis from the point of view of translation studies', *Journal of Language and Politics*, 3 (1), 117–150.

Schlesinger, A. M., Jr. (1959) *The Coming of the New Deal* (Boston, MA: Houghton-Mifflin).

Schlesinger, R. (2008) *White House Ghosts: Presidents and Their Speechwriters* (New York: Simon & Schuster Paperbacks).

Scott, M. (2004) *WordSmith Tools version 4* (Oxford: Oxford University Press).

Semino, E. (2008) *Metaphor in Discourse* (Cambridge/New York: Cambridge University Press).

Semino, E. and M. Masci (1996) 'Politics is football: Metaphor in the discourse of Silvio Berlusconi in Italy', *Discourse & Society*, 7 (2), 243–69.

Sharifian, F. (2007) 'Politics and/of translation: Case studies between Persian and English', *Journal of Intercultural Studies*, 28 (4), 413–24.

Sharifian, F. (2009) 'Figurative language in international political discourse: The case of Iran', *Journal of Language and Politics*, 8 (3), 416–32.

Sharifian, F. (2011) *Cultural Conceptualizations and Language: Theoretical Framework and Applications* (Amsterdam/Philadelphia: Benjamins).

Shenhav, S. R. (2009) 'We have a place in a long story. Empowered narratives and the construction of communities: The case of US presidential debates', *Narrative Inquiry*, 19 (2), 199–218.

Shore, B. (1996) *Culture in Mind: Cognition, Culture and the Problem of Meaning* (Oxford: Oxford University Press).

Simons, H. W. and A. A. Aghazarian (eds) (1986) *Form, Genre, and the Study of Political Discourse* (Columbia, SC: University of South Carolina Press).

Smith, C. A. and K. B. Smith (1994) *The White House Speaks: Presidential Leadership as Persuasion* (Westport, CT: Praeger).

Steen, G. J. (2011) 'The contemporary theory of metaphor – now new and improved!', *Review of Cognitive Linguistics*, 9 (1), 26–64.

Stefanowitsch, A. and S. T. Gries (eds) (2006) *Corpus-based Approaches to Metaphor and Metonymy* (Berlin/New York: Mouton de Gruyter).

Stockwell, S. (2005) *Political Campaign Strategy. Doing Democracy in the 21st Century* (Melbourne: Australian Scholarly).

Straehle, C., Weiss, G., Wodak, R., Muntigl, P. and M. Sedlak (1999) 'Struggle as metaphor in European Union discourses on unemployment', *Discourse & Society*, 10 (1), 67–99.

Stuckey, M. E. (1990) *Playing the Game: The Presidential Rhetoric of Ronald Regan* (New York: Praeger).

Stuckey, M. E. (1991) *The President as Interpreter-in-Chief* (New York: Chatham House).

Tannen, D. (1994) *Talking from 9 to 5: How Women's and Men's Conversational Styles Affect Who Gets Heard, Who Gets Credit, and What Gets Done at Work* (New York: William Morrow).

Tannen, D. (2007) *Talking Voices. Repetition, Dialogue and Imagery in Conversational Discourse*, 2nd edn (Cambridge: Cambridge University Press).

Teten, R. L. (2003) 'Evolution of the modern rhetorical presidency: Presidential presentation and development of the State of the Union Address', *Presidential Studies Quarterly*, 33 (2), 333–46.

Thomas, G. (2008) *Yes We Can. A Biography of President Barack Obama* (New York: Feiwel and Friends).

Thornborrow, J. (1993) 'Metaphors of security: A comparison of representation in defense discourse in post-Cold War France and Britain', *Discourse & Society*, 4 (1), 99–119.

Trent, J. S. and R. V. Friedenberg (2000) *Political Campaign Communication. Principles and Practices* (Westport, CT: Praeger).

Tulis, J. (1987) *The Rhetorical Presidency* (Princeton, NJ: Princeton University Press).

Tuman, J. S. (2008) *Political Communication in American Campaigns* (Thousand Oaks, CA: Sage).

van Dijk, T. A. (1997) 'What is political discourse analysis'. In J. Blommaert and C. Bulcaen (eds), *Political Linguistics* (Amsterdam/Philadelphia: Benjamins), pp. 11–52.

Vertessen, D. and C. De Landtsheer (2008) 'A metaphorical election style: Use of metaphor at election time'. In T. Carver and J. Pikalo (eds), *Political Language and Metaphor. Interpreting and Changing the World* (London/New York: Routledge), pp. 271–85.

Wilson, J. (1990) *Politically Speaking: The Pragmatic Analysis of Political Language* (London: Blackwell).

Windt, T. and B. Ingold (eds) (1987) *Essays in Presidential Rhetoric* (Dubuque, IA: Kendall/Hunt).

Wodak, R. (ed.) (1989) *Language, Power and Ideology* (Amsterdam/Philadelphia: Benjamins).

Wolfe, A. (1998) *One Nation After All: What Middle-Class Americans Really Think about God, Country, Family, Racism, Welfare, Immigration, Homosexuality, Work, the Right, the Left and Each Other* (New York: Penguin).

Wood, D. B. (2007) *The Politics of Economic Leadership. The Causes and Consequences of Presidential Rhetoric* (Princeton, NJ: Princeton University Press).

Zarefsky, D. (2002) 'The presidency has always been a place for rhetorical leadership'. In L. G. Dorsey (ed.), *The Presidency and Rhetorical Leadership* (College Station: Texas A&M University), pp. 20–41.

Zashin, E. (1974) 'The uses of metaphor and analogy: toward a renewal of political language', *The Journal of Politics*, 36 (2), 290–326.

Zinken, J. (2003) 'Ideological imagination: Intertextual and correlational metaphors in political discourse', *Discourse & Society*, 14 (4), 507–23.

Index

308

Printed and bound by CPI Group (UK) Ltd, Croydon, CR0 4YY